Classic Edition

Sources

Multicultural Education

McGraw Hill

Connect
Learn
Succeed™

Classic Edition

Sources

Multicultural Education

Edited by

JANA NOEL
California State University, Sacramento

CLASSIC EDITION SOURCES: MULTICULTURAL EDUCATION, THIRD EDITION

Published by McGraw-Hill, a business unit of The McGraw-Hill Companies, Inc., 1221 Avenue of the Americas, New York, NY 10020. Copyright © 2012 by The McGraw-Hill Companies, Inc. All rights reserved. Previous editions © 2008 and 2007. No part of this publication may be reproduced or distributed in any form or by any means, or stored in a database or retrieval system, without the prior written consent of The McGraw-Hill Companies, Inc., including, but not limited to, in any network or other electronic storage or transmission, or broadcast for distance learning.

Some ancillaries, including electronic and print components, may not be available to customers outside the United States.

Classic Edition Sources® is a registered trademark of the McGraw-Hill Companies, Inc.
Classic Edition Sources is published by the **Contemporary Learning Series** group within the McGraw-Hill Higher Education division.

1 2 3 4 5 6 7 8 9 0 QDB/QDB 1 0 9 8 7 6 5 4 3 2 1

ISBN 978-0-07-802621-8
MHID 0-07-802621-0
ISSN 1525-3724 (print)
ISSN 2159-1105 (online)

Managing Editor: *Larry Loeppke*
Developmental Editor: *Dave Welsh*
Permissions Coordinator: *DeAnna Dausener*
Marketing Specialist: *Alice Link*
Project Manager: *Robin A. Reed*
Design Coordinator: *Margarite Reynolds*
Buyer: *Nicole Baumgartner*
Media Project Manager: *Sridevi Palani*

Compositor: Laserwords Private Limited

Advisory Board

Members of the Advisory Board are instrumental in the final selection of articles for each edition of CLASSIC EDITION SOURCES. Their review of articles for content, level, currentness, and appropriateness provides critical direction to the editor and staff. We think that you will find their careful consideration well reflected in this volume.

Editor

JANA NOEL
California State University, Sacramento

Adboard Members

JORGE OSTERLING
George Mason University

ANNE MARIE RAKIP
South Carolina State University

WILLIAM LAY
Western Washington University

LOIS SALMON
Grand Canyon University

JANA NOEL
California State University, Sacramento

JANA NOEL is a Professor of Teacher Education at California State University, Sacramento. She also serves as the provost's Fellow for Community and Civic Engagement as well as the university's Community Engagement Faculty Scholar. She was previously Associate Professor of Educational Foundations and Multicultural Education at Montana State University, Bozeman. She received her PhD in philosophy of education at UCLA in 1991. Her research focuses on urban and multicultural education and teacher education. She received her university's Outstanding Community Service Award in 2008, and the Research and Creative Activities Capstone Award in 2010, in recognition of research and scholarship at the national level. Her Urban Teacher Education Center received the 2008 California Quality Educational Partnership Award for Distinguished Service to Children and the Preparation of Teachers. She is the author of the textbook *Developing Multicultural Educators* (Waveland Press, 2005), and she has published in such journals as *Journal of Teacher Education*, *Educational Theory*, *Journal of Negro Education*, *Multicultural Perspectives*, and *The Urban Review*.

Preface

*T*his third edition of *Classic Edition Sources: Multicultural Education* has been updated to include selections addressing some of the most critical issues within education that have developed more prominently since the previous edition of the book. The third edition incorporates recent writings by some of the most influential writers in the field of multicultural education. Chapters and selections have been added, deleted, and re-organized to reflect the direction of the field of multicultural education today.

Four new selections addressing our changing society have been added. A selection on Sexual Orientation has been included (Selection 21) from *The Right to Be Out: Sexual Orientation and Gender Identity in America's Public Schools,* by Stuart Biegel, a leading author in this emerging field of literature. This selection lays out some of the historical court cases and legislative acts regarding GLBT (Gay, Lesbian, Bisexual, Transgender) students and schools, and describes how to ensure that school and classroom climate are respectful of all students. Additionally within this selection, a discussion of bullying reflects an unfortunate increase in reports of bullying in U.S. schools. A selection on education for newcomer immigrants by Súarez-Orozco, Pimentel, and Martin (Selection 26) describes the state of education for newly immigrated students, as well as the impact of educational practices on both the academic achievement and the aspirations and identities of new immigrants.

Religion is the topic for an entirely new section of the third edition. A selection from the Pew Foundation Forum on Religion and Public Life (Selection 29) traces the issues and court cases addressing some of the key, and most passionately argued, debates regarding religion and schools: school prayer, the Pledge of Allegiance, religion in the curriculum, and religious rights in and out of the classroom. The conflict between religions and culture is discussed in terms of Christian and non-Christian privilege and oppression and is addressed in the selection by Khyati and Joshi (Selection 30).

Several additional selections have been updated to present more recent writings of several influential writers whose works were in the previous edition. The selections were updated using newer editions of books, newer books, or newer articles written by the same authors, in order to keep abreast of their continued contributions to the field of multicultural education. This includes updated selections by the American Association of University Women (AAUW) on Gender Equity (Selection 20), Valerie Ooka Pang on Asian American education (Selection 25), and Jim Cummins on Language and Bilingual Education (Selection 27).

New directions within the theory of multicultural education have been represented by new authors and topics. Daniel Solorzano lays out the field of Critical Race Theory (Selection 19), which has undergirded much new research in the field of multicultural education. Lisa Delpit describes the "culture of power" in schools (Selection 10), and how differential issues of power affect children of color. A new selection by William Bennett, Chester Finn, and John Cribb presents the conservative tradition of education, discussing the perceived lack of parental involvement and moral development within U.S. schools (Selection 17). Hersh C. Waxman, Yolanda N. Padrón, and Andres García provide a recent update on the issues and effective practices for teaching Hispanic students (Selection 24).

The third edition of *Classic Edition Sources: Multicultural Education* is intended to present some classic articles as well as the work of the most influential writers within the field of multicultural education. The majority of the text contains the same selections as in the previous edition, but the text also includes updated selections, re-organized chapters, and new chapters addressing both the emerging theories of multicultural education and the issues of critical importance to schools and society today.

Acknowledgments

I want to thank David Welsh, developmental editor from McGraw-Hill, who worked with me on this third edition. He has been helpful and patient in assisting me in this process.

And on a personal note, I want to give special thanks to my husband David Powell and to my parents Jim and Jan Noel, who have all given me love, support, and encouragement not only in this book but in all of my personal and professional endeavors.

Contents

Gender and Orientation

97

Race and Immigration

109

Selection 22 **GLORIA LADSON-BILLINGS,** from "The Power of Pedagogy: Does Teaching Matter?" in William H. Watkins, James H. Lewis, and Victoria Chow, *Race and Education: The Roles of History and Society in Educating African American Students* (Allyn & Bacon, 2001)

110

"[Research] identifies cultural solidarity, linking classroom content to students' experiences, a focus on the whole child, a use of familiar cultural patterns, and the incorporation of culturally compatible communication patterns as key elements of success in teaching African American urban students."

Selection 23 **CORNEL PEWEWARDY,** from "Learning Styles of American Indian/ Alaska Native Students: A Review of Literature and Implications for Practice," *Journal of American Indian Education* (2002)

115

"Traditional American Indian/Alaska Native learning focuses on process over product, legends, and stories as traditional teaching paradigms, knowledge obtained from self, and cognitive development through problem-solving techniques."

Selection 24 **HERSH C. WAXMAN, YOLANDA N. PADRÓN, AND ANDRES GARCÍA,** from "Educational Issues and Effective Practices for Hispanic Students," in Susan J. Paik and Herbert J. Walberg, *Narrowing the Achievement Gap: Strategies for Educating Latino, Black, and Asian Students* (Springer, 2007)

121

"Another important characteristic found in effective schools serving predominantly Hispanic students is that they provide a number of different instructional strategies . . . providing language support in the students' first language . . . use of collaboration, student-centered instruction, incorporating individual learning styles, providing more teacher support and classroom order, and having more instructional interactions with students."

Selection 25 **VALERIE OOKA PANG,** from "Fighting the Marginalization of Asian American Students with Caring Schools: Focusing on Curricular Change," *Race, Ethnicity & Education* (2006)

128

"Caring teachers consider why and how Asian Americans are marginalized in the curriculum, educational practices, and school policies. They examine how the needs of AA students are often ignored or not addressed . . . Curriculum content and strategies can be used in schools to fight the issue of marginalization."

Language *140*

Religion *155*

Social Class *166*

14 Multicultural Classrooms and Schools   178

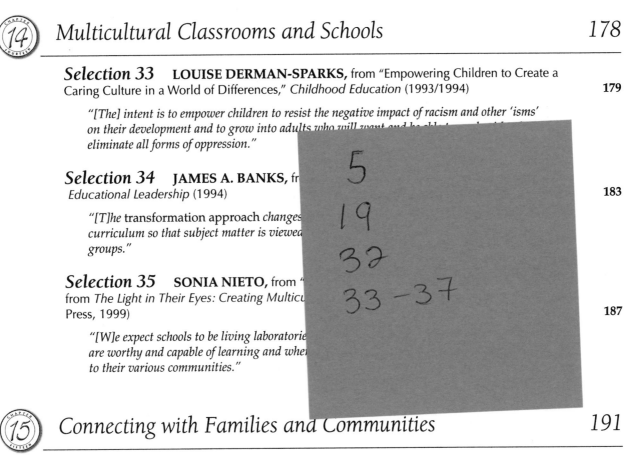

15 Connecting with Families and Communities   191

Correlation Guide

*E*ach volume in the *Classic Edition Sources* series brings together over 35 selections of enduring intellectual value—classic articles, book excerpts, and research studies—that have shaped a discipline of study. Edited for length and level, the selections are organized topically around the major areas of study within the discipline. For more information on *Classic Edition Sources* and other *McGraw-Hill Contemporary Learning Series* titles, visit www.mhhe.com/cls.

This convenient guide matches the Parts in **Classic Edition Sources: Multicultural Education, 3/e** with the corresponding chapters in two of our best-selling McGraw-Hill Multicultural Education textbooks by Cushner et al. and Kottak/Kozaitis.

Classic Edition Sources: Multicultural Education, 3/e	Human Diversity in Education: An Integrative Approach, 7/e by Cushner et al.	On Being Different: Diversity and Multiculturalism in the North American Mainstream, 4/e by Kottak/Kozaitis
Chapter 1: Historical and Philosophical Perspectives on Multicultural Education	**Chapter 1:** Education in a Changing Society **Chapter 2:** Multicultural Education: Historical and Theoretical Perspectives	**Chapter 1:** Introduction **Chapter 4:** The Multicultural Society
Chapter 2: Sociological and Anthropological Perspectives on Multicultural Education		
Chapter 3: Ethnographic Perspectives on Multicultural Education	**Chapter 7:** The Classroom as a Global Community: Nationality and Region	**Chapter 5:** Ethnicity
Chapter 4: Culture	**Chapter 3:** Culture and the Culture-Learning Process	**Chapter 4:** The Multicultural Society
Chapter 5: Racism and Prejudice	**Chapter 6:** Creating Classrooms That Address Race and Ethnicity	**Chapter 8:** Race: Its Social Construction
Chapter 6: Identity Development	**Chapter 10:** Developing a Collaborative Classroom: Gender and Sexual Orientation	**Chapter 3:** Globalization and Identity **Chapter 10:** Sexual Orientation
Chapter 7: The Conservative Tradition	**Chapter 2:** Multicultural Education: Historical and Theoretical Perspectives	
Chapter 8: Critical Pedagogy	**Chapter 11:** Creating Developmentally Appropriate Classrooms: The Importance of Age and Developmental Status	

Chapter 9: Gender and Orientation	**Chapter 10:** Developing a Collaborative Classroom: Gender and Sexual Orientation	**Chapter 9:** Gender
Chapter 10: Race and Immigration	**Chapter 6:** Creating Classrooms That Address Race and Ethnicity **Chapter 7:** The Classroom as a Global Community: Nationality and Region	**Chapter 3:** Globalization and Identity **Chapter 7:** Race: Its Biological Dimensions **Chapter 8:** Race: Its Social Construction
Chapter 11: Language	**Chapter 8:** Developing Learning Communities: Language and Learning Style	**Chapter 15:** Linguistic Diversity
Chapter 12: Religion	**Chapter 9:** Religious Pluralism in Secular Classrooms	**Chapter 6:** Religion
Chapter 13: Social Class	**Chapter 13:** Improving Schools for All Children: The Role of Social Class and Social Status in Teaching and Learning	**Chapter 13:** Class
Chapter 14: Multicultural Classrooms and Schools	**Chapter 2:** Multicultural Education: Historical and Theoretical Perspectives **Chapter 7:** The Classroom as a Global Community: Nationality and Region	
Chapter 15: Connecting with Families and Communities	**Chapter 7:** The Classroom as a Global Community: Nationality and Region	**Chapter 16:** Families

Internet References

Chapter 1

The History of Education Society promotes improved teaching of, and scholarly research in, the history of education. The Society's homepage offers links to its journal the *History of Education Quarterly* as well as resources for teaching and research in the field.
www.historyofeducation.org/

The Philosophy of Education Society (PES) is the national organization of philosophers of education in the United States. This website offers links to articles, issues, and resources of interest to those studying philosophy of education and other foundations of education fields.
http://philosophyofeducation.org/

The American Educational Studies Association (AESA) is an educational organization comprised of teachers, researchers, professors, and students who focus on the foundations of education fields of history, philosophy, sociology, anthropology, politics, economics, and comparative/international studies.
www.educationalstudies.org/

Chapter 2

The American Sociological Association has a subgroup focusing on Sociology of Education. The website for that section of the Association includes links to publications, funding opportunities, universities that offer Sociology of Education, and links to blogs for discussion of issues within education.
www2.asanet.org/soe/

This website is the home page of the American Anthropological Association, which includes a number of links and reports related to anthropology of education, with a focus on race, class, and ethnography.
www.aaanet.org/index.htm

Chapter 3

There are many on-line sources of information about Jonathan Kozol and his work. The following link connects to a website dedicated to presenting Kozol's work through a variety of avenues, including written, video, audio, and photographic images of Kozol.
www.learntoquestion.com/seevak/groups/2002/sites/kozol/Seevak02/ineedtogoHOMEPAGE/homepage.htm

Ethnographic research is distinct from other types of qualitative and quantitative research. The following link provides an article clearly laying out the key features of ethnographic research in education.
www.readingonline.org/articles/Purcell-gates/

Chapter 4

The National Association for Multicultural Education (NAME) brings together educators from all levels of education, preschool through university, who have an interest in multicultural education. The association holds conferences, publishes, serves as a place to gather ideas for instruction, and is involved in advocating for educational equity.
www.nameorg.org/

The International Journal of Multicultural Education is an open-access e-journal with articles and book reviews on multicultural education from around the world. The journal can be read, free of charge, at the following website.
http://ijme-journal.org/index.php/ijme

Chapter 5

The Anti-Defamation League (ADL) was organized for the purpose of helping to secure justice and fair treatment for all people. It gathers information and develops materials that help people learn how to fight prejudice and racism.
www.adl.org

The Southern Poverty Law Center is a nonprofit organization that combats hate, intolerance, and discrimination through education and litigation. The organization provides a number of resources for educators to help teach about these issues.
www.splcenter.org

Chapter 6

In this website, Andrea Ayvazian and Beverly Daniel Tatum (Tatum is the author of Selection 15) provide cross-racial vignettes as the foundation for how public dialogue can be established regarding race, identity, and opportunity. They also give suggestions on how to plan a public forum to discuss racism in one's community.
www.sojo.net/index.cfm?action=magazine.article&issue=soj9601&article=960111

This website provides links to resources related to White privilege, cultural sensitivity, human rights, tolerance, and racism and stereotyping. Included are links to articles, organizations, statements, and teaching materials.
www.chlive.org/pbeck/eastlibrary/WHITEPRIVILEGE&RACISMRESOURCES.htm

Chapter 7

The website for the Association for Moral Education provides information about conferences, awards, grants, and publications, and provides a set of links to other organizations and publications addressing moral education.
www.amenetwork.org/about.html

The Goodcharacter.com website provides free resources, materials, and lesson plans related to character education. The site also provides a list of character education organizations for educators as well as a list of character-building activities and organizations for students.
www.goodcharacter.com/

The following is a link to a nearly three-hour interview with William Bennett, which aired on July 4, 2010, on the television program BookTV, on channel C-Span2. In this free-to-watch program, Bennett talks about his life and career as well as his books and beliefs on education.
www.c-spanvideo.org/program/294333-1

Chapter 8

This website is devoted to critical pedagogy. It includes an overview of the field, with definitions, history, key concepts, and major theorists, and it includes links to other critical pedagogy websites.
http://mingo.info-science.uiowa.edu/%7Estevens/critped/index.htm

The website of the "Critical Multicultural Pavilion" lists and provides links to over 30 multicultural education organizations and associations.
www.edchange.org/multicultural/sites/orgs.html

Chapter 9

The American Association of University Women (AAUW) is a national organization that promotes education and equity for all women and girls. It sponsors research, community action projects, fellowships and grants, and funds for legal efforts.
www.aauw.org

The Gay, Lesbian and Straight Education Network (GLSEN) works with educators, policymakers, community leaders, and students to address anti-LGBT behavior and bias in schools. GLSEN's website provides information on programs to address such issues in schools and provides updates on LGBT-related policies.
www.glsen.org/cgi-bin/iowa/all/about/index.html

Chapter 10

The following website presents a "Culturally Relevant Pedagogy Primer." The site includes a description of culturally relevant pedagogy, a facilitator's guide to help enhance understanding of the pedagogy, and examples of culturally relevant pedagogy in classrooms.
www.tolerance.org/tdsi/culturally-relevant-pedagogy-primer

The U.S. Department of Education reports the findings of the most recent National Assessment of Education Progress (NAEP). The following link presents the statistics on the achievement gap between Blacks and Whites, as well as resources for reducing the achievement gap. The report on the achievement gap between Hispanics and Whites will also appear on this website when it becomes available.
http://nces.ed.gov/nationsreportcard/studies/gaps/

The California Center for Applied Linguistics keeps a database of Secondary School Newcomer Programs offered throughout the United States. This searchable database allows website visitors to find information about more than 60 programs in 23 states.
www.cal.org/CALWebDB/newcomer/

Chapter 11

The National Clearinghouse for English Language Acquisition and Language Instruction Educational Programs (NCELA) works to collect, analyze, and disseminate information relating to the effective education of linguistically and culturally diverse learners in the United States. It works with local districts and states to develop educational programs.
www.ncela.gwu.edu/

The National Association for Bilingual Education (NABE) advocates for bilingual and English Language Learners and their families. NABE hosts conferences, produces publications, and works to affect policy change for bilingual education.
www.nabe.org/

Chapter 12

The First Amendment Center publishes a number of articles and information items related to the First Amendment "right to free speech" on its website. Included are articles about efforts to restrict religion and religious rights in schools, and how the fear of non-Christian religions plays into elections.
www.firstamendmentcenter.org/default.aspx

Teaching Tolerance, a free publication of the Southern Poverty Law Center dedicated to helping teachers teach multicultural education, has produced an on-line document with links that assists teachers in learning how to teach religious tolerance within the bounds of the Constitution and law.
www.tolerance.org/activity/maintain-neutrality

Chapter 13

The U.S. Census Bureau website includes a section documenting the level of poverty in the U.S., with links to their statistics related to number and percentage of children and families in poverty within each state and in the nation.
http://factfinder.census.gov/servlet/ACSSAFFPeople?_submenuId=people_9&_sse=on

A series by the *New York Times* analyzed how social class—income, education, wealth, and occupation—affects the lives of children and families. The following link is to that series of reports.
www.nytimes.com/pages/national/class/index.html

Chapter 14

Teaching Tolerance is a free magazine that provides educators with ideas, information, and resources for promoting multicultural understanding in schools and communities.
www.teachingtolerance.org

Author James Banks directs the Center for Multicultural Education at the University of Washington. Their website contains ideas for classrooms, academic resources, recent publications in the field of multicultural education, and links to a variety of additional multicultural education resources.
http://depts.washington.edu/centerme/home.htm

The following website presents an annotated bibliography of multicultural children's literature, as well as links to additional information and activities that can be used to teach multicultural topics. The site also contains illustrations of some book covers and some children's multicultural artwork.
www.multiculturalchildrenslit.com/

Chapter 15

The Center on School, Family, and Community Partnerships conducts studies on school–university partnerships, coordinates a network of such partnerships, and provides professional development on creating partnerships between school, university, and community.
www.csos.jhu.edu/P2000/center.htm

The National Coalition for Parent Involvement in Education provides resources, research, legislative updates, and programs, all for the purpose of advocating for the involvement of parents and families in their children's education, to foster relationships between home, school, and community.
www.ncpie.org/

Historical and Philosophical Perspectives on Multicultural Education

The Great Civil Rights Movement and the New Culture Wars

Joel Spring

Joel Spring has published over 20 books that critically examine a wide range of issues in education, from politics of education, to Native American education, to the history of education. His work on politics and education focuses on issues of corporate models of education and on the intersection of education and the global economy. With a family history within the Choctaw Nation, Spring writes about Native American culture and history. And his books on the history of education look at that history through a multicultural lens. A Professor at City University of New York Graduate Center, his books include *Education and the Rise of the Global Economy* (Lawrence Erlbaum Associates, 1998), *Conflict of Interests: The Politics of American Education* (McGraw-Hill, 2005), and *The Cultural Transformation of a Native American Family and Its Tribe 1763–1995: A Basket of Apples* (Lawrence Erlbaum Associates, 1996).

In the following selection from the book *Deculturalization and the Struggle for Equality: A Brief History of the Education of Dominated Cultures in the United States,* 4th ed. (McGraw-Hill, 2004), Spring describes the efforts of a number of minority groups to gain civil and educational equality. He has included sections on African American, Native American, Asian American, and Mexican American efforts. He focuses especially on school desegregation efforts and on the call for recognition of the cultures and languages of all students. He describes many of the legal cases and court decisions, the groups and individuals involved in the efforts, and the types of activities undertaken, such as nonviolent protests. He introduces and describes Martin Luther King, Jr., the Southern Christian Leadership Conference, the American Indian Movement, and the Mexican American Legal Defense and Education Fund, among others, as leading the efforts to gain civil and educational rights for all.

Key Concept: efforts toward civil and educational rights

School segregation, and cultural and linguistic genocide were central issues in the great civil rights movement of the 1950s and 1960s.

African and Mexican Americans were primarily concerned with ending racial segregation in the schools. Native and Mexican Americans, and Puerto Ricans wanted to reverse previous efforts by federal and state governments to destroy their languages and cultures. They banded together in demands for public schools to maintain and teach Spanish and Native American languages. They also wanted schools to provide positive images of their cultural traditions. Asian Americans were still struggling with the negative public images created by the mass media. Japanese Americans were at a particular disadvantage because of the anti-Japanese movies made during World War II. In addition, Asian Americans wanted equal educational opportunities.

The great civil rights movement confronted traditional opposition to integration and to protection of minority cultures and languages. In the 1950s, the costs of integration were the killing of civil rights workers, church bombings, and race riots. There still persisted the argument that Protestant Anglo-American culture would be the dominant culture of the United States.

School Desegregation

The desegregation of American schools was the result of over a half-century of struggle by the African and Hispanic/Latino communities. Since its founding in the early part of the twentieth century, the NAACP had struggled to end discriminatory practices against minority groups. The school desegregation issue was finally decided by the U.S. Supreme Court in 1954 in *Brown v. Board of Education of Topeka.*

In this particular case, Oliver Brown's daughter was denied the right to attend a white elementary school within five blocks of her home and forced to cross railroad tracks and travel 21 blocks to attend an all-black school. The federal district court in Kansas ruled against Oliver Brown, using the argument that the segregated schools named in the suit were substantially equal and thus fell within the separate but equal doctrine.

In preparing its brief for the Supreme Court, the NAACP defined two important objectives: (1) to show that the climate of the times required an end to segregation laws and (2) to show that the separate but equal doctrine contained a contradiction in terms—that is, that separate facilities were inherently unequal.

The Supreme Court argued in the *Brown* decision, "In the field of public education the doctrine of 'separate but equal' has no place. Separate educational facilities are inherently unequal."

In 1955 the Supreme Court issued its enforcement decree for the desegregation of schools. One problem facing the Court was the lack of machinery for supervising and ensuring the desegregation of vast numbers of segregated school districts.

Consequently, integration occurred at a slow pace until additional civil rights legislation was passed in the 1960s and the mounting frustrations in the black community fed the flames of a militant civil rights movement.[1]

The evolution of the mass media in the 1950s was an important factor in the civil rights movement because it became possible to turn local problems into national issues.

Concern over America's international image grew as pictures of racial injustice flashed around the world, and the president's public image was often threatened when examples of racial injustice were shown to millions of television viewers.

The most dramatic technique used by civil rights groups was nonviolent confrontation. The massive non-violent demonstrations by blacks and whites were met by cursing southern law enforcement units using an array of cattle prods, clubs, and fire hoses. These scenes were broadcast on television around the world. The Congress on Racial Equality (CORE); the Student Nonviolent Coordinating Committee (SNCC); and the Southern Christian Leadership Conference (SCLC), led by the Reverend Martin Luther King, Jr., forced the passage of national civil rights legislation.

CORE, a major organization in the civil rights movement, was organized at the University of Chicago in 1942. The two basic doctrines of the early CORE movement were commitment to racial integration and the use of Christian nonviolent techniques.

CORE did not rise to national prominence until the late 1950s, when another Christian leader, Dr. Martin Luther King, Jr., made nonviolent confrontation the central drama of the civil rights movement.

Like the early members of CORE, King became convinced that nonviolent resistance "was the only morally and practically sound method open to oppressed people in their struggle for freedom."[2]

The incident that launched Martin Luther King, Jr.'s, civil rights activities and provided scope for his Gandhian form of the social gospel occurred on 1 December 1955. On that date, Rosa Parks, who had worked a regular day as a seamstress in one of the leading department stores in Montgomery, Alabama, boarded a bus and took the first seat behind the section reserved for whites. During the journey home, several white passengers boarded the bus. The driver ordered Rosa Parks and three other black passengers to stand so that the white passengers could have seats. Rosa Parks refused and was arrested. The black ministers in the community quickly organized in response to this incident, and on 5 December the Montgomery bus boycott began.

The bus boycott lasted for over a year and finally ended on 21 December 1956, when, after a Supreme Court decision against segregation on buses, the Montgomery transit system was officially integrated. King emerged from the struggle a national hero among dominated groups. In 1957 he organized the Southern Christian Leadership Conference (SCLC), which became the central organization in the civil rights struggle.

After SCLC was formed, boycotts and nonviolent demonstrations began to occur throughout the South.

The march on Washington symbolized to Congress and the American people the growing strength of the civil rights movement and provided the stage for television coverage of speeches by civil rights leaders.

The result of these activities was the Civil Rights Act of 1964. Under 11 different titles, the power of federal regulations was extended in the areas of voting rights, public accommodations, education, and employment.

Native Americans

As African Americans were leading the fight against segregated schooling, Native Americans were attempting to gain control of the education of their children and restore their cultural heritage and languages to the curriculum. Native Americans shared a common interest with Mexican Americans and Puerto Rican Americans in supporting bilingual and multicultural education.

During the 1940s and 1950s, federal Indian policy was directed at termination of tribes and reservations.

Termination policies attempted to break up tribal relations by relocating Indians to urban areas. Relocation to urban areas was similar to the nineteenth-century federal policy that sent Native Americans to Indian Territory and reservations. But, in this case, Indians were to be "civilized" by being dispersed throughout the general population.

While resisting termination policies, Native Americans began to demand greater self-determination.

One of the results of the drive for self-determination was the creation of the Rough Rock Demonstration School in 1966. Established on a Navajo reservation in

Arizona, the school was a joint effort of the Office of Economic Opportunity and the Bureau of Indian Affairs. One of the major goals of the demonstration school was for Navajo parents to control the education of their children and participate in all aspects of their schooling.[3]

Besides tribal control, one of the important features of the Rough Rock Demonstration School was the attempt to preserve the Navajo language and culture. In contrast to the deculturalization efforts of the nineteenth and early twentieth centuries, the goal of learning Navajo and English was presented as a means of preparing children to "fend successfully in both cultures and see the Navajo way as part of a universal system of values."[4]

The struggle for self-determination was aided by the development of a Pan-Indian movement in the United States. The Pan-Indian movement was based on the assumption that Native American tribes shared a common set of values and interests. Similar to the role played by CORE and SCLC among African Americans, Pan-Indian organizations, such as the American Indian Movement (AIM) and the Indians of All Tribes, led demonstrations demanding self-determination.

Indian Education: A National Tragedy

Throughout the 1960s and 1970s, federal administrators gave support to Indian demands for self-determination. During his election campaign in 1968, Richard M. Nixon declared, "The right of self-determination of the Indian people will be respected and their participation in planning their own destiny will actively be encouraged."[5]

It was in this climate of civil rights activism and political support for Indian self-determination that the U.S. Senate Committee on Labor and Public Welfare issued in 1969 the report *Indian Education: A National Tragedy— A National Challenge.*

After a lengthy review of the failure of past educational policies, the report's first recommendation was "maximum participation and control by Indians in establishing Indian education programs."[6] In its second recommendation, the report called for maximum Indian participation in the development of educational programs in federal schools and local public schools. These educational programs were to include early childhood education, vocational education, work-study, and adult literacy education. Of special importance was the recommendation to create bilingual and bicultural education programs.

Native American demands for bilingual and bicultural education were aided by the passage of Title 7 of the Elementary and Secondary Education Act of 1968 or, as it was also called, the Bilingual Education Act. This was a product of political activism by Mexican American groups. Native Americans used funds provided under this legislation to support bilingual programs in Indian languages and English.

The most important piece of legislation supporting self-determination was the 1975 Indian Self-Determination and Education Assistance Act, which gave tribes the power to contract with the federal government to run their own education and health programs.

The Indian Self-Determination and Education Assistance Act strengthened Indian participation in the control of education programs. The legislation provided that, in a local school district receiving funds for the education of Indian students that did not have a school board having a majority of Indians, the district had to establish a separate local committee composed of parents of Indian students in the school. This committee was given the authority over any Indian education programs contracted with the federal government.

Efforts to protect Indian culture were strengthened with the passage in 1978 of a congressional resolution on American Indian religious freedom. Remember that missionaries and federal policies from the seventeenth to the early twentieth centuries attempted to eradicate Indian religions and replace them with Christianity. The resolution recognized these earlier attempts to abridge Indian rights to religious freedom, stating: "That henceforth it shall be the policy of the United States to protect and preserve for American Indians their inherent right of freedom to believe, express and exercise traditional religions . . . and the freedom to worship through ceremonial and traditional rites."[7]

In addition to the protection of religion, the federal government committed itself to promoting traditional languages with the passage of the Native American Languages Act of 1990. This act commits the federal government to "preserve, protect, and promote the rights and freedom of Native Americans to use, practice, and develop Native American languages."[8]

Asian Americans: Educating the "Model Minority"

In a sharp break with the previous public image of Asian American students as "deviants" and a "yellow peril," the model minority image presented the Asian American as possessing the "ideal" public school personality traits of obedience, punctuality, neatness, self-discipline, and high-achievement motivation.

Critics of the model minority image claimed it was being used to cover up the continuing racism in U.S. society. The disparity between educational achievement and income highlighted how education could be used to achieve the American dream in schooling but not in the workplace.

I would argue that the model minority image created in the 1960s and 1970s might have distorted the image European Americans had of Asian immigrants arriving from Southeast Asia, particularly the Hmong and Cambodians. Assuming that these Asian immigrants would live up to the model minority image, European

American educators might have neglected the real educational problems confronting these populations. For instance, the children of some Cambodian immigrants were easily recruited during the 1980s and 1990s into existing violent-youth gangs in the Los Angeles area. One reason was the continuation of racist attitudes toward Asian Americans. Describing his school experience in Stockton, California, in the 1980s, Sokunthy Pho complained, "I hated my parents for bringing me and my sisters . . . to America because we were always being picked on by the white kids at our school. . . . They spat at us, sneaked behind us and kicked us. . . . We didn't respond. . . . Instead, we kept quiet and walked home with tears running down our brown cheeks."[9]

Asian Americans: Language and the Continued Struggle for Equal Educational Opportunity

School problems for Asian Americans continued despite popular media extolling the virtues of the model Asian American student. The continuing struggle against educational discrimination was dramatized by events surrounding the historic 1974 U.S. Supreme Court decision *Lau v. Nichols*. The decision guaranteed equal educational opportunity to non-English-speaking students by requiring public schools to provide special assistance to these students to learn English so that they could equally participate in the educational process.

Despite recognizing the problem, school authorities did little to alleviate it. In 1970, only one-fourth of the limited-English-speaking Chinese American students in the San Francisco school system were receiving help.

Enraged by the neglect of their children's educational problems, the families of Kinney Kinmon Lau and 12 other Chinese American students in 1970 sued in federal district court asking that the San Francisco school system provide special English classes taught by bilingual teachers. The school district objected to the demand and claimed that receiving help in learning the English language was not a legal right. The district court agreed with the school district and argued that limited- and non-English-speaking students were receiving equal educational opportunity because they were receiving the same education as all students in the district.

After the district court ruling, the case hinged on the question of whether students are entitled to special instruction as part of the right to equal educational opportunity. The case was appealed to the U.S. Court of Appeals for the Ninth Circuit. Again, the appeals court agreed with the school district that the legal responsibility of the school district extended "no further than to provide them with the same facilities, textbooks, teachers and curriculum as is provided to other children in the district."[10]

In 1974, the U.S. Supreme Court overturned the decisions of the lower courts and argued that sometimes equal educational opportunity requires special programs for students. In language that would have a profound impact on the education of all limited- and non-English-speaking students, the Supreme Court maintained, "There is no equality of treatment merely by providing students with the same facilities, textbooks, teachers, and curriculum; for students who do not understand English are effectively foreclosed from any meaningful education."[11]

The *Lau* decision did not end the educational problems faced by the Chinese American community in San Francisco. Led by the Chinese for Affirmative Action, the local community had to struggle with the school district to implement the Lau decision.

Hispanic/Latino Americans

The struggles of Mexican Americans and Puerto Rican Americans increased the opportunities for Hispanic/Latino immigrants arriving after the 1960s. Similar to African Americans, Mexican Americans turned to the courts to seek redress for their grievances.

In 1946 a U.S. District Court ruled in *Mendez et al. v. Westminster School District of Orange County* that Mexicans were not Indians as claimed under the 1935 California law. The judge argued that the only possible argument for segregation was the special educational needs of Mexican American children. These needs centered around the issue of learning English. Completely reversing the educational justification for segregation, the judge argued that "evidence clearly shows that Spanish-speaking children are retarded in learning English by lack of exposure to its use by segregation."[12] Therefore, the court ruled that segregation was illegal because it was not required by state law and because there was no valid educational justification for segregation.[13]

Heartened by the *Mendez* decision, LULAC forged ahead in its legal attack on segregation in Texas. With support from LULAC, a group of parents in 1948 brought suit against the Bastrop independent school district, charging that local school authorities had no legal right to segregate children of Mexican descent and that this segregation was solely because the children were of Mexican descent. In *Delgado v. Bastrop Independent School District*, the court ruled that segregating Mexican American children was illegal and discriminatory. The ruling required that the local school district end segregation. The court did give local school districts the right to separate some children in the first grade only if scientific tests showed that they needed special instruction in English and the separation took place on the same campus.[14]

While the *Mendez* and *Delgado* decisions did hold out the promise of ending segregation of Mexican Americans, local school districts used many tactics to avoid integration, including manipulation of school district lines, choice plans, and different forms of second-generation segregation.

In *All Deliberate Speed: Segregation and Exclusion in California Schools, 1855–1975*, Charles Wollenberg estimates that in California by 1973 more Mexican and Mexican American children attended segregated schools than in 1947.[15]

The continuation of de facto forms of segregation resulted in the formation in 1967 of the Mexican American Legal Defense and Education Fund (MALDEF).

The case brought by MALDEF, *Rodriguez v. San Antonio Independent School District*, had major implications for financing of schools across the country. In the case, a group of Mexican American parents brought a class action against the state of Texas for the inequitable funding of school districts. In 1971, a federal district court ruled that the Texas school finance system was unconstitutional.

The U.S. Supreme Court overturned the decision on 12 March 1973 with the argument that school finance was not a constitutional issue. This Supreme Court decision meant that all school finance cases would have to be dealt with in state courts. Since 1973, numerous cases involving inequality in the financing of public schools have been argued in state courts.[16]

In 1970, Mexican Americans were officially recognized by the federal courts as an identifiable dominated group in the public schools in a MALDEF case, *Cisneros v. Corpus Christi Independent School District*. A central issue in the case was whether the 1954 school desegregation decision could be applied to Mexican Americans. The original *Brown* decision had dealt specifically with African Americans segregated by state and local laws. In his final decision, Judge Owen Cox ruled that blacks and Mexican Americans were segregated in the Corpus Christi school system law and that Mexican Americans were an identifiable dominated group because of their language, culture, religion, and Spanish surnames.[17]

Bilingual Education: The Culture Wars Continued

Since the efforts of Noah Webster in the late eighteenth and early nineteenth centuries to create a national language, Native Americans and Spanish-speaking residents were concerned about preserving their languages. In the 1960s, a new chapter in the culture wars was opened when Native Americans, Mexican Americans, and Puerto Ricans joined in efforts to have the public schools implement bilingual education programs. Those opposed to multicultural education quickly reacted to the bilingual education movement by arguing that the official language of the United States should be English.

La Raza Unida was formed in 1967 when a group of Mexican Americans boycotted federal hearings on the conditions of Mexican Americans and started their own conference. At the conference, La Raza Unida took a militant stand on the protection of the rights of Mexican Americans and the preservation of their culture and language. A statement drafted at the first conference proclaimed: "The time of subjugation, exploitation, and abuse of human rights of La Raza in the United States is hereby ended forever."[18]

La Raza Unida's statement on the preservation of culture and language reflected the growing mood in the Mexican American community that public schools needed to pay more attention to dominated cultures and languages. The statement drafted at the first conference affirmed "the greatness of our heritage, our history, our language, our traditions, our contributions to humanity and our culture."[19]

Native Americans, along with Mexican Americans and Puerto Ricans, welcomed the idea of bilingual education. The legislation promised that their cultures and languages would be preserved by the public schools.

By the 1980s, the two major U.S. political parties were divided over bilingual education. Traditionally, organized ethnic groups, including Mexican Americans and Puerto Ricans, were a strong force in the Democratic party. In contrast, bilingual education became a major target of attack during the Republican administrations of the 1980s and 1990s. Some members of the Republican party joined a movement opposing bilingual education and supporting the adoption of English as the official language of the United States.

Within the Reagan administration, Secretary of Education William Bennett attempted to reduce support for bilingual education by appointing opponents of it to the government's National Advisory and Coordinating Council on Bilingual Education. The new appointees expressed a preference for immersing non-English-speaking children in the English language, rather than teaching them in a bilingual context. In addition, the new appointees favored giving more power to local officials to determine programs. Such a policy would undercut the power the Hispanic community had gained by working with the federal government. Originally, Hispanics had turned to the federal government for assistance because they lacked power in local politics.[20]

Despite opposition from civil rights organizations and professional organizations, including the National Association of Bilingual Education, the National Council of Teachers of English, the Linguistics Society of America, and the Modern Language Association, efforts to make English the official language continue at the state and national levels. In 1923, Nebraska made English the official state language, followed by Illinois in 1969. In 1978, Hawaii made English and Hawaiian the official state languages. Indicative of the concerns of the 1980s, between 1984 and 1988 fourteen other states made English the official state language.[21]

The major target of those supporting English as the official language is the ballot. Extensions to the 1965 Voting Rights Act granted citizens the right to voting information in their native languages. In communities where 5 percent or more of the population speak languages other than English, voting material must be provided in those languages.

Besides the issue of political power, language is considered a cultural issue by Mexican Americans, Puerto Ricans, and Native Americans. A person's cultural perspective is directly related to attitudes regarding making English the official language.

The Next Chapter in the Culture Wars: No Child Left Behind Act of 2001

The No Child Left Behind Act of 2001 dealt a severe blow to those advocating the protection of minority cultures and languages. First, it mandated that states use high-stakes standardized tests to measure educational outcomes. By their very definition and construction, high-stakes standardized tests given in elementary, middle, and high schools represent only a single culture. Given to all students, test questions could not be based on knowledge known only to students in a minority culture. Since teachers must teach to the best to ensure that their students are able to be promoted or graduated, teachers are forced to teach the culture embedded in the test items.

In addition, the No Child Left Behind Act undercuts attempts to preserve the usage of minority languages. The legislation requires that the name of the Office of Bilingual Education be changed to the Office of English Language Acquisition. Bilingual advocates wanted the schools to maintain minority languages as a means of maintaining minority cultures. The No Child Left Behind Act mandated that minority languages would be used as a vehicle for learning English.

What about segregation? In 1999 Gary Orfield, a long-time advocate of school desegregation, issued a report with the ominous title "Resegregation in American Schools." The report states, "We are clearly in a period when many policymakers, courts and opinion makers assume that desegregation is no longer necessary. . . . Polls show that most white Americans believe that equal educational opportunity is being provided." Orfield's study found that segregation of schools in the South increased from 1988 to 1997 with the number of black students attending majority white schools declining from 43.5 percent to 34.7 percent. Hispanic students are now the most segregated group with about 75 percent attending schools with over 50 percent nonwhite students. On the average, white students attend schools that are 81 percent white. Orfield's report concludes, "We are floating back toward an educational pattern that has never in the nation's history produced equal and successful schools."

Conclusion: Human and Educational Rights

In the United States the historical issues of cultural and linguistic genocide and educational segregation are still alive in the twenty-first century. The problem is the inherent tendency of nation-states to use their educational systems to create uniform culture and language usage as a means of maintaining social order and control. Consequently, it is increasingly becoming the task of international organizations to protect equal educational opportunity and cultural and linguistic rights. Advocates of international human rights documents are forcing national educational systems to provide equal educational opportunity and to end the practice of cultural and linguistic genocide. These issues are specifically dealt with in the 1960 Convention Against Discrimination in Education released by the United Nations Educational, Scientific and Cultural Organization (UNESCO). The Convention defines "discrimination" as "any distinction, exclusion, limitation or preference."[22] Race, color, sex, language, social class, religion, political opinion, and national origin are identified as objects of discrimination in education.[23]

Notes

1. "The Effects of Segregation and the Consequences of Desegregation: A Social Science Statement," appendix to Appellants' Brief filed in the *School Segregation Cases* in the Supreme Court of the United States, October term, 1952, in *The Afro-Americans: Selected Documents*, edited by John Bracey, August Meier, and Elliott Rudwick (Boston: Allyn & Bacon, 1972), pp. 661–671.
2. Martin Luther King, Jr., *Stride Toward Freedom: The Montgomery Story* (New York: Harper & Row, 1958), pp. 94–97.
3. Jon Reyhner and Jeanne Eder, *A History of Indian Education* (Billings: Eastern Montana College, 1989), pp. 125–126.
4. Ibid., p. 126.
5. Prucha, p. 82.
6. U.S. Senate Committee on Labor and Public Welfare, *Indian Education: A National Tragedy—A National Challenge*, 91st Cong., 1st sess. 1969, p. 106.
7. "American Indian Religious Freedom. August 11, 1978," Prucha, pp. 288–289.
8. Quoted in Reyhner and Eder, p. 128.
9. Quoted in Joel Spring, *Intersections of Culture: Multicultural Education in the United States and the Global Economy* (New York: McGraw-Hill, 2000), p. 56.
10. Quoted in L. Ling-Chi Wang, "*Lau v. Nichols:* History of a Struggle for Equal and Quality Education," in *The Asian American Educational Experience*, edited by Don T. Nakanishi and Tina Yamano Nishida (New York: Routledge, 1995), p. 60.
11. Ibid., p. 61.
12. Reyhner and Eder, p. 128.
13. Ibid., pp. 127–129. Also see Gilbert G. Gonzalez, *Chicano Education in the Era of Segregation* (Philadelphia: Balch Institute Press, 1990), pp. 147–156.
14. Guadalupe San Miguel, Jr., *"Let All of Them Take Heed": Mexican Americans and the Campaign for Educational Equality in Texas, 1910–1981* (Austin: University of Texas Press, 1987), pp. 123–124.
15. Charles Wollenberg, *All Deliberate Speed: Segregation and Exclusion in California Schools, 1855–1975* (Berkeley: University of California Press, 1976), p. 134.
16. San Miguel, pp. 173–174.

17. Ibid., pp. 177–179.
18. San Miguel, p. 168.
19. Ibid.
20. James Crawford, "Administration Panel Praises Bennett's Bilingual-Education Stance," *Education Week 5,* no. 28 (9 April 1986), p. 9.
21. Rosalie Pedalino Porter, *Forked Tongue: The Politics of Bilingual Education* (New York: Basic Books, 1990), pp. 210–211.
22. "Convention Against Discrimination in Education, 1960," *Basic Documents on Human Rights Third Edition,* edited by Ian Brownlie (New York: Oxford University Press, 1992), p. 319.
23. Ibid., p. 319.

The Passions of Pluralism: Multiculturalism and the Expanding Community

Maxine Greene

Maxine Greene's approach to multicultural education is to see the diverse nation as a community. She uses literary works, the arts, and ethnographies to bring out the voices of people who have been unintentionally overlooked and purposefully silenced. She calls these omissions of diverse voices "gaps in our understandings." Greene would like for us to engage with others in explorations and discussions of what it means to be a person. From dialogue we learn about the many perspectives on life by the young and the old, the excluded and the powerless, and those in poverty. Her hope is that by helping students to look through multiple perspectives on life, to hear and read a wide range of human stories, those young people will want to transform society into a place where all voices are heard.

Greene is a Professor Emeritus at Teachers College, Columbia University in New York City, and in 2003 she founded the Maxine Greene Foundation for Social Imagination, the Arts and Education. She has received the American Educational Research Association's Lifetime Achievement Award. Her life prior to academia involved actively fighting for people's rights to be heard. She became involved in antifascist activities in Spain, and she served as legislative director of the American Labor Party in Brooklyn, New York. Thus her concern for bringing diverse voices to readers and teachers arises out of her own life experiences. Greene's aesthetic and literary approach to the study and practice of education has resulted in bringing the diverse stories of people to the attention of readers. Among her well-known books are *Landscapes of Learning* (Teachers College Press, 1978), *The Dialectic of Freedom* (Teachers College Press, 1988), and *Releasing the Imagination: Essays on Education, the Arts, and Social Change* (Jossey-Bass, 1995). The following selection is from her article "The Passions of Pluralism: Multiculturalism and the Expanding Community," *Educational Researcher* (January–February 1993).

Key Concept: engaging in dialogue to gain multiple perspectives on life

There have always been newcomers in this country; there have always been strangers. There have always been young persons in our classrooms we did not, could not see or hear. In recent years, however, invisibility has been refused on many sides. Old silences have been shattered; long-repressed voices are making themselves heard. Yes, we are in search of what John Dewey called "the Great Community" (1954, pp. 143ff), but, at once, we are challenged as never before to confront plurality and multiplicity. Unable to deny or obscure the facts of pluralism, we are asked to choose ourselves with respect to unimaginable diversities. To speak of passions in such a context is not to refer to the strong feelings aroused by what strikes many as a confusion and a cacophony. Rather, it is to have in mind the central sphere for the operation of the passions: "the realm of face-to-face relationships" (Unger, 1984, p. 107). It seems clear that the more continuous and authentic personal encounters can be, the less likely it will be that categorizing and distancing will take place. People are less likely to be treated instrumentally, to be made "other" by those around. I want to speak of pluralism and multiculturalism with concrete engagements in mind, actual and imagined: engagements with persons, young persons and older persons, some suffering from exclusion, some from powerlessness, some from poverty, some from ignorance, some from boredom. Also, I want to speak with imagination in mind, and metaphor, and art. Cynthia Ozick writes:

Through metaphor, the past has the capacity to imagine us, and we it. Through metaphorical concentration, doctors can imagine what it is to be their patients. Those who have no pain can imagine those who suffer. Those at the center can imagine what it is to be outside. The strong can imagine the weak. Illuminated lives can imagine the dark. Poets in their twilight can imagine the borders of stellar fire. We strangers can imagine the familiar hearts of strangers. (1989, p. 283)

Towards a Community of Persons

Passions, then, engagements, and imagining: I want to find a way of speaking of community, an expanding community, taking shape when diverse people, speaking as *who* and not *what* they are, come together in speech and action, as [historian] Hannah Arendt puts it, to constitute something in common among themselves. She writes: "Plurality is the condition of human action because we are all the same, that is, human, in such a way that nobody is ever the same as anyone else who ever lived, lives, or will live" (1958, p. 57). For her, those present on a common ground have different locations on that ground; and each one "sees or hears from a different position." An object—a classroom, a neighborhood street, a field of flowers—shows itself differently when encountered by a variety of spectators. The reality of that object (or classroom, or neighborhood, or field of flowers) arises out of the sum total of its appearances. Thinking of those spectators as participants in an ongoing dialogue, each one speaking out of a distinct perspective and yet open to those around, I find a kind of paradigm for what I have in mind. I discover another in the work of Henry Louis Gates, Jr., who writes about the fact that "the challenge facing America in the next century will be the shaping, at long last, of a truly common public culture, one responsive to the long-silenced cultures of color" (1991, p. 712). (It is not long, it will be remembered, since the same Professor Gates asked in a *New York Times* article, "Whose canon is it anyway?" See Gates, 1992.) More recently, he has evoked the philosopher Michael Oakeshott and his notion of a conversation with different voices. Education, Gates suggests, might be "an invitation into the art of this conversation in which we learn to recognize the voices, each conditioned by a different perception of the world." Then Gates adds: "Common sense says that you don't bracket out 90% of the world's cultural heritage if you really want to learn about the world" (1991, p. 712).

For many, what is common sense for Gates represents an attack on the coherence of what we think of as our heritage, our canon. The notion of different voices conditioned by different perspectives summons up the spectre of relativism; and relativism, according to Clifford Geertz, is the "intellectualist Grande Peur." It makes people uneasy, because it appears to subvert authority; it eats away at what is conceived of as objectively real. "If thought is so much out in the world as this," Geertz asks, as the uneasy might ask, "what is to guarantee its generality, its objectivity, its efficacy,

or its truth?" (1983, p. 153). There is irony in Geertz's voice, since he knows and has said: "For our time and forward, the image of a general orientation, perspective, *Weltanschauung,* growing out of humanistic studies (or, for that matter, out of scientific ones) and shaping the direction of the culture is a chimera." He speaks of the "radical variousness of the way we think now" and suggests that the problem of integrating cultural life becomes one of "making it possible for people inhabiting different worlds to have a genuine, and reciprocal, impact upon one another" (p. 161). This is troubling for people seeking assurances, seeking certainties. And yet they, like the rest of us, keep experiencing attacks on what is familiar, what James Clifford calls "the irruption of otherness, the unexpected" (1988, p. 13). It may well be that our ability to tolerate the unexpected relates to our tolerance for multiculturalism, for the very idea of expansion and the notion of plurality. . . .

The seer of the life of communion, according to Dewey, was Walt Whitman. Whitman wrote about the many shapes arising in the country in his time, "the shapes of doors giving many exits and entrances" and "shapes of democracy . . . ever projecting other shapes." In "Song of Myself" (in total contradiction to the fundamentalist version of the "American way") he wrote:

Through me many long dumb voices,

Voices of the interminable generations of prisoners
  and slaves,

Voices of the diseas'd and despairing and of thieves
  and dwarfs,

Voices of cycles of preparation and accretion,

And of the threads that connect the stars, and of wombs
  and of the father-stuff,

And of the rights of them the others are down
  upon. . . .

Through me forbidden voices. . . .

—(Whitman, 1931, p. 53)

He was, from all appearances, the seer of a communion arising out of "many shapes," out of multiplicity. There is no suggestion of a melting pot here, nor is there a dread of plurality.

Silence and Invisibility: The Need to Repair

For some of us, just beginning to feel our own stories are worth telling, the reminders of the "long dumb voices," the talk of "the rights of them the others are down upon" cannot but draw attention to the absences and silences that are as much a part of our history as the articulate voices, the shimmering faces, the images of emergence and success. Bartleby, the clerk who "prefers not to" in Herman Melville's story [Billy Budd] (1986), may suddenly become exemplary. What of those who said no, who found no place, who made no mark? Do they not say something about a society that closed too many doors, that allowed people to be abandoned like "wreckage in the mid-Atlantic" (Melville, 1986, p. 121)? What of those like Tod Clifton in Ralph Ellison's *Invisible Man*? A former youth leader in the so-called Brotherhood, he ends up selling Sambo dolls in front of the public library. When the police try to dislodge him, he protests; and they kill him. The narrator, watching, wonders:

> Why did he choose to plunge into nothingness, into the void of faceless faces, or soundless voices, lying outside history? . . . All things, it is said, are duly recorded—all things of importance, that is. But not quite; for actually it is only the known, the seen, the heard, and only those events that the recorder regards as important are put down. . . . But the cop would be Clifton's historian, his judge, his witness, his executioner, and I was the only brother in the watching crowd. (1952, p. 379)

The many who ended up "lying outside history" diminished the community, left an empty space on the common ground, left undefined an aspect of reality.

It is true that we cannot know all the absent ones, but they must be present somehow in their absence. Absence, after all, suggests an emptiness, a void to be filled, a wound to be healed, a flaw to be repaired. I think of E. L. Doctorow painting a landscape of denial at the beginning of *Ragtime,* appealing to both wonder and indignation, demanding a kind of repair. He is writing about New Rochelle in 1906 but he is presenting a past that reaches into the present, into *our* present, whether or not we ride trolleys anymore.

> Teddy Roosevelt was President. The population customarily gathered in great numbers either out of doors for parades, public concerts, fish fries, political picnics, social outings, or indoors in meeting halls, vaudeville theatres, operas, ballrooms. There seemed to be no entertainment that did not involve great swarms of people. Trains and steamers and trolleys moved them from one place to another. That was the style; that was the way people lived. Women were stouter then. They visited the fleet carrying white parasols. Everyone wore white in summer. There was a lot of sexual fainting. There were no Negroes. There were no immigrants. (1975, pp. 3–4)

The story has focally to do with a decent, intelligent Black man named Coalhouse Walker, who is cheated, never acknowledged, never understood, scarcely *seen,* and who begins his own fated strategy of vengeance which ends when promises are broken and he is shot down in cold blood. Why is he unseen? Why were there no Negroes, no immigrants? More than likely because of the condition of the minds of those in power, those in charge. Ellison may explain it when he attributes invisibility to "a peculiar disposition of the eyes of those with whom I come in contact. A matter of the construction of their inner eyes, those eyes with which they look through their physical eyes upon reality" (1952, p. 7). But that disposition must itself have been partly due to the play of power in discourse as well as in social arrangements. We may wonder even now what the assimilation or initiation sought by so many educators signified when there were so many blanked out spaces—"no Negroes . . . no immigrants," oftentimes no full-grown women.

Looking back at the gaps in our own lived experiences, we might think of silences like those Tillie Olsen had in mind when she spoke of literary history "dark with silences," of the "unnatural silences" of women who worked too hard or were too embarrassed to express themselves (1978, p. 6), of others who did not have the words or had not mastered the proper "ways of knowing" (Belenky, Clinchy, Goldberger, & Tarule, 1986). We might ponder the plight of young island women, like Jamaica Kincaid's Lucy from Antigua, forced to be "two-faced" in a post-colonial school: "Outside, I seemed one way, inside I was another; outside false, inside true" (1990, p. 18). For years we knew no more about people like her (who saw "sorrow and bitterness" in the face of daffodils because of the Wordsworth poem she had been forced to learn) than we did about the Barbadians Paule Marshall has described, people living their fragmented lives in Brooklyn. There was little consciousness of what Gloria Anzaldua calls *Borderlands/La Frontera* on which so many Latinos live (1987), or of the Cuban immigrants like the musicians in Oscar Hijuelos's *The Mambo Kings Sing Songs of Love* (1989). Who of us truly wondered about the builders of the railroads, those Maxine Hong Kingston calls "China Men," chopping trees in the Sandalwood and Sierra Nevada Mountains? Who of us could fill the gaps left by such a person as Ah Goong, whose "existence was outlawed by the Chinese Exclusion Acts"? His family, writes Kingston,

> did not understand his accomplishments as an American ancestor, a holding, homing ancestor of this place. He'd gotten the legal or illegal papers burned in the San Francisco earthquake and fire; he appeared in America in time to be a citizen and to father citizens. He had also been seen carrying a child out of the fire, a child of his own in spite of the laws against marrying. He had built a railroad out of sweat, why not have an American child out of longing? (1989, p. 151)

Did we pay heed to a person like Michelle Clift, an Afro-Caribbean woman who felt that speaking in words that were not her own was a form of speechlessness? Or to a child like Pecola Breedlove in Toni Morrison's (1972) *The Bluest Eye*, the unloved Black child who wanted to look like Shirley Temple so she could be included in the human reality? Or to a Mary Crow Dog, who finds her own way of saying in the autobiography, *Lakota Woman*? How many of us have been willing to suffer the experiences most recently rendered in Art Spiegelman's two-volume comic book called *Maus?* He tells about his father, the ill-tempered Vladek, a survivor of Auschwitz, and his resentful sharing of his Holocaust memories with his son. Every character in the book is an animal: the Jews, mice; the Germans, cats; the Poles, pigs. It is a reminder, not simply of a particular culture's dissolution. ("Anja's parents, the grandparents, her big sister Tosha, little Bibi, and our Richieu. . . . All what is left, it's the photos"; 1991, p. 115). It is a reminder of the need to recognize that everything is possible, something normal people (including school people) either do not know or do not want to know.

To open up our experience (and, yes, our curricula) to existential possibilities of multiple kinds is to extend and deepen what we think of when we speak of a community. If we break through and even disrupt surface equilibrium and uniformity, this does not mean that particular ethnic or racial traditions ought to replace our own. Toni Morrison writes of pursuing her freedom as a writer in a "genderized, sexualized, wholly racialized world," but this does not keep her from developing a critical project "unencumbered by dreams of subversion or rallying gestures at fortress walls" (1992, pp. 4–5). In her case, the project involves exploring the ways in which what we think of as our Americanness is in many ways a response to an Africanist presence far too long denied. She is not interested in replacing one domination by another; she is interested in showing us what she sees from her own perspective—and, in showing us, enriching our understanding not only of our own culture, but of ourselves. . . .

As Charles Taylor and Alasdair MacIntyre have written, we understand our lives in narrative form, as a quest. Taylor writes: "because we have to determine our place in relation to the good, therefore we cannot be without an orientation to it, and hence must see our life in stories" (1989, p. 51). Clearly, there are different stories connected by the same need to make sense, to make meaning, to find a direction.

To help . . . the diverse students we know articulate their stories is not only to help them pursue the meanings of their lives—to find out *how* things are happening, to keep posing questions about the why. It is to move them to learn the "new things" [Paulo] Freire spoke of, to reach out for the proficiencies and capacities, the craft required to be fully participant in this society, and to do so without losing the consciousness of who they are. That is not all. Stories . . . must break through into what we think of as our tradition or our heritage. They should with what Cornel West has in mind when he speaks about the importance of acknowledging the "distinctive cultural and political practices of oppressed people" without highlighting their marginality in such a way as to further marginalize them. Not only does he call attention to the resistance of Afro-Americans and that of other long-silenced people. He writes of the need to look at Afro-Americans' multiple contributions to the culture over the

generations. We might think of the music, Gospel, jazz, ragtime; we might think of the Black churches; we might summon up the Civil Rights movement and the philosophies, the dreams that informed it; we might ponder—looking back, looking around—the images of courage, the images of survival. West goes on to say:

> Black cultural practices emerge out of a reality they cannot not know—the ragged edges of the real, of necessity; a reality historically constructed by white supremacist practices in North America. . . . These ragged edges—of not being able to eat, not to have shelter, not to have health care—all this is infused into the strategies and styles of black cultural practices." (1989, p. 23)

Viewed in connection with the idea of multiculturalism, this does not mean that Afro-American culture in all its variousness can be defined mainly in terms of oppression and discrimination. One of the many reasons for opening spaces in which Afro-Americans can tell their own stories is that they, far more than those from other cultures, can explain the ways in which poverty and exclusion have mediated their own sense of the past. It is true that experiences of pain and abandonment have led to a search for roots and, on occasion, for a revision of recorded history. What is crucial is the provision of opportunities for telling all the diverse stories, for interpreting membership as well as ethnicity, for making inescapable the braids of experience woven into the fabric of America's plurality. . . .

Conclusion

Learning to look through multiple perspectives, young people may be helped to build bridges among themselves; attending to a range of human stories, they may be provoked to heal and to transform. Of course there will be difficulties in affirming plurality and difference and, at once, working to create community. Since the days of [Alexis] De Tocqueville, Americans have wondered how to deal with the conflicts between individualism and the drive to conform. They have wondered how to reconcile the impassioned voices of cultures not yet part of the whole with the requirements of conformity, how not to lose the integrity of those voices in the process, how not to allow the drive to conformity determine what happens at the end. But the community many of us hope for now is not to be identified with conformity. As in Whitman's way of saying, it is a community attentive to difference, open to the idea of plurality. Something life-affirming in diversity must be discovered and rediscovered, as what is held in common becomes always more many-faceted—open and inclusive, drawn to untapped possibility.

No one can predict precisely the common world of possibility, nor can we absolutely justify one kind of community over another. Many of us, however, for all the tensions and disagreements around us, would reaffirm the value of principles like justice and equality and free-dom and commitment to human rights since, without these, we cannot even argue for the decency of welcoming. Only if more and more persons incarnate such principles, we might say, and choose to live by them and engage in dialogue in accord with them, are we likely to bring about a democratic pluralism and not fly apart in violence and disorder. Unable to provide an objective ground for such hopes and claims, all we can do is speak with others as eloquently and passionately as we can about justice and caring and love and trust. Like Richard Rorty and those he calls pragmatists, we can only articulate our desire for as much intersubjective agreement as possible, "the desire to extend the reference of 'us' as far as we can" (1991, p. 23). But, as we do so, we have to remain aware of the distinctive members of the plurality, appearing before one another with their own perspectives on the common, their own stories entering the culture's story, altering it as it moves through time. We want our classrooms to be just and caring, full of various conceptions of the good. We want them to be articulate, with the dialogue involving as many persons as possible, opening to one another, opening to the world. And we want them to be concerned for one another, as we learn to be concerned for them. We want them to achieve friendships among one another, as each one moves to a heightened sense of craft and wide-awake-ness, to a renewed consciousness of worth and possibility.

With voices in mind and the need for visibility, I want to end with a call for human solidarity by Muriel Rukeyser, who—like many of us—wanted to "widen the lens and see/standing over the land myths of identity, new signals, processes." And then:

Carry abroad the urgent need, the scene,
to photograph and to extend the voice,
to speak this meaning.
Voices to speak to us directly. As we move.
As we enrich, growing in larger motion,
this word, this power.
—(Rukeyser, 1938, p. 71)

This power, yes, the unexplored power of pluralism, and the wonder of an expanding community.

References

Anzaldua, G. (1987). *Borderlands/La Frontera: The new mestiza.* San Francisco: Spinsters/Aunt Lute.

Arendt, H. (1958). *The human condition.* Chicago: University of Chicago Press.
Belenky, M. F., Clinchy, B., Goldberger, N., & Tarule, J. (1986). *Women's ways of knowing.* New York: Basic Books.
Clifford, J. (1988). *The predicament of culture.* Cambridge, MA: Harvard University Press.
Dewey, J. (1954). *The public and its problems.* Athens, OH: Swallow Press.
Doctorow, E. L. (1975). *Ragtime.* New York: Random House.
Ellison, R. (1952). *Invisible Man.* New York: Signet.
Gates, Jr., H. L. (1992). The master's pieces: On canon formation and the African-American tradition. In Gates, *Loose Canons* (pp. 17–42). New York: Oxford University Press.
Gates, Jr., H. L. (1991). Goodbye, Columbus? Notes on the culture of criticism. *American Literacy History,* 3(4), 711–727.
Geertz, C. (1983). *Local knowledge.* New York: Basic Books.
Hijuelos, O. (1989). *The mambo kings sing songs of love.* New York: Farrar, Straus, & Giroux.
Hughes, R. (1992, April 23). Art, morality & Mapplethorpe. *The New York Review of Books,* pp. 21–27.
Kincaid, J. (1990). *Lucy.* New York: Farrar, Straus, & Giroux.
Kingston, M. H. (1989). *China men.* New York: Vintage.
Melville, H. (1986). Bartleby. In H. Melville, *Billy Budd, sailor and other stories* (pp. 95–130). New York: Bantam Books.
Morrison, T. (1972). *The bluest eye.* New York: Pocket Books.
Morrison, T. (1992). *Playing in the dark: Whiteness and the literary imagination.* Cambridge, MA: Harvard University Press.
Olsen, T. (1978). *Silences.* New York: Delacorte.
Ozick, C. (1989). *Metaphor and memory.* New York: Knopf.
Rorty, R. (1991). Solidarity or objectivity? In Rorty, *Objectivity, relativism, and truth.* Cambridge, England: Cambridge University Press.
Rukeyser, M. (1983). *The book of the dead.* New York: Covici-Friede.
Schlesinger, Jr., A. M. (1992). *The disuniting of America: Reflections on a multicultural society.* New York: Norton.
Spiegelman, A. (1991). *Maus II.* New York: Pantheon Books.
Taylor, C. (1989). *Sources of the self.* Cambridge, MA: Harvard University Press.
Unger, R. M. (1984). *Passion: An essay on personality.* New York: Free Press.
Walker, A. (1982). *The color purple.* New York: Washington Square Press.
West, C. (1989). Black culture and postmodernism. In B. Kruger & P. Mariani (Eds.), *Remaking history.* Seattle: Bay Press.
Whitman, W. (1931). *Leaves of grass.* New York: Aventine Press.

The Promise of Cultural Studies of Education

Kathy Hytten

Kathy Hytten has turned the attention of scholars and educators toward the field of Cultural Studies of Education in several publications, including the current selection from "The Promise of Cultural Studies of Education," *Educational Theory* (Fall 1999). In this selection, she lays out the field of cultural studies, which is drawn from fields such as sociology, anthropology, philosophy, literary criticism ethnic studies, and education. She frames her writing with the question "What should be the ultimate purposes of education in a democratic society?" Hytten draws from several texts within cultural studies to describe the central focus of cultural studies on the critical examination of popular culture and on critical literacy in general. She points out that within the framework of cultural studies, educators must model critical literacy and social engagement as a way to directly address issues of inequality and oppression. And finally, Hytten ties the field of cultural literacy to the field of multicultural education and the study of diversity, with a discussion of issues such as racism, sexism, heterosexism, and white privilege.

Hytten is currently Professor and Interim Chair in the Department of Educational Administration and Higher Education at Southern Illinois University, Carbondale, where she has taught courses in philosophy of education, sociology of education, cultural studies in education, and globalization. Hytten previously served as President of the American Educational Studies Association as well as the Executive Secretary of the Philosophy of Education Society. Her work has helped to frame the developing fields of cultural studies and of whiteness studies in education. In all of her work, there is a focus on social justice and critical pedagogy. Her articles have appeared in journals such as *Educational Theory, Educational Studies, Qualitative Studies in Education,* and the *Journal of Curriculum Studies.*

Key Concept: cultural studies in education

What should be the ultimate purposes of education in a democratic society? This seems like a simple question, yet when posed to educators, numerous, varied, and often contradictory responses are given. These range from gaining knowledge to developing skills, from finding a job to making a life, from social consciousness to social control, and from cultural transmission to critical citizenship. Certainly how we respond to this question influences what we do in the name of education, including how we design public schools and curricula. Surprisingly, however, this is a question not often asked by educators, nor one seriously addressed in schools of education. Asking about ultimate purposes is a metaphysical question, one that requires us to consider the reasons we do something—the why, or the end goal. Yet too often in education we neglect metaphysical questions and focus instead on engineering ones. Such questions are about means, about how we can best do something or how we can more efficiently reach some predetermined goal. Engineering questions are commonplace in education. Should students be able to choose their schools? How can we efficiently implement an educational strategy such as cooperative learning? What is the best way to teach biology? How can we better assess students? Some of these types of questions are more compelling than others, but "what they have in common is that they evade the issue of what schools are for. It is as if we are a nation of technicians, consumed by our expertise of how something should be done, afraid or incapable of thinking about why."

The failure to attend to questions of purpose is a significant concern of those who work within the emerging field of cultural studies of education. More so than many other traditions within education, cultural studies scholars begin with metaphysical concerns. They ask about what schools currently do to children and for what purposes, and they explore what schools might do differently and why. They begin with two premises: first, there is an integral relationship between education and the broader society; and second, schools and teachers play critical social and political roles. Within the more critically oriented cultural studies tradition in education, they also provide a vision for the ultimate purposes of education in society; a vision that involves challenging inequity and injustice and building a more humane society. This vision is based on a view of democracy that entails full participation by all citizens and that ensures equality of opportunity and an adequate standard of living for all. In practice, cultural studies practitioners explore the links between culture, knowledge, and power, and they aim to uncover disempowering educational and social practices. They claim that education does not provide equality of opportunity, but instead "generates a privileged narrative space for some social groups and a space of inequality and subordination for others."[1] Thus they challenge the ways in which schools currently function to reproduce the status quo (so that those groups with power retain power, and those that are marginalized or powerless remain so). Instead, cultural studies scholars suggest that minimally, "educational practice should participate in a social transformation that is aimed at securing fundamental human dignity."[2]

A Brief Orientation

It is difficult to trace briefly the development of cultural studies as a field largely because many different influences have led to its current state. Cultural studies draws from works in, and borrows methods from, many different academic fields, including sociology, anthropology, philosophy, literary criticism, ethnic studies, and education. Perhaps the most commonly agreed upon reference point in its development is the founding of the Birmingham Centre for Contemporary Cultural Studies in 1964.

Among the goals of those in the Centre were to understand how individuals make meaning of the world around them, to study how media and popular culture serve to influence and construct public opinion, to uncover the connections between economic structures and culture, and to examine the relations between culture and power.

In addition to the guiding desire to understand working class culture better, early cultural studies practitioners also sought to redefine the meaning of culture itself, aiming to move it away from its elitist connotations. It was their view that by studying the "real" world, and investigating how people make meaning in their everyday interactions, that they could uncover disabling and disempowering social practices and relations, and

consequently work toward altering them. In this sense, the tradition of cultural studies is not marked by "value-free scholarship but . . . political commitment."[3] It calls for academic work to make a difference in the world, and for the production of knowledge "that both helps people understand that the world is changeable and offers some direction how to change it."[4] While there is still much confusion over exactly what constitutes cultural studies as an approach to academic work, at its most basic level cultural studies historically was, and still is, a critical, interventionist, and ethical project that builds upon a fundamental commitment to disempowered populations. It is aligned with Left political movements that aim at exposing how power operates in society to privilege some and disempower others. As a critical project, practitioners interrogate the power dynamics behind the valuation of only certain forms of cultural capital and show how social institutions, the media, and schools often help to reproduce, rather than to challenge, inequitable social relations.

Cultural studies has been taken up by educators in a variety of ways. The two areas within education where cultural studies has been most visibly embraced are in the tradition of critical pedagogy and within ethnic and diversity studies. Despite the fact that many of the explicit links between cultural studies as a field and critical pedagogy are relatively recent, the overriding concerns of critical pedagogy certainly complement those of cultural studies. Critical pedagogues historically have sought to explore the connections between culture, knowledge, power, and authority, and have been guided by the goal of combating social inequities in the pursuit of greater social justice. Using a language of both critique and hope, they have shown how schools are culturally and socially reproductive, yet also how educators can resist problematic reproduction and create a more equitable and just social order. Recent theoretical developments in such fields as feminism, poststructuralism, and postmodernism have influenced the concerns of critical pedagogy more in the direction of cultural studies by exposing some of the limitations of critical pedagogy, particularly its seeming determinism and reductionist language.[5] Situating their work more firmly within a cultural studies tradition, many critical pedagogues are now more attentive to the complexity of notions such as oppression and empowerment and have argued that a critical investigation of schools should serve to "create a more ethically empowering world which encourages a greater awareness of the way in which power can be mobilized for the purposes of human liberation."[6]

Diversity studies within education have also drawn from, and been situated within, cultural studies. Moving beyond traditional additive notions of multiculturalism in education (where the goal is for curricula to be more inclusive, yet without challenging the dominant class ideologies and assumptions the curricula are based upon), critical diversity scholars have called for educators to rethink notions of difference, privilege, and power. They have challenged the implicit social norms of those with power and called for us to uncover (so as to alter) the operations of the culture of power. This culture casts whites as the mythical norm and concurrently, non-whites as deficient, deviant, and thus in need of compensatory programs. Peggy McIntosh writes that "whites are taught to think of their lives as morally neutral, normative, and average, and also ideal, so that when we work to benefit others, this is seen as work that will allow 'them' to be more like 'us.'"[7] A cultural studies approach to education has thus called for us to investigate the dominant culture critically so as to dismantle practices that silence voices and stifle diversity. Bell hooks argues that cultural studies offers a promising terrain for educators "to create ways to look at and talk about or study diverse cultures and peoples in ways that do not perpetuate exploitation or domination."[8] Within a critical, cultural studies approach to diversity "the intent is not to create a new center of authority based on a spurious unity of the marginalized, but rather to open up spaces for new ways of thinking about the dynamics of cultural power."[9]

The Popular as Pedagogical

The first association many people have with cultural studies as a field is the study of popular culture, which includes analyses of movies, television, books, magazines, advertisements, and electronic media. One of the legacies of the Birmingham school is a blurring of the distinctions between high or elite culture and its more popular manifestations. Popular culture was deemed crucial to understanding how people made meaning in their everyday lives, how they came to voice, and how they perceived possibilities. In short, the point of early cultural studies practitioners was that popular culture is a crucial force that helps to mold individuals and their perspectives of the world. This molding can occur somewhat passively or more critically. Cultural studies practitioners explore the meanings and messages behind popular cultural artifacts in order to reveal deleterious images, on the one hand, and to open up empowering options for critical reading, on the other. Implying that educators need to undertake a concerted effort to include popular culture within the curriculum, Giroux suggests that they "need to take up what it means to provide an ethical discourse from which to criticize those images, discourses, and representations that might be destructive to the psychological health of children or serve to undermine the normative foundations of a viable democracy" (CS, 60).

The argument that cultural studies of education scholars make is that the popular is pedagogical: "The electronic media—television, movies, music, and news—have become powerful pedagogical forces, veritable teaching machines in shaping the social imagination of students in terms of how they view themselves, others,

and the larger society" (CS, 109). It is therefore critical that educators investigate the ways in which popular culture affects students' lives and the ways in which they interact with knowledge and classroom learning. Popular culture is also a fruitful arena for exploring issues of diversity. Exemplifying this, Giroux provides a critical reading of the popular film about education, *Dangerous Minds*. He shows how behind the seemingly uplifting closing images of Latino children engaging and succeeding in schools, are coded images of minority children as intractable, out of control, hostile, dangerous, and in need of taming by white teachers through accepting the norms of "authority, orderliness, rationality, and control" (CS, 115). Kelly also talks about the pedagogical work that film can do in her analysis of the movie *Exotica*, which centers around the "disturbing relationship between male voyeurism and the murder and abuse of schoolgirls" (SD, 95). Critically reading this movie, she highlights the negatively portrayed images of social class, gender, sexuality, and race so that they may be "interrogated and redefined" and so that young people can "challenge such signfications and . . . resignify desire more firmly on their own terms and in their better interests" (SD, 97).

The news media is also a form of popular culture that cultural studies argues needs deconstructing. Marciano contends that the dominant forms of news media serve the interests of maintaining the status quo and of constructing a view of current events that is conducive to national interests. Referring to the news coverage of the Persian Gulf war, he asserts that a critical analysis of the mass media deserved "special attention" in schools, "for they propagandized the public and youth in a manner that undermined any attempt at civic literacy" (CIE, 167). With respect to popular media culture, the central message offered by advocates of a cultural studies approach to education is that popular culture does not simply provide passive entertainment or value neutral information, but contributes significantly to how people read and understand the world. Currently, popular culture is too often socially detrimental in that images of racism, sexism, classism, violence, and hyperindividualism are rampant. Yet cultural studies insists that there is hope, as educators can teach young people how to understand the negative effects of such images so as to rearticulate and recreate popular cultural spheres. In so doing, they can contribute to the development of "an ethical discourse in which cultural justice and rights can be seen as integral to expanding and democratizing popular forms and public spaces" (CS, 33). This type of critical reading is at the heart of cultural studies practice.

Critical Literacy

Kelly describes critical literacy well, distinguishing it from functional and cultural literacy—the predominant forms of literacy cultivated in schools. While a certain level of functional literacy is a prerequisite to critical literacy, what Kelly refers to when talking about functional literacy is the behavioristic, individualistic, and competitive nature in which it is nurtured, suggesting it is tied to the logic of the marketplace. *Functional* literacy is typically taught through pre-packaged curriculum materials and is premised on the development of value-neutral skills. Building from this base, *cultural* literacy is developed, which entails knowing the great ideas and literature that have shaped a culture or civilization. A curriculum for cultural literacy is typically closed, elitist, and based on the authority of tradition (*SD*, 10). Both of these approaches neglect the fact that when children are taught to read, they are taught to read in certain ways and, as Luke insists, "teaching the word, we selectively socialize students into versions of the world."[10] They both ask students to adopt certain norms, and especially with regard to cultural literacy, to internalize particular values and "social hierarchies" (*SD*, 11).

In contrast to these two approaches, *critical* literacy highlights the unavoidably political nature of knowledge, schooling, culture, and the making of identity. It aims not at adaptation to pre-existing norms, but at social transformation. Describing critical literacy, Kelly offers that "its curriculum is the everyday world as text and the analytic frameworks necessary to deconstruct it; its pedagogy is situated, interrogative, and counter-hegemonic" (*SD*, 10). She adds that critical literacy is empowering and transformative. This is because students are taught the relations among literacy, culture, and power and shown how culture works to shape individuals' understanding of knowledge and the world around them. A critically literate person can identify how this shaping occurs, and thus disrupt the problematic ways in which deleterious cultural practices (namely, racism, patriarchy, and classism) are encoded and transmitted in classrooms, in the media, and through popular culture. This type of critical literacy is also at the heart of Giroux's educational vision. He wants education to uncover commonsense and taken-for-granted understandings of the world and to challenge the ways in which negative representations of youth and of difference are socially reproduced. He asserts that "education works best when those experiences that shape and penetrate one's lived reality are jolted, unsettled, and made the object of critical analysis" (*CS*, 13).

The Roles of Educators and Intellectuals

Discussion of the role of intellectuals in social life is another common theme in cultural studies literature. Practitioners have written about the gulf between academic and real world concerns, the lack of obvious links between theory and practice, and the problematic posture of detached objectivity and neutrality that many

scholars and educators take with regard to crucial social and political issues. In contrast, while they do not always do it well, cultural studies practitioners call for academic life to be marked by intervention, engagement, and moral commitment. Emblematically, Carey writes that those who practice cultural studies must give up "the pose of observer" and instead must "undertake, explicitly, the task of using intelligence to change, modify, or reconstruct the social order."[11]

The message sent by this characteristic of cultural studies work is that as intellectuals, educators need to model critical literacy, engaged scholarly work, and social commitment. They also must seriously consider the broad public implications of their positions. Cultural studies of education calls for the breaking down of "rigid boundaries and binary oppositions between teaching and politics" (*ECS*, 6). In essence, the vision is of teachers as public intellectuals who play important social and political roles. Given that schools are perhaps the central social institutions through which societies' transmit knowledge, culture and values, teachers necessarily shape the meanings students make of the world and the priorities and goals they develop in their own lives. Moreover, "educators play a crucial role in shaping the identities, values, and beliefs of students who impact directly upon society" (*CS*, 150). For example, schools could implicitly encourage students to become competitive, selfish, and greedy, or conversely, to develop compassion, care, and social commitment. Giroux contends that teachers must link their "work to the moral horizon of public responsibility and progressive social change" (*CS*, 140).

Cultural studies offers a very different vision of teaching than is typically proffered in schools of education, where the emphasis is on content area expertise and technical pedagogical skills. In this sense, it is less concerned with engineering questions, and more concerned with questions of the purposes of education in society, and of the role that teachers can play in social reconstruction. The bottom line in a cultural studies of education perspective is that teaching is never value neutral. It always contributes to molding students in some ways and not others. It is therefore incumbent upon educators to be more conscious of the messages they do send, both in the overt and hidden curriculum, so that they can consciously work to bring about a more inclusively empowering democracy. This would enable greater equity and social justice, and contribute to a genuine respect for diversity and difference.

Rethinking Diversity as Pedagogy of Difference

Issues of difference and diversity are central in cultural studies of education. Beginning with a commitment to oppressed and marginalized populations, one key goal of cultural studies advocates is to create the conditions in which all peoples' lives and experiences are validated and legitimated, and not just those who are from the dominant culture. Furthermore, they show that in diversity there is strength, because multiple viewpoints and perspectives are enriching.

The guiding motifs of Kelly's pedagogy of difference provide a useful frame for how cultural studies of education, in general, approaches this topic. She begins with an exploration of how difference gets constructed in schools, and in whose interests. She highlights the fact that difference is always relational, that is, something or someone is only "different" in relation to something socially defined as the norm. For example, a person is not essentially learning disabled, but only becomes so in relation to what schools decide "abled" learning should look like. How this decision gets made is critical and consequential. This is particularly the case when the abilities, beliefs, and behaviors of minority children often get deemed "abnormal." Kelly writes that "the work of schooling, curriculum, and pedagogy is implicated in the making of social differences that make an *unjust* difference" (*SD*, 117, emphasis mine). From this base, she adds several corollaries to a pedagogy of difference which are particularly relevant in cultural studies of education. These include the need for critical reflexivity, an interrogation of privilege, and openness to all accounts of experience. In terms of critical reflexivity, she claims that the project of embracing difference is always contingent, limited, and provisional. It requires educators to be ever-vigilant of the impact of their pedagogies on all students in the classroom, not just those from the dominant culture.

The next two principles are related. They point to the imperative of studying both the experiences and accounts of marginalized groups while at the same time studying the privileges of the dominant social groups (in relation to which others become marginal). Schools of education have had some success with the first task, as curricula have become somewhat more inclusive and representative. Yet they often neglect the necessary corollary of studying the center of privilege (whiteness); as a result differences get exoticized and appropriated, but rarely result in a rethinking of the center of privilege itself. Giroux addresses this point as well in his discussion of the importance of whiteness studies. According to him, the goal of whiteness studies is to unmask domination and oppression by the dominant culture (which is synonymous with whiteness) so that racism and prejudice can be rooted out of both individuals and institutions: "Its primary aim is to unveil the rhetorical, political, cultural, and social mechanisms through which 'whiteness' is both invented and used to mask its power and privilege" (*CS*, 102). Consistent with other cultural studies scholars, both Giroux and Kelly call for a strategic educational approach to privilege in schools to serve as an integral complement to both a more representative canon and to a broader democratic vision.

Visions of Democracy

Taken together, the four overriding cultural studies of education themes that emerge from a review of contemporary works in this area—the need for attention to popular culture, critical literacy, engaged academic work, and a pedagogy of difference—are united in that they are all underscored by a vision of the possibility of developing a truly democratic social life in which the voices and contributions of all citizens are taken into account, and in which all forms of oppression and exploitation are diminished.

Most directly in this last theme, cultural studies of education practitioners address the question of the ultimate purposes of education. Accordingly, they argue that the central purposes of schools should be to educate people to create and take part in democratic life. At the same time, schools should be guided by the broad ethical goals of empowering the powerless and ensuring equitable treatment and a decent standard of living for all citizens. While there are allusions in all four books to the types of curricular practices that would best lead to these goals, the authors offer few specific claims of what to do or how best to engineer schools. Largely this is because there are a variety of viable ways to encourage the educational ends deemed worthwhile, particularly if schools have a clear vision of the types of citizens they hope to create and even more basically, of why we have public schools in the first place.

Cultural studies does offer educators distinct possibilities for rethinking their practices, as evidenced in the characterizing themes discussed here, and these have the potential to transform schooling and society. The challenge is to broaden the audience doing this rethinking so that cultural studies can better fulfill its promises. This is no small task.

Notes

1. Henry A. Giroux, "Doing Cultural Studies: Youth and the Challenge of Pedagogy," *Harvard Educational Review* 64 (1994): 279.
2. Roger I. Simon, *Teaching Against the Grain: Texts for a Pedagogy of Possibility* (New York: Bergin and Garvey, 1992), 17.
3. Alan O'Conner, "The Problem of American Cultural Studies," in *What is Cultural Studies? A Reader,* ed. John Storey (London: Arnold, 1996), 187.
4. Lawrence Grossberg, *Bringing it all Back Home: Essays on Cultural Studies* (Durham, N.C.: Duke University Press, 1997), 264.
5. I develop the connection between cultural studies and critical pedagogy more fully in Kathy Hytten, "The Ethics of Cultural Studies," *Educational Studies* 29, no. 3 (1998): 247–65. I argue that writings in critical pedagogy, most notably those by Giroux, are increasingly situated within the cultural studies literature. Responding to critiques that critical pedagogy is too reductionistic and deterministic, practitioners have developed more complex and multifaceted understandings of power dynamics and have

problematized such dichotomies as those of the oppressor versus the oppressed. They have exposed where the "reproductive theory of schooling has in some instances become a reactive mode of analysis, one that repeatedly oversimplifies the complexity of social and cultural life."

6. McLaren and Giroux, "Writing from the Margins," 21.
7. Peggy McIntosh, "White Privilege and Male Privilege: A Personal Account of Coming to See Correspondences through Work in Women's Studies," in *Readings in Sociocultural Studies in Education*, 2nd ed., ed. Kate Rousmaniere (New York: McGraw-Hill, College Custom Series, 1995), 190.
8. bell hooks, *Yearning: Race, Gender, and Cultural Politics* (Boston: South End Press, 1990), 128.
9. Russell Ferguson, "Introduction: Invisible Center," in *Out There: Marginalization and Contemporary Cultures*, ed. Russell Ferguson, Martha Gever, Trinh T. Minh-ha, and Cornel West (Cambridge: MIT Press, 1990), 9.
10. Allan Luke, "Literacies as Social Practices," *English Education* 3, no. 3 (1991), 139, cited in *SD*, 10.
11. James W. Carey, "Overcoming Resistance to Cultural Studies," in Storey, *What is Cultural Studies?* 73.

Sociological and Anthropological Perspectives on Multicultural Education

Unequal Education and the Reproduction of the Social Division of Labor

Samuel Bowles

Samuel Bowles has applied his knowledge in the fields of sociology and economics to the study of education. Most of his work is on understanding capitalism within a democracy, with a focus on the structure of labor, the organization of work, and the resulting inequities in society and schools. He is Professor Emeritus at the University of Massachusettsat Amherst, and currently serves as the Arthur Spiegel Research Professor and Director of the Behavioral Sciences Program at the Santa Fe Institute. His book *School in Capitalist America* was named Book of the Century in 1999 by the Museum of Education. Although Bowles is not first and foremost an educational scholar, his explanations of class distinctions and the role of schools to reproduce those class divisions have been widely studied and accepted within the fields of education and multicultural education. The following selection is from a chapter titled "Unequal Education and the Reproduction of the Social Division of Labor" in a book edited by Martin Carnoy, *Schooling in a Corporate Society: The Political Economy of Education in America,* 2nd ed. (McKay, 1975).

Bowles writes that unequal education is part of the capitalist society of the United States and is inherent within the class distinctions created by capitalism. He further contends that inequalities in the school system serve to reproduce the existing class structure, benefiting the upper strata of society. Schools have evolved in the way that they have, he believes, as a response to the needs of corporate society, producing a social division of labor with differences in rules, opportunities, and expectations of different classes of students. In discussing reform efforts in schools, Bowles asserts that reform efforts have failed because they have not challenged the basic class distinctions of capitalism.

Key Concept: education as the reproduction of class inequalities

The ideological defense of modern capitalist society rests heavily on the assertion that the equalizing effects of education can counter the disequalizing forces inherent in the free-market system. That educational systems in capitalist societies have been highly unequal is generally admitted and widely condemned. Yet educational inequalities are taken as passing phenomena, holdovers from an earlier, less enlightened era, which are rapidly being eliminated.

The record of educational history in the United States, and scrutiny of the present state of our colleges and schools, lend little support to this comforting optimism. Rather, the available data suggest an alternative interpretation. In what follows I argue (1) that schools have evolved in the United States not as part of a pursuit of equality, but rather to meet the needs of capitalist employers for a disciplined and skilled labor force, and to provide a mechanism for social control in the interests of

political stability; (2) that as the economic importance of skilled and well-educated labor has grown, inequalities in the school system have become increasingly important in reproducing the class structure from one generation to the next; (3) that the U.S. school system is pervaded by class inequalities, which have shown little sign of diminishing over the last half century; and (4) that the evidently unequal control over school boards and other decision-making bodies in education does not provide a sufficient explanation of the persistence and pervasiveness of inequalities in the school system. Although the unequal distribution of political power serves to maintain inequalities in education, the origins of these inequalities are to be found outside the political sphere, in the class structure itself and in the class subcultures typical of capitalist societies. Thus, unequal education has its roots in the very class structure which it serves to legitimize and reproduce. Inequalities in education are part of the web of capitalist society, and are likely to persist as long as capitalism survives. . . .

Class Inequalities in U.S. Schools

Unequal schooling reproduces the social division of labor. Children whose parents occupy positions at the top of the occupational hierarchy receive more years of schooling than working-class children. Both the amount and the content of their education greatly facilitates their movement into positions similar to those of their parents.

Because of the relative ease of measurement, inequalities in years of schooling are particularly evident. If we define social-class standing by the income, occupation, and educational level of the parents, a child from the 90th percentile in the class distribution may expect on the average to achieve over four and a half more years of schooling than a child from the 10th percentile.[1] . . . [S]ocial-class inequalities in the number of years of schooling received arise in part because a disproportionate number of children from poorer families do not complete high school.[2] . . . [T]hese inequalities are exacerbated by social-class inequalities in college attendance among those children who did graduate from high school: even among those who had graduated from high school, children of families earning less than $3,000 per year were over six times as likely *not* to attend college as were the children of families earning over $15,000.[3]

Because schooling, especially at the college level, is heavily subsidized by the general taxpayer, those children who attend school longer have access for this reason alone to a far larger amount of public resources than those who are forced out of school or who drop out early.[4] But social-class inequalities in public expenditure on education are far more severe than the degree of inequality in years of schooling would suggest. In the first place, per-student public expenditure in four-year colleges greatly exceeds that in elementary schools; those who stay in school longer receive an increasingly large *annual* public subsidy.[5] Second, even at the elementary level, schools attended by children of the poor tend to be less well endowed with equipment, books, teachers, and other inputs into the educational process. Evidence on the relationship between the level of school inputs and the income of the neighborhoods that the schools serve . . . indicate[s] that both school expenditures and more direct measures of school quality vary directly with the income levels of the communities in which the school is located.

Inequalities in schooling are not simply a matter of differences in years of schooling attained or in resources devoted to each student per year of schooling. Differences in the internal structure of schools themselves and in the content of schooling reflect the differences in the social-class compositions of the student bodies. The social relations of the educational process ordinarily mirror the social relations of the work roles into which most students are likely to move. Differences in rules, expected modes of behavior, and opportunities for choice are most glaring when we compare levels of schooling. Note the wide range of choice over curriculum, life style, and allocation of time afforded to college students, compared with the obedience and respect for authority expected in high school. Differentiation occurs also within each level of schooling. One needs only to compare the social relations of a junior college with those of an elite four-year college,[7] or those of a working-class high school with those of a wealthy suburban high school, for verification of this point.[8]

The various socialization patterns in schools attended by students of different social classes do not arise by accident. Rather, they stem from the fact that the educational objectives and expectations of both parents and teachers, and the responsiveness of students to various patterns of teaching and control, differ for students of different social classes.[9] Further, class inequalities in school socialization patterns are reinforced by the inequalities in financial resources documented above. The paucity of financial support for the education of children from working-class families not only leaves more resources to be devoted to the children of those with commanding roles in the economy; it forces upon the teachers and school administrators in the working-class schools a type of social relations which fairly closely mirrors that of the factory. Thus, financial considerations in poorly supported working-class schools militate against small intimate classes, against a multiplicity of elective courses and specialized teachers (except disciplinary personnel), and preclude the amounts of free time for the teachers and free space required for a more open, flexible educational environment. The lack of financial support all but requires that students be treated as raw materials on a production line; it places a high premium on obedience and punctuality; there are few opportunities for independent, creative work or individualized attention by teachers. The well-financed schools attended by the children of the rich can offer much greater opportunities for the development of the capacity for sustained independent work and the other characteristics required for adequate job performance in the upper levels of the occupational hierarchy.

Much of the inequality in American education exists between schools, but even within a given school different children receive different educations. Class stratification within schools is achieved through tracking, differential participation in extracurricular activities, and in the attitudes of teachers and guidance personnel who expect working-class children to do poorly, to terminate schooling early, and to end up in jobs similar to those of their parents.[10]

Not surprisingly, the results of schooling differ greatly for children of different social classes. The differing educational objectives implicit in the social relations of schools attended by children of different social classes has already been mentioned. Less important but more easily measured are differences in scholastic achievement. If we measure the output of schooling by scores on nationally standardized achievement tests, children whose parents were themselves highly educated outperform children of parents with less education by a wide margin. A recent study revealed, for example, that among white high school seniors, those whose parents were in the top education decile were on the average well over three grade levels ahead of those whose parents were in the bottom decile.[11] Although a good part of this discrepancy is the result of unequal treatment in school and unequal educational resources, much of it is related to differences in the early socialization and home environment of the children.

Given the great social-class differences in scholastic achievement, class inequalities in college attendance are to be expected. Thus one might be tempted to argue that the data . . . are simply a reflection of unequal scholastic achievement in high school and do not reflect any *additional* social-class inequalities peculiar to the process of college admission. This view, so comforting to the admissions personnel in our elite universities, is unsupported by the available data. . . . Access to a college education is highly unequal, even for children of the same measured "academic ability."

The social-class inequalities in our school system and the role they play in the reproduction of the social division of labor are too evident to be denied. Defenders of the educational system are forced back on the assertion that things are getting better, that inequalities of the past were far worse. And, indeed, some of the inequalities of the past have undoubtedly been mitigated. Yet, new inequalities have apparently developed to take their place, for the available historical evidence lends little support to the idea that our schools are on the road to equality of educational opportunity. For example, data from a recent U.S. Census survey . . . indicate that graduation from college has become increasingly dependent on one's class background. This is true despite the fact that the probability of high school graduation is becoming increasingly equal across social classes. On balance, the available data suggest that the number of years of schooling attained by a child depends upon the social-class standing of his father at least as much in the recent period as it did fifty years ago.[12]

The argument that our "egalitarian" education compensates for inequalities generated elsewhere in the capitalist system is so patently fallacious that few persist in maintaining it. But the discrepancy between the ideology and the reality of the U.S. school system is far greater than would appear from a passing glance at the . . . data. In the first place, if education is to compensate for the social-class immobility caused by the inheritance of wealth and privilege, education must be structured so as to yield a negative correlation between social-class background of the child and the quantity and quality of his schooling. Thus the assertion that education compensates for inequalities in inherited wealth and privilege is falsified not so much by the extent of the social-class inequalities

in the school system as by their very existence, or, more correctly, by the absence of compensatory inequalities.

Moreover, if we turn from the problem of intergenerational immobility to the problem of inequality of income at a given moment, a similar argument applies. In a capitalist economy, the increasing importance of schooling in the economy exercises a disequalizing tendency on the distribution of income even in the absence of social-class inequalities in quality and quantity of schooling. To see why this is so, consider a simple capitalist economy in which only two factors are used in production: uneducated and undifferentiated labor, and capital, the ownership of which is unequally distributed among the population. The only source of income inequality in this society is the unequal distribution of capital. As the labor force becomes differentiated by type of skill or schooling, inequalities in labor earnings contribute to total income inequality, augmenting the inequalities inherent in the concentration of capital. This will be the case even if education and skills are distributed randomly among the population. The disequalizing tendency will of course be intensified if the owners of capital also acquire a disproportionate amount of those types of education and training which confer access to high-paying jobs.[13] A substantial negative correlation between the ownership of capital and the quality and quantity of schooling received would have been required merely to neutralize the disequalizing effect of the rise of schooling as an economic phenomenon. And while some research has minimized the importance of social-class biases in schooling,[14] nobody has yet suggested that class and schooling were inversely related!

Notes

1. The data for this calculation refer to white males who were aged 25–34 in 1962. See S. Bowles, "Schooling and Inequality from Generation to Generation" (Paper presented at the Far Eastern Meetings of the Econometric Society, Tokyo, 1970).

2. [Data] understate the degree of social-class inequality in school attendance because a substantial portion of upper-income children not enrolled in public schools attend private schools. Private schools provide a parallel educational system for the upper class. I have not given much attention to these institutions as they are not quantitatively very significant in the total picture. Moreover, to deal extensively with them might detract attention from the task of explaining class inequalities in the ostensibly egalitarian portion of our school system.

3. For recent evidence on these points, see U.S. Bureau of the Census, *Current Population Reports* (Series P–20), nos. 183 and 185.

4. W. L. Hansen and B. Weisbrod, "The Distribution of Costs and Direct Benefits of Public Higher Education: The Case of California," *Journal of Human Resources* 5, no. 3 (Summer 1970): 361–370.

5. In the school year 1969–70, per-pupil expenditures of federal, state, and local funds were $1,490 for colleges

and universities and \$747 for primary and secondary schools. U.S. Office of Education, *Digest of Educational Statistics, 1969* (Washington, D.C.: Government Printing Office, 1969).

6. See also P. C. Sexton, *Education and Income* (New York: Viking Press, 1961).

7. See J. Binstock, *"Survival in the American College Industry"* mimeograph, 1971.

8. E. Z. Friedenberg, *Coming of Age in America* (New York: Random House, 1965). It is consistent with this pattern that the play-oriented, child-centered pedagogy of the progressive movement found little acceptance outside of private schools and public schools in wealthy communities. See Cohen and Lazerson, "Education and the Industrial Order."

9. That working-class parents seem to favor more authoritarian educational methods is perhaps a reflection of their own work experiences which have demonstrated that submission to authority is an essential ingredient in one's ability to get and hold a steady, well-paying job.

10. See, for example, A. B. Hollingshead, *Elmtown's Youth* (New York: John Wiley, 1949); W. L. Warner and P. S. Lunt, *The Social Life of a Modern Community* (New Haven: Yale University Press, 1941); R. Rosenthal and L. Jacobson, *Pygmalion in the Classroom* (New York: Holt, Rinehart, and Winston, 1968); and W. E. Schafer, C. Olexa, and K. Polk, "Programmed for Social Class: Tracking in High School," *Transaction* 7, no. 12 (October 1970): 39–46.

11. Calculation based on data in James S. Coleman et al., *Equality of Educational Opportunity*, vol. 2 (Washington, D.C.: U.S. Office of Education, 1966), and methods described in S. Bowles, "Schooling and Inequality from Generation to Generation."

12. See P. M. Blau and O. D. Duncan, *The American Occupational Structure* (New York: Wiley, 1967). More recent data do not contradict the evidence of no trend toward equality. A 1967 Census survey, the most recent available, shows that among high school graduates in 1965, the probability of college attendance for those whose parents had attended less than eight years of school. See U.S. Bureau of the Census, *Current Population Reports* (Series P–20), no. 185, 11 July 1969.

13. A simple statistical model will elucidate the main relationships involved.

    Let y (individual or family income) be the sum of w (earnings from labor, including embodied education and skills, L) and k (earnings from capital, K), related according to the equation $y = w + k = aK^A L^B$. The coefficients A and B represent the relative importance of capital and labor as sources of income. The variance of the logarithm of income (a common measure of inequality) can then be represented by the following expression:

    var log y = A^2var log K + B^2 var log L + $2AB$ covar (log L, log K).

    The first term on the right represents the contribution of inequalities in capital ownership to total inequality, the second measures that part of total income inequality due to inequalities of education and skills embodied in labor, and the third represents the contribution to income inequality of social class inequalities in the supply of skills and schooling. Prior to the educational differentiation of the labor force, the variance of labor was zero. All workers were effectively equal. The variance of the logarithm of income would then be owed entirely to capital inequality and would be exactly equal to A^2 var log K. The rise of education as a source of income and labor differentiation will increase the variance of the logarithm of embodied labor unless all workers receive identical education and training. This is true even if the third term is zero, indicating no social class inequalities in the provision of skills and education.

    To assert the conventional faith in the egalitarian influence of the rising economic importance of education, one would have to argue that the rise of education is likely to be associated with either (1) a fall in A, the relative importance of capital as a source of earnings; (2) a decrease in the size of the covariance of the logarithms of capital and labor; (3) a decrease in the inequality of capital ownerships; or (4) an increase in equality in the supply of education. While each is possible, I see no compelling reason why education should *produce* these results.

14. See, for example, Robert Hauser, "Educational Stratification in the United States," *Sociological Inquiry* 40 (Spring 1970): 102–29.

Adaptation to Minority Status and Impact on School Success

John U. Ogbu

John U. Ogbu (1939–2003), who was one of the world's leading educational anthropologists, specialized in the comparative study of minority education. He conducted research on the identities, experiences, and education of students, with a focus on minority status and class status. Ogbu's work has been recognized by numerous organizations and foundations. He was named Distinguished Scholar/Researcher on minority education by the American Educational Research Association. He received grants to further his research from a number of foundations, including the MacArthur Foundation, the Rockefeller Foundation, and the National Institute of Education. He was Alumni Distinguished Professor of Anthropology at the University of California, Berkeley. His last book published was *Black Students in an Affluent Suburb: A Study of Academic Engagement* (2003).

In the following selection, which has been taken from "Adaptation to Minority Status and Impact on School Success," *Theory Into Practice* (Autumn 1992), Ogbu explains why some minority groups, as groups, are more successful in school than other minority groups. He distinguishes between what he calls immigrant, or voluntary, minorities and nonimmigrant, or involuntary, minorities, and he goes on to discuss the community forces within these groups that differ both historically and currently. According to Ogbu, voluntary and involuntary minorities differ in terms of how they were initially incorporated into American society. Ogbu examines the degree of trust in whites that these minorities have developed over time, models of how to get ahead in U.S. society, and the strategies that the groups and individuals use in order to have a sense of self-esteem and group identity. The community forces that affect students different across different groups include historical experiences, cultural models, cultural frames of reference, degrees of trust, and educational strategies that are developed and used in schools.

Key Concept: community factors impacting minority student school performance

Community Forces

From my comparative research both in the United States and internationally, I suggest that an essential key to understanding the differences in the school adjustment and academic performance of minority groups is an understanding of (a) the *cultural models* a minority group has with regard to the U.S. society and schooling, (b) the *cultural and language frame of reference* of a minority group, (c) the *degree of trust or acquiescence* the minorities have for White Americans and the societal institutions they control, and (d) the *educational strategies* that result from the above elements. These four factors are dependent in part on the group's history, its present situation, and its future expectations. They are combined in the term *community forces*.

Cultural model is used to mean peoples' understandings of their world, which guide their interpretations of events in that world and their own actions in it. (Folk theory or folk model is a comparable term.) (See Ogbu, 1974; also, Bohannan, 1957; Holland & Quinn, 1987; Holy & Stuchlik, 1981.)

Cultural/language frames of reference are either ambivalent/oppositional or non-oppositional. Non-oppositional cultural/language frames of reference are due to *primary* cultural/language differences. These are differences that existed *before* a group became a minority, such as before immigrants from China, India, or Latin America arrived in the United States.

For example, before Punjabi Indians in Valleyside, California, arrived in the United States, they spoke Punjabi, practiced Sikh, Hindu, or Moslem religion, had arranged marriages, and the males wore turbans. The Punjabis also brought to America their own way of raising children. For example, they differ from White Americans in training children to make decisions and manage money (Gibson, 1988). The Punjabis continue to some extent these beliefs and practices in America.

Primary cultural differences result in a cultural frame of reference that is merely different, not oppositional. This frame of reference leads the bearers of primary cultural/language differences to interpret the cultural/language differences they encounter in school and workplace as *barriers to overcome* in order to achieve their goals.

Oppositional or ambivalent cultural frames of reference are due to *secondary* cultural/language differences. The latter are differences that arose *after* a group has become a minority, such as after Blacks were brought to America as slaves, or after an American Indian tribe was conquered, moved, and placed on a "reservation."

This type of cultural difference is thus the product of reactions to a contact situation, especially one that involves the subordination of one group by another. At the beginning of the contact, both the dominant group and the minority group are characterized by primary cultural differences. But subsequently, the minorities develop new cultural features and reinterpret old ones in order to cope with their subordination or oppression.

African Americans, for instance, spoke numerous African languages and practiced a variety of primary African cultural patterns at the time of their arrival in America as chattels of the dominant Whites. However, due to the subordination and oppressive conditions of the slavery period, the indigenous languages and cultural patterns eventually were mostly lost, reinterpreted, or replaced by new cultural and language forms.

These new cultural and language forms, behaviors, and meanings became the minorities' cultural frame of reference or ideal ways guiding behaviors. They became oppositional partly because the minorities were not rewarded for behaving like White Americans, were not permitted to behave like Whites, were punished for behaving like Whites, or, because under such circumstances the ideal way of behaving or cultural frame of reference symbolized their shared or collective sense of identity and self-worth.

Minorities with oppositional cultural/language frames of reference do not define cultural or language differences they encounter in society and school as barriers to overcome, but as markers of *identity to be maintained*. For these minorities, there is "a White way" and "a minority way" of talking and behaving. These minorities feel strongly that their way of talking, walking, etc., is an expression of their group identity; and that the "White way" is an expression of White identity (Ogbu, 1991a).

Degree of trust or acquiescence in a relationship with White Americans and their institutions is important. Some minorities have experienced many episodes in their relationship with Whites that have led them to believe that Whites and the institutions they control cannot be trusted; their comparative frame of reference is the education in White suburbs and they usually conclude that they are given different and inferior education.

Educational strategies encompass the attitudes, plans, and actions minorities use or do not use in their pursuit of formal education. Educational strategies are very much influenced by the minorities' cultural models, degree of trust or acquiescence, and cultural/language frames of reference.

An essential point of these community forces—i.e., cultural models, degree of trust or acquiescence, cultural/language frames of reference, and educational strategies—is that they are group or collective phenomena. Although they may be manifested at an individual level, they are characteristic of the group *qua* group. In other words, to understand minority students' (as well as minority parents') behaviors, decisions, or attitudes toward schooling, we need to understand the cultural models, degree of trust, cultural frames of reference, and educational strategies of the minority group from which they come.

Group Differences

All minority groups face certain similar barriers in school, including inferior curriculum, denigrating treatment, and cultural and language barriers, as well as social and economic barriers in the wider society. Yet some minorities are more able than others to adjust socially and do well academically in school.

As discussed above, factors that contribute to the differences in social adjustment and academic performance are the groups' differing cultural models, degree of trust, cultural frames of reference, and educational strategies, i.e., differing community forces. (See Fordham & Ogbu, 1986; Gibson, 1986, 1988; Gibson & Bhachu, 1991; Gibson & Ogbu, 1991; Lee, 1984; Schofield, 1982; Suarez-Orozco, 1987; Weis, 1985.) A major factor in these community forces appears to be the groups' histories and self-perceptions *vis-à-vis* the dominant group. To understand how history and self-perception shape these community forces, minority groups can be classified into the following: (a) autonomous; (b) immigrant or voluntary; and (c) non-immigrant or involuntary.

Autonomous minorities are minority groups that may be culturally or linguistically distinct but are not politically, socially, or economically subordinated to major degrees. These groups have relatively high rates of school success. White examples in the United States include Jews and Mormons; there are no non-White examples in the United States. Autonomous minorities are not discussed further in this article.

Immigrant or voluntary minorities are people who have moved more or less voluntarily to the United States because they believe that this would result in more economic well-being, better overall opportunities, and/or greater political freedom. Even though they experience subordination once here, the positive expectations they bring with them influence their perceptions of the U.S. society and schools controlled by Whites. Their children do not usually experience disproportionate and persistent problems in social adjustment and academic achievement. Examples in California are Chinese and Punjabi immigrants.

Refugees are not immigrant or voluntary minorities and are not the subject of this article. Yet I must note that there is a good deal of misunderstanding about refugees in the United States, especially Southeast Asian refugees, some of whom are doing well in school; others poorly. I have tried to explain elsewhere the distinction between refugees and immigrant minorities (Ogbu, 1991b). The point to stress here is that refugees are not synonymous with immigrants.

The third type is *non-immigrant or involuntary minorities*. Involuntary minorities are those groups that are a part of the United States society because of slavery, conquest, or colonization, rather than by choice because of expectations of a better future. They usually have no other "homeland" to which to return if their experiences in the United States become unbearable. It is these involuntary minorities that have the most difficulties with school adjustment and academic achievement. Examples of involuntary minorities include African Americans, Mexican Americans, Native Americans, and Native Hawaiians. (For the Mexican Americans, I consider those of Southwest origins, rather than immigrants from Mexico, see Ogbu, 1978; Ogbu & Matute-Bianchi, 1986.)[1]

Comparative research suggests that voluntary minorities, such as Chinese, Punjabi, and South American immigrants, have cultural models, degree of trust, cultural/language frames of reference, and educational strategies that differ from those of involuntary minorities, such as African Americans, Mexican Americans, Native Americans, and Native Hawaiians.

Voluntary minorities have cultural models that lead them to accept uncritically mainstream folk theory and strategies of getting ahead in the United States and to interpret their economic hardships as temporary problems they can and will overcome through education and hard work. Additionally they tend to acquiesce in their relationship with school personnel and White authorities controlling other societal institutions. Their cultural/ language frames of reference enable them to interpret cultural and language barriers in school as barriers to be overcome in order to achieve their immigration goals. Finally, these voluntary minorities do make concerted efforts to overcome the cultural and language barriers they experience in school and mainstream society.

Under these circumstances, one finds in voluntary minority communities an educational climate or orientation that strongly endorses academic success as a means of getting ahead in the United States. Equally important, one also finds culturally sanctioned high and persistence academic efforts. In these communities, social, peer, and psychological pressures not only encourage students to perform like Whites but also to surpass Whites in academic achievement.

In contrast, one finds in the communities of involuntary minorities cultural models that make them skeptical that they can get ahead merely through mainstream beliefs and strategies, even though they verbally endorse education as a means of getting ahead. Their cultural models lead them to attribute their economic and other difficulties to *institutionalized discrimination*, which, in their opinion, will not necessarily be eliminated by hard work and education alone.

Involuntary minorities tend to distrust school personnel and White people (or their minority representatives) who control other societal institutions. Their cultural/ language frames of reference lead them to interpret the cultural and language differences they encounter in school as symbols of their group identity to be maintained, and to consciously and/or unconsciously avoid crossing cultural and language boundaries (see Fordham & Ogbu, 1986; Ogbu, 1982, 1985, 1991a; Ogbu & Matute-Bianchi, 1986). Unlike voluntary minorities, involuntary minorities are the groups likely to demand or need culturally compatible curriculum, teaching and learning styles, communication style, and interactional style, rather than accept the school counterparts or, as Gibson puts it, "play by the rules" (Au, 1981; Moll & Diaz, 1987; Erickson & Mohatt, 1982; Gibson, 1988; Philips, 1983). . . .

Impact on School Outcomes

These differing elements of the community forces of the minority groups work in combination with societal factors to ultimately produce educational strategies that either enhance or discourage school success. This process occurs in a step-wise fashion as follows: Initially, a minority group's understanding of its place in United States society is partially determined by its initial terms of incorporation (voluntary or involuntary) and subsequent subordination; these understandings, in turn, determine the group's cultural model of schooling. Its cultural model also determines the group members' coping responses to the U.S. society as a whole, as well as in a given locality. These coping responses, expressed in the forms of folk theories about making it, and alternative or survival strategies, tend to require and promote adaptational attitudes, skills, and role models that may or may not be compatible with the pursuit of academic success. The initial terms of incorporation and subsequent treatment also determine the degree of trust the minorities have for the schools and Whites (or their minority representatives) who control the schools.

Additionally a minority group's cultural frame of reference and collective identity may lead its members to interpret the cultural and language differences they encounter as barriers to be overcome or as markers of group identity to be maintained. Those who interpret the cultural and language differences as barriers to be overcome will usually make concerted efforts and, with appropriate assistance from the schools, acquire the standard language and behavioral norms of the school. Those who interpret these differences as identity symbols and boundary-maintaining may consciously or unconsciously perceive learning the standard English language and cultural behaviors of the school as detrimental to their language and cultural identity and make little or no effort to cross cultural and language boundaries. . . .

Conclusion

Many who study literacy problems among African-American children and similar minorities focus on what goes on within the school, classroom, or family. This is probably due to the American cultural orientation of explaining educational behavior in terms of what takes place in these settings. It is also because of emphasis on remediation or improvement research, rather than research to understand the nature and scope of the problem, especially in comparative perspective. The assumption of this article is that in order to understand the disproportion and persistence of the literacy problems of African Americans and similar minorities, we must go beyond the events and situations in the school, classroom, and home. We must examine the historical and structural contexts of these events and situations in a comparative framework.

Voluntary and involuntary minorities differ not only in initial terms of incorporation into American society but also in their cultural models of what it means to be a minority, how to get ahead, and the role of education in getting ahead in the United States. They differ in the degree to which they trust White Americans and the institutions, such as schools, that are controlled by Whites; and they differ in collective identity and cultural frame of reference for judging appropriate behavior and affirmation of group membership and solidarity.

These distinguishing beliefs and practices affect the cultural knowledge, attitudes, and behaviors that minority parents employ in preparing their children for school and minority children bring to school. The latter interact with school factors and together they influence the children's social adjustment and academic performance.

Note

1. We classify Mexican Americans as an involuntary minority group because they were initially incorporated by conquest: The "Anglos" conquered and annexed the Mexican territory where Chicanos were living in the southwest, acts that were completed by the Treaty of Quadalupe Hildago in 1948 (see Acuna, 1981; Ogbu & Matute-Bianchi, 1986). Mexicans coming to the United States from Mexico are immigrants and may be properly designated as *Mexicanos* until they assume the identity or sense of peoplehood of the conquered group.

We also classify Puerto Ricans on the mainland United States as an involuntary minority group because they are more or less a "colonized group." The United States conquered or colonized Cuba, Puerto Rico, and the Philippines in 1898. Both Cuba and the Philippines later gained independence; for this reason Cubans and Filipinos coming to the United States come more or less as immigrants or refugees. The status of Puerto Rico is ambiguous: It is neither a state within the U.S. policy nor an independent nation in the real sense. Many Puerto Ricans feel that their "country" is still a colony of the United States (see Ogbu, 1978, 1990).

In summary, we classify a minority group as "voluntary" if its members have chosen to come to the United States and have not been forced by White Americans to become a part of the country through conquest, slavery, or colonization. That people are "forced" to flee their country by war, famine, political upheaval, etc., is not relevant to our classification. What matters is that members of the minority group do not interpret their presence in the United States as forced on them by White Americans. The distinction between the groups usually shows up in ethnographic studies focusing on the minority groups themselves.

References

Acuna, R. (1981). *Occupied America: The Chicano's struggle toward liberation.* San Francisco: Canfield Press.

Au, K. H. (1981). Participant structure in a reading lesson with Hawaiian children: Analysis of a culturally appropriate instructional event. *Anthropology and Education Quarterly, 10,* 91–115.

Bohannan, P. (1957). *Justice and judgment among the Tiv.* London: Oxford University Press.

Erickson, F., & Mohatt, J. (1982). Cultural organization of participant structure in two classrooms of Indian students. In G. D. Spindler (Ed.), *Doing the ethnography of schooling: Educational anthropology in action* (pp. 132–175). New York: Holt, Rinehart & Winston.

Fordham, S., & Ogbu, J. U. (1986). Black students' school success: Coping with the burden of "acting White." *Urban Review, 18*(3), 1–31.

Gibson, M. A. (1986). Playing by the rules. In G. Spindler (Ed.), *Education and cultural process* (2nd ed., pp. 274–281). Prospect Heights, IL: Waveland Press.

Gibson, M. A. (1988). *Accommodation without assimilation: Sikh immigrants in an American high school and community.* Ithaca, NY: Cornell University Press.

Gibson, M. A., & Bhachu, P. (1991). The dynamics of educational decision making. In M. A. Gibson & J. U. Ogbu (Eds.), *Minority status and schooling: A comparative study of immigrant vs. involuntary minorities* (pp. 63–95). New York: Garland.

Gibson, M. A., & Ogbu, J. U. (1991). *Minority status and schooling: A comparative study of immigrant vs. involuntary minorities.* New York: Garland.

Holland, D. C., & Quinn, N. (1987). Introduction. In N. Quinn & D. C. Holland (Eds.), *Cultural models in language and thought* (pp. 3–40). New York: Cambridge University Press.

Holy, L., & Stuchlik, M. (1981). The structure of folk models. In L. Holy & M. Stuchlik (Eds.), *The structure of folk models* (pp. 1–34). New York: Academic Press.

Lee, Y. (1984). *A comparative study of East Asian American and Anglo American academic achievement: An ethnographic study.* Unpublished doctoral dissertation, Department of Anthropology, Northwestern University.

Moll, L. C., & Diaz, S. (1987). Change as the goal of educational research. *Anthropology and Education Quarterly, 18,* 300–311.

Ogbu, J. U. (1974). *The next generation: An ethnography of education in an urban neighborhood.* New York: Academic Press.

Ogbu, J. U. (1978). *Minority education and caste: The American system in cross-cultural perspective.* New York: Academic Press.

Ogbu, J. U. (1982). Cultural discontinuities and schooling. *Anthropology and Education Quarterly, 13,* 290–307.

Ogbu, J. U. (1985). Research currents: Cultural-ecological influences on minority school learning. *Language Arts, 62,* 860–869.

Ogbu, J. U. (1990). Minority status and literacy in comparative perspective. *Daedalus, 119,* 141–168.

Ogbu, J. U. (1991a). Cultural diversity and school experience. In C. E. Walsh (Ed.), *Literacy as praxis: Culture, language, and pedagogy* (pp. 25–50). Norwood, NJ: Ablex.

Ogbu, J. U. (1991b). *Understanding cultural diversity and school learning.* Invited presentation at the annual meeting of the American Educational Research Association (Division D), Chicago.

Ogbu, J. U., & Matute-Bianchi, M. E. (1986). Understanding sociocultural factors in education: Knowledge, identity, and adjustment in schooling. In *Beyond language: Social and cultural factors in schooling language minority students* (pp. 73–142). Sacramento: California State Department of Education, Bilingual Education Office.

Philips, S. U. (1983). *The invisible culture: Communication in classroom and community on the Warm Springs Indian Reservation.* New York: Longman.

Schofield, J. W. (1982). *Black and White in school: Trust, tension, or tolerance.* New York: Praeger.

Suarez-Orozco, M. M. (1987). Becoming somebody: Central American immigrants in U.S. inner-city schools. *Anthropology and Education Quarterly, 18,* 287–299.

Weis, L. (1985). *Between two worlds: Black students in an urban community college.* Boston: Routledge & Kegan Paul.

Ethnographic Perspectives on Multicultural Education

Savage Inequalities: Children in America's Schools

Jonathan Kozol

Jonathan Kozol is a best-selling author whose books have contributed to both the public awareness and political discussion of educational inequities in the United States. Through his numerous books on the conditions of schools and communities, especially those of poverty, Jonathan Kozol brings to our attention the struggles and hopes of overlooked children within U.S. society. He is concerned with the extreme racial segregation in U.S. schools and the corresponding disparaging differences in funding, safety, and quality of schools. He employs an ethnographic approach, in which he spends time within the communities that he is studying. Kozol's most recent book, *The Shame of the Nation: The Restoration of Apartheid School in America*, examines the continued racial and economic disparities of schools today, pointing out that schools are still separate and unequal. Kozol has received several awards for his work, including the Robert F. Kennedy Book Award and the Conscience in Media Award.

In the following selection, drawn from the book *Savage Inequalities: Children in America's Schools* (Crown Publishers, 1991), Kozol applies his ethnographic approach to the schools and communities of several cities throughout the United States. He gives not only the details about the physical makeup of the schools and communities but also the words of the children who are impacted by those conditions. Kozol describes conditions ranging from the raw sewage contaminating the streets and schools in East St. Louis to the lack of medical and dental care. In describing the latter's impact on children, he writes "Children live for months with pain that grown-ups would find unendurable." Using these details and descriptions, Kozol argues for more equitable funding for schools across the country and urges legislators and educators to stop ignoring the needs of the millions of children who live in poverty in the United States.

Key Concept: ethnography of inequalities among U.S. schools and communities

It was a long time since I'd been with children in the public schools.

I had begun to teach in 1964 in Boston in a segregated school so crowded and so poor that it could not provide my fourth grade children with a classroom. We shared an auditorium with another fourth grade and the choir and a group that was rehearsing, starting in October, for a Christmas play that, somehow, never was produced. In the spring I was shifted to another fourth grade that had had a string of substitutes all year. The 35 children in the class hadn't had a permanent teacher since they entered kindergarten. That year, I was their thirteenth teacher.

The results were seen in the first tests I gave. In April, most were reading at the second grade level. Their math ability was at the first grade level.

In an effort to resuscitate their interest, I began to read them poetry I liked. They were drawn especially to poems of Robert Frost and Langston Hughes. One of the most embittered children in the class began to cry when she first heard the words of Langston Hughes.

What happens to a dream deferred?
Does it dry up
like a raisin in the sun?

She went home and memorized the lines.

The next day, I was fired. There was, it turned out, a list of "fourth grade poems" that teachers were obliged to follow but which, like most first-year teachers, I had never seen. According to school officials, Robert Frost and Langston Hughes were "too advanced" for children of this age. Hughes, moreover, was regarded as "inflammatory."

I was soon recruited to teach in a suburban system west of Boston. The shock of going from one of the poorest schools to one of the wealthiest cannot be overstated. I now had 21 children in a cheerful building with a principal who welcomed innovation.

After teaching for several years, I became involved with other interests—the health and education of farmworkers in New Mexico and Arizona, the problems of adult illiterates in several states, the lives of homeless families in New York. It wasn't until 1988, when I returned to Massachusetts after a long stay in New York City, that I realized how far I'd been drawn away from my original concerns. I found that I missed being with schoolchildren, and I felt a longing to spend time in public schools again. So, in the fall of 1988, I set off on another journey.

During the next two years I visited schools and spoke with children in approximately 30 neighborhoods from Illinois to Washington, D.C., and from New York to San Antonio. Wherever possible, I also met with children in their homes. There was no special logic in the choice of cities that I visited. I went where I was welcomed or knew teachers or school principals or ministers of churches.

What startled me most—although it puzzles me that I was not prepared for this—was the remarkable degree of racial segregation that persisted almost everywhere. Like most Americans, I knew that segregation was still common in the public schools, but I did not know how much it had intensified. The Supreme Court decision in *Brown v. Board of Education* 37 years ago, in which the court had found that segregated education was unconstitutional because it was "inherently unequal," did not seem to have changed very much for children in the schools I saw, not, at least, outside of the Deep South. Most of the urban schools I visited were 95 to 99 percent nonwhite. In no school that I saw anywhere in the United States were nonwhite children in large numbers truly intermingled with white children.

Moreover, in most cities, influential people that I met showed little inclination to address this matter and were sometimes even puzzled when I brought it up. Many people seemed to view the segregation issue as "a past injustice" that had been sufficiently addressed. Others took it as an unresolved injustice that no longer held sufficient national attention to be worth contesting. In all cases, I was given the distinct impression that my inquiries about this matter were not welcome.

None of the national reports I saw made even passing references to inequality or segregation. Low reading scores, high dropout rates, poor motivation—symptomatic matters—seemed to dominate discussion. In three cities—Baltimore, Milwaukee and Detroit—separate schools or separate classes for black males had been proposed. Other cities—Washington, D.C., New York and Philadelphia among them—were considering the same approach. Black parents or black school officials sometimes seemed to favor this idea. Booker T. Washington

was cited with increasing frequency, [W. E. B.] Du Bois never, and Martin Luther King only with cautious selectivity. He was treated as an icon, but his vision of a nation in which black and white kids went to school together seemed to be effaced almost entirely. Dutiful references to "The Dream" were often seen in school brochures and on wall posters during February, when "Black History" was celebrated in the public schools, but the content of the dream was treated as a closed box that could not be opened without ruining the celebration.

For anyone who came of age during the years from 1954 to 1968, these revelations could not fail to be disheartening. What seems unmistakable, but, oddly enough, is rarely said in public settings nowadays, is that the nation, for all practice and intent, has turned its back upon the moral implications, if not yet the legal ramifications, of the *Brown* decision. The struggle being waged today, where there is any struggle being waged at all, is closer to the one that was addressed in 1896 in *Plessy v. Ferguson,* in which the court accepted segregated institutions for black people, stipulating only that they must be equal to those open to white people. The dual society, at least in public education, seems in general to be unquestioned.

To the extent that school reforms such as "restructuring" are advocated for the inner cities, few of these reforms have reached the schools that I have seen. In each of the larger cities there is usually one school or one subdistrict which is highly publicized as an example of "restructured" education; but the changes rarely reach beyond this one example. Even in those schools where some "restructuring" has taken place, the fact of racial segregation has been, and continues to be, largely uncontested. In many cities, what is termed "restructuring" struck me as very little more than moving around the same old furniture within the house of poverty. The perceived objective was a more "efficient" ghetto school or one with greater "input" from the ghetto parents or more "choices" for the ghetto children. The fact of ghetto education as a permanent American reality appeared to be accepted.

Liberal critics of the Reagan era sometimes note that social policy in the United States, to the extent that it concerns black children and poor children, has been turned back several decades. But this assertion, which is accurate as a description of some setbacks in the areas of housing, health and welfare, is not adequate to speak about the present-day reality in public education. In public schooling, social policy has been turned back almost one hundred years.

These, then, are a few of the impressions that remained with me after revisiting the public schools from which I had been absent for a quarter-century. My deepest impression, however, was less theoretical and more immediate. It was simply the impression that these urban schools were, by and large, extraordinarily unhappy places. With few exceptions, they reminded me of "garrisons" or "outposts" in a foreign nation. Housing projects, bleak and tall, surrounded by perimeter walls lined with barbed wire, often stood adjacent to the schools I visited. The schools were surrounded frequently by signs that indicated DRUG-FREE ZONE. Their doors were guarded. Police sometimes patrolled the halls. The windows of the schools were often covered with steel grates. Taxi drivers flatly refused to take me to some of these schools and would deposit me a dozen blocks away, in border areas beyond which they refused to go. I'd walk the last half-mile on my own. Once, in the Bronx, a woman stopped her car, told me I should not be walking there, insisted I get in, and drove me to the school. I was dismayed to walk or ride for blocks and blocks through neighborhoods where every face was black, where there were simply *no white people anywhere.*

In Boston, the press referred to areas like these as "death zones"—a specific reference to the rate of infant death in ghetto neighborhoods—but the feeling of the "death zone" often seemed to permeate the schools themselves. Looking around some of these inner-city schools, where filth and disrepair were worse than anything I'd seen in 1964, I often wondered why we would agree to let our children go to school in places where no politician, school board president, or business CEO would dream of working. Children seemed to wrestle with these kinds of questions too. Some of their observations were, indeed, so trenchant that a teacher sometimes would step back and raise her eyebrows and then nod to me across the children's heads, as if to say, "Well, there it is! They know what's going on around them, don't they?"

It occurred to me that we had not been listening much to children in these recent years of "summit conferences" on education, of severe reports and ominous prescriptions. The voices of children, frankly, had been missing from the whole discussion.

This seems especially unfortunate because the children often are more interesting and perceptive than the grown-ups are about the day-to-day realities of life in school. For this reason, I decided, early in my journey, to attempt to listen very carefully to children and, whenever possible, to let their voices and their judgments and their longings find a place within [my] book—and maybe, too, within the nation's dialogue about their destinies. I hope that, in this effort, I have done them justice.

East St. Louis—which the local press refers to as "an inner city without an outer city"—has some of the sickest children in America. Of 66 cities in Illinois, East St. Louis ranks first in fetal death, first in premature birth, and third in infant death. Among the negative factors listed by the city's health director are the sewage running in the streets, air that has been fouled by the local plants, the high lead levels noted in the soil, poverty, lack of education, crime, dilapidated housing, insufficient health care, unemployment. Hospital care is deficient too. There is no place to have a baby in East St. Louis. The maternity ward at the city's Catholic hospital, a 100-year-old structure, was shut down some years ago. The only other hospital in town was forced by lack of funds to close in 1990. The closest obstetrics service open to the women here is seven miles away. The infant death rate is still rising.

As in New York City's poorest neighborhoods, dental problems also plague the children here. Although dental problems don't command the instant fears associated with low birth weight, fetal death or cholera, they do have the consequence of wearing down the stamina of children and defeating their ambitions. Bleeding gums, impacted teeth and rotting teeth are routine matters for the children I have interviewed in the South Bronx. Children get used to feeling constant pain. They go to sleep with it. They go to school with it. Sometimes their teachers are alarmed and try to get them to a clinic. But it's all so slow and heavily encumbered with red tape and waiting lists and missing, lost or canceled welfare cards, that dental care is often long delayed. Children live for months with pain that grown-ups would find unendurable. The gradual attrition of accepted pain erodes their energy and aspiration. I have seen children in New York with teeth that look like brownish, broken sticks. I have also seen teenagers who were missing half their teeth. But, to me, most shocking is to see a child with an abscess that has been inflamed for weeks and that he has simply lived with and accepts as part of the routine of life. Many teachers in the urban schools have seen this. It is almost commonplace.

Compounding these problems is the poor nutrition of the children here—average daily food expenditure in East St. Louis is $2.40 for one child—and the under immunization of young children. Of every 100 children recently surveyed in East St. Louis, 55 were incompletely immunized for polio, diphtheria, measles and whooping cough. In this context, health officials look with all the more uneasiness at those lagoons of sewage outside public housing. . . .

A 16-year-old student in the South Bronx tells me that he went to English class for two months in the fall of 1989 before the school supplied him with a textbook. He spent the entire year without a science text. "My mother offered to help me with my science, which was hard for me," he says, "but I could not bring home a book."

In May of 1990 he is facing final exams, but, because the school requires students to pass in their textbooks one week prior to the end of the semester, he is forced to study without math and English texts.

He wants to go to college and he knows that math and English are important, but he's feeling overwhelmed, especially in math. He asked his teacher if he could come in for extra help, but she informed him that she didn't have the time. He asked if he could come to school an hour early, when she might have time to help him, but security precautions at the school made this impossible.

Sitting in his kitchen, I attempt to help him with his math and English. In math, according to a practice test he has been given, he is asked to solve the following equation: "$2x - 2 = 14$. What is x?" He finds this baffling. In English, he is told he'll have to know the parts of speech. In the sentence "Jack walks to the store," he is unable to identify the verb.

He is in a dark mood, worried about this and other problems. His mother has recently been diagnosed as having cancer. We leave the apartment and walk downstairs to the street. He's a full-grown young man, tall and quiet and strong-looking; but out on the street, when it is time to say good-bye, his eyes fill up with tears.

In the fall of the year, he phones me at my home. "There are 42 students in my science class, 40 in my English class—45 in my home room. When all the kids show up, five of us have to stand in back."

A first-year English teacher at another high school in the Bronx calls me two nights later: "I've got five classes—42 in each! We have no textbooks yet. I'm using my old textbook from the seventh grade. They're doing construction all around me so the noise is quite amazing. They're actually *drilling* in the hall outside my room. I have more kids than desks in all five classes."

"A student came in today whom I had never seen. I said, 'We'll have to wait and see if someone doesn't come so you can have a chair.' She looked at me and said, 'I'm leaving.' "

The other teachers tell her that the problem will resolve itself. "Half the students will be gone by Christmastime, they say. It's awful when you realize that the school is *counting* on the failure of one half my class. If they didn't count on it, perhaps it wouldn't happen. If I *began* with 20 students in a class, I'd have lots more time to spend with each of them. I'd have a chance to track them down, go to their homes, see them on the weekends. . . . I don't understand why people in New York permit this."

One of the students in her class, she says, wrote this two-line poem for Martin Luther King:

He tried to help the white and black.
Now that he's dead he can't do jack.

Another student wrote these lines:

America the beautiful,
Who are you beautiful for?

"Frequently," says a teacher at another crowded high school in New York, "a student may be in the wrong class for a term and never know it." With only one counselor to 700 students system-wide in New York City, there is little help available to those who feel confused. It is not surprising, says the teacher, "that many find the experience so cold, impersonal and disheartening that they decide to stay home by the sad warmth of the TV set."

. . . Surely there is enough for everyone within this country. It is a tragedy that . . . good things are not more widely shared. All our children ought to be allowed a stake in the enormous richness of America. Whether they were born to poor white Appalachians or to wealthy Texans, to poor black people in the Bronx or to rich people in Manhasset or Winnetka, they are all quite wonderful and innocent when they are small. We soil them needlessly.

Jocks and Burnouts: Social Categories and Identity in the High School

Penelope Eckert

Penelope Eckert is Professor of Linguistics at Stanford University. In her work, Eckert focuses on the relation between social identity and linguistic variation. Through her extensive ethnographic work with adolescents, she has detailed how language conveys local social meaning. She has discovered that there are local dynamics within linguistic patterns, and that these dynamics relate to such social constructs as class, gender, age, race, ethnicity, social networks, social categories, and communities of linguistic practice.

In her ethnographic study *Jocks and Burnouts: Social Categories and Identity in the High School* (Teachers College Press, 1989), Eckert provides insights into the lives, thoughts, and words of students as the students define and label each other as "jocks" and "burnouts." In addition to quoting the students, she helps to construct the socioeconomic patterns of the community and school as well. In the following selection from *Jocks and Burnouts*, Eckert describes how many aspects of school and community life help to reinforce the labels given to each other by students. Economic status can be laid directly over the jock-burnout distinction, with jocks generally coming from middle-class families and burnouts coming from the working classes. Eckert provides an analysis of not only how the housing patterns within the community differentiate jocks and burnouts but also the way in which the different students make use of the physical aspects of the neighborhoods. Even the different parts of the school serve various functions for the students of different labels. This ethnographic study has much to say to educators today about students' perceptions of the "haves" and "have-nots" amidst a growing split and increasing violence among students.

Key Concept: conditions related to student-created labels for each other

Introduction

So what is a jock then?

Someone who gets into school, who does her homework, who, uh, goes to all the activities, who's in Concert Choir, who has her whole day surrounded by school. You know, "tonight I'm gonna go to concert choir practice and today maybe I'll go watch track, and then early this morning maybe, oh, I'll go help a teacher or something." You know. . . .

Although Jocks and Burnouts take their names from athletics and drugs, respectively, these are neither necessary nor sufficient criteria for category membership. The term *Jock* originated in sports, which are so central to the high school culture. Indeed, varsity athletes are seen as serving the interests of the school and the community, representing the school in the most visible arena, and symbolizing all that is thought to be healthy

and vigorous in American culture. . . . Most important school activities center around sports events, and in common usage the term *Jock* has extended beyond athletes to all students who make those activities run. Although Jock is a common term for "athlete" in our culture, it is generally applied to people for whom athletics is a way of life. A Jock may be simply a person who engages regularly in some sport, but in general usage the term is used for someone whose life-style embraces a broader ideal associated in American culture with sports. The ideal Jock is good at more than one sport, trains regularly, follows the "clean" life-style considered necessary for maintaining physical fitness, and generally embraces American ideals of athletic fair play and competition. In the high school, this ideal of the squeaky-clean, all-American individual is given an even broader interpretation. The high school Jock embodies an attitude—an acceptance of the school and its institutions as an all-encompassing social context, and an unflagging enthusiasm and energy for working within those institutions. An individual who never plays sports, but who participates enthusiastically in activities associated with student government, unquestioningly may be referred to by all in the school as a Jock.

Another name in Belten High for Burnouts is "Jells," shortened from "Jello Brains" and alluding to the degenerative effects of drugs. But just as there are Jocks who are not athletes, there are Burnouts who do not do drugs. Drugs are this generation's most frightening form of rebellion, and as such they are taken as a symbol by and for the school's alienated category. One might more properly consider that these alienated adolescents are "burned out" from long years of frustration encountered in an institution that rejects and stigmatizes them as it fails to recognize and meet their needs. The complexity of the connotations of the category names is reflected in their use. Although the terms *Jock* and *Burnout* are used in certain unambiguous contexts to refer to an athlete or a "druggie," they frequently must be disambiguated through compounding. Thus, such terms as "Jock-Jock," "Sports-Jock," and "Burned-out Burnout" are commonly used to refer to an athlete or a habitual drug user.

The names, and even the stereotypes, of the Jock and Burnout categories belie a broader distinction and a profound cultural split, which reflects in turn the split between the adult middle and working classes. This does not mean that category membership is strictly determined by class, or that all differences between the categories arise directly from class differences. However, the considerable extent to which class is salient to these categories conspires to elevate the category stereotypes to class stereotypes, to produce a polarization of attitudes toward class characteristics associated with either category within the value-laden atmosphere of the school, and hence to force a corresponding polarization of behavioral choice. In this way, the Jock and Burnout categories come to mediate adult social class within the adolescent context. . . .

The Setting of Belten High

I guess the thing about the different schools that—only thing different I guess is that Casper thinks of Belten as a punk rock school, and Simmons I guess they have—they're all Beatlemaniacs over there. Belten thinks that Casper people are stuck up . . . stuff like that. Other than that, the people are the same, really, the ones that I know.

Opened in the 1950s, Belten is the oldest of several high schools in Neartown, a suburb of Detroit. Belten's approximately 2000 students come from families ranging from solid working class through upper middle class. Part of Detroit's urban sprawl, Neartown is one section of a vast geographic and socioeconomic continuum. In the Detroit suburban area, geography and class are clearly tied along the north–south and east–west axes. With the notable exception of some wealthy waterfront areas

Table 1 Socioeconomic Class Makeup (in Percentages) of Each Social Category

	Jocks	In-Betweens	Burnouts
Working class	16	16	50
Lower middle class	34	42	22
Upper middle class	50	42	23

east of the city, socioeconomic status rises as one moves north and west from the primarily black and poor inner city. Near-town's northwest corner, the farthest from Detroit, is the most rural, most recently developed, and wealthiest. This pattern is repeated by and large within the sections of the town served by its several high schools.

The students of Belten High generally point to the less affluent eastern end of Neartown as "Burnout" neighborhoods, particularly those at the more densely populated southeast end. In fact, these neighborhoods yield Jocks, Burnouts, and In-Betweens, but there are certain factors that make them "Burnout" neighborhoods. First, there is somewhat of a concentration of Burnouts living in the southeast corner of town. In addition, the main local Burnout hangouts are in the eastern neighborhoods, particularly in the southeast: the parks and school yards where many Burnouts organize pickup games or hang out in good weather. The socioeconomic makeup of each category is not homogeneous, but the socioeconomic balance of the categories reflects clear differentiation. Table 1 shows the percentages of members of the central Jock and Burnout clusters, as well as of a range of In-between clusters, from three socioeconomic strata. These percentages are based on students' reports, in the 118 tape-recorded interviews of Belten students, of their parents' education and occupation. It should be noted that the percentages did not change significantly when the determination of class was based on information about a working mother, a working father, or both. The percentages show a clear difference in the overall socioeconomic makeup of the polarized categories and suggest an intermediate status for the In-Betweens.

The Jock and Burnout categories are more than a simple reflection of parents' socioeconomic identity; they are pivotal in the transition from childhood to adult status, and both upward and downward mobility are achieved through the mediation of these categories. Of course there will be changes once a cohort has graduated from high school, but the current aspirations of the members of each category are more closely related to class than to actual origins. While almost all of the Jocks intend to go on to college, only 10 percent of the Burnouts expressed interest in college, and a number of them were not enrolled in college preparatory curricula. As Table 2 shows, the balance of choice of curriculum reflects these differences in aspiration. This table is based on school records of second semester junior year enrollments for 102 students clearly belonging to Jock and Burnout network clusters.

Table 2 Course Enrollments (in Percentages) Within Each Social Category

	Academic Courses				Vocational Courses			
	AP	**A-B**	**C**	**R**	**M-A**	**VOC**	**BUS**	**F-L**
Male Jocks	5	71	12	0	4	5	3	0
Male Burnouts	0	36	14	9	6	33	3	0
Female Jocks	11	70	7	0	7	0	2	4
Female Burnouts	0	19	28	7	11	9	5	21

AP   Advanced placement courses
A-B-C   Letters refer, in descending order, to the level of difficulty as listed in the school catalog
R   Remedial
M-A   Music and art
BUS   Business courses
F-L   Family life (traditional home economics courses and courses in child care)
VOC   Other vocational courses

The Local Environment

Neartown itself is a continuum: There is no town center, only interspersed industrial, commercial, and residential areas, with scattered shopping centers. Hangouts are fast-food restaurants and shopping centers, parks, and rollerskating rinks. Some of the most salient differences between social categories in Belten are closely involved with differences in geographic orientation and in the exploitation of local resources. The adolescent population must carve a relatively uninteresting geographic continuum into a world with significant areas, and they do this as part of the expression of their social identities.

. . . [O]ne of the important differences between Jocks and Burnouts is geographic orientation. Both categories use restaurants and particularly fast-food restaurants. But while the Burnouts make regular use of other local public space— parks, streets, skating rinks, pool halls—the Jocks confine their activities largely to movie theatres, homes, and the school. To a great extent, the Jocks' small use of local geography is a function of their intense involvement in school, which serves as the center of most of their leisure activities. Mobility beyond Neartown is equally telling. Most middle class Neartowners have turned their backs on Detroit and discourage their children from visiting or taking an interest in the city. The parental upward mobility that brought people from Detroit to Neartown dictates the abandonment of urban orientation and ties. To a great extent, Jocks visit other towns only in connection with sports events and to go to shopping malls and restaurants. The latter two take them not east to Detroit, but generally to more affluent suburban areas. Most Jocks rarely go to Detroit; of those who do, most limit their use of their city to public facilities, particularly sports arenas. A few go to museums and concerts, Greektown, and the Renaissance Center. Burnouts, on the other hand, cautiously extend their activities beyond Neartown toward Detroit. As they get older and more mobile, Burnouts expand their use of public space into the suburbs closer to Detroit, and into Detroit itself, gravitating to areas that provide contact with people from other towns.

This difference in geographic orientation stems from a variety of factors. Perhaps the clearest of these is the large number of Burnouts that have moved recently to the suburbs from Detroit. Some of them still have friends in Detroit and still visit their old neighborhoods. The urban migration that creates suburban populations plays a clear role in the Jock–Burnout split, even in schools such as Belten, much of whose population moved there at one time or another from Detroit or its closer suburbs. More than half of Belten's students were born outside of Neartown, most of them in Detroit. Based on the reports of 94 students, 40 percent began school before coming to Neartown, and about 24 percent moved to Neartown after the fifth grade. These numbers are not evenly distributed between the social categories: 17 percent of the Jocks, 23 percent of the In-Betweens, and 36 percent of the Burnouts moved after fifth grade.

A further aspect of the differential geographic orientation of Jocks and Burnouts is adaptive. While most of the Jocks' next life stage will be in an isolated and specialized institution similar to the high school, most Burnouts will leave school and directly begin to compete with adults in the workplace. While the high school negotiates the next life stage for its Jocks, it is of little use to Burnouts in finding a place in the job market. Participation in school activities is an important qualification for college admission, but it does little to enhance an individual's qualification for a blue-collar job, and while the school plays an active role in advising about college admission, it does little toward placing students in blue-collar jobs. In finding employment, most Burnouts expect to rely on contacts outside of school, particularly on relatives and friends already in the work force. Therefore, it is not in a Burnout's interests to pursue social activities in school; it is in his or her interests to pursue activities and contacts that provide access to the local work force. This work force is centered not in the affluent suburbs, but in the urban center and the closer, more urban suburbs. A work force orientation, therefore, is in many ways an urban orientation.

Finally, the Burnouts look at Detroit as a source of personal autonomy. While the Jocks seek autonomy in the occupation of institutional roles, the Burnouts seek it in the personal freedoms associated with adult status and in an independent relation with the larger environment. To some extent this can be linked to the difference in the salience of the adolescent life stage between those who will remain in educational institutions and those who are emerging into the work force. With adult responsibilities looming in the near future, the Burnouts can see no reason to postpone the pleasures of adult status. Adult status represents both personal freedom and interaction in the "real world," both of which are highly circumscribed in the school. Finally, there is the simple love of freedom, excitement, and, for some, danger. These various factors weigh differently for different Burnouts, but ultimately they all conspire to lead Burnouts into the urban area.

The sociogeographic continuum of the metropolitan area provides adolescents with a clear perspective on their place in the world. Belten High School lies squarely in the average socioeconomic range in American society. When individuals compare themselves with those surrounding communities, they develop more of a perspective on their "real-world" social status. Burnouts can look to the relative poverty of friends in Detroit, with their greater problems and lower aspirations; Jocks can look to those in more westerly and northerly suburbs who do not have jobs, who drive fancy cars and wear designer clothes, and who may even plan to go out of state to college. The local environment polarizes Jocks and Burnouts, but at the same time it protects them from the threat of comparison with those in surrounding communities who represent greater socioeconomic and behavioral extremes. Within the limitations of the local context, Jocks can avoid feeling poor and unsophisticated in comparison with their more affluent neighbors in suburbs to the north and west, and Burnouts can feel independent and rebellious without facing the dangers and insecurities of those living closer to Detroit. During high school, the confrontation with the world outside the community is still mitigated by the familiar and relatively safe context of the school. For this reason, many of those who hate school most are nonetheless loyal to their school. In part, this is a loyalty to what the students see as the school's socioeconomic mean, as reflected in one student's discussion of Neartown's wealthier school:

> They're a lot richer and they're really stuck up and they are better at a lot of things, but I'd rather be worse and proud of Belten than go to Simpson.

Each school seems to pride itself on its socioeconomic characteristics—Belten staff and students alike quote the broad socioeconomic range of its student body as its main advantage and as accounting for what they consider to be the school's very special character. . . .

Daily Routines

Use of the building is closely tied to the daily schedule. The class schedule outlines a routine for each student, organizing encounters with other students as well as movements into and though various parts of the building. The school day is divided into three 54-minute class periods in the morning, a noon period of approximately $1\frac{1}{2}$ hours, and two 54-minute class periods in the afternoon. Six minutes are allowed between class periods for changing rooms. The fourth (lunch) period is divided into three half-hour segments, two of which are spent in class and one at lunch. Fourth-hour classes are staggered so that some meet during the first two segments, some during the last two, and some during the first and third, with the lunch segment in the middle. Following disturbances in the school parking lot in the late 1970s, the administration imposed a "closed campus" policy, forcing students to remain in the school building during school hours except for authorized travel to curricular programs in other schools. Although students may not leave the building during the lunch hour, they are free to gather in the south wing and the courtyard, and with permission they may go to the library. The intersections between the south wing and the north–south halls are monitored during this time, as are the north, south, and middle (leading to the library) exits from the back hall.

Students work their social routines around their class schedules. They also work their class schedules around their social lives, by trying to get into classes with their friends. Thus classes are not simply part of the educational routine, but strategic points in the students' daily social encounters. Changing classes is punctuated with routine social encounters at designated places—in the hall, in the courtyard, at the lockers. Students know whom they can expect to pass in the hall on the way from one class to the next and can adjust their route or speed to guarantee meeting those they particularly wish to see. Depending on the period, individuals may rush to a designated spot for a quick encounter with a group, a friend, or a boyfriend/girlfriend; or they may do their route slowly, greeting a variety of people on the way. One particular class change might be the highpoint of a student's day. By and large, groups meet at set times and places before and after school, and virtually all students have a lunchtime routine, going to the same place with the same people, sometimes migrating at an appointed time to another place to wait for the bell to ring at the end of the period.

To a great extent, the individual's enjoyment of school routine is a function of the size of his or her social network. Those who have only a small group of friends are limited in their encounters to times of mutual availability. Some students have no group of school friends and must move through their day in isolation. Changing classes is not much of a problem for people with limited networks, since they can move with purpose through a crowd, but lunchtime can be a difficult and painful time. The smaller one's social network, the smaller are one's chances of having the same lunch period as one's friends, and the individual who eats alone or walks in the halls alone during this period of heightened visibility is stigmatized. Those who find themselves alone manage as best they can by making themselves inconspicuous, drifting as an unwelcome guest among established groups, or simply hiding. They do not, however, escape notice:

> We'd make fun of people that walked too close to the wall. We'd always call them "wall huggers." Because they didn't, they wouldn't walk down the middle of the hall. If they were walking by themselves, they walked by the wall, like it was their friend . . . It just seems like anybody who's alone usually stands right next to the wall. Just a little thing we noticed.

Loners can protect themselves by adopting a philosophical attitude, as the following girl who recognizes that people notice her solitude:

> They always have to be with someone because they're worried about what other people would think if they were walking down the hall alone, which is no big deal. It doesn't hurt.

But it does hurt, as one girl who finds lunch company by imposing on relatively inhospitable groups poignantly described:

> I just have friends that I say "hello" to and are acquaintances, but I don't have any best friends. . . . I just see them a lot in school, because like they're, they got their own very good friends. I'm just, you know, like to the people I know, I'm just a friend. I'm not a person you'd call up and invite to parties and get stoned with, you know. I wish I was, though. I mean I feel, at weekends I feel so left out, I sit there and, you know, "Ma, I'm so depressed, I want friends," you know. But, you know, there are some times, some times I think, uh, I'm better off not having too many friends because one can get just bogged down with all their "Oh, can you come over to my house today"; "No, I'm coming over her house, sorry." You know, I don't know. They just don't like me for what I am.

Lunch for the first day of the semester is stressful for most high school students, as they worry about whom they're going to eat with. The degree of stress varies inversely with the extensiveness of one's social networks. "Who has the same lunch" is a major preoccupation that can serve as a factor in choosing classes.

> See, this semester I was really bummed out. I wanted to get a change to fourth hour, because there's nobody in my lunch hour that I really know. But I sit, like, at a table with a bunch of girls that I know, but I don't really know. Um, Joan Smith, Judy—I don't know her last name, shows how well I know her. Those are really the only two that I even know that sit there. The rest of them just . . .

How did you start eating with them?

> Well, I don't know. Um, I went in the first day, and I was going to sit with Daphne Brown. But she was hanging around all the people that are on the swimming team. And like, I don't know them, you know.

The contrast between being a longer and being a member of the vast networks that constitute the Jock and Burnout categories can be the difference between social night and day. By virtue of their extensive networks, the Jocks and the Burnouts suffer the least at lunchtime. Intensive consultation lets Jocks know whom they will be eating with before they arrive in the cafeteria. There is always at least one girl Jock and one boy Jock table in each lunch hour, and Jocks find both security and visibility in their ability to sit at that table.

> Well see, well you find out, you know, before you go in there. And it's like, Joe Sloan, he played basketball with us, Alan Marsten did, and Peter Brown. And like I know Dan Jones, and Mark Johnson, I knew them already. So you know, Joe and Alan and those guys that play basketball, I knew what they had, you know, what lunch. So I was, I went in there looking for them. . . . Everyone asks what lunch you eat to find out who they can sit with.

The Burnouts do not even have to find out ahead of time who has the same lunch, since they know that their friends will be in the courtyard.

This [selection] deals more with Jocks and Burnouts than with the people who make up the majority of the student population—the many In-Betweens who find their way between and around the categories. It also does not deal with the people who never find their niche in high school—people who don't fit in and who feel lucky if they can remain sufficiently invisible to escape community ridicule. [There are] social dynamics that make extreme isolation possible. If a Jock is the opposite of a Burnout, a nerd is the opposite of both. While the Jocks and the Burnouts are no more interesting than the rest of the student body, the concentration of social energy in the maintenance of their oppositional identities not only limits their own freedom but that of everyone else in the school.

The Town, the School, and the Students

Guadalupe Valdés

Guadalupe Valdés is Professor of Education and of Spanish and Portuguese at Stanford University. She is also a Senior Partner for the Carnegie Foundation for the Advancement of Teaching. Much of her work is in the areas of sociolinguistics and applied linguistics, with a focus on bilingualism, especially among Spanish and English speakers. She addresses the process of becoming bilingual, and of maintaining one's native language, especially in immigrant communities. She has also addressed the role of national policies in bilingual and immigrant education. She serves on editorial boards for several prominent journals in bilingual education, such as *Bilingual Review* and the *International Journal of Bilingualism and Bilingual Education*. Her well-known books include *Con Respeto: Bridging the Distances Between Culturally Diverse Families and Schools: An Ethnographic Portrait* (Teachers College Press, 1996) and *Learning and Not Learning English: Latino Students in American Schools* (Teachers College Press, 2000), from which the following selection is drawn.

Valdés begins her ethnography of Mission Vista by describing a day in the life of a recent immigrant from Mexico as he attempts to be selected for a day labor position for the day. He stands on a street corner with a group of men, hoping to get a job for the day. The families and children of recent immigrants to Mission Vista have a different style of life and a different economic level from that of the long-time residents of the town. The resulting conflicts led the long-time residents to set-up exclusionary practices within the town, often guised as being better for the newcomers. The two groups rarely interact in the town, and the children are isolated from each other in their school. This ethnography illustrates the complex process of two groups learning to become part of a shared community and school, a process becoming more common across the country as immigration increases throughout all parts of the nation.

Key Concept: conflicts between a town's long-time residents and new immigrants

At 11:00 in the morning, Victor Andrade is still hopeful. After riding his bicycle for almost an hour, he has been standing at the intersection of Hacienda Avenue and San Martin Road in Mission Vista since 6:00. He knows that if he is lucky, he will be hired to do a day's work in construction, or gardening, or painting. Victor isn't picky. Like the other Latino men standing on the corner, he hopes for a day's wages, maybe $50 for 8 hours of hard work.

Many area residents know about the men standing on the corner because they are a source of enthusiastic cheap labor. Contractors, landscapers, and plumbers often come by early in the morning and hire a dozen men. Other area residents who just need one or two men for hauling, digging, and loading come by the intersection later.

At 11:30, a pickup truck pulls up and a man puts out his hand. "*Cuatro*," he shouts in Spanish, holding up four fingers, as the waiting men run toward the truck. Six or seven men climb aboard, but the man is firm. "*Cuatro*," he insists, "*cuatro*." Three men jump out of the truck. Victor is one of them. This time, he wasn't fast enough. He walks slowly back to the corner and joins the ten or fifteen men who still wait. He is tired and he is hungry.

Victor is one of many men who gather every day on one corner in a small shopping center in the city of Mission Vista. They are *jornaleros*, men who do a day's work for a stated wage. They stand on the corner much like they did in Mexico, where the contracting of jornaleros on the street is a normal occurrence. The men want work, and they have no other way of contacting potential employers. By standing on the corner and eagerly running toward every car that slows down, the men want to impress potential employers with their eagerness and enthusiasm. They are hard workers. They will spend hours in the sun, in the rain, and in the cold. They chop wood, dig trenches, dig up tree stumps, clean warehouses. They are not proud. Work is work, and they need money for their families.

Businessowners in the small shopping center, however, are angry and complain that their clients are frightened away by the presence of the Mexican workers. Some claim that their customers are pestered; others claim that the men are dirty and unsightly; still others claim that they are intimidated by what they suspect to be illegal aliens in their community.

In the surrounding community, feelings about immigrant day workers run high. Area residents have protested the presence of Mexican workers on their street corners. One town has passed an antiloitering ordinance forbidding several people from congregating on street corners. Another town has passed a law banning solicitation of work from vehicles.

In the community where this study took place, defenders of the day laborers attempted to appease businessowners and angry residents by raising money for a workers' center. They claimed that such a center would remove workers from in front of businesses and still provide them with the opportunity of finding work. They also argued that a center would protect laborers from unscrupulous contractors who ordinarily hired them for very low wages.

Citizens angry about the workers' presence in their community, in turn, claimed that most men were illegal aliens, led unstable lives, and, because they spoke no English, had little opportunity for other jobs. They accused workers of loitering, littering, drinking, urinating in public, and intimidating women. According to one newspaper story, members of one activist group, which strongly opposed the job center proposal, photographed workers and wrote down license plate numbers of employers as a way of pressuring "illegal" workers to get off the streets. They then pressed immigration officials to conduct raids.

Elisa, Lilian, Bernardo, and Manolo, the focal children in this study, all lived and went to school in the town that I call Mission Vista. They felt the tensions present in the community through their parents, their relatives, and their friends. While it is not clear that they understood what these tensions meant, every day they walked to the middle-class part of town to attend a school that until a few years before had been almost exclusively White. They saw other students arrive in Mercedes-Benzes and BMWs, delivered lovingly at school by well-dressed and confident parents. Immigrant children, on the other hand, walked to school, no matter where they lived. School bus service had been discontinued in the district as a cost-cutting measure.

What happened in the community among both majority and minority residents, what happened in government agencies and religious institutions, and what was reported by the mass media were directly related to what happened to the four children in school. As Cortes (1986) has suggested, in order to understand a school context, the wider context in which a school is located must be examined carefully. What happens in the schoolyard, in attendance offices, in PTA meetings, and at school board meetings directly reflects the beliefs and values of the community and its residents. In the case of communities such as Mission Vista where rapid population shift had resulted in a changing community, established middle-class residents necessarily come into contact with people who are very different from themselves. Often established residents struggle to retain control of the schools. At other times, they simply give up and decide to send their children to private schools. They abandon institutions that they had helped support and maintain for many years.

The process of confronting and adjusting to change is a painful one. In the face of rapid population shift, the entire character of both the community and the schools change. "New" children are unlike the "old" children. Expectations that teachers have about study habits, background knowledge, language, and discipline are found to be inaccurate. Assumptions about children's futures must be questioned. Views about curriculum and standards, as well as opportunities to learn, cannot be taken for granted. Some teachers feel angry. They feel cheated at not having the "good" students they once had. They join together to complain to the principal. The solution, they argue, is to hire more new teachers to handle students who are not up to their standards. Principals, however, do not have easy solutions. Sometimes they, too, wish that the new children would simply go away.

New Immigrants in Mission Vista

Mission Vista is located in California. It is home to numerous high-technology companies as well as retail stores, executive offices, research and development firms, and professional service companies. The brochures mailed out by the Chamber of Commerce depict an attractive community blessed with a desirable climate, a good transportation network, and two nearby international airports. At the time that the study took place, the average price of a single family home was $394,971. A studio or one-bedroom apartment rented for $600 to $850. Apartments with two to four bedrooms rented for $800 to $2,100. Residences—including apartments and single-family homes—in the community were 35.5% owner-occupied and 64.5% renter-occupied.

Beginning in late 1980s, Mission Vista schools experienced a rapid population change. Large numbers of Latino immigrants of largely Mexican background moved into the community primarily because of the availability of apartment rentals. The arrival of Mexican immigrants from a largely rural background was felt in many ways by the community. Large sections of the town suddenly took on a different character. Apartment buildings that were built as luxury rentals 20 or 30 years earlier became the heart of the immigrant community. Blocks and blocks of two-story apartment complexes were slowly neglected by their owners. Swimming pools were emptied or boarded over. Buildings were not repainted. Two or three families often occupied two-bedroom apartments, and dozens of young children played in the dirt and mud surrounding the run-down buildings. Old cars lined the streets, and mothers pushing strollers—with three or four young children in tow—could be seen walking many blocks to the grocery store. On weekends, very large extended families invaded the city parks and took over the picnic grounds and the grassy areas for noisy games of soccer. Hamburger franchises and supermarket chains found themselves competing with hole-in-the-wall Mexican restaurants and tiny grocery stores. Permanent residents were not prepared for the changes when they happened. What had once been a largely middle-class community saw itself slowly sliding into an identity that it did not want. Very few things appeared to be sacred. Even the area soccer leagues were threatened. Through the school, immigrant parents requested that their children be allowed to play. Middle-class soccer parents in Mission Vista, however, were not ready to mingle with immigrant parents. They lobbied the community youth sports association to insist on the customary $50-dollar-per-child fee. When the school raised money to pay the required fees, separate teams were organized for Latino children.

Much attention in the community was also directed at "gang" activity. A gang was defined as an association of youngsters who dressed alike and spent time together in groups. It was assumed in both the community and the school that gang membership was a problem for Latino students in particular. While it is not clear that all youngsters who dressed in certain colors or drew particular symbols on their notebooks were affiliated with gangs, the Mission Vista police department organized itself to inform schools about gang "wannabe" activities that needed to be monitored. Reflecting in part the rising anti-immigrant sentiment in California and in part the changes that surrounded them, residents of Mission Vista engaged in a not-so-subtle campaign to keep their communities "safe," their parks clean, and their schools organized primarily to serve the needs of their own children.

Many battles were fought at school board meetings. School administrators fought to implement new programs that could serve immigrant children's needs and to prepare mainstream teachers to cope with their new students. Hiring decisions were painful. Latino principals and teachers were scarce; mainstream teachers were tenured. Educators—as members of both the community and the wider society—reflected what Cortes (1986)

has called the societal curriculum. They had internalized views and perceptions about change and about the challenge to California of educating a rapidly growing number of new immigrant students. Some teachers saw immigrant students as defenseless and as needing help and support. Others, however, saw them as intruders, as freeloaders, and as part of a group that simply refused to become American. They were strongly sympathetic to the activities of anti-immigrant groups in California that were actively beginning to promote a series of state initiatives that would directly impact on Latino immigrants.

The feelings and the views of mainstream parents, school administrators, and teachers were widely shared by others in the town of Mission Vista as well as by many others in California. Concerns about immigrants—both legal and illegal—were increasing. To be fair, many of these worries and concerns were legitimate and valid. People had a right to ask such questions as: Have we lost control of our borders? Can this country support an unlimited number of new workers? Will native-born workers of all backgrounds (e.g., African American, Latino, European American) be displaced by persons willing to work for lower wages? Do new immigrants understand what it means to be American? Are they willing to learn English?

The School

The same uncertainties and concerns present in the community were played out in numerous ways in the schools. Nevertheless, Garden Middle School was a pleasant place. The buildings, while not new, had recently been painted. The grounds were clean, and the playing fields surrounding the school were well maintained. The classrooms were located in four separate one-story buildings. Each classroom had both a front and a back door, each opening to the patio area between each building. The main office, the attendance office, the multipurpose room, and the library were also located in separate but closely adjacent buildings.

Between classes students sat and talked on the patios or in the outside lunch area. Students enrolled in mainstream classes normally congregated together. This group included children of the original residents of the area—who were White, well dressed, and very much engaged in extra-curricular activities—as well as students from Asia and India and even Latin America who were middle-class and had been here for many years. This latter group of students was made up of fluent English speakers who seldom associated with the students who did not speak English.

Newly arrived immigrant students also kept mainly to themselves. Outside the classroom they spoke in Spanish to one another—sometimes loudly, sometimes in a whisper—and in certain ways mirrored the "American" behavior of their mainstream peers. Their dress, their demeanor, and their comportment, however, were not quite American. The girls either wore a little too much makeup and clothes that were a little too tight or they dressed very much like little children. The older boys strutted about ogling the girls and making the kinds of remarks to each other that they might have made on the streets of their towns in Mexico. The younger boys appeared to be shy and quiet and generally looked down respectfully when addressed by an adult. The most newly arrived youngsters looked uncomfortable. To outsiders they seemed shy and insecure.

As in other schools in which population shifts have rapidly changed the composition of the student body, there were tensions at Garden Middle School. The increasing number of non-English- or limited-English-speaking children had made demands on the staff and on the curriculum that had not been anticipated. Because of the increased enrollment of non-English-speaking children, the single ESL teacher had been joined by a colleague. Together, the two ESL teachers served every child in the school who was not yet fully fluent in English. Their classes generally enrolled 35 to 40 students.

Overall, the administration had worked hard to try to provide a program in which NEP (non-English-proficient) and LEP (limited-English-proficient) children could have access to the curriculum. They had designed a NEP and LEP core in which these students received instruction in both ESL (English as a second language) and social studies, and they had made an effort to provide other "real" subject-matter courses for these students. While many of the teachers who had never worked with ELL students still did not want to work with them, it is noteworthy that a number of subject-matter teachers in science, math, and computers offered "sheltered" content classes at different levels. Classes in science, math, and computers could be taken by NEP students who understood very little English. As might be imagined, the challenges faced by these content teachers were many.

During the years in which the study took place, Garden Middle School was a school in transition. It was a mainstream community's sole public middle school, a school where a few years earlier children of the neighborhood had felt comfortable and safe. Because of the population shift, this was changing. According to the former superintendent, the school was at the beginning of intensive "White flight." More and more middle-class parents were enrolling their children in private schools. They were afraid of the dropping standards, of the problems that might accompany non-English-background students, of gangs, of violence, and of interethnic romance.

In a very significant way, Garden Middle School is representative of schools all over the country that are changing as a result of the dramatic increase of "diverse" populations in many communities. Its almost all-White faculty had little experience with diversity. According to one teacher who worked closely with the Latino community, most teachers at Garden could predict few of the problems their "new" students would encounter. Most knew little about poverty. They had little notion of why working parents might not be able to make midday appointments with their children's teachers. They suspected lack of interest, apathy, and even antagonism and were baffled and troubled by the failure of these parents to "care" about their children.

The "new" students, on the other hand, did not quite yet know how to be American middle school students. They knew little about school spirit. They were not sure why being in the band or in chorus or in the computer club might be important. They frequently confused teachers' friendly demeanor with permissiveness, and they quickly found themselves in trouble. They understood little of what went on around them, and they often became discouraged and uninterested.

Reference

Cortes, C. E. (1986). The education of language minority students: A contextual interaction model. In Bilingual Education Office (Ed.), *Social and cultural factors in schooling language minority students* (pp. 3–33). Los Angeles: Evaluation, Dissemination and Assessment Center, California State University.

Culture

Selection 9
EDWARD T. HALL, from "What Is Culture?" *The Silent Language*

Selection 10
LISA DELPIT, from"The Silenced Dialogue: Power and Pedagogy in Educating Other People's Children," *Other People's Children: Cultural Conflict in the Classroom*

What Is Culture?

Edward T. Hall

In his book *The Silent Language* (Doubleday, 1981), from which the following selection has been taken, anthropologist Edward T. Hall proposes that culture is a form of communication. Culture is the way that adults communicate to their children the important parts of their society. Culture is what we often subconsciously communicate to each other by our actions. In the following selection, Hall emphasizes that the study of culture is the study of our own lives, of our own ways of thinking and living. Because the study of culture is the study of ourselves, he explains, it is difficult to comprehend. It is easier to think of culture as a description of someone else's culture, to see culture as exotic customs. But, says Hall, it is crucial to study our own culture in order to understand ourselves and our society. This study of culture has the purpose of making us self-conscious, of making known to ourselves what it is that makes up everyday life.

Throughout his writings, Hall has focused on the different styles of cultural groups. He has written about proxemics—the study of the space that people surround themselves with and their communication and interaction patterns. In addition to *The Silent Language,* his leading books include *The Hidden Dimension* (Doubleday, 1966) and *Beyond Culture* (Anchor Press, 1976).

Key Concept: the study of one's own culture

Culture is a word that has so many meanings already that one more can do it no harm. . . . For anthropologists culture has long stood for the way of life of a people, for the sum of their learned behavior patterns, attitudes, and material things. Though they subscribe to this general view, most anthropologists tend to disagree however, on what the precise substance of culture is. In practice their work often leads some of them to a fascination with a single category of events among the many which make up human life, and they tend to think of this as the essence of all culture. Others, looking for a point of stability in the flux of society, often become preoccupied with identifying a common particle or element which can be found in every aspect of culture. In sum, though the concept of culture was first defined in print in 1871 by E. B. Tylor, after all these years it still lacks the rigorous specificity which characterizes many less revolutionary and useful ideas.

Even more unfortunate is the slowness with which the concept of culture has percolated through the public consciousness. Compared to such notions as the unconscious or repression, to use two examples from psychology, the idea of culture is a strange one even to the informed citizen. The reasons for this are well worth noting, for they suggest some of the difficulties which are inherent in the culture concept itself.

. . . Culture is not an exotic notion studied by a select group of anthropologists in the South Seas. It is a mold in which we are all cast, and it controls our daily lives in many unsuspected ways. In my discussion of culture I will be describing the part of human behavior which we take for granted—the part we don't think about, since we assume it is universal or regard it as idiosyncratic.

Culture hides much more than it reveals, and strangely enough what it hides, it hides most effectively from its own participants. Years of study have convinced me that the real job is not to understand foreign culture but to understand our own. I am also convinced that all that one ever gets from studying foreign culture is a token understanding. The ultimate reason for such study is to learn more about how one's own system works. The best reason for exposing oneself to foreign ways is to generate a sense of vitality and awareness—an interest in life which can come only when one lives through the shock of contrast and difference.

Simply learning one's own culture is an achievement of gargantuan proportions for anyone. By the age of twenty-five or thirty most of us have finished school, been married, learned to live with another human being, mastered a job, seen the miracle of human birth, and started a new human being well on his way to growing up. Suddenly most of what we have to learn is finished. Life begins to settle down.

Yet our tremendous brain has endowed us with a drive and a capacity for learning which appear to be as strong as the drive for food or sex. This means that when a middle-aged man or woman stops learning he or she is often left with a great drive and highly developed capacities. If this individual goes to live in another culture, the learning process is often reactivated. For most Americans tied down at home this is not possible. To forestall atrophy of their intellectual powers people can begin learning about those areas of their own culture which have been out of awareness. They can explore the new frontier.

The problem which is raised in talking about American culture without reference to other cultures is that an audience tends to take the remarks personally. I once addressed a group of school principals on the subject of culture. We were discussing the need for Americans to progress in their jobs, to get ahead, and to receive some recognition so that they would know in a tangible way that they were actually getting some place. One of the audience said to me, "Now you are talking about something interesting, you're talking about me." When the man in the audience learned something about himself, the study of culture got lost in the shuffle. He did not seem to realize that a significant proportion of the material which was highly personal to him was also relevant cultural data.

A knowledge of his own culture would have helped this same man in a situation which he subsequently described for the audience. In the middle of a busy day, it seems, his son had kept him waiting for an hour. As a result he was aware that his blood pressure had risen rather dangerously. If both the father and the son had

had a cultural perspective on this common and infuriating occurrence the awkward quarrel which followed might have been avoided. Both father and son would have benefited if the father had understood the cultural basis of his tension and explained, "Now, look here. If you want to keep me waiting, O.K., but you should know it is a real slap in the face to anyone to be kept waiting so long. If that's what you want to communicate, go ahead, but be sure you know that you are communicating an insult and don't act like a startled fawn if people react accordingly."

The best reason for the lay person to spend time studying culture is that he/she can learn something useful and enlightening about himself/herself. This can be an interesting process, at times harrowing but ultimately rewarding. One of the most effective ways to learn about oneself is by taking seriously the cultures of others. It forces you to pay attention to those details of life which differentiate them from you.

For those who are familiar with the subject the remarks I have just made should be a clear indication that [these ideas are] not simply a rehash of what previous writers on the subject of culture have said. The approach is new. It involves new ways of looking at things. Indians and natives of the South Pacific, the hallmarks of most anthropological texts, are used. However, they are introduced solely to clarify points about our own way of life, to make what we take for granted stand out in perspective. . . . The complete theory of culture as communication is new and has not been presented in one place before.

. . . The language of culture speaks as clearly as the language of dreams Freud analyzed, but, unlike dreams, it cannot be kept to oneself. When I talk about culture I am not just talking about something in the abstract that is imposed on mankind and is separate from individuals, but about humans themselves, about you and me in a highly personal way.

The Silenced Dialogue: Power and Pedagogy in Educating Other People's Children

Lisa Delpit

Lisa Delpit uses the debate over process-oriented versus skills-oriented writing instruction as the starting-off point to examine the "culture of power" that exists in society in general and in the educational environment in particular. She analyzes five complex rules of power that explicitly and implicitly influence the debate over meeting the educational needs of Black and poor students on all levels. Delpit concludes that teachers must teach all students the explicit and implicit rules of power as a first step toward a more just society. This article is an edited version of a speech presented at the Ninth Annual Ethnography in Education Research Forum, University of Pennsylvania, Philadelphia, Pennsylvania, February 5–6, 1988.

I have found what I believe to be a connecting and complex theme: what I have come to call "the culture of power." There are five aspects of power I would like to propose as given for this presentation:

- Issues of power are enacted in classrooms.
- There are codes or rules for participating in power; that is, there is a "culture of power."
- The rules of the culture of power are a reflection of the rules of the culture of those who have power.
- If you are not already a participant in the culture of power, being told explicitly the rules of that culture makes acquiring power easier.
- Those with power are frequently least aware of—or least willing to acknowledge—its existence. Those with less power are often most aware of its existence.

The first three are by now basic tenets in the literature of the sociology of education, but the last two have seldom been addressed. The following discussion will explicate these aspects of power and their relevance to the schism between liberal educational movements and that of non-White, non-middle-class teachers and communities.

1. Issues of power are enacted in classrooms.

These issues include: the power of the teacher over the students; the power of the publishers of textbooks and of the developers of the curriculum to determine the view of the world presented; the power of the state in enforcing compulsory schooling; and the power of an individual or group to determine another's intelligence or "normalcy." Finally, if schooling prepares people for jobs, and the kind of job a person has determines her or his economic status and, therefore, power, then schooling is intimately related to that power.

2. There are codes or rules for participating in power; that is, there is a "culture of power."

The codes or rules I'm speaking of relate to linguistic forms, communicative strategies, and presentation of self; that is, ways of talking, ways of writing, ways of dressing, and ways of interacting.

3. The rules of the culture of power are a reflection of the rules of the culture of those who have power.

This means that success in institutions—schools, workplaces, and so on—is predicated upon acquisition of the culture of those who are in power. Children from middle-class homes tend to do better in school than those from non-middle-class homes because the culture of the school is based on the culture of the upper and middle classes—of those in power. The upper and middle classes send their children to school with all the accoutrements of the culture of power; children from other kinds of families operate within perfectly wonderful and viable cultures but not cultures that carry the codes or rules of power.

4. If you are not already a participant in the culture of power, being told explicitly the rules of that culture makes acquiring power easier.

In my work within and between diverse cultures, I have come to conclude that members of any culture transmit information implicitly to co-members. However, when implicit codes are attempted across cultures, communication frequently breaks down. Each cultural group is left saying, "Why don't those people say what they mean?" as well as, "What's wrong with them, why don't they understand?"

Anyone who has had to enter new cultures, especially to accomplish a specific task, will know of what I speak. When I lived in several Papua New Guinea villages for extended periods to collect data, and when I go to Alaskan villages for work with Native Alaskan communities, I have found it unquestionably easier, psychologically and pragmatically, when some kind soul has directly informed me about such matters as appropriate dress, interactional styles, embedded meanings, and taboo words or actions. I contend that it is much the same for anyone seeking to learn the rules of the culture of power. Unless one has the leisure of a lifetime of "immersion" to learn them, explicit presentation makes learning immeasurably easier.

And now, to the fifth and last premise:

5. Those with power are frequently least aware of—or least willing to acknowledge—its existence. Those with less power are often most aware of its existence.

For many who consider themselves members of liberal or radical camps, acknowledging personal power and admitting participation in the culture of power is distinctly uncomfortable. On the other hand, those who are less powerful in any situation are most likely to recognize the power variable most acutely. My guess is that the White colleagues and instructors of those previously quoted did not perceive themselves to have power over the nonwhite speakers. However, either by virtue of their position, their numbers, or their access to that particular code of power of calling upon research to validate one's position, the White educators had the authority to establish what was to be considered "truth" regardless of the opinions of the people of color, and the latter were well aware of that fact.

A related phenomenon is that liberals (and here I am using the term "liberal" to refer to those whose beliefs include striving for a society based upon maximum individual freedom and autonomy) seem to act under the assumption that to make any rules or expectations explicit is to act against liberal principles, to limit the freedom and autonomy of those subjected to the explicitness.

. . . I would like to present several statements typical of those made with the best of intentions by middle-class liberal educators. To the surprise of the speakers, it is not unusual for such content to be met by vocal opposition or stony silence from people of color. My attempt here is to examine the underlying assumptions of both camps.

"I want the same thing for everyone else's children as I want for mine."

To provide schooling for everyone's children that reflects liberal, middle-class values and aspirations is to ensure the maintenance of the status quo, to ensure that power, the culture of power, remains in the hands of those who already have it. Some children come to school with more accoutrements of the culture of power already in place—"cultural capital," as some critical theorists refer to it[2]—some with less. *Many liberal educators hold that the primary goal for education is for children to become autonomous, to develop fully who they are in the classroom setting without having arbitrary, outside standards forced upon them. This is a very reasonable goal for people whose children are already participants in the culture of power and who have already internalized its codes.*

But parents who don't function within that culture often want something else. It's not that they disagree with the former aim, it's just that they want something more. *They want to ensure that the school provides their children with discourse patterns, interactional styles, and spoken and written language codes that will allow them success in the larger society.*

. . . I do not advocate a simplistic "basic skills" approach for children outside of the culture of power. It would be (and has been) tragic to operate as if these children were incapable of critical and higher-order thinking and reasoning. Rather, I suggest that schools must provide these children the content that other families from a different cultural orientation provide at home. This does not mean separating children according to family background, but instead, ensuring that each classroom incorporates strategies appropriate for all the children in its confines.

And I do not advocate that it is the school's job to attempt to change the homes of poor and nonwhite children to match the homes of those in the culture of power. That may indeed be a form of cultural genocide. I have frequently heard schools call poor parents "uncaring" when parents respond to the school's urging, saying, "But that's the school's job." What the school personnel fail to understand is that if the parents were members of the culture of power and lived by its rules and codes, then they would transmit those codes to their children. In fact, they transmit another culture that children must learn at home in order to survive in their communities.

Racism and Prejudice

Selection 11
CORNEL WEST, from *Race Matters*

Selection 12
PEGGY MCINTOSH, from "White Privilege: Unpacking the Invisible Knapsack," *Peace and Freedom*

Selection 13
JANA NOEL, from "Stereotyping, Prejudice, and Racism," *Developing Multicultural Educators*

Race Matters

Cornel West

Cornel West is Professor of Religion at Princeton University and teaches in the Center for African American Studies. This follows a publicly well-known dispute with the president of Harvard University, where he was professor of Afro-American Studies and Philosophy of Religion. His work focuses on black critical thought, cultural criticism, social theory, and the future of American youth. He is known, both within academia and in the general public, for his ideas on how to overcome crises in black communities. He is the author of over 15 books, including *Race Matters* (Beacon Press, 1993) and *Democracy Matters: Winning the Fight against Imperialism* (Penguin Press, 2004). He has also participated in popular culture, with his CD titled *Sketches of My Culture* and as an actor in *The Matrix Trilogy*, having been invited to play an elder of the community.

In this introduction from *Race Matters*, West explores how to set up a discussion of race in America today. He first asserts that race is not a single, separate factor in American society. Rather, it is tied to economic and political issues and lethargy as part of the complex mix in U.S. life. He then says that before we can have open discussions of race, we must move away from labeling blacks as "them" and basing discussions on how they can fit in. West believes that we must move away from seeing blacks as "problems" in society. Using the Rodney King trial and ensuing riots as an initiating point for discussion, he discusses how current feelings about race in America have been heightened by the effects of media, materialism, and violence. He worries about "the collapse of meaning in life" and states that we must learn compassion and understanding of the history that has led us here.

Key Concept: preparing for discussions of race

What happened in Los Angeles in April of 1992 was neither a race riot nor a class rebellion. Rather, this monumental upheaval was a multiracial, trans-class, and largely male display of justified social rage. For all its ugly, xenophobic resentment, its air of adolescent carnival, and its downright barbaric behavior, it signified the sense of powerlessness in American society. Glib attempts to reduce its meaning to the pathologies of the black underclass, the criminal actions of hoodlums, or the political revolt of the oppressed urban masses miss the mark. Of those arrested, only 36 percent were black, more than a third had full-time jobs, and most claimed to shun political affiliation. What we witnessed in Los Angeles was the consequence of a lethal linkage of economic decline, cultural decay, and political lethargy in American life. Race was the visible catalyst, not the underlying cause.

Introduction

The meaning of the earthshaking events in Los Angeles is difficult to grasp because most of us remain trapped in the narrow framework of the dominant liberal and conservative views of race in America, which with its wornout vocabulary leaves us intellectually debilitated, morally disempowered, and personally depressed. The astonishing disappearance of the event from public dialogue is testimony to just how painful and distressing a serious engagement with race is. Our truncated public discussions of race suppress the best of who and what we are as a people because they fail to confront the complexity of the issue in a candid and critical manner. The predictable pitting of liberals against conservatives, Great Society Democrats against self-help Republicans, reinforces intellectual parochialism and political paralysis.

The liberal notion that more government programs can solve racial problems is simplistic—precisely because it focuses *solely* on the economic dimension. And the conservative idea that what is needed is a change in the moral behavior of poor black urban dwellers (especially poor black men, who, they say, should stay married, support their children, and stop committing so much crime) highlights immoral actions while ignoring public responsibility for the immoral circumstances that haunt our fellow citizens.

The common denominator of these views of race is that each still sees black people as a "problem people," in the words of Dorothy I. Height, president of the National Council of Negro Women, rather than as fellow American citizens with problems. Her words echo the poignant "unasked question" of W. E. B. Du Bois, who, in *The Souls of Black Folk* (1903), wrote:

> They approach me in a half-hesitant sort of way, eye me curiously or compassionately, and then instead of saying directly, How does it feel to be a problem? they say, I know an excellent colored man in my town. . . . Do not these Southern outrages make your blood boil? At these I smile, or am interested, or reduce the boiling to a simmer, as the occasion may require. To the real question, How does it feel to be a problem? I answer seldom a word.

Nearly a century later, we confine discussions about race in America to the "problems" black people pose for whites rather than consider what this way of viewing black people reveals about us as a nation.

This paralyzing framework encourages liberals to relieve their guilty consciences by supporting public funds directed at "the problems"; but at the same time, reluctant to exercise principled criticism of black people, liberals deny them the freedom to err. Similarly, conservatives blame the "problems" on black people themselves—and thereby render black social misery invisible or unworthy of public attention.

Hence, for liberals, black people are to be "included" and "integrated" into "our" society and culture, while for conservatives they are to be "well behaved" and "worthy of acceptance" by "our" way of life. Both fail to see that the presence and predicaments of black people are neither additions to nor defections from American life, but rather *constitutive elements of that life.*

To engage in a serious discussion of race in America, we must begin not with the problems of black people but with the flaws of American society—flaws rooted in historic inequalities and longstanding cultural stereotypes. How we set up the terms for discussing racial issues shapes our perception and response to these issues. As long as black people are viewed as a "them," the burden falls on blacks to do all the "cultural" and "moral" work necessary for healthy race relations. The implication is that only certain Americans can define what it means to be American—and the rest must simply "fit in."

The emergence of strong black-nationalist sentiments among blacks, especially among young people, is a revolt against this sense of having to "fit in." The variety of black-nationalist ideologies, from the moderate views of Supreme Court Justice Clarence Thomas in his youth to those of Louis Farrakhan today, rest upon a fundamental truth: white America has been historically weak-willed in ensuring racial justice and has continued to resist fully accepting the humanity of blacks. As long as double standards and differential treatment abound—as long as the rap performer Ice-T is harshly condemned while former Los Angeles Police Chief Daryl F. Gates's anti-black comments are received in polite silence, as long as Dr. Leonard Jeffries's anti-Semitic statements are met with vitriolic outrage while presidential candidate Patrick J. Buchanan's anti-Semitism receives a genteel response—black nationalisms will thrive.

Afrocentrism, a contemporary species of black nationalism, is a gallant yet misguided attempt to define an African identity in a white society perceived to be hostile. It is gallant because it puts black doings and sufferings, not white anxieties and fears, at the center of discussion. It is misguided because—out of fear of cultural hybridization and through silence on the issue of class, retrograde views on black women, gay men, and lesbians, and a reluctance to link race to the common good—it reinforces the narrow discussions about race.

To establish a new framework, we need to begin with a frank acknowledgment of the basic humanness and Americanness of each of us. And we must acknowledge that as a people—*E Pluribus Unum*—we are on a slippery slope toward economic strife, social turmoil, and cultural chaos. If we go down, we go down together. The Los Angeles upheaval forced us to see not only that we are not connected in ways we would like to be but also, in a more profound sense, that this failure to connect binds us even more tightly together. The paradox of race in America is that our common destiny is more pronounced and imperiled precisely when our divisions are deeper. The Civil War and its legacy speak loudly here. And our divisions are growing deeper. Today, eighty-six percent of white suburban Americans live in neighborhoods that are less than 1 percent black, meaning that the prospects for the country depend largely on how its cities fare in the hands of a suburban electorate. There is no escape from our interracial interdependence, yet enforced racial hierarchy dooms us as a nation to collective paranoia and hysteria—the unmaking of any democratic order.

The verdict in the Rodney King case which sparked the incidents in Los Angeles was perceived to be wrong by the vast majority of Americans. But whites have often failed to acknowledge the widespread mistreatment of black people, especially black men, by law enforcement agencies, which helped ignite the spark. The verdict was merely the occasion for deep-seated rage to come to the surface. This rage is fed by the "silent" depression ravaging the country—in which real weekly wages of all American workers since 1973 have declined nearly 20 percent, while at the same time wealth has been upwardly distributed.

The exodus of stable industrial jobs from urban centers to cheaper labor markets here and abroad, housing policies that have created "chocolate cities and vanilla suburbs" (to use the popular musical artist George Clinton's memorable phrase), white fear of black crime, and the urban influx of poor Spanish-speaking and Asian immigrants—all have helped erode the tax base of American cities just as the federal government has cut its supports and programs. The result is unemployment, hunger, homelessness, and sickness for millions.

And a pervasive spiritual impoverishment grows. The collapse of meaning in life—the eclipse of hope and absence of love of self and others, the breakdown of family and neighborhood bonds—leads to the social deracination and cultural denudement of urban dwellers, especially children. We have created rootless, dangling people with little link to the supportive networks—family, friends, school—that sustain some sense of purpose in life. We have witnessed the collapse of the spiritual communities that in the past helped Americans face despair, disease, and death and that transmit through the generations dignity and decency, excellence and elegance.

The result is lives of what we might call "random nows," of fortuitous and fleeting moments preoccupied with "getting over"—with acquiring pleasure, property, and power by any means necessary. (This is not what Malcolm X meant by this famous phrase.) Post-modern culture is more and more a market culture dominated by gangster mentalities and self-destructive wantonness. This culture engulfs all of us—yet its impact on the disadvantaged is devastating, resulting in extreme violence in everyday life. Sexual violence against women and homicidal assaults by young black men on one another are only the most obvious signs of this empty quest for pleasure, property, and power.

Last, this rage is fueled by a political atmosphere in which images, not ideas, dominate, where politicians spend more time raising money than debating issues. The functions of parties have been displaced by public polls, and politicians behave less as thermostats that determine the climate of opinion than as thermometers registering the public mood. American politics has been rocked by an unleashing of greed among opportunistic public officials—who have followed the lead of their counterparts in the private sphere, where, as of 1989, 1 percent of the population owned 37 percent of the wealth and 10 percent of the population owned 86 percent of the wealth—leading to a profound cynicism and pessimism among the citizenry.

And given the way in which the Republican Party since 1968 has appealed to popular xenophobic images—playing the black, female, and homophobic cards to realign the electorate along race, sex, and sexual-orientation lines—it is no surprise that the notion that we are all part of one garment of destiny is discredited. Appeals to special interests rather than to public interests reinforce this polarization. The Los Angeles upheaval was an expression of utter fragmentation by a powerless citizenry that includes not just the poor but all of us.

What is to be done? How do we capture a new spirit and vision to meet the challenges of the post-industrial city, post-modern culture, and post-party politics?

First, we must admit that the most valuable sources for help, hope, and power consist of ourselves and our common history. As in the ages of Lincoln, Roosevelt, and King, we must look to new frameworks and languages to understand our multilayered crisis and overcome our deep malaise.

Second, we must focus our attention on the public square—the common good that undergirds our national and global destinies. The vitality of any public square ultimately depends on how much we *care* about the quality of our lives together. The neglect of our public infrastructure, for example—our water and sewage systems, bridges, tunnels, highways, subways, and streets—reflects not only our myopic economic policies, which impede productivity, but also the low priority we place on our common life.

The tragic plight of our children clearly reveals our deep disregard for public well-being. About one out of every five children in this country lives in poverty, including one out of every two black children and two out of every five Hispanic children. Most of our children—neglected by overburdened parents and bombarded by the market values of profit-hungry corporations—are ill-equipped to live lives of spiritual and cultural quality. Faced with these facts, how do we expect ever to constitute a vibrant society?

One essential step is some form of large-scale public intervention to ensure access to basic social goods—housing, food, health care, education, child care, and jobs. We must invigorate the common good with a mixture of government, business, and labor that does not follow any existing blueprint. After a period in which the private sphere has been sacralized and the public square gutted, the temptation is to make a fetish of the public square. We need to resist such dogmatic swings.

Last, the major challenge is to meet the need to generate new leadership. The paucity of courageous leaders—so apparent in the response to the events in Los Angeles—requires that we look beyond the same elites and voices that recycle the older frameworks. We need leaders—neither saints nor sparkling television personalities—who can situate themselves within a larger historical narrative of this country and our world, who can grasp the complex dynamics of our peoplehood and imagine a future grounded in the best of our past, yet who are attuned to the frightening obstacles that now perplex us. Our ideals of freedom, democracy, and equality must be invoked to invigorate all of us, especially the landless, propertyless, and luckless. Only a visionary leadership that can motivate "the better angels of our nature," as Lincoln said, and activate possibilities for a freer, more efficient, and stable America—only that leadership deserves cultivation and support.

This new leadership must be grounded in grass-roots organizing that highlights democratic accountability. Whoever *our* leaders will be as we approach the twenty-first century, their challenge will be to help Americans determine whether a genuine multiracial democracy can be created and sustained in an era of global economy and a moment of xenophobic frenzy.

Let us hope and pray that the vast intelligence, imagination, humor, and courage of Americans will not fail us. Either we learn a new language of empathy and compassion, or the fire this time will consume us all.

White Privilege: Unpacking the Invisible Knapsack

Peggy McIntosh

Peggy McIntosh is Associate Director of the Wellesley College Center for Research on Women and cofounder of the Rocky Mountain Women's Institute. Additionally, she is founder and co-director of the national SEED (Seeking Educational Equity and Diversity) Project on Inclusive Curriculum. In these projects, she works internationally with college and school faculty in creating gender-fair and multicultural curricula.

Perhaps McIntosh's most influential work is her paper "White Privilege and Male Privilege: A Personal Account of Coming to See Correspondences through Work in Women's Studies." Her most well-known contributions have come in the pointing-out of the idea of *privilege,* or that set of "taken-for-granted" practices that members of the dominant gender, race, and sexual orientation with the United States seem to have in their lives. The following selection is from an excerpt of "White Privilege and Male Privilege" that published in the July/August 1988 issue of *Peace and Freedom.* In it, McIntosh straightforwardly lists what she calls privileges of being white and heterosexual in the United States. She asserts that these are privileges that are not earned but merely exist by virtue of one's being born white into U.S. society. Although her list is straightforward, McIntosh argues that it is difficult for white heterosexuals to recognize these as unearned privileges that only they are able to receive. She explains that whites are not taught to recognize their own privileges, and they thus deny the resulting advantages that they receive in society. This set of privileges is institutionalized and embedded within society, concludes McIntosh.

Key Concept: whites' privileges in U.S. society

Through work to bring materials from Women's Studies into the rest of the curriculum, I have often noticed men's unwillingness to grant that they are over-privileged, even though they may grant that women are disadvantaged. They may say they will work to improve women's status, in the society, the university, or the curriculum, but they can't or won't support the idea of lessening men's. Denials which amount to taboos surround the subject of advantages which men gain from women's disadvantages. These denials protect male privilege from being fully acknowledged, lessened or ended.

Thinking through unacknowledged male privilege as a phenomenon, I realized that since hierarchies in our society are interlocking, there was most likely a phenomenon of white privilege which was similarly denied and protected. As a white person, I realized I had been taught about racism as something which puts others at a disadvantage, but had been taught not to see one of its corollary aspects, white privilege, which puts me at an advantage.

I think whites are carefully taught not to recognize white privilege, as males are taught not to recognize male privilege. So I have begun in an untutored way to ask what it is like to have white privilege. I have come to see white privilege as an invisible package of unearned assets which I can count on cashing in each day, but about which I was 'meant' to remain oblivious. White privilege is like an invisible weightless knapsack of special provisions, maps, passports, codebooks, visas, clothes, tools and blank checks.

Describing white privilege makes one newly accountable. As we in Women's Studies work to reveal male privilege and ask men to give up some of their power, so one who writes about having white privilege must ask, "Having described it, what will I do to lessen or end it?"

After I realized the extent to which men work from a base of unacknowledged privilege, I understood that much of their oppressiveness was unconscious. Then I remembered the frequent charges from women of color that white women whom they encounter are oppressive. I began to understand why we are justly seen as oppressive, even when we don't see ourselves that way. I began to count the ways in which I enjoy unearned skin privilege and have been conditioned into oblivion about its existence.

My schooling gave me no training in seeing myself as an oppressor, as an unfairly advantaged person, or as a participant in a damaged culture. I was taught to see myself as an individual whose moral state depended on her individual moral will. My schooling followed the pattern my colleague Elizabeth Minnich has pointed out: whites are taught to think of their lives as morally neutral, normative, and average, and also ideal, so that when we work to benefit others, this is seen as work which will allow "them" to be more like "us."

I decided to try to work on myself at least by identifying some of the daily effects of white privilege in my life. I have chosen those conditions which I think in my case *attach somewhat more to skin-color privilege* than to class, religion, ethnic status, or geographical location, though of course all these other factors are intricately intertwined. As far as I can see, my African American co-workers, friends and acquaintances with whom I come into daily or frequent contact in this particular time, place, and line of work cannot count on most of these conditions.

1. I can if I wish arrange to be in the company of people of my race most of the time.
2. If I should need to move, I can be pretty sure of renting or purchasing housing in an area which I can afford and in which I would want to live.
3. I can be pretty sure that my neighbors in such a location will be neutral or pleasant to me.
4. I can go shopping alone most of the time, pretty well assured that I will not be followed or harassed.
5. I can turn on the television or open to the front page of the paper and see people of my race widely represented.
6. When I am told about our national heritage or about "civilization," I am shown that people of my color made it what it is.
7. I can be sure that my children will be given curricular materials that testify to the existence of their race.
8. If I want to, I can be pretty sure of finding a publisher for this piece on white privilege.
9. I can go into a music shop and count on finding the music of my race represented, into a supermarket and find the staple foods which fit with my cultural traditions, into a hairdresser's shop and find someone who can cut my hair.
10. Whether I use checks, credit cards, or cash, I can count on my skin color not to work against the appearance of financial reliability.
11. I can arrange to protect my children most of the time from people who might not like them.
12. I can swear, or dress in second hand clothes, or not answer letters, without having people attribute these choices to the bad morals, the poverty, or the illiteracy of my race.
13. I can speak in public to a powerful male group without putting my race on trial.
14. I can do well in a challenging situation without being called a credit to my race.
15. I am never asked to speak for all the people of my racial group.
16. I can remain oblivious of the language and customs of persons of color who constitute the world's majority without feeling in my culture any penalty for such oblivion.
17. I can criticize our government and talk about how much I fear its policies and behavior without being seen as a cultural outsider.
18. I can be pretty sure that if I ask to talk to "the person in charge," I will be facing a person of my race.
19. If a traffic cop pulls me over or if the IRS audits my tax return, I can be sure I haven't been singled out because of my race.
20. I can easily buy posters, postcards, picture books, greeting cards, dolls, toys, and children's magazines featuring people of my race.
21. I can go home from most meetings of organizations I belong to feeling somewhat tied in, rather than isolated, out-of-place, outnumbered, unheard, held at a distance, or feared.
22. I can take a job with an affirmative action employer without having co-workers on the job suspect that I got it because of race.
23. I can choose public accommodation without fearing that people of my race cannot get in or will be mistreated in the places I have chosen.
24. I can be sure that if I need legal or medical help, my race will not work against me.
25. If my day, week, or year is going badly, I need not ask of each negative episode or situation whether it has racial overtones.
26. I can choose blemish cover or bandages in "flesh" color and have them more or less match my skin.

I repeatedly forgot each of the realizations on this list until I wrote it down. For me white privilege has turned out to be an elusive and fugitive subject. The pressure to avoid it is great, for in facing it I must give up the myth of meritocracy. If these things are true, this is not such a free country; one's life is not what one makes it; many doors open for certain people through no virtues of their own.

In unpacking this invisible knapsack of white privilege, I have listed conditions of daily experience which I once took for granted. Nor did I think of any of these perquisites as bad for the holder. I now think that we need a more finely differentiated taxonomy of privilege, for some of these varieties are only what one would want for everyone in a just society, and others give licence to be ignorant, oblivious, arrogant and destructive.

I see a pattern running through the matrix of white privilege, a pattern of assumptions which were passed on to me as a white person. There was one main piece of cultural turf; it was my own turf, and I was among those who could control the turf. *My skin color was an asset for any move I was educated to want to make.* I could think of myself as belonging in major ways, and making social systems work for me. I could freely disparage, fear, neglect, or be oblivious to anything outside of the dominant cultural forms. Being of the main culture, I could also criticize it fairly freely.

In proportion as my racial group was being made confident, comfortable, and oblivious, other groups were likely being made inconfident, uncomfortable, and alienated. Whiteness protected me from many kinds of hostility, distress, and violence, which I was being subtly trained to visit in turn upon people of color.

For this reason, the word "privilege" now seems to me misleading. We usually think of privilege as being a favored state, whether earned or conferred by birth or luck. Yet some of the conditions I have described here work to systematically overempower certain groups. Such privilege simply *confers dominance* because of one's race or sex.

I want, then, to distinguish between earned strength and unearned power conferred systemically. Power from unearned privilege can look like strength when it is in fact permission to escape or to dominate. But not all of the privileges on my list are inevitably damaging. Some, like the expectation that neighbors will be decent to you, or that your race will not count against you in court, should be the norm in a just society. Others, like the privilege to ignore less powerful people, distort the humanity of the holders as well as the ignored groups.

We might at least start by distinguishing between positive advantages which we can work to spread, and negative types of advantages which unless rejected will always reinforce our present hierarchies. For example, the feeling that one belongs within the human circle, as Native Americans say, should not be seen as privilege for a few. Ideally it is an *unearned entitlement.* At present, since only a few have it, it is an *unearned advantage* for them. This paper results from a process of coming to see that some of the power which I originally saw as attendant on being a human being in the U.S. consisted in *unearned advantage* and *conferred dominance.*

I have met very few men who are truly distressed about systemic, unearned male advantage and conferred dominance. And so one question for me and others like me is whether we will be like them, or whether we will get truly distressed, even outraged, about unearned race advantage and conferred dominance and if so, what we will do to lessen them. In any case, we need to do more work in identifying how they actually affect our daily lives. Many, perhaps most, of our white students in the U.S. think that racism doesn't affect them because they are not people of color; they do not see "whiteness" as a racial identity. In addition, since race and sex are not the only advantaging systems at work, we need similarly to examine the daily experience of having age advantage, or ethnic advantage, or physical ability, or advantage related to nationality, religion, or sexual orientation.

Difficulties and dangers surrounding the task of finding parallels are many. Since racism, sexism, and heterosexism are not the same, the advantaging associated with them should not be seen as the same. In addition, it is hard to disentangle aspects of unearned advantage which rest more on social class, economic class, race, religion, sex and ethnic identity than on other factors. Still, all of the oppressions are interlocking, as the Combahee River Collective Statement of 1977 continues to remind us eloquently.

One factor seems clear about all of the interlocking oppressions. They take both active forms which we can see and embedded forms which as a member of the dominant group one is taught not to see. In my class and place, I did not see myself as a racist because I was taught to recognize racism only in individual acts of meanness by members of my group, never in invisible systems conferring unsought racial dominance on my group from birth.

Disapproving of the systems won't be enough to change them. I was taught to think that racism could end if white individuals changed their attitudes. [But] a "white" skin in the United States opens many doors for whites whether or not we approve of the way dominance has been conferred on us. Individual acts can palliate, but cannot end, these problems.

To redesign social systems we need first to acknowledge their colossal unseen dimensions. The silences and denials surrounding privilege are the key political tool here. They keep the thinking about equality or equity incomplete, protecting unearned advantage and conferred dominance by making these taboo subjects. Most talk by whites about equal opportunity seems to me now to be about equal opportunity to try to get into a position of dominance while denying that *systems* of dominance exist.

It seems to me that obliviousness about white advantage, like obliviousness about male advantage, is kept strongly inculturated in the United States so as to maintain the myth of meritocracy, the myth that democratic choice is equally available to all. Keeping most people unaware that freedom of confident action is there for just a small number of people props up those in power, and serves to keep power in the hands of the same groups that have most of it already.

Though systemic change takes many decades, there are pressing questions for me and I imagine for some others like me if we raise our daily consciousness on the perquisites of being light-skinned. What will we do with such knowledge? As we know from watching men, it is an open question whether we will choose to use unearned advantage to weaken hidden systems of advantage, and whether we will use any of our arbitrarily-awarded power to try to reconstruct power systems on a broader base.

Stereotyping, Prejudice, and Racism

Jana Noel

Jana Noel is Provost's Fellow for Community and Civic Engagement and Professor of Teacher Education at California State University, Sacramento. She was the co-creator and coordinator of the Sacramento State Urban Teacher Education Center, which received the 2008 California Quality Education Partnership for Distinguished Service to Children and the Preparation of Teachers. Her research focuses on urban and multicultural education, teacher education, and school-community-university engagement. She is the author of the textbook *Developing Multicultural Educators* (Waveland Press, 2005), from which the following selection is drawn, and she has published in such journals as *Journal of Teacher Education, Educational Theory, Journal of Negro Education, Multicultural Perspectives,* and *The Urban Review.*

Noel approaches the concept of prejudice by asking readers to consider how their own identities have helped lead to, and are impacted by, prejudice. She lays out five theories of how prejudice may form within an individual: racial and cultural difference, economic competition, traumatic experience, frustration-aggression, and social control. She gives examples of each type of prejudice, to explain how each theory of prejudice works. But she also discusses how none of these theories can stand on their own to explain prejudice, but instead how the complex concept of prejudice is formed through a combination of several of these theories.

Key Concept: theories of the formation of prejudice

Prejudice

For the past 40 years, researchers have studied the possible reasons why people form prejudices. Some have posited the idea that some experiences can lead to prejudice formation. Others have pointed to the prejudice found within society as a general foundation within which people draw from and form their prejudices. And still other researchers have proposed that people with certain personality types will be most likely to develop prejudices. Following here are five theories of prejudice formation, summarized largely in Banks (1982). As you read through these theories, reflect upon whether any or all of them help explain why your prejudice was formed.

Forming Prejudices

Racial and Cultural Difference Theory

People have an instinctive fear and dislike of individuals who are physically and culturally different from themselves. Going back again to social identity theory, we are reminded that people seem to form in-groups from which they gain their self-esteem. Those who are not within that comfortable in-group then are disliked or feared. It may also be that we are uncertain about the beliefs and behaviors of people whom we do not know; thus there is discomfort when asked to talk about or interact with those others.

Does this theory help explain any of your prejudices? Do you feel this instinctive concern about a group of people different from yourself? This theory may help explain the prejudice formed by some individuals; however, it will not fully explain all prejudice. In studies of the social interactions of young children, for instance, it has been found that while children do see differences among people, they do not make judgments based upon those differences. For example, a fairly common response of young White children who have never seen a person of color is to ask a parent: "Why is that man black?" upon seeing an African American for the first time. These young children recognize color but do not understand the concept of race. They recognize male and female distinctions, but do not understand the concept of gender. Young children only begin to display signs of judging people when they have learned many of society's judgments of groups of people, when they hear the social and political meanings of race and gender.

Economic Competition Theory

Prejudice results from antagonism caused by competition among various groups for jobs and other economic rewards (housing, services, and so on). This theory sheds light on many historical and current examples of prejudice, at each of the national, local community, and individual levels. A 1994 instantiation of this theory at the state level is California's passage of Proposition 187, which states that individuals who are living illegally in the United States (who are not yet citizens or do not have work visas) can no longer receive social services, education, or health care. This means that approximately 400,000 school-aged children would not be allowed to go to school, and would not be allowed to receive the free inoculations against disease that all other children are allowed to receive. It further means that their parents would get no assistance such as Medicare to help pay for such things as dental care and basic medical checkups. The economic competition-based prejudice that gave origins to this proposition were stated very clearly in the actual text of the bill. The text begins: "The People of California find and declare as follows: That they have suffered and are suffering economic hardship caused by the presence of illegal aliens in this state." It is clear in this legislation that those people who voted for Proposition 187 feel "antagonism caused by competition among various groups for jobs and other economic rewards (such as housing, services, etc.)," which is the definition of the economic-based theory of prejudice.

At a more local community-based level, members of communities who have for generations shared a sense of similar values and traditions may develop prejudice against members of a community-designated out-group based on a real or perceived feeling that the out-group is threatening that sense of tradition and security. As can be seen by these examples, it may be more likely that the prejudice resulting from economic competition will arise and develop especially in times of national, political, or personal turmoil. This prejudice can arise mainly as a response to the feeling of a loss of control, with a corresponding need to figure out why these hardships are occurring.

Allport (1958), a leading scholar on the origins of prejudice, has described this phenomenon as scapegoating. In other words: someone or something outside my control is causing my struggles and misfortunes.

Does this theory help explain any of your prejudices? Are your prejudices based to any extent on this sense of loss of economic stability? This theory does seem to explain a number of prejudices. But similar to the objection to the first theory described here, this theory will not be able to explain all examples or types of prejudice. In particular, economic competition theory fails to explain why an individual or a group continues to hold certain prejudices even when it no longer profits economically from doing so.

Traumatic Experience Theory

Prejudice emerges in an individual following a traumatic experience involving a member of another group. Does this theory help explain any of your prejudices? Have you ever had an actual experience with someone within the group against whom you hold a prejudice? This theory may operate on two different levels. If you actually have had a direct traumatic experience with one or more members of a particular group, you may have developed a prejudice based on that primary experience. Many of these primary experiences are related to violent acts. For instance, a woman who has been raped may develop a prejudice against men. This prejudice may be against all men or only against the particular race of the man who raped her, or his income level, body shape, nationality, or language spoken. At whatever level of prejudice, the prejudice is the result of an actual, physical experience. The theory may also operate on a second level. This level does not involve actual physical trauma of the individual. Rather, we may take on the prejudices of others, especially those close to us, who have themselves had a traumatic experience and then pass on their views to us. This secondary sense could be called experience with a traumatized individual. This secondary sense of prejudice can help explain why children will most likely take on the prejudices of their parents or community, rather than the prejudices of an unrelated group of people. Which of these levels of traumatic experience theory—the primary or secondary sense—is closest to a possible reason that you may have formed your prejudice?

Once again, the traumatic experience theory will not explain every instance of prejudice, for the theory does not help explain why only some people who have traumatic experiences will develop prejudice as a result, whereas others will never form that prejudice. An additional component needs to be examined to further understand the formation of prejudice: the conditions under which that prejudice was formed. For the formation of prejudice occurs not in a vacuum, but only within a complex web of personal beliefs, desires, and perceptions of a situation. As Middlebrook (1974) describes:

> The forming of an impression of something involves a complicated interaction between the person forming the impression, the situation in which it is formed, and the objective attributes of the person or thing being consi dered. . . . The impression derived reflects the past history, culture, interests, motives, and beliefs of the person as much as the actual characteristics of the person or situation being judged.
>
> (From Campbell, 1967, pp. 120–121)

Frustration–Aggression Theory

Prejudice results when individuals become frustrated because they are unable to satisfy real or perceived needs; this leads to aggression directed at other groups. This highly psychological theory, called a personality theory of prejudice, basically says that a certain type of personality is more prone to being prejudice. This theory was promoted early by Adorno (1950) in what he called the authoritarian personality. In reviewing multiple studies, Adorno summarized what he believed to be the characteristics of the prejudiced person.

Allport (1958) echoes the idea that there can be a prejudiced personality. In his review of the research on prejudice, he lays out the characteristics of authoritarianism in combination with a need for concrete and definiteness in all situations. Because the prejudiced personality needs such definiteness, this type of person will see rules, actions, and behaviors in strict "right or wrong" determinations. This personality "grows overconcerned with sin in others" (Allport, 1958, p. 375) because he or she sees anyone who is different as breaking the rules. Allport continues: "when he sees any lapses from the conventional code in others he grows anxious. He wishes to punish the transgressor" (p. 375). The personality thus becomes prejudiced through this combination of needs for a uthoritarian and definite standards of right and wrong.

There are two key criticisms of this personality-based theory of prejudice. The first criticism is that the studies that created the base for this theory have, themselves, been criticized over time. Questions have been raised such as how the "prejudiced" people were selected for the studies, who judged them to be prejudiced, and how their characteristics were ascertained. Since the original studies have been questioned, the results of those studies must also raise some concerns about their accuracy. Questions have arisen that ask whether this identification of a supposed set type of personality is a form of stereotyping.

The second criticism is that this theory proposes a sort of free-floating feeling of prejudice, with the resulting aggression not really aimed at or focused on any specific target group. The idea behind this theory is that the prejudiced individual has such a feeling of frustration that he or she will lash out at any nearby or highly visible groups. But once again this theory cannot on its own explain prejudice entirely, for there is still the question of why one group becomes a target rather than another group. If the frustration and aggression were to be truly randomly distributed, then all people would be equally violated. In reality, however, certain groups of people are more commonly targeted for violence than others. Each year, FBI keeps track of reported hate crimes; crimes in which the offender targets a member of a specific group, and makes that target status clear through verbal or written attacks on that person's group membership. According to the FBI statistics for 1995, certain groups are clearly targeted more frequently, based on their group membership. The statistics show that 38 percent of all hate crimes are targeted toward Blacks. The clear distinction based on race can be seen when Asians are the targets of 5 percent and Hispanics the targets of 3 percent of hate crimes. Another group that is very clearly the frequent target of hate crimes is based on sexual orientation; specifically, 13 percent of hate crimes are aimed at homosexuals and bisexuals. And finally, another highly targeted group for hate crimes are individuals of the Jewish religion, with 12 percent of hate crimes aimed at anti-Jewish activity.

Social Control Theory

Because individuals are forced to conform to society's traditions and norms, they are taught and socialized to hold prejudices. This theory takes the emphasis off the personality of the individual and recognizes instead the crucial impact of society upon the individual. The theory points out the critical interactions of person, family, community, and social institutions such as schools, government, and the media.

The City Kids Foundation, a multicultural youth group founded in 1895 by Laurie Medoff, specifically addresses these issues of society and individual interaction. In their book *City Kids Speak on Prejudice,* they write about their experiences and views on the development and effects of prejudice. The following is a poem by 15-year-old Brigitte:

Meet Kim	*Kim is not black*	*Kim is not white*	*Kim does not see color*
Meet Kim	*Kim is not Christian*	*Kim is not Muslim*	*Kim knows no religion*
Meet Kim	*Kim is not rich*	*Kim is not poor*	*Kim does not understand the meaning of money*
Meet Kim	*Kim is not a Crip*	*Kim is not a Blood*	*Kim belongs to no gang*
Meet Kim	*Kim hates no one*	*All this will change when Kim grows up*	

Can you identify the societal factors that will likely affect Kim's beliefs about others as she grows up? Might she hear negative opinions about targeted groups from her friends? Could her parents hold the same prejudice while unintentionally passing it on to her? Will her prejudice also be the one that is negatively emphasized by the media? What would be your answers to all these questions regarding your own prejudices?

Social Foundations of Prejudice

Research has indicated that a positive and well-developed understanding of identity enables people to more readily accept those who are culturally different, while being less likely to develop and continue prejudices. Hoare (1991) lays out this view: "in the Western world, a well-grounded, mature psychosocial identity is nec-essary for the acceptance of persons who are culturally different and who may have different cultural realities" (p. 45). Streitmatter and Pate (1989) have examined this idea, studying the level of identity and prejudice, and found in their study of 182 early adolescents that there are "significant and direct relationships between 'cognitive prejudice' or stereotypical thinking and lower levels of psychosocial identity development" (p. 48). Pate goes even further and says that the way to defend against prejudice is to have high self-esteem, to have a positive view of self.

Summary of Prejudice

This chapter has presented five theories about how prejudice may form within us. Some of these focus on the psychological variables involved in prejudice formation, others focus on the role that society plays in this process, and still others draw out the ways that individuals react to events within society. The five theories presented here explain possible reasons for the development of prejudice: racial and cultural difference, economic competition, traumatic experience, frustration-aggression, and social control. As discussed here, none of these theories is adequate on its own to fully explain prejudice. Some problems with each of the theories are also described, making clear that prejudice formation is not a simple matter. It is more likely that there is going to be a complex interaction between the society, the person who is the target of a prejudice, and the person who holds the prejudice.

References

Adorno, Theodore W., Frenkel-Brunswil, Else, Levinson, Daniel J., and Sanford, R. Nevitt., *The Authoritarian Personality* (New York: Harper & Row, 1950).

Allport, Gordon W., *The Nature of Prejudice* (Garden City, NY: Doubleday Anchor, 1958).

Banks, James A., *Reducing Prejudice in Students: Theory, Research, and Strategies,* paper presented at the Kamloops Spring Institute for Teacher Education Lecture Series, Burnaby, British Columbia, February 1982.

Campbell, Donald, "Stereotypes and the Perception of Group Differences," *American Psychologist, 22* (1967): 817–829.

CityKids Speak on Prejudice (New York: Random House, 1994).

Hoare, Carol H., "Psychosocial Identity Development and Cultural Others," *Journal of Counseling and Development, 70* (1991): 45–53.

Middlebrook, Patricia Niles, *Social Psychology and Modern Life* (New York: Alfred A. Knopf, 1974).

Streitmatter, Janice L. and Pate, Glenn S., "Identity Status Development and Cognitive Prejudice in Early Adolescents," *Journal of Early Adolescence, 9* (1–2)(1989): 142–152.

Identity Development

Selection 14
JEAN S. PHINNEY, from "Ethnic Identity in Adolescents and Adults: Review of Research," *Psychological Bulletin*

Selection 15
BEVERLY DANIEL TATUM, from "Teaching White Students About Racism: The Search for White Allies and the Restoration of Hope," *Teachers College Record*

Ethnic Identity in Adolescents and Adults: Review of Research

Jean S. Phinney

The study of ethnic identity development seeks to answer the question, "How do we come to know who we are ethnically?" In this selection, from "Ethnic Identity in Adolescents and Adults: Review of Research," *Psychological Bulletin* (1990), Jean S. Phinney provides a review of over 70 articles on the topic of ethnic identity development, in particular on the ethnic identity of minority adolescents and adults. Phinney points out that the development of one's identity is not a static process, but rather is constantly undergoing change throughout one's lifetime. According to a stage model presented in the following selection, individuals may go through a stage in which they have not thought much about, or examined, their ethnic identity. Some individuals may also go through a time when they explore their identity and may finally come to a deeper understanding of what their ethnicity means to their identity.

Phinney has served as Professor of Psychology at California State University, Los Angeles. Her articles are published in journals such as *Journal of Cross-Cultural Psychology, Journal of Youth and Adolescence,* and *Journal of Social Issues.* She has focused much of her research on the development of ethnic and bicultural identity among adolescents. Her interests lie in identifying the factors that influence the development of psychological well-being among minority youth. She is a recipient of a research grant from the National Institutes of Health, with which she has developed a measure of identity development that is currently being used with adolescents around the world.

Key Concept: review of ethnic identity development

The growing proportion of minority group members in the United States and other Western countries has resulted in an increasing concern with issues of pluralism, discrimination, and racism in the media. However, psychological research on the impact of these issues on the individual is uneven. Most of the research dealing with psychological aspects of contact between racial or ethnic groups has focused on attitudes toward racial or ethnic groups other than one's own and particularly on stereotyping, prejudice, and discrimination. The emphasis has been on attitudes of members of the majority or dominant group toward minority group members; this is a research area of great importance in face of the daily evidence of ethnic tensions and racial violence.

A far less studied aspect of diversity has been the psychological relationship of ethnic and racial minority group members with their own group, a topic dealt with under the broad term *ethnic identity*. The study of attitudes about one's own ethnicity has been of little interest to members of the dominant group, and little attention has

been paid by mainstream, generally White researchers to the psychological aspects of being a minority group member in a diverse society.

Recent concern with ethnic identity has derived in part from the ethnic revitalization movements in the 1960s. Growing awareness in society of differences associated with ethnic group membership (e.g, lower educational and occupational attainment) has been accompanied by social movements leading to increased ethnic consciousness and pride (Laosa, 1984). Attitudes toward one's ethnicity are central to the psychological functioning of those who live in societies where their group and its culture are at best poorly represented (politically, economically, and in the media) and are at worst discriminated against or even attacked verbally and physically; the concept of ethnic identity provides a way of understanding the need to assert oneself in the face of threats to one's identity (Weinreich, 1983). The psychological importance of ethnic identity is attested to by numerous literary writings of ethnic group members about the struggle to understand their ethnicity (e.g, Du Bois, 1983; Kingston, 1976; Malcolm X, 1970; Rodriguez, 1982).

The issue of ethnic identity has also been brought to the fore by changing demographics, including differential birthrates and increasing numbers of immigrants and refugees throughout the world. Projections suggest that by the mid-1990s, minority youth will constitute more than 30% of the 15- to 25-year-olds in the United States (Wetzel, 1987). The topic not only has important implications within psychology (e.g., Ekstrand, 1986) but also has broad political significance. In response, Canada has developed an explicit policy of multiculturalism and supports continuing study of the issue (Berry, Kalin, & Taylor, 1977). Many European countries will be dealing for years to come with struggles of ethnic minorities to maintain or assert their identities (Kaplan, 1989).

Within the social sciences, many writers have asserted that ethnic identity is crucial to the self-concept and psychological functioning of ethnic group members (e.g., Gurin & Epps, 1975; Maldonado, 1975). Critical issues include the degree and quality of involvement that is maintained with one's own culture and heritage; ways of responding to and dealing with the dominant group's often disparaging views of their group; and the impact of these factors on psychological well-being. These issues have been addressed conceptually from a variety of perspectives (e.g., Alba, 1985; Arce, 1981; Atkinson, Morten, & Sue, 1983; Dashefsky, 1976; DeVos & Romanucci-Ross, 1982; Frideres & Goldenberg, 1982; Mendelberg, 1986; Ostrow, 1977; Parham, 1989; Staiano, 1980; Tajfel, 1978, 1981; Weinreich, 1988; Yancey, Ericksen, & Juliani, 1976; Zinn, 1980).

However, the theoretical writing far outweighs empirical research. Most of the empirical work on ethnic identity has concentrated on young children, with a focus on minority children's racial misidentification or preference for White stimulus figures. This work has been widely discussed and reviewed (e.g., Aboud, 1987; Banks, 1976; Brand, Ruiz, & Padilla, 1974) and is not addressed here. Far less work has been done on ethnic identity beyond childhood and particularly the transition from childhood to adulthood; this gap has been recently noted (Kagitcibasi & Berry, 1989). In published studies on ethnic identity in adolescents and adults, researchers have generally focused on single groups and have used widely discrepant definitions and measures of ethnic identity, which makes generalizations and comparisons across studies difficult and ambiguous. The findings are often inconclusive or contradictory.

The topic is of sufficient importance to warrant serious research attention, but in order for the research to yield useful and meaningful results, greater conceptual and methodological clarity is needed. The primary goal of this article is to provide such clarity through a review of the empirical literature on ethnic identity in adolescents and adults. I describe the definitions and conceptual frameworks that have guided empirical research, the way in which the construct has been defined and measured, and the empirical findings. The article concludes with recommendations for future research. . . .

Definitions of Ethnic Identity

Ethnic identity was defined in many ways in the research reviewed. The fact that there is no widely agreed-on definition of ethnic identity is indicative of confusion about the topic. A surprisingly number of the articles reviewed (about two thirds) provided no explicit definition of the construct. The definitions that were given reflected quite different understandings or emphases regarding what is meant by *ethnic identity*.

In a number of articles, ethnic identity was defined as the ethnic component of social identity, as defined by Tajfel (1981): "that part of an individual's self-concept which derives from his knowledge of his membership of a social group (or groups) together with the value and emotional significance attached to that membership" (p. 255). Some writers considered self-identification the key aspect; others emphasized feelings of belonging and commitment (Singh, 1977; Ting-Toomey, 1981; Tzuriel & Klein, 1977), the sense of shared values and attitudes (White & Burke, 1987, p. 311), or attitudes toward one's group (e.g., Parham & Helms, 1981; Teske & Nelson, 1973). In contrast to the focus by these writers on attitudes and feelings, some definitions emphasized the cultural aspects of ethnic identity: for example, language, behavior, values, and knowledge of ethnic group history (e.g., Rogler, Cooney, & Ortiz, 1980). The active role of the individual in developing an ethnic identity was suggested by several writers who saw it as a dynamic product that is achieved rather than simply given (Caltabiano, 1984; Hogg, Abrams, & Patel, 1987; Simic, 1987).

In summary researchers appeared to share a broad general understanding of ethnic identity, but the specific aspects that they emphasized differed widely. These differences are related to the diversity in how researchers have conceptualized ethnic identity and in the questions they have sought to answer; these issues are reviewed in the next section.

Conceptual Frameworks for the Study of Ethnic Identity

About a quarter of the studies suggested no theoretical framework, but most of the studies were based on one of three broad perspectives: social identity theory, as presented by social psychologists; acculturation and culture conflict, as studied by social psychologists, sociologists, or anthropologists; and identity formation, drawn from psychoanalytic views and from developmental and counseling psychology. There is considerable overlap among the frameworks on which the studies were based, as well as great variation in the extent to which the relevant framework or theory was discussed and applied to the research. However, these three approaches provide a background for understanding the empirical research.

Ethnic Identity and Social Identity Theory

Much of the research on ethnic identity has been conducted within the framework of social identity as conceptualized by social psychologists. One of the earliest statements of the importance of social identity was made by Lewin (1948), who asserted that individuals need a firm sense of group identification in order to maintain a sense of well-being. This idea was developed in considerable detail in the social identity theory of Tajfel and Turner (1979). According [to] the theory, simply being a member of a group provides individuals with a sense of belonging that contributes to a positive self-concept.

However, ethnic groups present a special case of group identity (Tajfel, 1978). If the dominant group in a society holds the traits or characteristics of an ethnic group in low esteem, then ethnic group members are potentially faced with a negative social identity. Identifying with a low-status group may result in low self-regard (Hogg, Abrams, & Patel, 1987; Ullah, 1985). An extensive literature deals explicitly with the notion of "self-hatred" among disparaged ethnic groups, generally with reference to Black Americans (Banks, 1976; V. Gordon, 1980). Much of the research reviewed was concerned with this issue: that is, whether or to what extent membership in, or identification with, an ethnic group with lower status in society is related to a poorer self-concept. A number of studies addressed these issues (Grossman, Wirt, & David, 1985; Houston, 1984; Paul & Fischer, 1980; Tzuriel & Klein, 1977; White & Burke, 1987); the specific findings are discussed later in the article.

Tajfel (1978) asserted that members of low-status groups seek to improve their status in various ways. Individuals may seek to leave the group by "passing" as members of the dominant group, but this solution may have negative psychological consequences. Furthermore, this solution is not available to individuals who are racially distinct and are categorized by others as ethnic group members. Alternative solutions are to develop pride in one's group (Cross, 1978), to reinterpret characteristics deemed "inferior" so that they do not appear inferior (Bourhis, Giles, & Tajfel, 1973), and to stress the distinctiveness of one's own group (Christian, Gadfield, Giles, & Taylor, 1976; Hutnik, 1985).

Social identity theory also addresses the issue of potential problems resulting from participation in two cultures. Both Lewin (1948) and Tajfel (1978) discussed the likelihood that identification with two different groups can be problematic for identity formation in ethnic group members because of the conflicts in attitudes, values, and behaviors between their own and the majority group (Der-Karabetian, 1980; Rosenthal & Cichello, 1986; Salgado de Snyder, Lopez, & Padilla, 1982; Zak, 1973). The issue in this case is whether individuals must choose between two conflicting identities or can establish a bicultural ethnic identity and, if so, whether that is adaptive.

A distinct but related approach to ethnic identity is based on symbolic interactionism and identity theory (Stryker, 1980). Research in this framework emphasizes the importance of shared understandings about the meaning of one's ethnic identity, which derive both from one's own group and from a "countergroup" (White & Burke, 1987).

Acculturation as a Framework for Studying Ethnic Identity

Ethnic identity is meaningful only in situations in which two or more ethnic groups are in contact over a period of time. In an ethnically or racially homogeneous society, ethnic identity is a virtually meaningless concept. The broad area of research that has dealt with groups in contact is the acculturation literature.

The term *ethnic identity* has sometimes been used virtually synonymously with *acculturation*, but the two terms should be distinguished. The concept of acculturation deals broadly with changes in cultural attitudes, values, and behaviors that result from contact between two distinct cultures (Berry, Trimble, & Olmedo, 1986). The level of concern is generally the group rather than the individual, and the focus is on how minority or immigrant groups relate to the dominant or host society. Ethnic identity may be thought of as an aspect of acculturation, in which the concern is with individuals and the focus is on how they relate to their own group as a subgroup of the larger society.

Two distinct models have guided thinking about these questions: a linear, bipolar model and a two-dimensional model. In the linear model, ethnic identity is conceptualized along a continuum from strong ethnic ties at one extreme to strong mainstream ties at the other (Andujo, 1988; Makabe, 1979; Simic, 1987; Ullah, 1985). The assumption underlying this model is that a strengthening of one requires a weakening of the other; that is, a strong ethnic identity is not possible among those who become involved in the mainstream society, and acculturation is inevitably accompanied by a weakening of ethnic identity.

In contrast to the linear model, an alternative model emphasizes that acculturation is a two-dimensional process, in which both the relationship with the traditional or ethnic culture and the relationship with the new or dominant culture must be considered, and these two relationships may be independent. According to this view, minority group members can have either strong or weak identifications with both their own and the mainstream cultures, and a strong ethnic identity does not necessarily imply a weak relationship or low involvement with the dominant culture.

This model suggests that there are not only the two acculturative extremes of assimilation or pluralism but

Table 1   Terms Used for Four Orientations, Based on Degree of Identification with Both One's Own Ethnic Group and the Majority Group

Identification with majority group	Identification with ethnic group	
	Strong	**Weak**
Strong	Acculturated Integrated Bicultural	Assimilated
Weak	Ethnically identified Ethnically embedded Separated Dissociated	Marginal

at least four possible ways of dealing with ethnic group membership in a diverse society (Berry et al., 1986). Strong identification with both groups is indicative of integration or biculturalism; identification with neither group suggests marginality. An exclusive identification with the majority culture indicates assimilation, whereas identification with only the ethnic group indicates separation. Table 1 is an illustration of this model and some of the terms that have been used for each of the four possibilities in empirical research. A number of the studies reviewed were based on this model (e.g., M. Clark, Kaufman, & Pierce, 1976; Hutnik, 1986; Ting-Toomey, 1981; Zak, 1973), and in some the authors explored empirical evidence for the bipolar versus the two-dimensional models (e.g., Elias & Blanton, 1987; Zak, 1976). Research on this issue is summarized later.

An important empirical issue in this area has been the question of the extent to which ethnic identity is maintained over time when a minority ethnic group comes in contact with a dominant majority group (DeVos & Romanucci-Ross, 1982; Glazer & Moynihan, 1970; M. Gordon, 1964) and the impact of the process on psychological adjustment (e.g., Berry, Kim, Minde, & Mok, 1987). Underlying both these issues is the theme of culture conflict between two distinct groups and the psychological consequences of such conflicts for individuals. How such conflicts are dealt with at the individual level is part of the process of ethnic identity formation.

Ethnic Identity Formation

Both the social identity and the acculturation frameworks acknowledge that ethnic identity is dynamic, changing over time and context. In a similar vein, several of the definitions cited earlier include the idea that ethnic identity is achieved through an active process of decision making and self-evaluation (Caltabiano, 1984; Hogg et al., 1987; Simic, 1987). In a conceptual chapter, Weinreich (1988) asserted that ethnic identity is not an entity but a complex of processes by which people construct their ethnicity. However, in research based on the social identity or acculturation frameworks, investigators in general have not examined ethnic identity at the level of individual change—that is, developmentally.

A developmental framework was provided by Erikson's (1968) theory of ego identity formation. According to Erikson, an achieved identity is the result of a period of exploration and experimentation that typically takes place during adolescence and that leads to a decision or a commitment in various areas, such as occupation, religion, and political orientation. The ego identity model, as operationalized by Marcia (1966, 1980), suggests four ego identity statuses based on whether people have explored identity options and whether they have made a decision. A person who has neither engaged in exploration nor made a commitment is said to be *diffuse*; a commitment made without exploration, usually on the basis of parental values, represents a *foreclosed* status. A person in the process of exploration without having made a commitment is in *moratorium*; a firm commitment following a period of exploration is indicative of an *achieved identity* (see Table 2). Although Erikson alluded to the importance of culture in identity formation, this model has not been widely applied to the study of ethnic identity.

The formation of ethnic identity may be thought of as a process similar to ego identity formation that takes place over time, as people explore and make decisions about the role of ethnicity in their lives. A number of conceptual models have described ethnic identity development in minority adolescents or adults. Cross (1978) described a model of the development of Black consciousness in college students during the Civil Rights era. In a dissertation, Kim (1981) described Asian American identity development in a group of young adult Asian American women. A model of ethnic identity formation based on clinical experience was proposed by Atkinson et al. (1983), and Arce (1981) conceptualized the issues with regard to Chicanos.

In a recent article, Phinney (1989) examined commonalities across various models and proposed a three-stage progression from an unexamined ethnic identity through a period of exploration to an achieved or committed ethnic identity (see Table 2). According to this model, early adolescents and perhaps adults who have not been exposed to ethnic identity issues are in the first stage, an unexamined ethnic identity. According to Cross (1978) and others (e.g., Atkinson et al., 1983; Kim, 1981), this early stage is characterized for minorities by a preference for the dominant culture. However, such a preference is not a necessary characteristic of this stage. Young people may simply not be interested in ethnicity and may have given it little thought (their ethnic identity is diffuse). Alternatively, they may have absorbed positive ethnic attitudes from parents or other adults and therefore may not show a preference for the majority group, although they have not thought through the issues for themselves—that is, are foreclosed (Phinney, 1989).

A second stage is characterized by an exploration of one's own ethnicity, which is similar to the moratorium

Table 2 Marcia's Ego Identity Statuses (Top) and Proposed Stages of Ethnic Identity (Bottom)

Marcia (1966, 1980)	Identity diffusion	Identity foreclosure	Identity crisis[a]	Moratorium	Identity achievement
Cross (1978)		Pre-encounter	Encounter	Immersion/emersion	Internalization
Kim (1981)		White identified	Awakening to social political awareness	Redirection to Asian American consciousness	Incorporation
Atkinson et al. (1983)		Conformity: Preference for values of dominant culture	Dissonance: Questioning and challenging old attitudes	Resistance and immersion: Rejection of dominant culture	Synergetic articulation and awareness
Phinney (1989)	Unexamined ethnic identity:		Ethnic identity search (Moratorium):		Achieved ethnic identity
	Lack of exploration of ethnicity. Possible subtypes:		Involvement in exploring and seeking to understand meaning of ethnicity for oneself		Clear, confident sense of own ethnicity
	Diffusion: Lack of interest in or concern with ethnicity	Foreclosure: Views of ethnicity based on opinions of others			

[a]Identity crisis is not one of Marcia's original four statuses.

status described by Marcia (1980). This may take place as the result of a significant experience that forces awareness of one's ethnicity ("encounter" according to Cross, 1978, or "awakening," according to Kim, 1981). It involves an often intense process of immersion in one's own culture through activities such as reading, talking to people, going to ethnic museums, and participating actively in cultural events. For some people it may involve rejecting the values of the dominant culture.

The stage model suggests that as a result of this process, people come to a deeper understanding and appreciation of their ethnicity—that is, ethnic identity achievement or internalization. This culmination may require resolution or coming to terms with two fundamental problems for ethnic minorities: (a) cultural differences between their own group and the dominant group and (b) the lower or disparaged status of their group in society (Phinney, Lochner, & Murphy, 1990). The meaning of ethnic identity achievement is undoubtedly different for different individuals and groups because of their different historical and personal experiences. However, achievement does not necessarily imply a high degree of ethnic involvement; one could presumably be clear about and confident of one's ethnicity without wanting to maintain one's ethnic language or customs. A recent conceptual article suggested that the process does not necessarily end with ethnic identity achievement but may continue in cycles that involve further exploration or rethinking of the role or meaning of one's ethnicity (Parham, 1989). A similar idea has been suggested with regard to ego identity (Grotevant, 1987).

Empirical research based on these models has involved describing changes over time in a person's attitudes and understanding about his or her ethnicity. In addition, researchers have looked at factors related to ethnic identity formation, such as parental attitudes and social class, and at correlates, including self-esteem or adjustment and attitudes toward counselors. . . .

Empirical Findings

Because of the different conceptualizations, definitions, and measures that have been used in the study of ethnic identity, empirical findings are difficult or impossible to compare across studies. Not surprisingly, the findings are often inconsistent.

Self-Esteem, Self-Concept, and Psychological Adjustment

A key issue in conceptual writing about ethnic identity has been the role of group identity in the self-concept: Specifically, does a strong identification with one's ethnic group promote a positive self-concept or self-esteem? Or, conversely, is identification with an ethnic group that is held in low regard by the dominant group likely to lower one's self-esteem? Furthermore, is it possible to hold negative views about one's own group and yet feel good about oneself?

Early interest in these questions stemmed from the work of K. Clark and M. Clark (1947), which showed that young Black children tended to prefer White dolls to Black dolls. The meaning of such findings continues to be debated, and a number of reviewers have discussed the findings (Aboud, 1987; Banks, 1976; Brand et al., 1974; V. Gordon, 1980). However, this controversy has been dealt with almost entirely in studies with children, and there has been little extension of the work into adolescence and adulthood, the topic of the current review. Given the theoretical importance of this issue, it is surprising that in only 11 of the studies reviewed, the researchers assessed self-esteem or a related construct and examined its relationship to some measure of ethnic identity. The researchers who did address this question presented conflicting results.

Three of the studies suggested positive effects of ethnic identity, although the measures used were different in each case. Among Black early adolescents (ages 13–14) of low socioeconomic status (SES), "acceptance of racial identity," as measured by six items (no reliability given), was found to be significantly related to self-concept as measured by the Tennessee Self Concept Scale (Paul & Fischer, 1980). A study with Anglo-American and Mexican-American junior high school students revealed a positive relationship between self-esteem, assessed by Rosenberg's (1979) Self-Esteem Scale, and ethnic esteem, as measured by adjective ratings of one's own group (Grossman et al., 1985). Among Israeli high school students, ego identity, which is suggestive of good adjustment, was higher among those with high ethnic group identification than among those with low identification (on a scale with reliability of alpha equal to .60), especially among the Oriental Jews, a minority group in Israel (Tzuriel & Klein, 1977).

Four studies revealed no relationship between ethnic identity and various measures of adjustment. A study of Black and White college students revealed no relationship between self-esteem (Rosenberg scale) and ethnic identity, measured in terms of similarity-to-group scores on semantic differential ratings of Blacks and Whites—that is, similarity to a stereotype of one's own group (White & Burke, 1987). Also, for Black college students, "Black consciousness," measured by attitudes toward Blacks and Whites, was unrelated to two measures of self-esteem (Houston, 1984). Among Arab-Israeli college students, self-esteem (Rosenberg scale) was not related to measures of Arab identity (scale reliability = .81) or Israeli identity (scale reliability = .83; Zak, 1976). Finally, a study of Italian Australians revealed "Italian identity" (scale reliability = .89) to be unrelated to psychosocial adjustment, according to the Offer Self-Image Questionnaire and the Erikson Psychosocial Stage Inventory (Rosenthal & Cichello, 1986). In summary, these studies of ethnic identity, in which a variety of measures of ethnic identity as a state were used, permit no definitive conclusion about its role in self-esteem.

In contrast to the preceding studies, researchers in four studies examined self-esteem in relation to the stage model of ethnic identity. By analogy with the ego-identity literature, in which positive psychological outcomes have been associated with an achieved identity (Marcia, 1980), the developmental model predicts higher self-esteem in subjects with an achieved ethnic identity. This prediction was supported in a study with 10th-grade Black,

Asian American, and Mexican-American adolescents, in which subjects at higher stages of ethnic identity, as assessed by interviews, were found to have significantly higher scores on all four subscales of a measure of psychological adjustment (self-evaluation, sense of mastery, family relations, and social relations), as well as on an independent measure of ego development (Phinney, 1989). A similar relationship between ethnic identity search and commitment (scale reliabilities = .69 and .59, respectively) and self-esteem was found among college students from four ethnic groups (Asian American, Black, Mexican American, and White); the relationship was stronger among minority group students than among their White peers (Phinney & Alipuria, 1990). A study with Black college students, which was based on Cross's (1978) process model, revealed that low self-esteem was related to the earliest (pre-encounter) stage and to the immersion (moratorium) stage, whereas high self-esteem was associated with the encounter stage, which involves events that precipitate a search or immersion (Parham & Helms, 1985a). In a related study, the pre-encounter and immersion stages were found to be related to feelings of inferiority and anxiety (Parham & Helms, 1985b). These studies suggest that a positive self-concept may be related to the process of identity formation—that is, to the extent to which people have come to an understanding and acceptance of their ethnicity.

Ethnic Identity in Relation to the Majority Culture

The acculturation framework for studying ethnic identity suggests that for understanding ethnic identity, it is necessary to consider also the individual's relationship to the dominant or majority group. Whereas a number of the studies reviewed focused on a single ethnic group, without reference to the dominant group (e.g., Asbury, Adderly-Kelly, & Knuckle, 1987; Constantinou & Harvey, 1985; Garcia & Lega, 1979; Keefe, 1986; Masuda, Hasegawa, & Matsumoto, 1973), many researchers took into consideration the relationship to the dominant group.

A central question, as discussed earlier, is whether ethnic identity is directly related to degree of acculturation or whether, conversely, it is independent, so that, for example, one could have a strong ethnic identification and also have strong ties to the dominant culture (see Table 1). Several studies suggest that the two are independent. In a study with adolescent girls of East Indian extraction who were living in England, Hutnik (1986) assessed separately self-identification (as Indian or British) and Indian and British cultural behaviors; the results showed the two dimensions to be unrelated. A similar picture emerged from a study of seven White ethnic groups in Canada (Driedger, 1976). Group scores demonstrated varying degrees of ethnic affirmation and denial for each group, which resulted in three types of ethnic identity, depending on degree of ethnic identification or denial: majority assimilator, ethnic identifiers, and ethnic marginals. Similarly, studies of Armenian Americans (Der-Karabetian, 1980), Jewish Americans (Zak, 1973), and Chinese Americans (Ting-Toomey, 1981) revealed ethnic identity and American identity to be independent dimensions.

However, other studies gave different results. A comparison of bipolar and orthogonal models of ethnic identity among Israelis living in the United States suggested that attitudes and behaviors relative to being Israeli, Jewish, or American were not independent (Elias & Blanton, 1987). Affective measures of the three aspects of identity were positively intercorrelated, whereas behavioral measures were negatively related; subjects who engaged in many typical American behaviors showed fewer Israeli behaviors. In another study of Israelis residing in the United States (Elizur, 1984), Jewish and American identity tended to be negatively related.

More complex results emerged from two studies in which qualitative data were used. An extensive study of Mexican-American and Asian American adults (M. Clark et al., 1976) revealed six profiles representing different combinations of attitudes, behaviors, and knowledge relative to one's own culture and American culture. A qualitative study of Mexican-American high school students (Matute-Bianchi, 1986) demonstrated five types of ethnic identity, depending on the students' degree of involvement in their own ethnic culture and in the mainstream culture of the high school. Moreover, the types of identity were related to school achievement. Those students who were more embedded in the barrio culture were the least successful academically.

The value of studies such as these, in which mainstream as well as ethnic orientation is assessed, has been in emphasizing that ethnic identity is not necessarily a linear construct; it can be conceptualized in terms of qualitatively different ways of relating to one's own and other groups. A problem in using this more complex conceptualization is in assessing the attributes of the contrast group. The characteristics of mainstream culture are far more difficult to define than those of a particular subculture. The issue of measurement of mainstream attitudes belongs properly to the topic of acculturation; these measurement issues were thoroughly discussed by Berry et al. (1986).

The two-dimensional model provides some clarification of the importance of ethnic identity to the self-concept. Some of the contradictions and inconsistencies noted in this review may be a function of differences in the degree to which researchers have considered identification with both the ethnic group and the mainstream culture. For example, although ethnic identity, in the sense of identification with one's ethnic group, can range from strong to weak, an understanding of how ethnic identity is related to self-concept may require also determining an individual's relationship to the majority group. There is some evidence that the acculturated or integrated option may be the most satisfactory and the

marginal, the least (Berry et al., 1987). However, the other two possibilities, assimilation and separation, may also provide the basis for a good self-concept, if the person is comfortable with these alternatives and is in an environment that supports them (Phinney et al., 1990).

Changes in Ethnic Identity Related to Generation of Immigration

A second focus of research within the acculturation framework is the way in which ethnic identity changes with contact with another group. Writers generally have agreed that ethnic identity is a dynamic concept, but relatively few have studied it over time. However, a number of researchers have examined changes related to generational status among immigrant groups.

Studies of generational differences in ethnic identity have shown a fairly consistent decline in ethnic group identification in later generations descended from immigrants (Constantinou & Harvey, 1985; Fathi, 1972). Ethnic identity was found to be similarly weaker among those who arrived at a younger age and had lived longer in the new country (Garcia & Lega, 1979; Rogler et al., 1980) and among those with more education (Rogler et al., 1980). However, a study of third- and fourth-generation Japanese-American youth revealed virtually no generational difference (Wooden, Leon, & Toshima, 1988), and a study of Chinese Americans suggests a cyclical process whereby ethnic identity became more important in third- and fourth-generation descendents of immigrants (Ting-Toomey, 1981). A recent study (Rosenthal & Feldman, in press) found that among adolescent Chinese immigrants, ethnic knowledge and behavior decreased between the first and second generations, but that there was no change in the importance or positive valuation of ethnicity. The authors suggest that although some behavioral and cognitive elements of ethnic identity decline, immigrants retain a commitment to their culture. Furthermore, specific programs can foster ethnic identity (Zisenwine & Walters, 1982).

A study of three age groups in Japan (Masuda et al., 1973) illustrates the possible confounding of generation with age and cultural change. Older Japanese scored higher than did younger people in a measure of Japanese identification, in results similar to the generational differences among Japanese immigrants. Comparisons between younger (second-generation) and older (first-generation) subjects may thus tap age as well as cohort differences. In a retrospective interview study with elderly Croatians, Simic (1987) noted an intensification of ethnic sentiments during later life.

Ethnic Identity and Gender

Gender may be a variable in acculturation in those cultures in which men are more likely to get jobs in the mainstream culture while the women remain at home. There may also be different cultural expectations for men and women, such as the assumption that women are the carriers of ethnic traditions. The very little research that addresses this issue suggests a greater involvement in ethnicity by women than by men. Research with Chinese-American college students revealed women to be more oriented to their ancestral culture than were men (Ting-Toomey, 1981), and a drawing study showed higher Black identification in women (Bolling, 1974). Among Irish adolescents in England, girls were significantly more likely than boys to adopt an Irish identity (Ullah, 1985). Japanese girls and women tended to score higher than boys and men on Japanese ethnic identity (Masuda et al., 1973).

In contrast, Jewish boys in Canada were found to show greater preference for Jewish norms than did girls (Fathi, 1972), a fact that the author suggested may be related to the Jewish emphasis on male dominance. Among East Indian and Anglo-Saxon adolescents in England, girls were more inclined than boys to mix with their own group, but they were also more willing to invite home someone from a different group (Hogg et al., 1987). Gender was found to interact with ethnic identity on attitudes toward counseling (Ponterotto, Anderson, & Grieger, 1986) and on a measure of visual retention (Knuckle & Asbury, 1986).

In the sparse literature on identity formation, Parham and Helms (1985b) found that Black men were more likely than Black women to endorse attitudes from the earliest stages and less likely to show evidence of the highest stage. A similar trend among Black adolescents was noted by Phinney (1989). These fragmentary results clearly allow no conclusions about sex differences in ethnic identity.

Contextual Factors in Ethnic Identity

Ethnic identity is to a large extent defined by context; it is not an issue except in terms of a contrast group, usually the majority culture. The particular context seems to be an essential factor to consider, yet relatively few researchers have examined it in any detail. There is some evidence that ethnic identity varies according to the context (e.g., Vermeulen & Pels, 1984) and the characteristics of the group (Rosenthal & Hrynevich, 1985). Adolescents report that their feelings of being ethnic vary according to the situation they are in and the people they are with (Rosenthal & Hrynevich, 1985). Ethnic identity is positively related to the ethnic density of the neighborhood (Garcia & Lega, 1979) and negatively to the occupational and residential mobility of subjects (Makabe, 1979); it varies among communities within the same state (Teske & Nelson, 1973).

Some writers have suggested that ethnic identity is less likely to be maintained among middle-SES than among lower-SES ethnic group members. Among second-generation Irish adolescents in England, those from lower socioeconomic backgrounds were significantly more likely to identify themselves as Irish than were middle-SES youth, perhaps because they lived in areas with a higher concentration of Irish immigrants. However, research based on the developmental model has revealed no relationship between stages of ethnic identity and social class among high school students (Phinney, 1989) or college students (Phinney & Alipuria, 1990), and racial identity attitudes were not predictive of socioeconomic status among Black college students (Carter & Helms, 1988).

The impact of the context on Black identity has been investigated through studies of transracial adoption. Racial identity was more of a problem for Black children and adolescents adopted into White homes than for those adopted by Black parents, although the self-esteem of the two groups did not differ (McRoy, Zurcher, Lauderdale, & Anderson, 1982). Transracially adopted Hispanic adolescents were similarly likely to identify themselves as Americans, whereas those adopted by Mexican-American couples overwhelmingly called themselves Mexican-American (Andujo, 1988). Furthermore, the parental attitudes and perceptions had an important impact on the racial identity of transracial adoptees (McRoy, Zurcher, & Lauderdale, 1984).

There has been little research on such presumably important factors as the relative size of the ethnic group (at the local or the national level) or its status in the community.

Ethnic Identity Formation

The developmental model assumes that with increasing age, subjects are more likely to have an achieved ethnic identity. Although there is little empirical support for this assumption, some results suggest that there is a developmental progression. In an interview study with Black and White 8th graders, about a third of the subjects showed evidence of ethnic identity search (Phinney & Tarver, 1988); among 10th graders in a related study, the comparable figure was about half (Phinney, 1989). Thus it appeared that the older students had done more searching. In a study based on Cross's (1978) model, Black college students reported their perceptions of themselves over the past, present, and future as shifting from lower to higher levels of Black identity (Krate et al., 1974). Both longitudinal and cross-sectional studies are needed to examine changes toward higher levels of ethnic identity formation.

Although the process model of ethnic identity has not been validated, it provides an alternative way of thinking about ethnic identity. Both attitudes and behaviors with respect to one's own and other groups are conceptualized as changing as one develops and resolves issues and feelings about one's own and other groups. Differing ethnic attitudes and behaviors may therefore reflect different stages of development, rather than permanent characteristics of the group or the individuals studied. Some discrepancies in the findings regarding relationships among components of ethnic identity, reported earlier in this review, may result from studying subjects at different stages of development.

Another topic of interest in this area has been the impact of ethnic identity stages on attitudes regarding the ethnicity of counselors. Black college students in the early stages preferred White counselors (Parham & Helms, 1981), whereas those in the intermediate stages showed a preference for Black counselors (Morten & Atkinson, 1983; Parham & Helms, 1981). Results for subjects at the highest stage are mixed; they may show Black preference (Parham & Helms, 1981) or no preference (Morten & Atkinson, 1983). Stages of ethnic identity development in Blacks are also related to perceptions of White counselors (Pomales, Claiborn, & LaFromboise, 1986).

In examining the relationship of stages of Black identity to Black value orientations, Carter and Helms (1987) found that certain values could be predicted from the stages; for example, the highest stage, internalization, was associated with a belief in harmony with nature.

The study of stages of ethnic identity is at present rudimentary; however, a developmental perspective may be able eventually to provide a more complete understanding of this phenomenon across age. . . .

Summary

In a world where the populations of most countries are increasingly diverse, both ethnically and racially, it is essential to understand the psychological impact of such diversity (Albert, 1988). Although attitudes of the majority toward minority ethnic groups have received most attention, it is equally important to understand how ethnic group members deal with being part of a group that may be disparaged or discriminated against, that must struggle to maintain its own customs and traditions, and that is not well represented in the media, among other problems. The task of understanding ethnic identity is complicated by the fact that the uniqueness that distinguishes each group and setting makes it difficult to draw general conclusions across groups.

There are important research questions to be addressed, such as the role of ethnic identity in self-esteem, its relationship to acculturation, and its place in the development of personal identity. Currently, researchers can offer few answers to these questions because of widely differing approaches to the study of ethnic identity, including lack of agreement on what constitutes its essential components, varying theoretical orientations that have guided the research, and measures that are unique to each group. It is hoped that this article brings some conceptual clarity to this important area and stimulates further research on ethnic identity.

References

Aboud, F. (1987). The development of ethnic self-identification and attitudes. In J. Phinney & M. Rotheram (Eds.), *Children's ethnic socialization: Pluralism and development* (pp. 32–55). Newbury Park, CA: Sage.

Alba, R. (1985). *Ethnicity and race in the U.S.A.* London: Routledge & Kegan Paul.

Albert, R. (1988). The place of culture in modern psychology. In P. Bronstein & K. Quina (Eds.), *Teaching a psychology of people: Resources for gender and sociocultural awareness* (pp. 12–18). Washington, DC: American Psychological Association.

Andujo, E. (1988). Ethnic identity of transethnically adopted Hispanic adolescents. *Social Work, 33,* 531–535.

Arce, C. (1981). A reconsideration of Chicano culture and identity. *Daedalus, 110*(2), 177– 192.

Asbury, C., Adderly-Kelly, B., & Knuckle, E. (1987). Relationship among WISC-R performance categories and measured ethnic identity in Black adolescents. *Journal of Negro Education, 56,* 172–183.

Atkinson, D., Morten, G., & Sue, D. (1983). *Counseling American minorities.* Dubuque, IA: Wm. C. Brown.

Banks, W. (1976). White preference in Blacks: A paradigm in search of a phenomenon. *Psychological Bulletin, 83,* 1179–1186.

Berry, J., Kalin, R., & Taylor, D. (1977). *Multiculturalism and ethnic attitudes in Canada.* Ottawa, Canada: Minister of Supply and Services.

Berry, J., Kim, U., Minde, T., & Mok, D. (1987). Comparative studies of acculturative stress. *International Migration Review, 21,* 492–511.

Berry, J., Trimble, J., & Olmedo, E. (1986). Assessment of acculturation. In W. Lonner & J. Berry (Eds.), *Field methods in cross-cultural research* (pp. 291–324). Newbury Park, CA: Sage.

Bolling, J. (1974). The changing self-concept of Black children. *Journal of the National Medical Association, 66,* 28–31, 34.

Bourhis, R., Giles, H., & Tajfel, H. (1973). Language as a determinant of Welsh identity. *European Journal of Social Psychology, 3,* 447–460.

Brand, E., Ruiz, R., & Padilla, A. (1974). Ethnic identification and preference: A review. *Psychological Bulletin, 86,* 860–890.

Caltabiano, N. (1984). Perceived differences in ethnic behavior: A pilot study of Italo-Australian Canberra residents. *Psychological Reports, 55,* 867–873.

Carter, R., & Helms, J. (1987). The relationship of Black value-orientations to racial identity attitudes. *Measurement and Evaluation in Counseling and Development, 19,* 185–195.

Carter, R., & Helms, J. (1988). The relationship between racial identity attitudes and social class. *Journal of Negro Education, 57,* 22–30.

Christian, J., Gadfield, N., Giles, H., & Taylor, D. (1976). The multidimensional and dynamic nature of ethnic identity. *International Journal of Psychology, 11,* 281–291.

Clark, K., & Clark, M. (1947). Racial identification and preference in Negro children. In T. Newcomb and E. Hartley (Eds.), *Readings in social psychology* (pp. 551–560). New York: Holt.

Clark, M., Kaufman, S., & Pierce, R. (1976). Explorations of acculturation: Toward a model of ethnic identity. *Human Organization, 35,* 231–238.

Constantinou, S., & Harvey, M. (1985). Dimensional structure and intergenerational differences in ethnicity: The Greek Americans. *Sociology and Social Research, 69,* 234–254.

Cross, W. (1978). The Thomas and Cross models of psychological nigrescence: A literature review. *Journal of Black Psychology, 4,* 13–31.

Dasheksky, A. (Ed.) (1976). *Ethnic identity in society.* Chicago: Rand McNally.

Der-Karabetian, A. (1980). Relation of two cultural identities of Armenian-Americans. *Psychological Reports, 47,* 123–128.

DeVos, G., & Romanucci-Ross, L. (1982). *Ethnic identity: Cultural continuities and change.* Chicago: University of Chicago Press.

Driedger, L. (1976). Ethnic self-identity: A comparison of in-group evaluations. *Sociometry, 39,* 131–141.

Du Bois, W. E. B. (1983). *Autobiography of W. E. B. Du Bois.* New York: International Publishing.

Ekstrand, L. (1986). *Ethnic minorities and immigrants in a cross-cultural perspective.* Lisse, Netherlands: Swets & Zeitlinger.

Elias, N., & Blanton, J. (1987). Dimensions of ethnic identity in Israeli Jewish families living in the United States. *Psychological Reports, 60,* 367–375.

Elizur, D. (1984). Facet analysis of ethnic identity: The case of Israelis residing in the United States. *Journal of General Psychology, 111,* 259–269.

Erikson, E. (1968). *Identity: Youth and crisis.* New York: Norton.

Fathi, A. (1972). Some aspects of changing ethnic identity of Canadian Jewish youth. *Jewish Social Studies, 34,* 23–30.

Frideres, J., & Goldenberg, S. (1982). Myth and reality in Western Canada. *International Journal of Intercultural Relations, 6,* 137–151.

Garcia, M., & Lega, L. (1979). Development of a Cuban ethnic identity questionnaire. *Hispanic Journal of Behavioral Sciences, 1,* 247–261.

Glazer, N., & Moynihan, D. (1970). *Beyond the melting pot.* Cambridge, MA: Harvard University Press.

Gordon, M. (1964). *Assimilation in American life.* London: Oxford University Press.

Gordon, V. (1980). *The self-concept of Black Americans.* Lanham, MD: University Press America.

Grossman, B., Wirt, R., & Davids, A. (1985). Self-esteem, ethnic identity, and behavioral adjustment among Anglo and Chicano adolescents in West Texas. *Journal of Adolescence, 8,* 57–68.

Grotevant, H. (1987). Toward a process model of identity formation. *Journal of Adolescent Research, 2,* 203–222.

Gurin, P., & Epps, E. (1975). *Black consciousness, identity, and achievement.* New York: Wiley.

Hogg, M., Abrams, D., & Patel, Y. (1987). Ethnic identity, self-esteem, and occupational aspirations of Indian and Anglo-Saxon British adolescents. *Genetic, Social, and General Psychology Monographs, 113,* 487–508.

Houston, L. (1984). Black consciousness and self-esteem. *Journal of Black Psychology, 11,* 1–7.

Hutnik, N. (1985). Aspects of identity in a multi-ethnic society. *New Community, 12,* 298–309.

Hutnik, N. (1986). Patterns of ethnic minority identification and modes of social adaptation. *Ethnic and Racial Studies, 9,* 150–167.

Kagitcibasi, C., & Berry, J. (1989). Cross-cultural psychology: Current research and trends. In M. Rosenzweig & L. Porter (Eds.), *Annual review of psychology* (Vol. 40, pp. 493–531). Palo Alto, CA: Annual Reviews.

Kaplan, R. (1989, July). The Balkans: Europe's third world. *The Atlantic, 263,* 16–22.

Keefe, S. (1986). Southern Appalachia: Analytical models, social services, and native support systems. *American Journal of Community Psychology, 14,* 479–498.

Kim, J. (1981). *The process of Asian American identity development: A study of Japanese American women's perceptions of their struggle to achieve positive identities.* Unpublished doctoral dissertation, University of Massachusetts.

Kingston, M. (1976). *The woman warrior.* South Yarmouth, MA: J. Curley.

Knuckle, E., & Asbury, C. (1986). Benton revised visual retention test: Performance of Black adolescents according to age, sex, and ethnic identity. *Perceptual and Motor Skills, 63,* 319–327.

Krate, R., Leventhal, G., & Silverstein, B. (1974). Self-perceived transformation of Negro-to-Black identity. *Psychological Reports, 34,* 1071–1075.

Laosa, L. (1984). Social policies toward children of diverse ethnic, racial and language groups in the United States. In H. Stevenson & A. Siegel (Eds.), *Child development research and social policy* (pp. 1–109). Chicago: University of Chicago Press.

Lewin, K. (1948). *Resolving social conflicts.* New York: Harper.

Makabe, T. (1979). Ethnic identity scale and social mobility: The case of Nisei in Toronto. *The Canadian Review of Sociology and Anthropology, 16,* 136–145.

Malcolm X. (1965). *Autobiography of Malcolm X.* New York: Golden Press.

Maldonado, D., Jr. (1975). Ethnic self-identity and self-understanding. *Social Casework, 56,* 618–622.

Marcia, J. (1966). Development and validation of ego-identity status. *Journal of Personality and Social Psychology, 3,* 551–558.

Marcia, J. (1980). Identity in adolescence. In J. Adelson (Ed.), *Handbook of adolescent psychology* (pp. 159–187). New York: Wiley.

Masuda, M., Hasegawa, R., & Matsumoto, G. (1973). The ethnic identity questionnaire: A comparison of three Japanese age groups in Tachikawa, Japan, Honolulu, and Seattle. *Journal of Cross-Cultural Psychology, 4,* 229–244.

Matute-Bianchi, M. (1986). Ethnic identities and pattern of school success and failure among Mexican-descent and Japanese-American students in a California high school: An ethnographic analysis. *American Journal of Education, 95,* 233–255.

McRoy, R., Zurcher, L., & Lauderdale, M. (1984). The identity of transracial adoptees. *Social Casework, 65,* 34–39.

McRoy, R., Zurcher, L., Lauderdale, M., & Anderson, R. (1982). Self-esteem and racial identity in transracial and inracial adoptees. *Social Work, 27,* 522–526.

Mendelberg, H. (1986). Identity conflict in Mexican-American adolescents. *Adolescence, 21,* 215–222.

Morten, G., & Atkinson, D. (1983). Minority identity development and preference for counselor race. *Journal of Negro Education, 52,* 156–161.

Ostrow, M. (1977). The psychological determinants of Jewish identity. *Israel Annals of Psychiatry and Related Disciplines, 15,* 313–335.

Parham, T. (1989). Cycles of psychological nigrescence. *The Counseling Psychologist, 17,* 187–226.

Parham, T., & Helms, J. (1981). The influence of Black student's racial identity attitudes on preferences for counselor's race. *Journal of Counseling Psychology, 28,* 250–257.

Parham, T., & Helms, J. (1985a). Attitudes of racial identity and self-esteem of Black students: An exploratory investigation. *Journal of College Student Personnel, 26,* 143–147.

Parham, T., & Helms, J. (1985b). Relation of racial identity attitudes to self-actualization and affective states of Black students. *Journal of Counseling Psychology, 32,* 431–440.

Paul, M., & Fischer, J. (1980). Correlates of self-concept among Black early adolescents. *Journal of Youth and Adolescence, 9,* 163–173.

Phinney, J. (1989). Stages of ethnic identity in minority group adolescents. *Journal of Early Adolescence, 9,* 34–49.

Phinney, J., & Alipuria, L. (1990). Ethnic identity in older adolescents from four ethnic groups. *Journal of Adolescence, 13.*

Phinney, J., Lochner, B., & Murphy, R. (1990). Ethnic identity development and psychological adjustment in adolescence. In A. Stiffman & L. Davis (Eds.), *Ethnic issues in adolescent mental health.* Newbury Park, CA: Sage.

Phinney, J., & Tarver, S. (1988). Ethnic identity search and commitment in Black and White eighth graders. *Journal of Early Adolescence, 8,* 265–277.

Pomales, J., Claiborn, C., & LaFromboise, T. (1986). Effect of Black students' racial identity on perceptions of White counselors varying in cultural sensitivity. *Journal of Counseling Psychology, 33,* 57–61.

Ponterotto, J., Anderson, W., & Grieger, I. (1986). Black students' attitudes toward counseling as a function of racial identity. *Journal of Multicultural Counseling and Development, 14,* 50–59.

Rodriguez, R. (1982). *Hunger of memory.* Boston: Godine.

Rogler, L., Cooney, R., & Ortiz, V. (1980). Intergenerational change in ethnic identity in the Puerto Rican family. *International Migration Review, 14,* 193–214.

Rosenberg, M. (1979). *Conceiving the self.* New York: Basic Books.

Rosenthal, D., & Cichello, A. (1986). The meeting of two cultures: Ethnic identity and psychosocial adjustment of Italian-Australian adolescents. *International Journal of Psychology, 21,* 487–501.

Rosenthal, D., & Feldman, S. (in press). The nature and stability of ethnic identity in Chinese youth: Effects of length of residence in two cultural contexts. *Journal of Cross-Cultural Psychology.*

Rosenthal, D., & Hrynevich, C. (1985). Ethnicity and ethnic identity: A comparative study of Greek-, Italian-, and Anglo-Australian adolescents. *International Journal of Psychology, 20,* 723–742.

Salgado de Snyder, N., Lopez, C. M., & Padilla, A. M. (1982). Ethnic identity and cultural awareness among the offspring of Mexican interethnic marriages. *Journal of Early Adolescence, 2,* 277–282.

Simic, A. (1987). Ethnicity as a career for the elderly: The Serbian-American case. *Journal of Applied Gerontology, 6,* 113–126.

Singh, V. (1977). Some theoretical and methodological problems in the study of ethnic identity: A cross-cultural perspective. *New York Academy of Sciences: Annals, 285,* 32–42.

Staiano, K. (1980). Ethnicity as process: The creation of an Afro-American identity. *Ethnicity, 7,* 27–33.

Stryker, S. (1980). *Symbolic interactionism: A social structural version.* Menlo Park, CA: Benjamin Cummings.

Tajfel, H. (1978). *The social psychology of minorities.* New York: Minority Rights Group.

Tajfel, H. (1981). *Human groups and social categories.* Cambridge, England: Cambridge University Press.

Tajfel, H., & Turner, J. (1979). An intergrative theory of intergroup conflict. In W. Austin & S. Worchel (Eds.), *The social psychology of intergroup relations* (pp. 34–47). Monterey, CA: Brooks/Cole.

Teske, R., & Nelson, B. (1973). Two scales for the measurement of Mexican-American identity. *International Review of Modern Sociology, 3,* 192–203.

Ting-Toomey, S. (1981). Ethnic identity and close friendship in Chinese-American college students. *International Journal of Intercultural Relations, 5,* 383–406.

Tzuriel, D., & Klein, M. M. (1977). Ego identity: Effects of ethnocentrism, ethnic identification, and cognitive complexity in Israeli, Oriental, and Western ethnic groups. *Psychological Reports, 40,* 1099–1110.

Ullah, P. (1985). Second generation Irish youth: Identity and ethnicity. *New Community, 12,* 310–320.

Vermeulen, H., & Pels, T. (1984). Ethnic identity and young migrants in The Netherlands. *Prospects, 14,* 277–282.

Weinreich, P. (1983). Emerging from threatened identities. In G. Breakwell (Ed.), *Threatened identities* (pp. 149–185). New York: Wiley.

Weinreich, P. (1988). The operationalization of ethnic identity. In J. Berry & R. Annis (Eds.), *Ethnic psychology: Research and practice with immigrants, refugees, native peoples, ethnic groups and sojourners* (pp. 149–168). Amsterdam: Swets & Zeitlinger.

Wetzel, J. (1987). *American youth: A statistical snapshot.* Washington, DC: William T. Grant Foundation.

White, C., & Burke, P. (1987). Ethnic role identity among Black and White college students: An interactionist approach. *Sociological Perspectives, 30,* 310–331.

Wooden, W., Leon, J., & Toshima, M. (1988). Ethnic identity among Sansei and Yonsei church-affiliated youth in Los Angeles and Honolulu. *Psychological Reports, 62,* 268–270.

Yancey, W., Ericksen, E., & Juliani, R. (1976). Emergent ethnicity: A review and reformulation. *American Sociological Review, 41,* 391–403.

Zak, I. (1973). Dimensions of Jewish-American identity. *Psychological Reports, 33,* 891–900.

Zak, I. (1976). Structure of ethnic identity of Arab-Israeli students. *Psychology Reports, 38,* 239–246.

Zinn, M. (1980) Gender and ethnic identity among Chicanos. *Frontiers, 5,* 18–24.

Zisenwine, D., & Walters, J. (1982). Jewish identity: Israel and the American adolescent. *Forum on the Jewish People, Zionism, and Israel, 45,* 79–84.

Teaching White Students About Racism: The Search for White Allies and the Restoration of Hope

Beverly Daniel Tatum

Beverly Daniel Tatum predicts that the development of ethnic identity for whites in the United States will take a different path than for minorities. Because of a political and social system that places whites in positions of power, she says, their struggles with coming to understand who they are ethnically deal with different issues. For instance, one struggle is when individuals move beyond the point of thinking that they are "normal," that everyone is just like them, to the recognition that they live in a society that validates their ethnicity while devaluing other ethnicities. In laying out the six-stage model developed by Janet Helms, Tatum asserts that for whites there are two major developmental tasks in the process of identity development. First, whites must recognize and then work to abandon individual racism. Later, though, there is a difficult effort to develop a positive white identity. Tatum includes the words of her teacher education students as examples of the various stages of the development of white identity.

Tatum is currently President of Spelman College, a renowned Historically Black College. Prior to her appointment at Spelman, she was a Professor of Psychology and Education at Mount Holyoke College in South Hadley, Massachusetts. Her work focuses on racial identity development and its impact on the classroom. She has widespread recognition in both the academic and popular arenas for her writings and presentations, and she was one of three authors to appear with President Bill Clinton at a 1997 national town meeting on race. The following selection is from her article "Teaching White Students About Racism: The Search for White Allies and the Restoration of Hope," *Teachers College Record* (Summer 1994). Tatum's publications also include best-sellers *Can We Talk About Race? And Other Conversations in an Era of School Resegregation* (2007) and *Why Are All the Black Kids Sitting Together in the Cafeteria? And Other Conversations About Race* (1997).

Key Concept: white identity development

Understanding White Identity Development

As Janet Helms explains in her model of white racial identity development, "racial identity development theory concerns the psychological implications of racial group membership, that is belief systems that evolve in reaction to perceived differential racial-group membership."[1] In U.S. society, where racial-group membership is emphasized, it is assumed that the development of a racial identity will occur in some form in everyone. However, the process will unfold in different ways for whites and people of color because of the different social positions they occupy in this society.

For whites, there are two major developmental tasks in this process, the abandonment of individual racism and the recognition of and opposition to institutional and cultural racism. Helms writes: "Concurrently, the person must become aware of her or his Whiteness, learn to accept Whiteness as an important part of herself or himself, and to internalize a realistically positive view of what it means to be White."[2] Helms's six-stage model can then be divided into two major phases, the first being the abandonment of racism (a process that begins with the Contact stage and ends with the Reintegration stage). The second phase, defining a positive white identity, begins with the Pseudo-Independent stage and reaches fruition at the Autonomy stage.

Contact Stage

The first stage of racial identity for whites (the Contact stage) is a stage at which there is little attention paid to the significance of one's racial group membership. Individuals at this stage of development rarely describe themselves as white. If they have lived, worked, or gone to school in predominantly white settings, they may simply think of themselves as like the majority of those around them. This view is exemplified by the comment one of my white students made when asked to describe herself in terms of her class and ethnic background. She summed up her middle-class, white European background by saying, "I'm just normal." This sense of being part of the racial norm is taken for granted without conscious consideration of the systematically conferred advantages given to whites simply because of their racial group membership.[3]

While they have been influenced by the prevailing societal stereotypes of people of color, there is typically limited awareness of this socialization process. Often individuals at the Contact stage perceive themselves as completely free of prejudice, unaware of their own assumptions about other racial groups. I would describe the majority of the white men and women I have had in my course over the last twelve years as being in this stage of development at the start of the semester.

Disintegration Stage

However, participating in a classroom where the social consequences of racial group membership are explicitly discussed as part of the course content typically propels white students from the first stage to the next, referred to by Helms as the Disintegration stage.[4] At this stage, white students begin to see how much their lives and the lives of people of color have been affected by racism in our society. The societal inequities they now notice are in direct contradiction to the idea of an American meritocracy, a concept that has typically been an integral part of their earlier socialization. The cognitive dissonance that results is part of the discomfort experienced at this stage. One response to this discomfort is to deny the validity of the information that is being presented to them, or to withdraw from the class psychologically, if not physically.[5] However, if they remain engaged, white students at the Disintegration stage typically want to deal with the guilt and other uncomfortable feelings by doing something, by taking action of some sort to interrupt the racism they now see around them. If students have learned (as I hope they have) that racism can take both active forms (e.g., verbal harassment, physical violence, intentional acts of discrimination) and passive forms (e.g., silence in the presence of another's racist remarks, unexamined policies and practices that disproportionately impact people of color, the failure to acknowledge the contributions of people of color), then they recognize that an active response to racism is required to interrupt its perpetuation in our society.

"But what action can I take?" is a common question at this point in their development. Jerri, a white woman from an upper-middle-class family, expressed this sentiment clearly in her journal:

> Another thing I realized when I got to college was the privileges attached to being white. My family had brought me up trying to make me aware of other people and their differences—but they never explained the power I had. I do not take advantage of my power—at least I try not to, but it seems inevitable. I feel helpless. There is so much I want to do—to help. What can I do? I do not want to help perpetuate racism, sexism and stereotypes.

Helping students think this question through for themselves is part of our responsibility as educators who have accepted the challenge of teaching about racism. Heightening student awareness about racism without also providing some hope for social change is a prescription for despair. We all have a sphere of influence, some domain in which we exercise some level of power and control. For students, the task may be to identify what their own sphere of influence is (however large or small) and to consider how it might be used to interrupt the cycle of racism.[6]

However, once again, students find that they can think of many more examples of racist behavior than they can think of examples of antiracist behavior. Many white students have experienced their most influential adult role models, their parents, as having been the source of overtly expressed racial prejudices. The following excerpts from the journals of two students illustrate this point:

> Today was the first class on racism. . . . Before today I didn't think I was exposed to any form of racism. Well, except for my father. He is about as prejudiced as they come. [Sally, a white female]
>
> It really bothers me that stereotypes exist because it is from them that I originally became uninformed. My grandmother makes all kinds of decisions based on stereotypes—who to hire, who to help out. When I was growing up, the only black people that I knew were adults [household help], but I admired them just as much as any other adult. When I expressed these feelings to my parents, I was always told that the black people that I knew were the exceptions and that the rest of the race were different. I, too, was taught to be afraid. [Barbara, a white woman]

Others experienced their parents as passively silent on the subject of racism, simply accepting the status quo. As one young man from a very privileged background wrote:

> It is easy to simply fade into the woodwork, run with the rest of society, and never have to deal directly with these problems. So many people I know from home . . . have simply accepted what society has taught them with little if any question. My father is a prime example of this.

His overriding preaching throughout my childhood dealt with simply accepting reality. [Carl, a white male]

Those white students whose parents actively espoused antiracist values still felt unprepared for addressing racism outside of the family circle, a point highlighted by the following journal entry, written by Annette, a white female college senior:

Talking with other class members, I realized how exceptional my parents were. Not only were they not overtly racist but they also tried to keep society's subtle racism from reaching me. Basically I grew up believing that racism was no longer an issue and all people should be treated as equals. Unfortunately, my parents were not being very realistic as society's racism did begin to reach me. They did not teach me how to support and defend their views once I was interacting in a society without them as a buffer.

How do they learn how to interrupt someone else's racist (or sexist/anti-Semitic/homophobic) joke or challenge someone's stereotype if they have never seen anyone else do it? Despite the lack of examples, many students will begin to speak up about racism to their friends and family members. They often find that their efforts to share their new knowledge and heightened awareness with others are perceived negatively. Alice, a white woman, wrote:

I never realized how much sexism and racism there still is on TV. I don't know if I'll ever be able to watch TV in the same way again. I used to just watch TV shows, laugh at the funny jokes, and not think about sexism or racism. . . . I know my friends and family probably don't think I'm as much fun as I used to be because I can't watch TV without making an issue of how racist and sexist most shows are.

The fear of being alienated from these friends and family members is real, and is part of the social pressure experienced by those at the Disintegration stage of development to back away from this new awareness of racism. The dilemma of noticing racism and yet feeling the societal pressure not to notice, or at least not to speak up, is resolved for some at the Reintegration stage.

Reintegration Stage

At the Reintegration stage, whites may turn to explanations for racism that put the burden of change on those who are the targets of racism.

Race-related negative conditions are assumed to result from Black people's inferior social, moral, and intellectual qualities, and thus it is not unusual to find persons in the Reintegration stage selectively attending to and/or reinterpreting information to conform to societal stereotypes of black people.[7]

As Wellman clearly illustrates, such thinking allows the white individual to relieve himself or herself of guilt as well as responsibility for working toward social change.[8]

Because the pressure to ignore racism and to accept the socially sanctioned stereotypes is so great, unless we talk about the interpersonal challenges that often confront students at this point in their understanding, we place them at risk of getting stuck in the Reintegration stage. Identifying these challenges for students does not solve the problem for them, but it does help them to recognize the source of some of the discomfort they may experience. It is hoped that this recognition allows them to respond in ways that will allow for continued growth in their own racial identity development.

Pseudo-Independent Stage

Continued, ongoing dialogue about race-related issues is one way to promote such growth. As the students' understanding of the complexity of institutional racism in our society deepens, the likelihood of resorting to "blame-the-victim" explanations lessens. Such deepening awareness is associated with the commitment to unlearn one's own racism, and marks the movement into the next stage of development in Helms's model, the Pseudo-independent stage. This stage marks the beginning of the second phase of this developmental process, creating a positive definition of whiteness.

At the Pseudo-independent stage, the individual may try to deal with some of the social pressures experienced at earlier stages by actively seeking friendships with those who share an antiracist perspective. In particular, some white students may want to distance themselves psychologically from their own racial group by seeking out relationships with people of color. An example of this can be seen in the following journal entry:

One of the major and probably most difficult steps in identity development is obtaining or finding the consciousness of what it means to be white. I definitely remember many a time that I wished I was not white, ashamed of what I and others have done to the other racial groups in the world. . . . I wanted to pretend I was black, live with them, celebrate their culture, and deny my whiteness completely. Basically, I wanted to escape the responsibility that came with identifying myself as "white." [Lisa, a white female]

How successful these efforts to escape whiteness via people of color are will depend in part on the racial-identity development of the people of color involved.[9] However, even if these efforts to build interracial relationships are successful, the individual must eventually confront the reality of his or her own whiteness.

We all must be able to embrace who we are in terms of our racial cultural heritage, not in terms of assumed superiority or inferiority, but as an integral part of our daily experience in which we can take pride. But for many white students who have come to understand the reality of racism in all of our lives, whiteness is still at this stage experienced as a source of shame rather than a source of pride. Efforts to define a positive white identity are still tentative. The confusion experienced at this stage is clearly expressed by Bob, a white male struggling with these issues. Five weeks into the semester, he wrote:

> There have been many talk shows on in the past week that have focused on race. Along with the readings I'm finding that I'm looking at the people and topics in very different ways than I had in the past. I'm finding that this idea of white identity is more important than I thought. Yet white identity seems very hard to pin hole. I seem to have an idea and feel myself understanding what I need to do and why and then something presents itself that throws me into mass confusion. I feel that I need some resource that will help me through the process of finding white identity.

Immersion/Emersion Stage

The next stage of white racial identity development, Immersion/Emersion, is a stage at which individuals intensify their efforts to create a positive self-definition as a white person. Helms writes, "The person in this stage is searching for the answers to the questions: 'Who am I racially?' and 'Who do I want to be?' and 'Who are you really?'"[10] Students at this stage actively seek white role models who might provide examples for nonoppressive ways of being white. Such examples might be found in the form of biographies or autobiographies of white individuals who have been engaged in a similar process. Unfortunately, these materials are not easily found because the lives of white antiracists or "allies" have not generally been subjects of study. . . .

Participation in white consciousness-raising groups organized specifically for the purpose of examining one's own racism is often helpful in this process. At Mount Holyoke College, where I currently teach, such a group was formed (White Women Against Racism) following the 1992 acquittal of the Los Angeles police officers involved in the beating of Rodney King. Support groups of this nature help to combat the social isolation antiracist whites often experience, and provide encouragement for continued development of a self-definition as a white ally.

It is at this stage that the feelings of guilt and shame are replaced with feelings of pride and excitement. Helms writes,

> The person may begin to feel a euphoria perhaps akin to a religious rebirth. These positive feelings not only help to buttress the newly developing White identity, but

provide the fuel by which the person can truly begin to tackle racism and oppression in its various forms.[11]

Mary, a senior writing her last journal entry of the semester, reflected this excitement at the changes she was observing in herself:

> This past weekend I went to New York. . . . As always we drove through Harlem on our way downtown. For the first time in four years I didn't automatically feel nervous when we turned that corner. For the first time I took an active interest in what was going on in the neighborhood and in the neighborhood itself. When the bus driver pointed out some points of interest like the Apollo, I actually recognized the names and was truly appreciative that the driver had pointed them out. I know this doesn't sound like much to get excited about, and in all honesty it doesn't really excite me either. In a way though, I guess this serves as an object lesson of sorts for me; I CAN unlearn the racism that I've been taught. It required some thought beforehand, but it certainly wasn't difficult by any means. Clearly, the next step is to identify something new to focus on and unlearn THAT as well. I can't help feeling like this is how a toddler must feel—each step is a challenge and although sometimes you fall, you don't usually hurt yourself. But overwhelmingly, each step is exciting and an accomplishment.

Notes

1. Janet E. Helms, *Black and White Racial Identity: Theory, Research and Practice* (Westport, Conn.: Greenwood Press, 1990).
2. Ibid., p. 55.
3. For further discussion of the concept of white privilege and the advantages systematically conferred on whites, see Peggy McIntosh's working paper, *White Privilege and Male Privilege: A Personal Account of Coming to See Correspondences through Work in Women's Studies* (Wellesley, Mass.: Wellesley College Center for Research on Women).
4. Helms, *Black and White Racial Identity*, chap. 4, p. 58.
5. Tatum, "Talking about Race, Learning about Racism."
6. For a discussion of the use of action-planning projects in a course on racism, see ibid.
7. Helms, *Black and White Racial Identity*, p. 60.
8. David Wellman, *Portraits of White Racism* (New York: Cambridge University Press, 1977).
9. For further discussion of the interaction effect of stages of racial-identity development for people of color and for whites, see Tatum, "Talking about Race, Learning about Racism."
10. Helms, *Black and White Racial Identity*, p. 62.
11. Ibid.

The Conservative Tradition

Selection 16

ARTHUR M. SCHLESINGER, JR., from "The Disuniting of America,"
American Educator

Selection 17

WILLIAM J. BENNETT, CHESTER E. FINN, JR., AND JOHN T.E. CRIBB, JR., from
The Educated Child: A Parent's Guide from Preschool through Eighth Grade

The Disuniting of America: Reflections on a Multicultural Society

Arthur M. Schlesinger, Jr.

Arthur M. Schlesinger, Jr. (1917–2007) was a well-known historian and author. He combined his scholarly work with political work, gaining the description "scholar-activist." He was a professor at Harvard University, and he also worked for presidents of the United States, including as advisor to John F. Kennedy. He also wrote a number of presidential speeches over the years, and he worked for the Office of War Information during World War II. He is perhaps best known for his presidential histories, most famously his biographies of the Kennedys. Schlesinger also wrote books on the Andrew Jackson and Franklin D. Roosevelt presidencies. He has twice won the Pulitzer Prize for his writings on history. The following selection is from an article in the Winter 1992 issue of *American Educator*, titled "The Disuniting of America: Reflections on a Multicultural Society."

One of Schlesinger's key concerns in his writings is the "cult of ethnicity" and his fear that the focus on ethnicity has fragmented society and is threatening to destroy America's common core and America itself. Schlesinger begins his selection by laying out some of the inconsistencies in beliefs throughout U.S. history. For example, one creed says that all men are created equal, yet America allowed slavery. With an Anglo-Saxon domination throughout history, ethnic groups started standing up for civil rights. This created what Schlesinger calls an "ethnic upsurge," and he gives this movement credit for correcting many inequities. But his main point in this selection is that too much of a focus on ethnicity emphasizes difference, puts walls between peoples, and tries to revise history in incorrect ways. Schlesinger also describes the role of historians in defining and shaping a national identity.

Key Concept: concerns about the "cult of ethnicity"

hat then, is the American, this new man?" This was the question famously asked two centuries ago by French immigrant J. Hector St. John de Crevecoeur in his book *Letters from an American Farmer*.

Crevecoeur ruminated over the astonishing diversity of the settlers—"a mixture of English, Scotch, Irish, French, Dutch, Germans, and Swedes," a "strange mixture of blood" that you could find in no other country. "From this promiscuous breed," he wrote, "that race now called Americans has arisen."

What, Crevecoeur mused, were the characteristics of this suddenly emergent American race? He provided a classic answer to his own question: "He is an American, who leaving behind him all his ancient prejudices and manners, receives new ones from the new mode of life he has embraced, the new government he obeys, and the new rank he holds. The American is a new man, who acts upon new principles. . . . *Here individuals of all nations are melted into a new race of men.*"

Crevecoeur's conception was of a brand-new nationality created by individuals who, in repudiating their homelands and joining to make new lives, melted away ancient ethnic differences. Most of those intrepid Europeans who had torn up their roots to brave the wild Atlantic saw America as a transforming nation, banishing old loyalties and forging a new national identity based on common political ideals.

This conception prevailed through most of the two centuries of the history of the United States. But lately a new conception has arisen. The escape from origins has given way to the search for roots. The "ancient prejudices and manners" disclaimed by Crevecoeur have made a surprising comeback.

The new gospel condemns Crevecoeur's vision of individuals of all nations melted into a new race in favor of an opposite vision: a nation of groups, differentiated in their ancestries, inviolable in their diverse identities. The contemporary ideal is shifting from assimilation to ethnicity, from integration to separatism.

The ethnic upsurge has had some healthy consequences. The republic has at last begun to give long-overdue recognition to the role and achievements of groups subordinated and ignored during the high noon of male Anglo-Saxon dominance—women, Americans of South and East European ancestry, black Americans, Indians, Hispanics, Asians. There is far better understanding today of the indispensable contributions minorities have made to American civilization.

But the cult of ethnicity, pressed too far, exacts costs. Instead of a transformative nation with an identity all its own, America increasingly sees itself as preservative of old identities. Instead of a nation composed of individuals making their own free choices, America increasingly sees itself as composed of groups more or less indelible in their ethnic character. The national ideal had once been *e pluribus unum*. Are we now to belittle *unum* and glorify *pluribus*? Will the center hold? Or will the melting pot yield to the Tower of Babel?

A struggle to redefine the national identity is taking place in many arenas—in our politics, our voluntary organizations, our churches, our language—and in no arena more crucial than our system of education. The schools and colleges of the republic train the citizens of the future. They have always been battlegrounds for debates over beliefs, philosophies, values.

What students learn in schools vitally affects other arenas of American life—the way we see and treat other Americans, the way we conceive the purpose of the republic. The debate about the curriculum is a debate about what it means to be an American. What is ultimately at stake is the shape of the American future.

I.

How could Crevecoeur's "promiscuous breed" be transformed into a "new race"? This question preoccupied another young Frenchman who arrived in America three quarters of a century after Crevecoeur. "Imagine, my dear friend, if you can," Alexis de Tocqueville wrote back to France, "a society formed of all the nations of the world . . . people having different languages, beliefs, opinions: in a word, a society without roots, without memories, without prejudices, without routines, without common ideas, without a national character, yet a hundred times happier than our own." What alchemy could make this miscellany into a single society?

The answer, Tocqueville concluded, lay in the commitment of Americans to democracy and self-government. Civic participation, Tocqueville argued in *Democracy in America*, was the great educator and the great unifier. Immigrants, Tocqueville said, become Americans through the exercise of the political rights and civic responsibilities bestowed on them by the Declaration of Independence and the Constitution.

Half a century later, when the next great foreign commentator on American democracy James Bryce wrote *The American Commonwealth*, immigration had vastly increased and diversified. What struck Bryce was what had struck Tocqueville: "the amazing solvent power which American institutions, habits, and ideas exercise upon newcomers of all races . . . quickly dissolving and assimilating the foreign bodies that are poured into her mass."

A century after Tocqueville, another foreign visitor, Gunnar Myrdal of Sweden, called the cluster of ideas, institutions, and habits "the American Creed." Americans "of all national origins, regions, creeds, and colors," Myrdal wrote in 1944, hold in common "the *most explicitly expressed* system of general ideals" of any country in the West: the ideals of the essential dignity and equality of all human beings, of inalienable rights to freedom, justice, and opportunity.

The schools teach the principles of the Creed, Myrdal said; the churches preach them; the courts hand down judgments in their terms. Myrdal saw the Creed as the bond that links all Americans, including nonwhite minorities, and as the spur forever goading Americans to live up to their principles. "America," Myrdal said, "is continuously struggling for its soul."

The new race received its most celebrated metaphor in 1908 in a play by Israel Zangwill, an English writer of Russian Jewish origin. *The Melting-Pot* tells the story of a young Russian Jewish composer in New York. David Quixano's artistic ambition is to write a symphony expressing the vast, harmonious interweaving of races in America, and his personal hope is to overcome racial barriers and marry Vera, a beautiful Christian girl. "America," David cries, "is God's crucible, the great Melting-Pot where all the races of Europe are melting and re-forming! . . . God is making the American."

Yet even as audiences cheered *The Melting-Pot*, Zangwill's metaphor raised doubts. One had only to stroll around the great cities to see that the melting process was incomplete. Ethnic minorities were forming their own *quartiers* in which they lived in their own way—not quite that of the lands they had left but not that of Anglocentric America either: Little Italy, Chinatown, Yorkville, Harlem, and so on.

In having his drama turn on marriage between people of different races and religions, Zangwill, who had himself married a Christian, emphasized where the melting pot must inexorably lead: to the submergence of separate ethnic identities in the new American race. Soon ethnic spokesmen began to appear, moved by real concern for distinctive ethnic values and also by real if unconscious vested interest in the preservation of ethnic constituencies. Even some Americans of Anglo-Saxon descent deplored the obliteration of picturesque foreign strains for the sake of insipid Anglocentric conformity. The impression grew that the melting pot was a device to impose Anglocentric images and values upon hapless immigrants—an impression reinforced by the rise of the "Americanization" movement in response to the new polyglot immigration.

Gunnar Myrdal in 1944 showed no hesitation in declaring the American Creed the common possession of all Americans, even as his great book, *An American Dilemma,* provided a magistral analysis of America's most conspicuous failure to live up to the Creed: the treatment by white Americans of black Americans.

Noble ideals had been pronounced as if for all Americans, yet in practice they applied only to white people. White settlers had systematically pushed the American Indians back, killed their braves, seized their lands, and sequestered their tribes. They had brought Africans to America to work their plantations and Chinese to build their railroads. They had enunciated glittering generalities of freedom and withheld them from people of color. Their Constitution protected slavery, and their laws made distinctions on the basis of race. Though they eventually emancipated the slaves, they conspired in the reduction of the freedmen to third-class citizenship. Their Chinese Exclusion acts culminated in the total prohibition of Asian immigration in the Immigration Act of 1924. It occurred to damned few white Americans in these years that Americans of color were also entitled to the rights and liberties promised by the Constitution.

Yet what Bryce had called "the amazing solvent power" of American institutions and ideas retained its force, even among those most cruelly oppressed and excluded. Myrdal's polls of Afro-America showed the "determination" of blacks "to hold to the American Creed." Ralph Bunche, one of Myrdal's collaborators, observed that every man in the street—black, red, and yellow as well as white—regarded America as the "land of the free" and the "cradle of liberty." The American Creed, Myrdal surmised, meant even more to blacks than to whites, since it was the great means of pleading their unfulfilled rights.

The second world war gave the Creed new bite. Hitler's racism forced Americans to look hard at their own racial assumptions. Emboldened by the Creed, blacks organized for equal opportunities in employment, opposed segregation in the armed forces, and fought in their own units on many fronts. After the war, the civil rights revolution, so long deferred, accelerated black self-reliance. So did the collapse of white colonialism around the world and the appearance of independent black states.

Across America minorities proclaimed their pride and demanded their rights. Women, the one "minority" that in America constituted a numerical majority, sought political and economic equality. Jews gained new solidarity from the Holocaust and then from the establishment of a Jewish state in Israel. Changes in the immigration law dramatically increased the number arriving from Hispanic and Asian lands, and, following the general example, they asserted their own prerogatives. American Indians mobilized to reclaim their rights and lands long since appropriated by the white man; their spokesmen even rejected the historic designation in which Indians have taken deserved pride and named themselves Native Americans. The civil rights revolution provoked new expressions of ethnic identity by the now long-resident "new migration" from southern and eastern Europe—Italians, Greeks, Poles, Czechs, Slovaks, Hungarians.

The pressure for the new cult of ethnicity came less from the minorities en masse than from their often self-appointed spokesmen. Most ethnics, white and nonwhite, saw themselves primarily as Americans. Still, ideologues, with sufficient publicity and time, could create audiences. Spokesmen with a vested interest in ethnic identification turned against the ideal of assimilation. The melting pot, it was said, injured people by undermining their self-esteem. It denied them heroes—"role models," in the jargon—from their own ethnic ancestries. Praise now went to the "unmeltable ethnics."

In 1974, after testimony from ethnic spokesmen denouncing the melting pot as a conspiracy to homogenize America, Congress passed the Ethnic Heritage Studies Program Act—a statute that, by applying the ethnic ideology to all Americans, compromised the historic right of Americans to decide their ethnic identities for themselves. The act ignored those millions of Americans—surely a majority—who refused identification with any particular ethnic group.

The ethnic upsurge (it can hardly be called a revival because it was unprecedented) began as a gesture of protest against the Anglocentric culture. It became a cult, and today it threatens to become a counter-revolution against the original theory of America as "one people," a common culture, a single nation.

II.

... The great American asylum, as Crevecoeur called it, open, as George Washington said, to the oppressed and persecuted of all nations, has been from the start an experiment in a multi-ethnic society. This is a bolder experiment than we sometimes remember. History is littered with the wreck of states that tried to combine diverse ethnic or linguistic or religious groups within a single sovereignty. Today's headlines tell of imminent crisis or impending dissolution in one or another multi-ethnic polity—the Soviet Union, India, Yugoslavia, Czechoslovakia, Ireland, Belgium, Canada, Lebanon, Cyprus, Israel, Ceylon, Spain, Nigeria, Kenya, Angola, Trinidad, Guyana. . . . The list is almost endless.

The ethnic revolt against the melting pot has reached the point, in rhetoric at least, though not I think in reality, of a denial of the idea of a common culture and a single society. If large numbers of people really accept this, the republic would be in serious trouble. The question poses itself: how to restore the balance between *unum* and *pluribus?*

The old American homogeneity disappeared well over a century ago, never to return. Ever since, we have been preoccupied in one way or another with the problem, as Herbert Croly phrased it eighty years back in *The Promise of American Life,* "of keeping a highly differentiated society fundamentally sound and whole."

The genius of America lies in its capacity to forge a single nation from peoples of remarkably diverse racial, religious, and ethnic origins. It has done so because democratic principles provide both the philosophical bond of union and practical experience in civic participation. The American Creed envisages a nation composed of individuals making their own choices and accountable to themselves, not a nation based on inviolable ethnic communities. The Constitution turns on individual rights, not on group rights. Law, in order to rectify past wrongs, has from time to time (and in my view often properly so) acknowledged the claims of groups; but this is the exception, not the rule.

Our democratic principles contemplate an open society founded on tolerance of differences and on mutual respect. In practice, America has been more open to some than to others. But it is more open to all today than it was yesterday and is likely to be even more open tomorrow than today. The steady movement of American life has been from exclusion to inclusion.

Historically and culturally this republic has an Anglo-Saxon base; but from the start the base has been modified, enriched, and reconstituted by transfusions from other continents and civilizations. The movement from exclusion to inclusion causes a constant revision in the texture of our culture. The ethnic transfusions affect all aspects of American life—our politics, our literature, our music, our painting, our movies, our cuisine, our customs, our dreams.

Black Americans in particular have influenced the ever-changing national culture in many ways. They have lived here for centuries, and, unless one believes in racist mysticism, they belong far more to American culture than to the culture of Africa. Their history is part of the Western democratic tradition, not an alternative to it. No one does black Americans more disservice than those Afrocentric ideologues who would define them out of the West.

The interplay of diverse traditions produces the America we know. "Paradoxical though it may seem," Diane Ravitch has well said, "the United States has a common culture that is multicultural." That is why unifying political ideals coexist so easily and cheerfully with diversity in social and cultural values. Within the overarching political commitment, people are free to live as they choose, ethnically and otherwise. Differences will remain; some are reinvented; some are used to drive us apart. But as we renew our allegiance to the unifying ideals, we provide the solvents that will prevent differences from escalating into antagonism and hatred.

One powerful reason for the continuing movement in America from exclusion to inclusion is that the American Creed facilitates the appeal from the actual to the ideal. When we talk of the American democratic faith, we must understand it in its true dimensions. It is not an impervious, final, and complacent orthodoxy, intolerant of deviation and dissent, fulfilled in flag salutes, oaths of allegiance, and hands over the heart. It is an ever-evolving philosophy, fulfilling its ideals through debate, self-criticism, protest, disrespect, and irreverence; a tradition in which all have rights of heterodoxy and opportunities for self-assertion. The Creed has been the means by which Americans have haltingly but persistently narrowed the gap between performance and principle. It is what all Americans should learn, because it is what binds all Americans together.

Americans of whatever origin should take pride in the distinctive inheritance to which they have all contributed, as other nations take pride in their distinctive inheritances.

Our schools and colleges have a responsibility to teach history for its own sake—as part of the intellectual equipment of civilized persons—and not to degrade history by allowing its contents to be dictated by pressure groups, whether political, economic, religious, or ethnic. The past may sometimes give offense to one or another minority; that is no reason for rewriting history. Properly taught, history will convey a sense of the variety, continuity, and adaptability of culture, of the need for understanding other cultures, of the ability of individuals and peoples to overcome obstacles, of the importance of critical analysis and dispassionate judgment in every area of life.

It has taken time to make our values real for all our citizens, and we still have a good distance to go, but we have made progress. If we now repudiate the quite marvelous inheritance that history bestows on us, we invite the fragmentation of the national community into a quarrelsome spatter of enclaves, ghettos, tribes. The bonds of cohesion in our society are sufficiently fragile, or so it seems to me, that it makes no sense to strain them by encouraging and exalting cultural and linguistic apartheid.

The question America confronts as a pluralistic society is how to vindicate cherished cultures and traditions without breaking the bonds of cohesion—common ideals, common political institutions, common language, common culture, common fate—that hold the republic together. Our task is to combine due appreciation of the splendid diversity of the nation with due emphasis on the great unifying Western ideas of individual freedom, political democracy, and human rights. These are the ideas that define the American nationality and that today empower people of all continents, races, and creeds.

The Educated Child: A Parent's Guide from Preschool through Eighth Grade

William J. Bennett, Chester E. Finn, Jr., and John T. E. Cribb, Jr.

William J. Bennett, Chester E. Finn, Jr., and John T.E. Cribb all served in the U.S. Department of Education in the Reagan administration. Bennett also served as the Chairman of the National Endowment for the Humanities from 1981–1985 and the Director of the National Drug Control Policy ("Drug Czar") from 1989–1991. In recent years he has hosted radio and television weekly commentary programs. Chester E. Finn, Jr. is a Senior Fellow at the Stanford University Hoover Institution and is also President of the Thomas B. Fordham Foundation. He has long been involved in education and public policy, serving in several legislative positions at the federal and state levels, followed by serving as a Professor of Education and Public Policy at Vanderbilt University. John T. E. Cribb is a writer and president of Palmetto Creative Group, a communications firm. Cribb is co-author with William Bennett of *The American Patriot's Almanac*.

In the following selection from their book *The Educated Child: A Parent's Guide from Preschool through Eighth Grade* (The Free Press, 1999), the authors address parents, telling them that "You Are Your Child's Most Important Teacher." They urge parents to instill in their children the ideals of hard work, responsibility, and respect for legitimate authority. They continue by telling readers that schools have low expectations and that for teachers in contemporary society, "Their overriding concern is to demonstrate how tolerant they are of others' behavior and choices." They summarize that "Many schools no longer possess a moral center." Instead, they claim, schools are responsible for transmitting the "common culture" of America, "the things that bind Americans together as one people."

Key Concept: common culture and moral center

You Are Your Child's Most Important Teacher

There is an old saying that a parent's heart is the child's schoolroom. Your dreams, your efforts, your examples and loving exhortations—these set the boundaries of your child's education. The seminal lessons taught in the home stay with children as they make their way through school and life, shaping their interests, ideals, and enthusiasm for learning. Parents are children's first and most important teachers. Raising your child is your number one job. Seeing that he gets a good education is, in many respects, the crux of that task.

The pressures of time, work, and competing interests tempt us to hand more and more of our educational responsibilities to others. Parents often get a subtle, alluring, but deeply damaging message from today's culture: your role is not quite so important after all. You can delegate. You can outsource. Children will suffer no harm—in fact, they may reap some benefits—when they get more of their care and guidance from others. Specialists and experts can fill in for you, pay attention for you, make decisions for you, give guidance where you cannot. Let others take charge of education: curriculum directors, counselors, child care professionals, even children themselves. It is a seductive siren song. It gives the green light for surrendering part of a sacred duty.

You must resist these temptations. For good or ill, you are always your child's most influential teacher. Even when he reaches school age, you are still the dean-at-home, the chief academic officer. The more involved you are, the better your child's chances of getting a good education. If you begin to remove yourself from the learning process, those chances start to plummet. If you turn over your most important responsibilities to others, you may doom his school career. That amounts to educational abandonment, a pernicious form of child neglect. You need to be in charge of your child's education. So take charge.

Several critical elements can come only from you. First among these is your love. The psychologist Urie Bronfenbrenner says that the one indispensable condition for a child's successful upbringing is that at least one adult must have a deep and irrational attachment to him. In other words, someone must be absolutely crazy about that child. Children are put on this earth to be loved. They need unconditional devotion (*not* unconditional approval). When they grow up knowing that an adult is always there as guardian angel and guide, they thrive. When they sense that such devotion is missing, things can begin to go terribly wrong with their educations and their lives.

Your attitude about education is another key predictor of academic success. Your child looks to you for cues about what is important in life. He is always watching for your approval or disapproval, for your interest or indifference. If you care, he cares. If he sees that you value learning, he will probably do the same. If he observes you putting education second or third, he may not take his schoolwork seriously. Consistent reinforcement means everything. The messages you send determine in no small way how well your child reads, writes, and thinks. Every morning, you must send him off to school with a good night's sleep, a decent breakfast, and a positive attitude toward learning.

Instilling the highest ideals is crucial: Belief in the value of hard work. A strong sense of responsibility. A willingness to keep trying until success finally comes. Respect for legitimate authority. Such traits are the engines that power learning at school, in college, and in life. Academic success depends on them. Transmission of these virtues is more than just part of the territory of parenthood. It is a fundamental obligation.

Your expectations are all important. Children strive to clear the bars that their parents set. So long as those standards are fair and reasonable, they help kids flourish. Parents' expectations determine whether children finish homework on time and study for tests. They separate good students from bad. They help set the course of life. It is said that Abraham Lincoln's mother told him over and over again what kind of good, hardworking man she hoped he would become. Many years later Lincoln observed, "All that I am, and all that I hope to be, I owe to my angel mother." Setting standards for children is not placing a burden on them. It is an expression of love and confidence.

Good students usually come from homes where moms and dads have tried to create a rich learning environment. They've stimulated their children's curiosity by showing them that the world is a fascinating place and helping them explore it. This does not require you to spend lots of money or have a degree in education. It mostly consists of seeing that your child grows up with interesting things to do. It means reading aloud to him, and listening to him

read aloud. It means playing games, asking and answering questions, explaining things as best you can. It means exposing him to varied experiences and visiting places together—taking walks in the woods, working in the garden, occasionally going to a museum or monument. Such activities turn children into curious students.

Education success comes from putting enough time into the right work. What one spends time on is what one ends up knowing. If your child spends endless hours playing video games, he will know all the ins and outs of video games. If he spends time on math and science, then that's what he will know. Academic achievement also hinges, to no small degree, on the time *you* devote to education. If you spend time helping your loved one learn to read, master those multiplication tables, and listen carefully when others are talking, his chances of doing well in school are much better.

Know what your child is doing—where he is, who his friends are, what book he reads, what movies he sees. Keep track of schoolwork—what he is learning, whether he's finishing his assignments, if he's prepared for that upcoming test. The parents of good students keep an eye on what the school teaches. They have a sense of the expectations it maintains, the discipline it requires. Your child's education demands your vigilance. You must stay alert. No one else will do it for you. When a parent's attention wanders, a child may quickly veer off the learning track. It may be harder than you think to get him back on.

You teach by example. Aesop tells a wonderful fable about a crab and his son scurrying over the sand. The father chastised his child: "Stop walking sideways! It's much more becoming to stroll straightforward." The young crab replied: "I will, father dear, just as soon as I see how. Show me the straight way, and I'll walk in it behind you." There is nothing like the quiet power of intellectual example and moral example. Parents teach in everything they do. More often than not, your child will walk it the way you walk it.

For most moms and dads, faith is a crucial part of education. Believing that children are moral and spiritual beings, they want their loved ones to be educated in a way that reflects those beliefs. Public schools, by law, cannot be of help in the inculcation of faith. But there are other institutions—churches, synagogues, mosques, and of course religious schools—that can be critical teachers. Bear in mind that religious training can help young people become better students, and there is ample evidence that faith safeguards children from threats that wreck educations at an early age, such as drugs, alcohol, and sexual experimentation.

The rules you maintain lie at the foundations of a good education—rules such as "All schoolwork must be finished before you talk to your friends on the phone," and "Always speak politely to teachers." Without clear direction from parents, most students do not know how to conduct themselves.

Rules about television are *especially* critical to academic success. In this country, television has become an enemy of education. In many homes, it is a constant interference with learning. Television is not only a distraction and sometimes a cesspool, but watching it also means your child is losing the opportunity to do something more valuable. Almost anything else—reading, exercising, playing a game, talking with parents, even sleeping—is a better use of your child's time. The research is clear: excessive television hurts a youngster's school achievement. A TV set on all the time is a sign of parental indifference. Yes, there is some good TV, but if you care about education, your youngster cannot sit slack-jawed hour after hour in front of the tube.

These, then, are the fundamentals. Your love. Your attitude about education. Your efforts to stimulate your child's curiosity. Your ideals, rules, and expectations. The time and attention you pay, and the examples you set. These themes are at the core of this book. They are necessary ingredients on your end. They do not guarantee academic achievement, but they make it much more likely. They put your child's education in the hands best able to direct it: yours.

Lessons That Good Schools Teach

Parents often attach the most importance to higher education, yet elementary school has a far greater impact. Except for family and church no institution is so influential. We ask elementary schools to help shape our students' first and lasting ideas about themselves, their country, and the world. We expect them to teach basic knowledge and nourish the appetite for learning. In the K-8 years, children gain—or fail to gain—skills they will need throughout their educations and careers. They develop habits and values they will carry the rest of their days. Elementary school is an invitation and encouragement to a fulfilled life. In educational significance, its mission dwarfs all others.

The authors have visited hundreds of schools across the country. We have learned that good elementary schools share a certain character or ethos. They teach certain lessons and uphold certain ideals. It takes no expertise to recognize whether a school is doing right by its students. You can begin to get a good sense of it just by spending a little time in its classrooms and corridors.

Good schools attend to the basic subjects: English, history, geography, math, science, art, and music. They focus on these academic fundamentals. They don't clutter the curriculum with so many other topics that the basics get pushed aside. Students know that learning this core curriculum is serious business.

Good elementary schools concentrate on essential skills. Perhaps most of all, that means teaching students how to comprehend the written word. Reading is the heart and soul of elementary education. If a child goes on to high school unable to read fluently, his chances for academic success are in great peril. Other vital skills also need to be mastered before eighth grade. We expect elementary schools to teach children to speak and write well; to add, subtract, multiply, divide, and measure things; to think logically and clearly; to ask good questions, analyze problems, and search for correct answers.

Knowledge is just as important as skills. Good elementary schools recognize that there are some facts and ideas that all American students should know. For example, they teach students what a right triangle is, what happened in 1776, where the earth is in our solar system, what a Trojan horse is. Good schools spell out for parents the fundamental knowledge they intend to transmit. Teaching it is serious work, not a chance by-product of learning skills.

Elementary schools hold the responsibility of transmitting to each new generation what may be called our "common culture," the things that bind Americans together as one people. In its highest form, this common culture is the sum of our intellectual inheritance, our legacy from all the ages that have gone before us. It is the knowledge, ideas, and aspirations that shape our understanding of who we are as a people. Our common culture is found in documents such as the Constitution and the Declaration of Independence; in principles such as the belief that all men are created equal; and in events from our past, such as the landings of the *Mayflower* at Plymouth and the *Eagle* on the moon. It lies in great stories and poems, such as Charles Dickens's *A Christmas Carol* and Emma Lazarus's "The New Colossus." Americans of all backgrounds want schools to acquaint children with our common legacy. As the journalist Walter Lippmann once observed, no culture can survive that is ignorant of its own traditions.

Teaching cultural literacy is part of the effort of raising good citizens. This task, too, belongs in considerable part to the elementary school: to help lay the groundwork for young people's eventual entry into the democratic community of responsible adults. Teachers acquaint pupils with their rights as well as their duties to their fellow citizens and their country. Teddy Roosevelt once said that "the first requisite of a good citizen in this republic of ours is that he shall be able and willing to pull his own weight." Good schools teach such civic virtues. They help children learn to live up to their obligations, not to shrink from toil, and to give others the respect they are due. They teach them to recognize America's faults, but also to offer this country the great honor it deserves. They help children become, in Madison's words, "loving critics."

In that vein, good elementary schools help parents develop character in children. They never lose sight of the fact that the formation of intellect and character go hand in hand. In training young hearts and minds toward the good, they make conscious efforts to inculcate virtues such as self-discipline, diligence, perseverance, and honesty. Teachers cultivate these traits largely through the formation of habits: getting to class on time, being thorough about assignments, saying "Yes, Ma'am" and "Yes, Sir" to teachers, cleaning up after oneself. They offer lessons that appeal to children's moral imaginations. They help students come to know virtue.

These are lessons that good elementary schools must teach. Our system of education is like a pyramid. Success at each level—high school, college, and beyond—depends on earlier preparation. Mediocrity at any stage will diminish possibilities for the next. A cracked foundation threatens the whole.

Will Your School Educate Your Child Well?

It is well documented that many U.S. schools are not meeting today's challenges. Surveys and test scores are disheartening. The National Assessment of Educational Progress reports that fewer than one third of fourth graders are "proficient" readers. Nearly 40 percent read below the "basic" level, which means they can barely read at all. In math, nearly 40 percent of eighth graders score below basic. Americans are now sadly accustomed to newspaper reports that fewer than one in five American children knows the purpose of the Declaration of Independence, or that one third of high school seniors can't identify the countries we fought during World War II.

Employers complain that many job applicants lack the basic reading and math skills they need to perform the jobs they are seeking. They say that many students come out of school with poor work habits, including disorganization, irresponsibility, and an inability to get to work on time. College officials voice similar concerns. Nationwide, about three in ten first-time college freshmen now have to take remedial courses in reading, writing, or mathematics. As Steven Sample, president of the University of Southern California, has observed, "A country that has the best universities in the world has among the worst elementary and secondary schools."

There are some bright spots in the academic record, particularly in the lower grades. In international math and science tests, for example, American fourth graders fare well compared with students in other nations. By the eighth grade, however, their performance is middling. By twelfth grade, they occupy the international cellar. In math and science, American seniors are among *the worst in the industrialized world.*

Clearly something is going wrong, particularly in the middle and high school grades. Unlike students in other countries, our kids seem to do worse the longer they stay in school. By the end of eighth grade, many are ill-prepared for the kind of high school education we want them to have.

The U.S. has been "reforming" its schools for the better part of two decades. We've tried a hundred different programs and a thousand gimmicks. We've poured in countless billions of dollars. Yet it's clearer than ever that none of these nostrums has worked—and some have made matters worse. It is deeply disturbing that in the most prosperous country in the world, our education system is failing so many of our children.

Low academic standards afflict many schools. Textbooks, tests, and assignments are watered down. "We're just demanding less and less, all the time," says a veteran North Carolina teacher. "I'm teaching lessons in the eighth grade that I used to teach in the sixth." Students learn to get by with less than their best. "No one corrects bad spelling or punctuation—and we're talking about third grade," says one worried mom. "Everyone gets a gold star." Some schools seem to have forgotten that there is a difference between making a lesson interesting and making it easy. "My seventh grader spent the last two weeks of social studies class cutting pictures out of magazines," another parent reports. "What is he learning? He's getting real handy with the scissors."

Some schools do not focus enough on basic subjects. Judging by their students' assignments, learning to cherish the rain forests, recognize ethnic foods, and feel good about oneself have become more important than mastering the three Rs. It's not that matters like respecting the environment are not important. They are. But too often they are used as an excuse not to tackle the tough academic fundamentals. Remember, education is largely time on task. We learn what we do. If a child does not work many math problems, we ought not be surprised that he doesn't know much math.

In many places, educators no longer take responsibility for stating which facts and lessons are most important to know. They no longer say: "Here is what we will teach your child before he leaves us. This is what a good education looks like." Instead, they talk about teaching students to "learn how to learn," and remain vague about exactly *what* they should learn. Some schools look largely to children's preferences, instincts, and feelings as teaching guides. For example, in one school saluted for its progressive attitude, the principal proudly announced that he uses "the smile gauge"—if students are smiling, they are doing their jobs. This is a questionable approach to teaching and learning, to say the least.

The poet Samuel Taylor Coleridge once invited a friend with such notions of education to view his garden. "But it is covered with weeds," his friend said in surprise. Coleridge explained that he was letting the garden make up its own mind about what to produce. "The weeds, you see, have taken the liberty to grow," the poet explained, "and I thought it unfair of me to prejudice the soil towards roses and strawberries." If schools do not spell out what a student should learn, you can count on his education being choked with weeds.

In some schools you find an unruly atmosphere. Kids act up, use foul language, talk rudely to teachers—and get away with it. The adults in charge are unwilling to tell them to sit down, be quiet, and get down to work. In some places, we've forgotten that self-discipline is not the enemy of learning—or of happiness. It is, rather, a necessary condition. We act as if young people cannot develop the self-control to pay attention, do what the teacher says, and stick with assignments until they get them right. We've given up the notion of insisting on studious, respectful children.

Many schools no longer possess a moral center. Their teachers have been discouraged from taking up character training in a direct fashion. They are reluctant to "impose their values" on students. Their overriding concern is to demonstrate how tolerant they are of others' behavior and choices. Saying to children "What you are doing is bad and wrong" might trample their rights, inflict feelings of shame, or damage their self-esteem. Meanwhile, more and more young Americans graduate with a shaky sense of right and wrong.

Let us be clear. The United States is blessed with a number of excellent elementary schools. Many, however, are mediocre, and there are some that we would not wish on any child. Here is the bottom line: you cannot automatically assume that your school is doing a good job teaching your child—even if it assures you that it is. You must pay attention and look to see exactly what sort of education your child is getting.

Our Schools and Our Culture

If we've learned anything in the last three decades, it is this: schools cannot take the place of moms and dads. When parents are distracted from their most important responsibilities, it is exceedingly difficult for teachers to fill the breach.

In the end, it is hard to escape the conclusion that what we see in our classrooms is a reflection of the larger culture, and that the mediocrity of our schools is part of a general lowering of standards. We have teachers who shy away from teaching right and wrong because they've been made to feel that the greatest sin is to be "judgmental." We have administrators who fear strict discipline because they don't want to get sued by parents. We have kids coming to class who've spent thousands of hours in the company of TV shows, movies, video games, and music which celebrate trash: profanity, violence, promiscuity, foul language, and rebellious attitudes. We have parents who rarely complain when their kids get lots of As in "fun" courses but turn plaintive when teachers try to give more homework or raise standards. If this is the world in which our schools have to operate, no wonder the education system has problems.

We repeat: many schools do a fine job. Likewise, millions of devoted parents want to do everything in their power to see that their children get good educations. Still, when we look at the cultural and educational landscape that our children are growing up in, like many Americans we find that things are not as they should be. This country is able to offer most of its young people a great deal materially, but is not necessarily giving them some of the things they need most. We are tolerating mediocrity on the hard, important lessons and trying to compensate with a kind of material lavishness that cannot plug the gap. We are doing well in many ways, but not nearly as well as we might in others. For all of this nation's greatness, it is not giving many students an education worthy of our ideals.

The good news is that it does not have to be this way. You can make a difference—all the difference—if you take certain steps and keep your eyes on certain goals. Education is not an enigmatic enterprise. There is no mystery about what makes good students and good schools. We spell out the basics in this book, together with steps you can take at home with your child, ways to see if your school is doing a good job, and strategies to adopt when things go wrong. James Madison said that "a people who mean to be their own governors must arm themselves with the power which knowledge gives." If you arm yourself with a little knowledge about what works in education, and take some of the actions described in these pages, the power is yours to help your loved one learn to his potential.

Please remember that, so long as you remain at the center to the education process, good things are likely to happen. Countless American parents prove it every school year, including those newly arrived on our shores. There will be bumps in the road, but your child is growing up in an amazing country and in an astonishing time. Despite our problems, the opportunities for education are more than plentiful. We hope this book is both informing and encouraging. We hope it bolsters your determination. We hope it helps you raise an educated child.

Ten Principles for Parents of Educated Children

These ten critical propositions will help you raise an educated child. Please take them to heart.

1. **Parents are the first and most important teachers.** The more involved you are, the better your child's chances of getting a good education. You can make the difference.
2. **Your teaching must not stop when schooling starts.** Some parents withdraw from involvement in education once their children reach school age. This is a mistake. Teachers cannot do a good job without your aid, support, and interest.
3. **The early years build the foundation for all later learning.** Make it sturdy. The first few years of life and then the first few years of school are critical. A solid education by eighth grade is a necessity or there will be trouble in high school and beyond.
4. **American schools are underperforming.** Many schools don't pay enough attention to academic basics, and standards are often too low. Trust but verify. Do not just assume that your school is doing a good job.

5. **Learning requires discipline; discipline requires values.** Too many classrooms are disrupted by disrespectful, unruly children. Too many kids have not been taught the virtues necessary to succeed in school.

6. **Follow your common sense.** Some people act as though it takes a special degree to know if a school is doing a good job. Wrong. You are the expert on your own child. Pay attention, talk to teachers and other parents, and trust your instincts.

7. **Content matters: what children study determines how well they learn.** Many schools are unwilling to say exactly which facts and ideas their students should know. This is a fundamental problem in American education. Some things are more important to learn in elementary school than others.

8. **Television is an enemy of good education.** In many homes, TV is the greatest obstacle to learning. We urge you to shut it off from Sunday evening until Friday evening during the school year.

9. **Education reform is possible.** You can change the system. If you are interested and engaged, there is much you can do to ensure that your child receives an excellent education. There are ways to improve your child's school, especially if you join forces with other parents.

10. **Aim high, expect much and children will prosper.** No parent, school, or child is perfect, but we all rise toward the level of expectations. The surest way to learn more is to raise standards.

Critical Pedagogy

Selection 18

PAULO FREIRE, from *Pedagogy of the Oppressed*

Selection 19

DANIEL G. SOLORZANO, from "Images and Words that Wound: Critical Race Theory, Racial Stereotyping, and Teacher Education," *Teacher Education Quarterly (1997)*

Pedagogy of the Oppressed

Paulo Freire

The writings of Paulo Freire (1921–1997) are a direct result of his life and circumstances in Brazil. His family lost their middle-class status during the depression of the 1930s, and he experienced poverty, hunger, malnourishment, and the accompanying falling behind in school. This life experience led him to work among the poor during his adolescent years to try to help peasants and workers in a project of liberation, a project he worked on for the rest of his life. In trying to help the poor to understand their legal rights, he turned his efforts to adult literacy programs and to methods of educating the poor and illiterate. In 1964, as a result of his work with the poor in Brazil, he was arrested, imprisoned, and then forced into exile. He returned 16 years later to become the appointed minister of education in Rio de Janeiro. He also served as a professor at Harvard University, and in 1986 he received the United Nations Educational, Scientific and Cultural Organization (UNESCO) Prize for Education. His books include *Pedagogy of the Oppressed* (Continuum, 1970), from which the following selection has been taken; *Education for Critical Consciousness* (Seabury Press, 1973); and *Pedagogy of Hope: Reliving Pedagogy of the Oppressed* (Continuum, 1994).

In the following selection, Freire introduces the "banking concept of education." As he describes it, "knowledge is a gift bestowed by those who consider themselves knowledgeable upon those whom they consider to know nothing." He continues that this equates to "Projecting an absolute ignorance onto others." To end this oppressive educational practice, Freire writes, teachers must engage with their students in "problem-posing" education, in which students become teachers and teachers become students. The resulting education is the "practice of freedom" rather than the "practice of domination."

Key Concept: critique of oppressive educational practices

A careful analysis of the teacher-student relationship at any level, inside or outside the school, reveals its fundamentally *narrative* character. This relationship involves a narrating Subject (the teacher) and patient, listening objects (the students). The contents, whether values or empirical dimensions of reality, tend in the process of being narrated to become lifeless and petrified. Education is suffering from narration sickness.

The teacher talks about reality as if it were motionless, static, compartmentalized, and predictable. Or else he expounds on a topic completely alien to the existential experience of the students. His task is to "fill" the students with the contents of his narration—contents which are detached from reality, disconnected from the totality that engendered them and could give them significance. Words are emptied of their concreteness and become a hollow, alienated, and alienating verbosity.

The outstanding characteristic of this narrative education, then, is the sonority of words, not their transforming power. "Four times four is sixteen; the capital of Pará is Belém." The student records, memorizes, and repeats these phrases without perceiving what four times four really means, or realizing the true significance of "capital" in the affirmation "the capital of Pará is Belém," that is, what Belém means for Pará and what Pará means for Brazil.

Narration (with the teacher as narrator) leads the students to memorize mechanically the narrated content. Worse yet, it turns them into "containers," into "receptacles" to be "filled" by the teacher. The more completely she fills the receptacles, the better a teacher she is. The more meekly the receptacles permit themselves to be filled, the better students they are.

Education thus becomes an act of depositing, in which the students are the depositories and the teacher is the depositor. Instead of communicating, the teacher issues communiqués and makes deposits which the students patiently receive, memorize, and repeat. This is the "banking" concept of education, in which the scope of action allowed to the students extends only as far as receiving, filing, and storing the deposits. They do, it is true, have the opportunity to become collectors or cataloguers of the things they store. But in the last analysis, it is the people themselves who are filed away through the lack of creativity, transformation, and knowledge in this (at best) misguided system. For apart from inquiry, apart from the praxis, individuals cannot be truly human. Knowledge emerges only through invention and re-invention, through the restless, impatient, continuing, hopeful inquiry human beings pursue in the world, with the world, and with each other.

In the banking concept of education, knowledge is a gift bestowed by those who consider themselves knowledgeable upon those whom they consider to know nothing. Projecting an absolute ignorance onto others, a characteristic of the ideology of oppression, negates education and knowledge as processes of inquiry. The teacher presents himself to his students as their necessary opposite; by considering their ignorance absolute, he justifies his own existence. The students, alienated like the slave in the Hegelian dialectic, accept their ignorance as justifying the teacher's existence—but, unlike the slave, they never discover that they educate the teacher.

The *raison d'être* of libertarian education, on the other hand, lies in its drive towards reconciliation. Education must begin with the solution of the teacher-student contradiction, by reconciling the poles of the contradiction so that both are simultaneously teachers *and* students.

This solution is not (nor can it be) found in the banking concept. On the contrary, banking education maintains and even stimulates the contradiction through the following attitudes and practices, which mirror oppressive society as a whole:

(a) the teacher teaches and the students are taught;
(b) the teacher knows everything and the students know nothing;
(c) the teacher thinks and the students are thought about;
(d) the teacher talks and the students listen—meekly;
(e) the teacher disciplines and the students are disciplined;
(f) the teacher chooses and enforces his choice, and the students comply;
(g) the teacher acts and the students have the illusion of acting through the action of the teacher;
(h) the teacher chooses the program content, and the students (who were not consulted) adapt to it;
(i) the teacher confuses the authority of knowledge with his or her own professional authority, which she and he sets in opposition to the freedom of the students;
(j) the teacher is the Subject of the learning process, while the pupils are mere objects.

It is not surprising that the banking concept of education regards men as adaptable, manageable beings. The more students work at storing the deposits entrusted to them, the less they develop the critical consciousness which would result from their intervention in the world as transformers of that world. The more completely they accept the passive role imposed on them, the more they tend simply to adapt to the world as it is and to the fragmented view of reality deposited in them.

The capability of banking education to minimize or annul the students' creative power and to stimulate their credulity serves the interests of the oppressors, who care neither to have the world revealed nor to see it transformed.

It follows logically from the banking notion of consciousness that the educator's role is to regulate the way the world "enters into" the students. The teacher's task is to organize a process which already occurs spontaneously, to "fill" the students by making deposits of information which he or she considers to constitute true knowledge. And since people "receive" the world as passive entities, education should make them more passive still, and adapt them to the world. The educated individual is the adapted person, because she or he is better "fit" for the world. Translated into practice, this concept is well suited to the purposes of the oppressors, whose tranquility rests on how well people fit the world the oppressors have created, and how little they question it.

The bank-clerk educator does not realize that there is no true security in his hypertrophied role, that one must seek to live *with* others in solidarity. One cannot impose oneself, nor even merely co-exist with one's students. Solidarity requires true communication, and the concept by which such an educator is guided fears and proscribes communication.

Yet only through communication can human life hold meaning. The teacher's thinking is authenticated only by the authenticity of the students' thinking. The teacher cannot think for her students, nor can she impose her thought on them. Authentic thinking, thinking that is concerned about *reality*, does not take place in ivory tower isolation, but only in communication. If it is true that thought has meaning only when generated by action upon the world, the subordination of students to teachers becomes impossible.

Those truly committed to liberation must reject the banking concept in its entirety, adopting instead a concept of women and men as conscious beings, and consciousness as consciousness intent upon the world. They must abandon the educational goal of deposit-making and replace it with the posing of the problems of human beings in their relations with the world. "Problem-posing" education, responding to the essence of consciousness—*intentionality*—rejects communiqués and embodies communication.

Indeed, problem-posing education, which breaks with the vertical patterns characteristic of banking education, can fulfill its function as the practice of freedom only if it can overcome the above contradiction. Through dialogue, the teacher-of-the-students and the students-of-the-teacher cease to exist and a new term emerges: teacher-student with students-teachers. The teacher is no longer merely the-one-who-teaches, but one who is himself taught in dialogue with the students, who in turn while being taught also teach. They become jointly responsible for a process in which all grow. In this process, arguments based on "authority" are no longer valid; in order to function, authority must be *on the side of* freedom, not *against* it. Here, no one teaches another, nor is anyone self-taught. People teach each other, mediated by the world, by the cognizable objects which in banking education are "owned" by the teacher.

Students, as they are increasingly posed with problems relating to themselves in the world and with the world, will feel increasingly challenged and obliged to respond to that challenge. Because they apprehend the challenge as interrelated to other problems within a total context, not as a theoretical question, the resulting comprehension tends to be increasingly critical and thus constantly less alienated. Their response to the challenge evokes new challenges, followed by new understandings; and gradually the students come to regard themselves as committed.

Education as the practice of freedom—as opposed to education as the practice of domination—denies that man is abstract, isolated, independent, and unattached to the world; it also denies that the world exists as a reality apart from people. Authentic reflection considers neither abstract man nor the world without people, but people in their relations with the world.

A deepened consciousness of their situation leads people to apprehend that situation as an historical reality susceptible of transformation. Resignation gives way to the drive for transformation and inquiry, over which men feel themselves to be in control. If people, as historical beings necessarily engaged with other people in a movement of inquiry, did not control that movement, it would be (and is) a violation of their humanity. Any situation in which some individuals prevent others from engaging in the process of inquiry is one of violence. The means used are not important; to alienate human beings from their own decision-making is to change them into objects.

This movement of inquiry must be directed towards humanization—the people's historical vocation. The pursuit of full humanity, however, cannot be carried out in isolation or individualism, but only in fellowship and solidarity; therefore it cannot unfold in the antagonistic relations between oppressors and oppressed. No one can be authentically human while he prevents others from being so.

Images and Words that Wound: Critical Race Theory, Racial Stereotyping, and Teacher Education

Daniel G. Solorzano

Daniel Solorzano is Professor of Social Sciences and Comparative Education at UCLA and Director of the University of California All Campus Consortium on Research for Diversity. His teaching and research interests include critical race and gender theory in education, with a special focus on education access, persistence, and graduation of students of color in the United States. He has published books, book chapters, and articles in journals such as *Harvard Educational Review*, *Teachers College Record*, *Equity and Excellence in Education*, and the *Journal of Latinos in Education*.

In the following selection titled "Images and Words that Wound: Critical Race Theory, Racial Stereotyping, and Teacher Education," from *Teacher Education Quarterly* (1997), Solorzano clearly lays out Critical Race Theory (CRT), a theory with growing prominence within the field of Multicultural Education. Critical Race Theory has been influential in its key focus on challenging dominant ideology in research and education and placing as central the knowledge and experience of communities of color. As Solorzano writes, "Critical race theory recognizes that the experiential knowledge of Women and Men of Color are legitimate, appropriate, and critical to understanding, analyzing, practicing, and teaching." CRT has thus opened up a wide number of disciplines to the importance of valuing communities of color. Solorzano concludes by proposing exercises that will enable readers to challenge racism and racial stereotyping in classrooms.

Key Concept: critical race theory

Critical Race Theory

Critical race theory draws from and extends a broad literature base that is often termed critical theory. Therefore, I borrow and adapt the works of Brian Fay (1987) and William Tierney (1991, 1993) and define critical theory as a framework or set of basic perspectives, methods, and pedagogy that seeks to identify, analyze, and transform those structural and cultural aspects of society that maintain the subordination and marginalization of People of Color.[1] Similarly, Mari Matsuda (1991) defines critical race theory as:

> . . . the work of progressive legal scholars of color who are attempting to develop a jurisprudence that accounts for the role of racism in American law and that work toward the elimination of racism as part of a larger goal of eliminating all forms of subordination. (p. 1331)

Specifically, critical race theory challenges the dominant discourse on race and racism as it relates to the law[2] by examining how legal doctrine is used to subordinate certain racial and ethnic groups (Bell, 1995; Calmore, 1992; Crenshaw, Gotanda, Peller, & Thomas, 1995; Delgado, 1995a, 1995b, 1996; Harris, 1994; Matsuda, Lawrence, Delgado, & Crenshaw, 1993).

Critical race theory has at least five themes that form its basic perspectives, research methods, and pedagogy:

1. The Centrality and Intersectionality of Race and Racism

Critical race theory starts from the premise that race and racism are endemic, permanent, and in the words of Margaret Russell (1992) "a central rather than marginal factor in defining and explaining individual experiences of the law" (pp. 762–63). Critical race theorists also take the position that racism has at least four dimensions: (1) it has micro and macro components; (2) it takes on institutional and individual forms; (3) it has conscious and unconscious elements; and (4) it has a cumulative impact on both the individual and group (Davis, 1989; Lawrence, 1987). Although race and racism are at the center of a critical race analysis, they are also viewed at their intersection with other forms of subordination such as gender and class discrimination (Crenshaw, 1989, 1993). As Robin Barnes (1990) has stated, "Critical Race Scholars have refused to ignore the differences between class and race as basis for oppression. . . . Critical Race Scholars know that class oppression alone cannot account for racial oppression" (p. 1868).

2. The Challenge to Dominant Ideology

Critical race theory challenges the traditional claims of the legal system to objectivity, meritocracy, colorblindness, race neutrality, and equal opportunity. The critical race theorists argue that these traditional claims arc a camouflage for the self-interest, power, and privilege of dominant groups in U.S. society (Calmore, 1992). In addition to challenging the way we examine race and racism, Kimberle Crenshaw and her colleagues have argued that critical race theory is also trying to "piece together an intellectual identity and a political practice that would take the form both of a left intervention into race discourse and a race intervention into left discourse" (Crenshaw et al., 1995, p. xix).

3. The Commitment to Social Justice

Critical race theory has an overall commitment to social justice and the limination of racism. In the critical race theorist's struggle toward social justice, the abolition of racism or racial subordination is part of the broader goal of ending other forms of subordination such as gender, class, and sexual orientation (Matsuda, 1991).

4. The Centrality of Experiential Knowledge

Critical race theory recognizes that the experiential knowledge of Women and Men of Color are legitimate, appropriate, and critical to understanding, analyzing, practicing, and teaching the law and its relation to racial subordination (Calmore, 1992). Indeed, critical race theory views this knowledge as a strength and draws explicitly on the Person of Color's lived experiences by including such methods as storytelling, family history, biographies, scenarios, parables, chronicles, and narratives (Bell, 1987; Delgado, 1989, 1995a, 1995b, 1996; Olivas, 1990).

5. The Interdisciplinary Perspective

Critical race theory challenges ahistoricism and the unidisciplinary focus of most analyses and insists on analyzing race and racism in the law by placing them in both an historical and contemporary context using interdisciplinary methods (Delgado, 1984, 1992; Garcia, 1995; Harris, 1994; Olivas, 1990).

Therefore, to paraphrase and extend Matsuda's definition, the overall goal of a critical race theory in teacher education focuses on the work of progressive Teacher Educators of Color and their Fellow Travelers who are trying to develop a pedagogy, curriculum, and research agenda that accounts for the role of race and racism in U.S. education and works toward the elimination of racism as part of a larger goal of eliminating all forms of subordination in education.

Defining Race, Racism, and Racial Stereotyping

In 1903, W.E.B. DuBois (1989) commented that "the problem of the 20th Century is the problem of the color-line" (p. 29). When we examine the popular and professional literature, and the political debates around immigration, welfare, crime, and affirmative action, it appears that DuBois's prophecy will continue into the twenty-first century. In dealing with the issue of "color" or race, history has shown that the U.S. has never been a "color-blind" society (Gotanda, 1991). The U.S. is very color conscious and color affects the way people view their separate and interrelated worlds (Dalton, 1987, 1995; Duster, 1993). A longitudinal investigation of public opinion polls on racial/ethnic and social issues illustrates that Blacks, Latinos, and Whites have very different positions on a variety of social issues (ABC News, 1996; Gates & West, 1996; Schuman, Steeh, & Bobo, 1985).

According to James Banks (1995), an examination of U.S. history reveals that the "color-line" or race is a socially constructed category, created to differentiate racial groups, and to show the superiority or dominance of one race over another. This position leads to the question: Does the dominance of a racial group require a rationalizing ideology? One could argue that dominant groups try to legitimate their interests through the use of an ideology (i.e., a set of beliefs that explains or justifies some actual or potential social arrangement). If racism is the ideology that justifies the dominance of one race over another, then how do we define racism? For our purpose, Audre Lorde (1992) may have produced the most concise definition of racism as "the belief in the inherent superiority of one race over all others and thereby the right to dominance" (p. 496). Manning Marable (1992) has also defined racism as "a system of ignorance, exploitation, and power used to oppress African Americans, Latinos, Asians, Pacific Americans, American Indians and other people on the basis of ethnicity, culture, mannerisms, and color" (p. 5). Indeed, embedded in the Lorde and Marable definitions of racism are at least three important points: (I) one group believes itself to be superior; (2) the group which believes itself to be superior has the power to carry out the racist behavior; and (3) racism effects multiple racial/ethnic groups. These two definitions take the position that racism is about institutional power, and People of Color in the United States have never possessed this form of power.

A critical race theory in teacher education seeks answers to the following questions: What forms does racism take in teacher education and how are these forms used to maintain the subordination of Students of Color? To answer this question, 1 begin by defining and examining racial stereotypes. Indeed, Gordon Allport (1979) has defined a stereotype as:

> An exaggerated belief associated with a category. Its function is to justify (rationalize) our conduct in relation to that category. (p. 191)

This definition provides a valuable tool for teacher educators to examine how racial stereotypes are used to justify certain attitudes and behaviors toward Students of Color.

The theoretical foundation for this line of deficit thinking comes from two traditions: the genetic determinist and cultural deficit models. The genetic determinist model takes the position that the low educational attainment of minority students can be traced to deficiencies in their genetic structure (Jensen, 1969; Kamin, 1974; Terman, 1916). In this scenario, there are few social policy options—lacking genetic transformation or total neglect—to raise the educational attainment of minority students. While seemingly out of favor in educational research and policy circles, there is a resurgence of interest in the genetic determinist model resulting from the works of Lloyd Dunn (1987; see Fernandez 1988), the Minnesota Twin Studies (Bouchard, Lykken, McGue, Segal, & Tellegen, 1990), Frederick Goodwin (see Breggin & Breggin, 1993), and Richard Hermstein and Charles Murray (1994).

The second and more widely used model in this deficit tradition is the cultural deficit model. The cultural deficit model contends that minority cultural values, as transmitted through the family, are dysfunctional, and therefore the reason for low educational and later occupational attainment. The model focuses on such deficient cultural values as present versus future time orientation, immediate instead of deferred gratification, an emphasis on cooperation rather than competition, and placing less value on education and upward mobility (see Carter & Segura, 1979).

The cultural deficit model also examines deficiencies in minority family internal social structure, such as large, disorganized, female-headed families; Spanish or nonstandard English spoken in the home; and patriarchal or matriarchal family structures. These models argue that since minority parents fail to assimilate and embrace the educational values of the dominant group, and continue to transmit or socialize their children with values that inhibit educational mobility, then they are to blame if the low educational attainment continues into succeeding generations.

This cultural deficit view of the minority student has become the "norm" in social scientific research, despite the fact there is little empirical evidence to support it (Kretovics & Nussel, 1994; Persell, 1977; Solorzano, 1991, 1992a, 1992b; Solorzano & Solorzano, 1995; Valencia, In Press). In practice, the deficit model gets applied in the classroom, and to Students of Color, by teachers who are professionally trained in colleges, and specifically in a teacher education curriculum that reflects an individualistic and cultural deficit explanation of low minority educational attainment (Kretovics & Nussel, 1994; Persell, 1977). The teacher education policy solutions that emerge from this model focus on the acculturation of minority students to the values and behaviors of the culturally dominant group; while criticizing, downplaying, or ignoring the values and behaviors of marginalized minority cultures.

Despite this history, claims that the cultural deficit model has been debunked and no longer widely used seem premature. In fact, the 1980s and 1990s have seen a revival of the cultural deficit model, under the rubric of the cultural "underclass" (Baca Zinn, 1989; Valencia & Solorzano, In Press). Indeed, Joseph Kretovics and Edward Nussel (1994) have stated: "At the highest levels of educational policy, we have moved from deficiency theory to theories of difference, back to deficiency theory" (p. x). The cultural deficit model, along with related popular and professional racial stereotypes, remains the hidden theory of choice at many elementary and secondary schools, teacher education departments, professional meetings, and settings where the topic of minority educational inequality is discussed.

Conclusion

Critical race theory provides a framework to challenge the genetic and cultural deficit theories. In fact, using the five themes of critical race theory, we can engage in the following four exercises to better understand and challenge race, racism, and racial stereotypes in our classrooms:

1. Examples of Concepts

We must define, analyze, and give examples for the concepts of race, racism, and racial stereotypes. Engaging in a discussion, analysis, and debate around these concepts is a critical first step. In this exercise, we can examine and give examples of racism in its institutional and individual forms, its macro and micro forms, conscious and unconscious elements, and its cumulative effects on both minority and non-minority students.

2. Identify Media Stereotypes

We must identify racial stereotypes in the popular media such as film, television, and print and show how they are used to justify attitudes and behavior toward Students of Color. For example, we can conduct a comparative analysis of three high school genre films—"Stand and Deliver" (1988), "Lean on Me" (1989), and "Dangerous Minds" (1995)—on the quantity and quality of Black and Latina/o characters. A discussion of these images can lead to the development of alternative story-lines and scripts for the portrayal of Students of Color in film. This same content analysis and alternative portrayals can be performed on television programs and news broadcasts.

Documentary films on the historical and contemporary condition of the Black and Chicano communities can provide an invaluable resource for developing an anti-racist and anti-sexist curriculum. For instance, such Public Broadcasting Service film series as the "Eyes on the Prize I: America's Civil Rights Years" (1986), "Eyes on the Prize II: America at the Racial Crossroads" (1990), and "Chicano: History of the Mexican American Civil Rights Movement" (1996) can serve as an important filmic base to challenge some of the racial and gender stereotypes related to Communities of Color.

3. Identify Professional Stereotypes

We must identify professional stereotypes, show their relationship to popular stereotypes, and then examine how both are used to justify the unequal treatment of Students of Color. For example, using the current state mandated language arts and social science elementary and secondary textbooks, students can conduct a content analysis of the quantity and quality of portrayals of Blacks, Chicanas/os, Native Americans, and Asian Americans (Council on Interracial Books for Children, 1977). As a follow-up, students can use contemporary and historical ethnic studies texts of People of Color to recreate alternative portraits to the state mandated textbooks.

4. Find Examples that Challenge

We must find examples within and about Communities of Color that challenge and transform racial stereotypes. In many Communities of Color, students can find and analyze street murals that artistically portray the positive and negative conditions in these communities. Also, in many of these communities there are elders who keep some of the history and traditions of the community alive. Both

street murals and elders can be invaluable resources to dispel the myths of an "uneducated" minority community. Also, information gathered by interviewing day laborers, who congregate in the mornings on certain street corners, can challenge the stereotype of the "lazy" minority worker. Moreover, there are rich sources of material in individual and family oral and pictorial histories, institutional and community studies, and artistic and cultural artifacts and ideologies that would challenge the racial stereotypes found in the popular and professional media.

Racial stereotypes, whether in the popular or professional literature, are continuing to increase. As educators, we must critically analyze their source, rationale, and impact on the people doing the stereotyping and on those being stereotyped. The discussion of race, racism, and racial stereotypes must be a continuing part of our teacher education discourse. In our classrooms, we must seek out popular, professional, and artistic images that depict People of Color in multiple contexts. As educators, we need to identify the resources and strengths of Students of Color and place them at the center of our research, curriculum, and teaching. The five elements of critical race theory provide a framework for teacher education faculty and students to utilize these resources in order to create, recreate, and recover knowledge and art in Communities of Color. In turn, critical race theory can empower teachers and students to better understand and challenge those racial stereotypical portrayals. Critical race theory is about strengths, and strengths are what we should be looking for within the Students and Communities of Color in order to combat and eliminate negative racial stereotypes. Finally, Cornel West (1995) has stated that "Critical Race Theory is the most exciting development in contemporary legal studies" (p. xi). I would argue that the same can be true for teacher education.

Notes

1. For this essay, People of Color are defined as those persons of African American, Chicana/o, Asian American, and Native American ancestry. I sometimes use this term synonymously with minority. Chicanas and Chicanos are defined as female and male persons of Mexican-origin living in the United States. Latinos are persons of Latin American origin living in the U.S.

CALIFORNIA COUNCIL ON TEACHER EDUCATION

Founded in 1945, the California Council on the Education of Teachers (now the California Council on Teacher Education as of July 2001) is a non-profit organization devoted to stimulating the improvement of the pre-service and in-service education of teachers and administrators. The Council attends to this general goal with the support of a community of teacher educators, drawn from diverse constituencies, who seek to be informed, reflective, and active regarding significant research, sound practice, and current public educational issues.

2. It is important to note that while critical race theory focusses on the law, we could easily insert other social institutions, such as schools, into these five guiding elements. See Richard Delgado and Jean Stefancic (1993, 1994) for two comprehensive appointed bibliographies on critical race theory.

References

Allport, G. (1979). *The Nature of Prejudice.* 25th Anniversary Edition. Reading, MA: Addison-Wesley.

ABC News. (1996, May 20–24). *Nightline: America in Black and White.* New York: American Broadcasting Company.

Baca Zinn, M. (1989). Family, Race, and Poverty in the Eighties. *Signs: Journal of Woman in Culture and Society,* 14, 856–874.

Banks, J. (1995). The Historical Reconstruction of Knowledge about Race: Implications for Transformative Teaching. *Educational Researcher,* 24, 15–25.

Barnes, R. (1990). Race Consciousness: The Thematic Content of Racial Distinctiveness in Critical Race Scholarship. *Harvard Law Review,* 103, 1864–1871.

Bell, D. (1987). *And We Will Not Be Saved: The Elusive Quest for Racial Justice.* New York: Basic Books.

Bell, D. (1995). Who's Afraid of Critical Race Theory? *University of Illinois Law Review,* 893–910.

Bouchard, T., Lykken, D., McGue, M., Segal, N.. & Tellegen, A. (1990). Sources of Human Psychological Differences: The Minnesota Study of Twins Reared Apart. *Science,* 250, 223–250.

Breggin, P. & Breggin, G. (1993). The Federal Violence Initiative: Threats to Black Children (and Others). *Psych Discourse,* 24, 8–11.

Calmore, J. (1992). Critical Race Theory, Archie Shepp, and Fire Music. Securing an Authentic Intellectual Life in a Multicultural World. *Southern California Law Review,* 65, 2129–2231.

Carter, T. & Segura, R. (1979). *The Mexican Americans in School: A Decade of Change.* New York: College Entrance Examination Board.

Council on Interracial Books for Children. (1977). *Stereotypes, Distortions and Omissions in U.S. History Textbooks.* New York: Council on Interracial Books for Children.

Crenshaw, K. (1989). Demarginalizing the Intersection of Race and Sex: A Black Feminist Critique of Antidiscrimination Doctrine, Feminist Theory and Antiracist Politics. *University of Chicago Legal Forum, 1989,* 139–167.

Crenshaw, K. (1993). Mapping the Margins: Intersectionality, Identity Politics, and the Violence Against Women of Color. *Stanford Law Review,* 43, 1241–1299.

Crenshaw, K., Gotanda, N., Peller, G., & Thomas, K. (Eds.). (1995). *Critical Race Theory: The Key Writings That Formed the Movement.* New York: The New Press.

Dalton, H. (1987). The Clouded Prism. *Harvard Civil Rights-Civil Liberties Law Review,* 22, 435–447.

Dalton, H. (1995). *Racial Healing: Confronting the Fear Between Blacks and Whites.* New York: Doubleday.

Davis, P. (1989). Law as Microaggression. *Yale Law Journal,* 98, 1559–1577.

Delgado, R. (1984). The Imperial Scholar: Reflections on a Review of Civil Rights Literature. *University of Pennsylvania Law Review,* 132, 561–578.

Delgado, R. (1989). Storytelling for Oppositionists and Others: A Plea for Narrative. *Michigan Law Review,* 87, 2411–2441.

Delgado, R. (1992). The Imperial Scholar Revisited: How to Marginalize Outsider Writing. *University of Pennsylvania Law Review,* 140, 1349–1372.

Delgado, R. (1995a). *The Rodrigo Chronicles: Conversations About America and Race.* New York: New York University Press.

Delgado, R. (Ed.). (1995b). *Critical Race Theory: The Cutting Edge.* Philadelphia, PA: Temple University Press.

Delgado, R. (1996). *The Coming Race War?: and Other Apocalyptic Tales of America After Affirmative Action and Welfare.* New York: New York University Press.

DuBois, W.E.B. (1989). *The Soul of Black Folks. New York:* Bantam. (Originally published in 1903).

Dunn, L. (1987). *Bilingual Hispanic Children on the Mainland: A Review of Research on Their Cognitive, Linguistic, and Scholastic Development.* Circle Pines, MN: American Guidance Service.

Duster, T. (1993). The Diversity of California at Berkeley: An Emerging Reformulation of "Competence" in an Increasingly Multicultural World. In B. Thompson & S. Tyagi, *Beyond a Dream Deferred: Multicultural Education and the Politics of Excellence* (pp. 231–255). Minneapolis, MN: University of Minnesota Press.

Fay, B. (1987). *Critical Social Science: Liberation and Its Limits.* Ithaca, NY: Cornell University Press.

Fernandez, R. (Ed.). (1988). Special Issue, Achievement Testing: Science vs. Ideology (Response to Lloyd Dunn). *Hispanic Journal of Behavioral Sciences,* 10, 179–323.

Gates, H. & West, C. (1996). *The Future of the Race.* New York: Alfred A. Knopf.

Gotanda, N. (1991). A Critique of "Our Constitution is Color-Blind." *Stanford Law Review,* 44, 1–68.

Harris, A. (1994). Forward: The Jurisprudence of Reconstruction. *California Law Review,* 82, 741–785.

Herrnstein, R. & Murray, C. (1994). *The Bell Curve: Intelligence and Class Structure in American Life.* New York: Free Press.

Jensen, A. (1969). How Much Can We Boost l.Q. and Scholastic Achievement? *Harvard Educational Review,* 39, 1–123.

Kamin, L. (1974). *The Science and Politics of l.Q.* New York: John Wiley & Sons.

Kretovics, J. & Nussel, E. (Eds.). (1994). *Transforming Urban Education.* Boston, MA: Allyn & Bacon.

Lawrence, C. (1987). The Id, the Ego, and Equal Protection: Reckoning with Unconscious Racism. *Stanford Law Review,* 39, 317–388.

Lorde, A. (1992). Age, Race, Class, and Sex: Women Redefining Difference. In M. Andersen & P. Hill Collins, *Race, Class, and Gender: An Anthology* (pp. 495–502). Belmont, CA: Wadsworth.

Marable, M. (1992). *Black America.* Westfield, NJ: Open Media.

Matsuda, M. (1991). Voices of America: Accent, Antidiscrimination Law, and a Jurisprudence for the Last Reconstruction. *Yale Law Journal,* 100, 1329–1407.

Matsuda, M., Lawrence, C., Delgado, R., & Crenshaw, K. (1993). *Words That Wound: Critical Race Theory, Assaultive Speech, and the First Amendment.* Boulder, CO: Westview Press.

Olivas, M. (1990). The Chronicles, My Grandfather's Stories, and Immigration Law: The Slave Traders Chronicle as Racial History. *Saint Louis University Law Journal,* 34, 425–441.

Persell, C. (1977). *Education and Inequality: The Roots and Results of Stratification in America's Schools.* New York: Free Press.

Russell, M. (1992). Entering Great America: Reflections on Race and the Convergence of Progressive Legal Theory and Practice. *Hastings Law Journal, 43,* 749–767.

Schuman, H., Steeh, C., & Bobo, L. (1985). *Racial Attitudes in America: Trends and Interpretations.* Cambridge, MA: Harvard University Press.

Solorzano, D. (1991). Mobility Aspirations Among Racial Minorities, Controlling for SES. *Sociology and Social Research, 75,* 182–188.

Solorzano, D. (1992a). An Exploratory Analysis of the Effect of Race, Class, and Gender on Student and Parent Mobility Aspirations. *Journal of Negro Education, 61,* 30–44.

Solorzano, D, (1992b). Chicano Mobility Aspirations: A Theoretical and Empirical Note. *Latino Studies Journal, 3,* 48–66.

Solorzano, D. & Solorzano, R. (1995). The Chicano Educational Experience: A Proposed Framework For Effective Schools in Chicano Communities. *Educational Policy, 9,* 293–314.

Terman, L. (1916). *The Measurement of Intelligence.* Boston, MA: Houghton Mifflin.

Tierney, W. (1991). Border Crossings: Critical Theory and the Study of Higher Education. In W. Tierney (Ed.), *Culture and Ideology in Higher Education* (pp. 3–15). New York: Praeger.

Tierney, W. (1993). *Building Communities of Difference: Higher Education in the Twenty-First Century.* Westport, CT: Bergin & Garvey.

Valencia, R. (Ed.). (In Press). *The Evolution of Deficit Thinking in Educational Thought and Practice.* Bristol, PA: Taylor & Francis.

Valencia, R. & Solorzano, D. (In Press). Contemporary Deficit Thinking. In R. Valencia (Ed.). *The Evolution of Deficit Thinking in Educational Thought and Practice.* Bristol, PA. Taylor & Francis.

West, C. (1995). Forward. In K. Crenshaw, N. Gotanda, G. Peller, and K. Thomas (Eds.), *Critical Race Theory: The Key Writings That Formed the Movement* (pp. xi–xii). New York: The New Press.

Gender and Orientation

Where the Girls Are: The Facts About Gender Equity in Education

Christianne Corbett, Catherine Hill, and Andresse St. Rose

The American Association of University Women (AAUW) is an organization founded in 1881 with the mission "to advance equity for women and girls through advocacy, education, and research." In addition to conducting and publishing research, the AAUW is actively involved in public policy advocacy, community programs, voter education, and leadership development for girls and women. The co-authors of the following selection are all researchers at AAUW. Catherine Hill was previously an Assistant Professor at the University of Virginia and is currently the Director of Research at AAUW. Christianne Corbett worked as a mechanical design engineer in the aerospace industry and is currently a research associate at AAUW. Andresse St. Rose, who is currently a research associate at AAUW, previously served as an academic counselor at Northeastern University and prior to that as a high school math and biology teacher in Trinidad.

The following selection, *Where the Girls Are: The Facts About Gender Equity in Education* (2008), is the most recent AAUW report to examine gender equity in education. In reviewing data from over 300,000 K-12 students, the report examines whether the gender gap that the AAUW pointed out in its previous studies still exists, and if it does, in what subject areas it is most prevalent. They discover that while some differences exist in boys' and girls' performances in math and reading, the greatest difference is seen in differential economic backgrounds. The authors explain that "Average differences by gender . . . were much smaller than differences between students from different family income levels."

Key Concept: gender equity in schools

*C*ommonly referred to as the Nation's Report Card, the National Assessment of Educational Progress (NAEP) tests U.S. students' knowledge and skills in reading, mathematics, and other subjects. This chapter uses this widely accepted barometer of student progress to consider evidence of a boys' crisis. The chapter charts trends in girls' and boys' scores on the NAEP and demonstrates that where the girls (and boys) are depends in large part on race/ethnicity and family income level.

This chapter presents data from two key NAEP assessments. The NAEP long-term trend (NAEP-LTT) assessment has been given every two to five years since the 1970s and was most recently given in 2004 to students ages 9, 13, and 17.[1] The NAEP-LTT was formulated to allow comparison of students' achievement from year to year and decade to decade and has remained essentially unchanged since its first administration (U.S. Department of Education, National Center for Education Statistics, 2007h).[2] The more recently developed main or national NAEP assessment was designed to evolve over time to reflect changes in curriculum and instruction. The main NAEP has been given every two to four years to students in grades 4, 8, and 12 in math since 1990 and reading since 1992 and was most recently given to 4th and 8th graders in 2007 and 12th graders in 2005 (ibid.).[3] The NAEP Data Explorer was used in this research to generate comparisons by gender, race/ethnicity, and family income level; where relevant, tests of significance were performed with the NAEP Data Explorer.[4]

Overall, average scores on the NAEP tests have risen during the past few decades, especially in math.[5] Gender differences persist, however, with boys generally outscoring girls on math tests by a small margin and girls consistently outscoring boys on reading tests by a larger, but still relatively small, margin.[6]

The Gender Gap Favoring Girls in Reading Is Neither Sudden Nor Increasing

Girls have consistently outperformed boys on the NAEP-LTT reading assessment since the test was first administered in 1971. Overall, the gender gap favoring girls on the reading assessment has narrowed or remained the same during the past three decades.[7] Nine-year-old boys scored higher on the reading assessment in 2004 than in any previous year, and 13- and 17-year-old boys' scores were either higher than or not significantly different from scores in the 1970s.

A Slight Gender Gap Favors Boys in Math

A gender gap favoring boys in math is small and inconsistent among younger students but more evident among older students. In the nine NAEP-LTT math assessments, 9-year-old girls outscored boys in 1978 and 1982, and boys scored higher than girls in 1996. In all other years, no difference appeared between 9-year-old girls' and boys' average scores. Among 13-year-olds, no differences appeared in six of the nine years, and boys outscored girls in 1994, 1996, and 2004. Among 17-year-olds, boys outscored girls in eight of the nine tests.

Increasing Percentages of Girls and Boys Are Scoring at Higher Levels of Proficiency

NAEP scores are reported by three levels of proficiency: basic, proficient, and advanced. **Basic** denotes partial mastery of the knowledge and skills that are fundamental for proficient work at each grade level. **Proficient** represents solid academic performance for each grade assessed. Students reaching this level have demonstrated competency over challenging subject matter, including subject-matter knowledge, application of such knowledge to real-world situations, and analytical skills appropriate to the subject matter. **Advanced** signifies superior performance (McGraw, Lubienski, & Strutchens, 2006; U.S. Department of Education, National Center for Education Statistics, 2007g).

Generally, more boys perform at the proficient or advanced level in math, while more girls perform at the proficient or advanced level in reading. For example, 41 percent of fourth-grade boys and 37 percent of fourth-grade girls scored at or above a proficient level on the main NAEP math exam in 2007, while 30 percent of fourth-grade boys and 36 percent of fourth-grade girls scored at or above a proficient level on the main NAEP reading exam. During the past 15 years, increasing

percentages of girls and boys have scored at higher levels of proficiency in math. In reading, trends are less consistent, but where changes have occurred, they have been positive for both girls and boys. Gender gaps are often more pronounced among higher-scoring students.

Large Gaps in Test Scores Exist by Race/Ethnicity

Consistently large gaps in NAEP test scores exist by race/ethnicity.[8] In most cases, however, these gaps have narrowed since the 1970s. Moreover, higher percentages of all students are reaching proficiency today than in the past, including students from disadvantaged groups. In 2007, a larger proportion of fourth and eighth graders in all racial/ethnic groups scored at or above a basic level of proficiency in both math and reading than did students in the same grades in 1992 (U.S. Department of Education, National Center for Education Statistics, 2007d). Still, large disparities remain, with a majority of African American (70 percent) and Hispanic (60 percent) 12th graders scoring *below* a basic level of proficiency in math, and a majority of white (70 percent) and Asian American (73 percent) 12th graders scoring *at or above* a basic level of proficiency in 2005. While gaps by race/ethnicity are narrowing, progress is slow, and troubling gaps among students by race/ethnicity persist.

Test Scores Are Closely Connected to Family Income Level

Eligibility for free or reduced-price school lunch is a commonly used indicator of family income level.[9] The proportion of eligible students is large and has been growing steadily during the past 10 years (U.S. Department of Education, National Center for Education Statistics, 2005d). In 2007, 42 percent of fourth graders taking the main NAEP math assessment and 41 percent of fourth graders taking the main NAEP reading assessment were eligible (U.S. Department of Education, National Center for Education Statistics, 2007g, 2007i).[10] When using this measure, gaps between students from higher-income and lower-income families on the most recent NAEP exam averaged 23 points in reading and 24 points in math for grades 4, 8, and 12 (authors' analysis of U.S. Department of Education, National Center for Education Statistics, 2007d).

Students from lower-income families are less likely to score at the proficient level in math and reading. A majority of 12th graders from lower-income families (61 percent) performed *below* a basic level of proficiency on the NAEP math assessment in 2005, while a majority of students from higher-income families (66 percent) performed *at or above* a basic level of proficiency. Still, trends are positive: Higher percentages of fourth and eighth graders from lower-income families scored at or above basic, at or above proficient, and at advanced levels in math in 2007 compared to 1996 (U.S. Department of Education, National Center for Education Statistics, 2007d).

Gender Differences Vary by Race/Ethnicity

On the NAEP-LTT math assessment, an advantage for boys is found most consistently between white girls and boys, much less often between Hispanic girls and boys, and not at all between African American girls and boys. Among 13- and 17-year-olds, white boys scored higher on average than white girls on 10 of the 18 tests. On average, 13- and 17-year-old Hispanic boys outscored Hispanic girls on three of the 18 tests, and no difference existed between African American girls and boys at any age from 1978 to 2004. For 9-year-olds, no gender differences existed within any racial/ethnic group during this period (ibid.).

On the NAEP-LTT reading assessment, girls tend to outperform boys in every racial/ethnic group; however, gender differences have been most consistent among white students, less consistent among African American students, and least consistent among Hispanic students. From 1975 to 2004, white girls outperformed white boys on 29 of the 30 tests for the three age groups, African American girls outperformed their male peers on 24 of the 30 tests, and Hispanic girls outperformed Hispanic boys less than half the time—on 14 of the 30 tests (ibid.).

The 2007 main NAEP eighth-grade math assessment provides an example of how gender differences in average test scores vary across racial/ethnic groups. Among students who took this exam, a small but statistically significant gender gap of two points favored boys. When broken down by race/ethnicity, a three-point gap favored boys over girls among white students, no significant gender gap appeared among Hispanic students, and a small but significant gap favored girls among African American students.

Girls and Boys from Similar Backgrounds Have Similar Scores

Large gaps exist between white girls and boys and their African American and Hispanic peers. On average, African American and Hispanic girls' scores are closer to African American and Hispanic boys' scores than to white girls' scores. Similar trends appear in proficiency levels by gender within the same racial/ethnic group. Few differences are found in the percentages of girls and boys of the same race/ethnicity scoring at or above a basic level of proficiency in math on the most recent main NAEP exams in 2005 and 2007. On the main NAEP

reading exams, however, higher percentages of girls tended to score at or above a basic level of proficiency than did boys of the same race/ethnicity for all three grades. Still, in both math and reading, African American and Hispanic girls scored more closely to African American and Hispanic boys than to white or Asian American girls.

The story is similar for family income level. Average scores of girls and boys from lower-income families tend to be closer than do scores of girls from higher-income families and girls from lower-income families, and the same is true for boys.

Math and Reading Scores Are Closely Tied to Family Income Level

In recent years, fourth- and eighth-grade boys have outscored girls within the same income group on the main NAEP math exam.[11] Average differences by gender within family income level, however, were much smaller than differences between students from different family income levels.

Family income level also has a strong influence on reading scores. Scores of girls and boys from the same family income level are more similar than are scores of girls or boys from different family income levels.[12] In all main NAEP reading assessments, girls and boys from higher-income families scored higher than did girls and boys from lower-income families at all three grade levels. Within family income levels, however, girls showed a consistent advantage in reading scores, outscoring boys in grades 4 and 8 in each of the past four tests and in grade 12 in the past three tests.

The effect of family income remains strong within racial/ethnic groups. For example, among white students, girls and boys from higher-income families outscored their lower-income peers in 4th and 8th grade in both math and reading and in 12th grade in math. The one exception is on the 12th-grade reading test, where no difference was found between white girls from lower-income families and white boys from higher-income families, although girls from higher-income families still outscored girls from lower-income families and boys from higher-income families still outscored boys from lower-income families.

Boys' advantage in math does not supersede the more substantial advantage of students from higher-income families over students from lower-income families. Similarly, girls' overall advantage in reading does not override the effect of family income level, although in 12th grade it comes close. The data show that boys from lower-income families perform behind the other groups in reading. Similarly, but to a lesser degree, girls from lower-income families score behind the other groups in math.

Geographic Patterns in NAEP Scores Refute a Boys' Crisis

Patterns in test scores across states provide further evidence that girls' success has not come at the expense of boys. In states where girls do well on tests, boys also do well, and states with low test scores among boys also tend to have low scores among girls. For example, test scores on the 2007 main NAEP fourth-grade math assessment by state show that the five highest-scoring states for boys—Massachusetts, New Jersey, New Hampshire, Kansas, and Minnesota—were also the highest-scoring states for girls. Similarly, three of the four states with the lowest scores for boys—Mississippi, New Mexico, and Alabama—were also three of the lowest-scoring states for girls (authors' analysis of U.S. Department of Education, National Center for Education Statistics, 2007g).

Where the Girls Are

The end of secondary school is a useful juncture to assess where the girls are. Which girls emerge from high school proficient in reading? in math? The indicators are not promising. On average, only among white girls in 2005 were at least half of 12th graders reading at or above a proficient level. In math, the numbers were less encouraging, with a clear majority of 12th-grade African American and Hispanic girls and girls from lower-income families scoring below a basic level of proficiency.

Math

A majority of 12th-grade white and Asian American/Pacific Islander girls and girls from higher-income families scored at or above the basic level of proficiency in math in 2005. A majority of African American and Hispanic girls and girls from lower-income families, however, scored below the basic level of proficiency. Only a minority of all groups of 12th-grade girls scored at or above the proficient level.

Reading

A majority of 12th-grade girls in all races/ethnicities and family income levels scored at or above a basic level of proficiency in reading in 2005. Half of all white girls but only 42 percent of Asian American/Pacific Islander, 23 percent of Hispanic, and 19 percent of African American girls scored at or above a proficient level. Additionally, 46 percent of girls from higher-income families compared to 23 percent of girls from lower-income families scored at or above a proficient level.

Summary

Overall, both girls and boys are performing better on NAEP assessments since the 1970s, especially in math.

The traditional gender differences persist, however, with boys generally outscoring girls on math tests by a small margin, and girls outscoring boys on reading tests by a larger, but still relatively small, margin. Increasing percentages of both girls and boys are performing at a proficient level in math. In reading, the percentages of girls and boys who achieve proficiency have remained about the same.

These generally positive trends, however, mask important variations by race/ethnicity and family income level. Girls from higher income families scored higher on average than did lower-income girls in both math and reading in all three grades and all years evaluated. In addition, while disparities by race/ethnicity and family income level are not increasing, the gaps are not closing at an acceptable rate. Large differences remain among students by race/ethnicity and family income level. Gender differences occur within all groups but appear to be larger and more consistent among white students. Nevertheless, even among white students, gender differences are small relative to gaps by race/ethnicity and family income level.

Notes

1. Between 1971 and 2004, the sample size for the NAEP-LTT math and reading assessments for a given age ranged from 3,500 (17-year-olds taking the math test in 1996) to 26,800 (17-year-olds taking the math test in 1978). Sample sizes for a given age in a given subject were larger (between 12,000 and 27,000) before 1986. Since 1986, sample sizes have ranged from 3,700 to 7,600 (U.S. Department of Education, National Center for Education Statistics, 2005a).

2. The next NAEP-LTT assessments will be given in 2008.

3. In 2007, 197,700 4th graders and 153,000 8th graders took the main NAEP math assessment (U.S. Department of Education, National Center for Education Statistics, 2007g) while 191,000 4th graders and 160,700 8th graders took the main NAEP reading assessment (U.S. Department of Education, National Center for Education Statistics, 2007i). In 2005, approximately 9,000 12th graders took the main NAEP math assessment while 12,000 12th graders took the main NAEP reading assessment (U.S. Department of Education, National Center for Education Statistics, 2007j).

4. The NAEP Data Explorer can be found on the website of the U.S. Department of Education National Center for Education Statistics at http://nces.ed.gov/nationsreportcard/naepdata. This analysis was conducted in August and September 2007.

5. The one exception is reading scores among 17-year-olds, which declined for most groups in 2004 compared to earlier years.

6. In a separate analysis using "Cohen's d," a widely accepted measure of effect size, Klecker (2006) shows that the gender differences in reading scores on the main NAEP exam from 1992 to 2003 fall within the "small" range for all three grades in each year.

7. For students age 9, the gender gap on the NAEP-LTT reading assessment decreased from 13 points in 1971 to 5 points in 2004. Students ages 13 and 17 showed no difference. While scores have declined for both girls and boys on the reading assessment at age 17 from a peak in the late 1980s and early 1990s and the gender gap narrowed during the 1980s and has since widened, the gender gap in reading at age 17 was not significantly different in 2004 from what it was in 1971.

8. When looking at NAEP-LTT trends, data for only African American, Hispanic, and white groups are presented because they are the only groups with sufficient sample size to lend themselves to statistically reliable comparisons (U.S. Department of Education, National Center for Education Statistics, 2005a).

9. Students from families with incomes at or below 130 percent of the poverty level are eligible for free lunch. Families with incomes between 131 percent and 185 percent of the poverty level are eligible for reduced-price school lunch, for which students can be charged no more than 40 cents (U.S. Department of Education, National Center for Education Statistics, 2007m). For the period July 1, 2006, through June 30, 2007, for a family of four, 130 percent of the poverty level was $26,000, and 185 percent was $37,000 (U.S. Department of Education, National Center for Education Statistics, 2007g).

10. In 2005, 70 percent of African American, 33 percent of Asian American/Pacific Islander, 73 percent of Hispanic, and 24 percent of white fourth graders were eligible for free or reduced-price school lunch (U.S. Department of Education, National Center for Education Statistics, 2007m).

11. Within family income levels, no gender difference appeared among 12th graders in the three most recent main NAEP math assessments for high school seniors.

12. The one exception to this trend is found in the 2002 reading scores of 12th graders, where the average score of boys from higher-income families was closer to the average score of boys from lower-income families than it was to that of girls from higher-income families.

The Right to Be Out: Sexual Orientation and Gender Identity in America's Public Schools

Stuart Biegel

Having received a J.D. and serving as a classroom teacher, Stuart Biegel's specialty is education and the law. He is a faculty member at UCLA, teaching in both the Graduate School of Education and Information Studies and the School of Law. He has served as Director of Teacher Education at UCLA as well as Special Counsel for the California Department of Education. Biegel is a leading, and well-respected, author on the issue of bullying and spokesman for improving the schooling experiences of lesbian, gay, bisexual, and transgender (LGBT) students.

The Right to Be Out: Sexual Orientation and Gender Identity in America's Public Schools (University of Minnesota, 2010), is Biegel's latest publication. The following selection from the book lays out some of the historical court cases and legislative acts regarding LGBT students and schools, and describes how to ensure that school and classroom climate are respectful of all students. Importantly, Biegel includes a discussion of bullying and anti-bullying programs and practices. In today's increasing awareness of school bullying, Biegel's discussion is helpful to educators attempting to interrupt bullying. In his discussion of setting a proactive strategy for improving school climate, Biegel describes that when educators are "setting the tone by demonstrating sensitivity to the needs of all students, including an open and explicit respect for LGBTs, then the possibilities for growth, development, and achievement are invariably maximized."

Key Concept: LGBT and bullying

The Legal Foundations of the Right to Be Out

The right to be out has emerged today as a strong and multifaceted legal imperative. . . .

The Intersection of the First and Fourteenth Amendments

At its heart, the right to be out is a combination of First Amendment and Fourteenth Amendment principles an analysis of gay identity issues appropriately involves *both* "freedom and equality: the freedom to express an individual gay identity without suffering the harms inflicted on members of subordinated groups."[4] It is at this intersection of free speech and equal protection, where both the freedom principle and the equality principle can operate simultaneously, that the right to be out

can be located for lesbian, gay, bisexual, and transgender persons in U.S. public education.

Additional Laws Bolstering Students' Right to Be Out

Most of the disputes involving LGBT students in the public schools directly or indirectly implicate safety concerns. Thus, students who are mistreated merely for the fact that they are open regarding their sexual and/or gender identity can also and often do rely on negligence law, threat law, harassment law, and a growing number of state statutes designed to maximize campus safety for everyone.

Negligence law is based on well-settled legal principles and is relatively consistent from jurisdiction to jurisdiction. K-12 educators typically have a duty to supervise and an obligation to act reasonably toward all students.

If students are injured in a school setting and the injury can be linked to the acts or omissions of school district employees, both the employees and the district can be held liable.[61]

Threat law has become increasingly prominent in the years since the tragic shootings at Columbine High School and the September 11, 2001, attacks on the nation. Not only do school officials have the option of suspending or expelling students for threatening their peers,[62] but criminal statutes also allow, and may in fact dictate, the arrest and prosecution of such perpetrators.[63] And if school officials do not intervene to put a halt to threatening behavior, or if they intervene to help some students but not others, they themselves may be found negligent for any subsequent injuries.

Harassment law has grown and developed over the past several decades, particularly with regard to the fine-tuning of frameworks governing hostile environment sexual harassment in the workplace. These frameworks have been applied to peer-to-peer harassment in a school setting under Title IX, and school districts may be found liable for deliberate indifference to known acts of harassment.[64] Peer-to-peer sexual harassment generally differs from peer mistreatment of LGBT persons in that the former is typically sexually charged while the latter tends to be what is commonly viewed as "gay bashing," yet many LGBTs are victimized by sexual harassment, especially openly lesbian and transgender youth. The strengthening of laws in this area provides additional protection for them if they choose to be out.[65]

In addition to these basic categories of law that apply nationwide, individual states may adopt legislation that sets forth precise mandates relating to campus safety for LGBT students. In recent years, a growing number of states have moved in this direction. By 2010, according to the Human Rights Campaign's state-by-state survey of school laws and policies, seventeen states plus the District of Columbia had passed laws that "address discrimination, harassment and/or bullying of students based on sexual orientation." Fourteen of these, plus D.C., have also added protection on the basis of gender identity, and it is noteworthy that ten of them did so in the years 2007–2010. The fourteen states include California, Colorado, Illinois, Iowa, Maine, Maryland, Minnesota, New Hampshire, New Jersey, New York, North Carolina, Oregon, Vermont, and Washington. Given the demographic makeup of these states, this means that the rights of approximately 40 percent of all the public school students in the country are strengthened even further in this area of the law.[66]

It is important to note that the state laws differ regarding the types of access to educational settings that are explicitly protected. They also differ as to the exact category of characteristics that are offered protection. Connecticut, for example, mandates for each child "an equal opportunity to participate in the activities, programs and courses of study offered in such public schools . . . without discrimination on account of race, color, sex, religion, national origin or sexual orientation."[67] Iowa and Minnesota, however, are much more specific. Iowa takes the affirmative step of proscribing "bullying" based on both sexual orientation and gender identity, and Minnesota adds a specific definition for gender identity.[68]

Proactive Strategies for Improving School Climate

The spirit of community that accompanies a positive school climate can be particularly important for students of color and LGBT students who may have self-image issues and may see themselves, incorrectly, as not capable or as less capable than others. Such students, vulnerable and at risk, are often among the first to be negatively impacted by a less-than-supportive school climate, which can lead them either to stop coming to school regularly or to simply drop out. The same students, situated in a positive and encouraging environment, can be among the greatest beneficiaries of these changes.[4]

As Rick Lipkin wrote in *Scientific American* in 2006, "Given our socially reactive brains, we must 'be wise,' and be aware of the ways that our moods influence the biology of each life we touch."[10] The implications of this for LGBT students and others who have often been viewed as outside of the mainstream are particularly poignant. If, for example, educators disseminate the prototypical message of disapproval—directly or indirectly—that the needs of gay and gender-nonconforming students are unimportant, that an LGBT identity does not really exist, and that queer students should keep their feelings to themselves, then such a message, magnified and further disseminated by other students who pick up on it, can have a devastating cumulative impact on the lives of young people just beginning to come to terms with who they are. But if the opposite is taking place, and educators are setting the tone by demonstrating sensitivity to the needs of all students, including an open and explicit respect for LGBTs, then the possibilities for growth, development, and achievement are invariably maximized.

Structured School Climate Programs

In addition to the proactive strategies for improving school climate across the board, structured programs are available that can serve the needs of particular campuses and communities.

Targeting Bullying, Peer Harassment, and Hate-Motivated Activity

Bullying is generally defined as behavior that can range from name-calling, threats, and social exclusion to serious criminal acts of libel and repeated physical attacks. Pervasive bullying is perhaps best seen as a type of peer harassment and mistreatment, and it continues to negatively affect persons of every race, ethnicity, gender, and sexual identity. Indeed, there is evidence that bullying is more prevalent than it was in the past.

Bullying remains a significant issue for LGBTs. A 2003 National Mental Health Association survey, for example, found that more than 75 percent of all teenagers witnessed bullying of classmates who were gay or thought to be gay. The same survey also asked students from twelve to seventeen years old, "Who gets bullied all the time?" The groups ranking highest were students with disabilities (6 percent), overweight students (11 percent), students "who dress differently" (12 percent), and students "who are gay or are thought to be gay" (24 percent).[27]

Yet the relevant research clearly shows that bullying is a problem for everyone, gay and straight alike. Gloria Moskowitz-Sweet, for example, who has worked in this area extensively over time, explains that "[a]ny child who does not fit narrow definitions of masculine or feminine behavior—or is not part of the dominant race, religion, culture, or appears different from the majority—is an easy target. Approximately 85 percent of children are affected by it: as perpetrators, recipients, or witnesses." She adds, "With the advent of electronic communications, the incidence of bullying has escalated into cyberspace, as our young people taunt through texting, Twittering, Facebook, MySpace, and other modern modes of communication." And she reports that "[m]ental health experts are now recognizing bullying's long-term effects." In 2009, for example, the American Academy of Pediatrics, for the first time, addressed the problem of childhood bullying when it published a policy statement on preventing school violence.[28]

One of the most volatile and relatively unexplored aspects of the bullying problem in K-12 schools is the potential for escalating violence. A single bullying event is often not an end point but the beginning of a series of events that may have truly tragic consequences for many people. The bullying of Lawrence King over time, for example, culminated in his tragic murder and also had a devastating impact on others, including (but not limited to) the virtual destruction of the life of the fourteen-year-old who shot him and the potentially career-ending consequences for the English teacher who was supervising the class when the shooting happened.[29] The bullying of eleven-year-olds Carl Walker-Hoover, in Springfield, Massachusetts, and Jaheem Herrera, in DeKalb, Georgia, led not only to their highly publicized suicides but also to still-undetermined repercussions in the lives of those who came in contact with them.[30]

Moreover, the aspect of bullying that very few appear willing to confront is that victims of bullying in the present era may, as a result, turn on their tormentors and on many others around them, striking back in the most violent of ways. There is evidence, for example, not only that perpetrators of some of the worst school violence at the K-12 level over the past ten to fifteen years were victims of bullying themselves, but also that they were targeted with anti-gay epithets meant to degrade and alienate them by suggesting a failure to meet gender- and sexuality-based expectations of masculinity. These include, among others, fourteen-year-old Michael Carneal, who killed three people in West Paducah, Kentucky, in 1997; high school seniors Eric Harris and Dylan Klebold, who killed fifteen, including themselves, at Columbine High School in Littleton, Colorado, in 1999; fifteen-year-old Charles Andrew Williams, who killed two people in Santee, California, in 2001; and sixteen-year-old Jeff Weise, who took his own life after killing seven people at the Red Lake Indian Reservation in Minnesota in 2005.[31]

Details emerging in subsequent news reports regarding these horrific events included reports that Carneal "endured years of anti-gay teasing after the school newspaper printed a rumor alleging he was gay and had a crush on another male student"; and that classmates of Harris and Klebold "said that they were often called 'gay' by athletes and other students. 'They're a bunch of homos. . . . If you want to get rid of someone, usually you tease 'em. So the whole school would call them homos,' a Columbine football player told *Time* magazine." And Williams "[w]as reportedly teased as 'gay' by students at his new high school, and was troubled by the homophobic bullying, according to an ex-girlfriend and her mother."[32] It should be noted that none of these students identified as LGBT, and no evidence indicated that they were anything other than straight. But they were victimized in this context nonetheless, as many are in K-12 schools across the country.

Summarizing the latest research in the area, Robert Kim explains that "[b]ullying of [LGBT students and those perceived as LGBT] stems largely from discomfort with students who do not conform to traditional gender roles in their appearance or behavior, i.e., who are gender-nonconforming. A student's actual sexual orientation may be far less relevant to his or her social victimization than his or her gender identity or gender expression."[33]

Not only has bullying by fellow students in a school setting consistently been found to have a negative impact on everyone's ability to learn, but recent research has also shown that bullying is more common and more potentially damaging to children than was previously thought. In fact, a definite link has been identified between bullying and later delinquent and criminal behavior.[34]

The Center for the Prevention of Hate Violence is a noteworthy example of an organization that coordinates training and educational programs designed to combat bullying and other forms of hate-related activity. Located in New England, the center works with businesses, non-profit organizations, schools, colleges, law enforcement agencies, and other institutions to prevent bias, harassment, and violence.[35] Center programs focusing on K-12 schools are particularly wide-ranging in scope. "Student leader workshops," for example, are designed to provide student leaders in grades 5 through 12 with the knowledge, confidence, and skills to safely intervene when they observe harassment at school. "Speech and facilitated discussion" empowers students to articulate the damage caused by harassment and to generate realistic solutions. "Controversial dialogues" are a series of workshops designed to highlight and address specific areas of conflict or tension between specific groups of students. "Bullying prevention workshops" take elementary students in the third and fourth grades through a series of interactive activities and role playing, helping them to recognize the impact of bullying and to learn how to prevent this behavior.[36]

Providing Support for LGBT Youth: Innovative Programs and Successful Approaches

Programs and activities with proven track records have been developed over the past several decades to assist school officials in providing needed support for LGBT youth at individual campuses. Most feature the active involvement of on-site faculty liaisons who agree to play prominent roles, and even those that have not involved faculty in the past may offer opportunities for such involvement in the future. Among the most successful approaches in this regard are safe zones, gay-straight alliances, suicide prevention programs, wellness programs geared toward students of particular races or ethnicities, and inclusive audiovisual materials developed by innovative media companies. In general, these initiatives focus on immediate issues of health and safety as well as on longer-term changes in both school culture and societal norms.

Safe Zones and Safe Spaces

Emerging over the past ten to fifteen years at both the K–12 and higher education levels, safe zones and safe spaces programs are very simple conceptually: identify spaces—typically a classroom at the K–12 level and an educator's office at the higher education level—where LGBT students can feel safe to be themselves and comfortable enough to talk about issues relating to their sexual and/or gender identities. Educators choosing to volunteer and participate in the training typically post pink triangles or some depiction of the rainbow flag on their doors, along with some language indicating that these are safe places for LGBT students. According to those who have planned and implemented such programs, "For many students, the presence of allies to whom they can turn for support—or even the simple knowledge that allies exist—can be a critical factor in developing a positive sense of self, building community, coping with bias, and working to improve school climate."[62]

Gay–Straight Alliances

Scholarly literature has documented the benefits of gay–straight alliances for all students in a pluralistic society today. A 2009 study builds on these findings, exploring how youth define and experience empowerment in youth-led organizations characterized by social justice goals. The study offers insights into the ways that empowerment may be experienced differently among youth as compared to adults.[63] In addition, related scholarship has examined the importance of teacher mentoring in the lives of LGBT youth, focusing in particular on "how significant teacher-mentors are to the educational resilience of sexual minority women of color."[64] The faculty adviser in a gay–straight alliance is often able to serve as a mentor in this context, enhancing the positive impact of the student organization.

GLSEN, the Gay, Lesbian, and Straight Education Network, has played a prominent role in the formation of these alliances from the beginning. The New York-based organization continues to provide a wealth of programmatic resources for K–12 educators, ranging from materials regarding safe zones and gay–straight alliances to national days of unification such as National Coming Out Day and the Day of Silence. GLSEN also provides professional-development materials for in-class activities, lessons, and curriculum.[65]

The California-based Gay–Straight Alliance Network has also contributed substantially to the work in this area. The network has gathered together an extensive collection of resources, ranging from steps that can be taken to form and maintain gay–straight alliances to programs empowering LGBT youth and their allies to help counter discrimination in this context.[66]

Suicide Prevention Programs and Initiatives

For some time now, research has found that the suicide rate for lesbian, gay, bisexual, and transgender youth is consistently higher than that of their straight counterparts. This takes into account both attempted suicides and completed suicides.[67] The problem is not limited to K–12 students. It is a major issue at the college and university level, and among persons beyond this age as well. Indeed, the current data might very well be an underestimate, skewed by the fact that many suicides may never be contextualized as LGBT-related, because the person attempting or committing suicide was highly closeted, perhaps even from him- or herself. In such instances, no one views the suicide as having anything to do with being gay, when in fact wrestling with sexual identity may have been a central factor.

Of course, suicide is not a problem in LGBT communities alone. Recent data, for example, has shown that young African American males and young Hispanic women are particularly at risk for suicide today. For those African American males and Hispanic women who are also LGBT, the circumstances are only compounded.[68]

Suicide prevention programs are not generally school-based, but they often involve express or implied partnerships with school officials, particularly those in the mental health field. Much work in this area is accomplished through telephone counseling, which persons contemplating suicide can tap via highly publicized hotlines. Schools across the country can and often do disseminate information regarding these hotlines.

In addition to suicide prevention programs designed for everyone, there are two noteworthy examples of programs that directly focus on LGBTs and their unique needs. The Trevor Project, which grew out of the success of the Academy Award-winning HBO film *Trevor*, is designed specifically to address suicide prevention among LGBT teenagers. It includes both a helpline and a Facebook page. The GLBT National Help Center includes both a national hotline and a national youth talkline.[69]

Aligning LGBT-Related Content with Statewide Content Standards

Increasingly, it is not possible to include anything in a formal public school curriculum that is not linked to standards that have been adopted by individual states. To that end, school officials focusing on LGBT issues have begun to identify the many ways that gay and transgender content ties in with such standards. A brief examination of four California standards for eleventh-grade U.S. history—standards that are representative of social studies content standards adopted nationwide—reveals that they offer numerous opportunities for the consideration of the contributions and struggles of gays and lesbians in the American story.[28]

- Standard 11.10.4 mandates "examin[ing] the roles of civil rights advocates." The story of Bayard Rustin, set forth in several recent highly acclaimed biographies and collected writings, has emerged in retrospect as a central feature of the civil rights movement.[29] A key organizer and intellectual force who worked closely with Martin Luther King Jr. and was in charge of putting together legendary nonviolent demonstrations such as the 1963 March on Washington, Rustin was also known to be a gay man during a time when tremendous stigma attached to this identity. Enemies of the civil rights movement such as segregationist senator Strom. Thurmond and FBI director J. Edgar Hoover attempted to use Rustin's sexual orientation to limit or discredit the movement. Rustin's achievements in spite of all the challenges cannot currently be found in any high school history text, but standards like this one provide an opportunity for teachers to include it.
- Standard 11.11.7 requires educators to "explain how ... government(s) have responded to demographic and social changes such as population shifts." Standards of this type provide an opportunity for teachers to reference the impact of LGBTs on urban planning, development, and renewal. Indeed, the extent to which areas of major U.S. cities such as the Castro and West Hollywood have been renovated, rebuilt, and in many instances transformed by gay residents and gay businesses is often pointed to as a model of what can be accomplished in other places.
- Standard 11.7.5 requires teachers to "discuss the ... response of the [Roosevelt] administration to Hitler's atrocities against the Jews and other groups." Too often, the extent to which Hitler's atrocities included the persecution, torture, and brutal murder of gay people is left out of the history books. A full treatment of the issues surrounding the U.S. response—or lack thereof—to ongoing reports from cities occupied by the Nazis and concentration camps run by the Nazis necessarily includes referencing what was nothing less than Hitler's effort to exterminate gays and lesbians.
- Standard 11.8.8 mandates "discuss[ing] forms of popular culture (e.g., jazz and other forms of popular music)." Such a discussion, on any level, would be incomplete without including an analysis of the increasing prevalence of LGBT themes in television, film, and theater, and without referencing the extent to which the work of composers and musicians such as Cole Porter, Billy Strayhorn, and Elton John was informed by their gay identity.[30]

In light of the opportunities afforded by the development of statewide curriculum standards, educators across the country are beginning to address the many ways that LGBT content can enrich the curriculum across subject areas in an age-appropriate manner.[31] Many individual teachers at local school sites across the nation, on their own initiative, have developed curriculum content that fits naturally within the prescribed courses of study.

Curriculum reform taken to this level can be central to the implementation of the emerging right to be out at local school sites on a day-to-day basis. By helping to reinforce a basic message that under current law LGBT identity can no longer be equated with outsider status and that the ongoing story of our society and culture has always included the story of gays, lesbians, and trans-gender people, an enhanced curriculum builds understandings and helps foster an appreciation of commonalities. In this manner, such reform strengthens and enriches the curriculum, providing a higher-quality education for everyone.

Notes

2. Kenneth L. Karst, "Myths of Identity: Individual and Group Portraits of Race and Sexual Orientation," *UCLA Law Review* 43 (1995): 263, 360.

4. See Karst, "Myths of Identity," 361.

61. These cases are generally brought under state law negligence principles and might vary from state to state because of immunity doctrines and differing statutory schemes.

62. See, e.g., *N.Y. Educ. Law* § 3214(3)(a), allowing the suspension of a pupil who "endangers the safety, morals, health or welfare of others"; and *Tex. Educ. Code* § 37.006(d)(2), allowing removal from the classroom and placement in a disciplinary program if a student's continued presence threatens the safety of others.

63. See, e.g., *Cal. Penal Code* § 422, regarding punishment for threatening statements meant as threats of death or great bodily harm, regardless of intent to carry the threat out; and *Mass. Gen. Law* ch. 275 § 2, allowing courts to examine the complaints of threat victims.

64. See *Davis v. Monroe County Bd. of Educ.*, 526 U.S. 629 (1999), which holds that Title IX may apply if peer-to-peer sexual harassment is so severe as to exclude the victim from an educational opportunity on the basis of sex.

65. See *L. W. v. Toms River Reg'l Sch. Bd. of Educ.*, 189 N.J. 381, 915 A.2d 535 (N.J. 2007), extending New Jersey's Law against Discrimination to recognize a cause of action against the school for sexual orientation discrimination by one student toward another student.

66. The states that provide protection against sexual orientation discrimination but as of 2010 had not added protection against gender-identity discrimination include Connecticut, Massachusetts, and Wisconsin. See, generally, Human Rights Campaign, "School Laws: State by State," Human Rights Campaign, http://www.hrc.org/documents/school_laws.pdf (accessed July 8, 2010).

67. *Conn. Gen. Stat.* 10-15c.

68. See *IA S.B.* 61; and *Minn. Stat.* § 363A.02. See, e.g., "GLSEN Hails Singing of Comprehensive Safe Schools Bill in IA," press release, Gay, Lesbian, and Straight Education Network, March 5, 2007, http://www.glsen.org/ (accessed March 6, 2007).

10. See Rick Lipkin, review of *Social Intelligence*, by Goleman, *Scientific American Mind*, December 2006–January 2007.

11. Goleman, interview.

26. See Robert Kim et al., *A Report on the Status of Gay, Lesbian, Bisexual, and Transgender People in Education: Stepping Out of the Closet, into the Light*, National Education Association, June 2009, http://www.nea.org/assets/docs/glbtstatus09.pdf (accessed July 4, 2009). See, generally, http://www.nea.org/home/ns/32071.htm (accessed July 31, 2009).

27. See Robert Tomsho, "Schools' Efforts to Protect Gays Face Opposition," *Wall Street Journal*, February 20, 2003. See also James T. Sears, *Homophobic Bullying* (Philadelphia: Haworth, 2007).

28. Gloria Moskowitz-Sweet, "Taking Bullying Seriously," *Bay Area Reporter*, June 19, 2009.

29. See, e.g., Catherine Saillant, "Oxnard Teacher Is Still Haunted by Student's Slaying," *Los Angeles Times*, July 19, 2009.

30. See, generally, Charles Blow, "Two Little Boys," *New York Times*, April 24, 2009.

31. See Ryan Lee, "'Boy Code' a Factor in Fatal School Shootings: Experts Say Masculinity Standards Overlooked in Search for Answers," *Washington Blade*, April 15, 2005.

32. See ibid.

33. Kim et al., *Report on the Status*.

34. See California Department of Education, "Bullying and Hate-Motivated Behavior Prevention," http://www.cde.ca.gov/ls/ss/se/bullyprev.asp (accessed July 30, 2007).

35. Stephen Wessler, interview by the author, April 16, 2008. http://www.preventinghate.org/ (accessed May 2, 2008).

36. In addition, the Center for the Prevention of Hate Violence also provides halfday workshops for faculty, staff, and administrators that provide critical information on the impact of harassment on student learning, as well as concrete strategies for responding to and preventing this problem at school.

62. "Safe Zone Programs," GLSEN, January 23, 2003, http://www.glsen.org/cgi-bin/iowa/all/library/record/1291.html (accessed September 10, 2007).

63. See Stephen T. Russell et al., "Youth Empowerment and High School Gay–Straight Alliances," *Journal of Youth and Adolescence* 38 (2009): 891–903.

64. See Billie Gastic and Dominique Johnson, "Teacher-Mentors and the Educational Resilience of Sexual Minority Youth," *Journal of Gay and Lesbian Social Services* 21, nos. 2–3 (2009): 219–31.

65. See GLSEN Web site, http://www.glsen.org/ (accessed August 2, 2009). See also "Project 10 at a Glance," Educational Equity Compliance Office, Los Angeles Unified School District, http://www.lausd.k12.ca.us/lausd/offices/eec/project10.htm (accessed May 14, 2008).

66. *Take It Back: A Manual for Fighting Slurs on Campus* (San Francisco: Tides Center/Gay–Straight Alliance Network, 2003). See http://gsanetwork.org/files/getinvolved/TakeItBack-Manual.pdf (accessed June 7, 2008).

67. See A. Damien Martin and Emery S. Hetrick, "The Stigmatization of the Gay and Lesbian Adolescent," *Journal of Homosexuality* 15, nos. 1–2 (1988): 163–83. See Arnold H. Grossman and Anthony R. D'Augelli, "Transgender Youth and Life-Threatening Behavior," *Suicide and Life-Threatening Behavior* 37, no. 5 (2007): 527–37.

68. The *Washington Post*, in its June 2006 series "Being a Black Man," reported that "the suicide rate among young black men has doubled since 1980." Steven A. Holmes and Richard Morin, "Poll Reveals a Contradictory Portrait Shaded with Promise and Doubt," *Washington Post*, June 4, 2006. "Young Latinas and a Cry for Help," editorial, *New York Times*, July 21, 2006.

69. The Trevor Helpline is at 1-866-488-7386 (1-866-4-U-TREVOR). For more information, see http://www.thetrevorproject.org/helpline.aspx. The Trevor Facebook page is at http://www.facebook.com/TheTrevorProject. The GLBT National Help Center is at http://www.glnh.org/ (all accessed July 31, 2009); its National Hotline is at 1-888-843-4564 (1-888-THE-GLNH), and its National Youth Talkline is at 1-800-246-7743 (1-800-246-PRIDE). The organization also offers an online Peer Support Chat.

28. http://www.cde.ca.gov/be/st/ss/documents/histsocscistnd.pdf (accessed July 13, 2010).

29. See, e.g., *Time on Two Crosses: The Collected Writings of Bayard Rustin*, ed. Devon W. Carbado and Donald Weise (San Francisco: Cleis, 2003).

Race and Immigration

Selection 22

GLORIA LADSON-BILLINGS, from "The Power of Pedagogy: Does Teaching Matter?" in *Race and Education: The Roles of History and Society in Educating African American Students*

Selection 23

CORNEL PEWEWARDY, from "Learning Styles of American Indian/Alaska Native Students: A Review of Literature and Implications for Practice," *Journal of American Indian Education*

Selection 24

HERSH C. WAXMAN, YOLANDA N. PADRÓN, AND ANDRES GARCÍA, from "Educational Issues and Effective Practices for Hispanic Students," in Susan J. Paik and Herbert J. Walberg, *Narrowing the Achievement Gap: Strategies for Educating Latino, Black, and Asian Students*

Selection 25

VALERIE OOKA PANG, from "Fighting the Marginalization of Asian American Students with Caring Schools: Focus on Curricular Change," *Race, Ethnicity & Education*

Selection 26

CAROLA SÚAREZ-OROZCO, ALLYSON PIMENTEL, AND MARGARY MARTIN, from "The Significance of Relationships: Academic Engagement and Achievement Among Newcomer Immigrant Youth," *Teachers College Record*

The Power of Pedagogy: Does Teaching Matter?

Gloria Ladson-Billings

Gloria Ladson-Billings lays out a vision of culturally relevant teaching in several of her articles and books. Culturally relevant teaching has as a key premise that teachers match their teaching styles, and schools match their curriculum, to the culture and home backgrounds of their students. In the following selection, from the article "The Power of Pedagogy: Does Teaching Matter?" in *Race and Education: The Roles of History and Society in Educating African American Students*, edited by William H. Watkins, James H. Lewis, and Victoria Chow (Allyn & Bacon, 2001), Ladson-Billings describes several key components of making education culturally relevant for African American students in urban settings.

Gloria Ladson-Billings is the Kellner Family Professor of Urban Education in the Department of Curriculum & Instruction at the University of Wisconsin-Madison, and she served as the 2005–2006 president of the American Educational Research Association. She has received several research awards, and was senior fellow in urban education of the Annenberg Institute for School Reform at Brown University. She writes on multicultural education in general and on race-related issues in particular. Her special focus is on African American education. Two of her most well-known books include *The Dreamkeepers: Successful Teachers of African American Children* (Jossey-Bass, 1997) *and Beyond the Big House: African American Educators on Teacher Education* (Teachers College Press, 2005).

Key Concept: making education culturally relevant for African American children

The Case for Culturally Relevant Teaching

Anthropologists have long had an interest in applying their research methodology to complex social institutions such as schools (Spindler, 1988). In an attempt to examine questions related to the denial of equal educational opportunity, anthropologists have looked at schools as agents of cultural transmission, arenas of cultural conflict, and sites of potential micro and macro level change (Wilcox, 1988). One of the areas of anthropological study that has proved fruitful for examining the experiences of marginalized students of color in the classroom is the attempt (or lack thereof) of teachers to find ways to match their teaching styles to the culture and home backgrounds of their students.

During the 1980s several terms emerged in the anthropology of education literature that describe these pedagogical strategies used by teachers in an effort to make the schooling experiences of students more compatible with their everyday lives. Those terms include "cultural congruence" (Mohatt & Erickson, 1981), "cultural appropriateness" (Au & Jordan, 1981), "cultural responsiveness" (Cazden & Legett, 1981; Erickson & Mohatt, 1982), "cultural compatibility" (Jordan, 1985; Vogt, Jordan, & Tharp, 1987), and "mitigating cultural discontinuity" (Macias, 1987).

Three of the terms employed by studies on cultural mismatch between school and home—"culturally appropriate," "culturally congruent," and "culturally compatible"—seem to connote accommodation of student culture to mainstream culture. Only the term "culturally responsive" appears to refer to a more dynamic or synergistic relationship between home/community culture and school culture. Erickson and Mohatt (1982) suggest their notion of culturally responsive teaching can be seen as a beginning step for bridging the gap between home and school:

> It may well be that, by discovering the small differences in social relations which make a big difference in the interactional ways children engage the content of the school curriculum, anthropologists can make practical contributions to the improvement of minority children's school achievement and to the improvement of the everyday school life for such children and their teachers. Making small changes in everyday participation structures may be one of the means by which more culturally responsive pedagogy can be developed. (p. 170)

Three examples of scholarship that focus on improving teaching for African American students are found in the work of Irvine (1990), Lee (1994), and Ladson-Billings (1994). Irvine developed the concept of "cultural synchronization" to describe the necessary interpersonal context that must exist between the teacher and African American students to maximize learning. Rather than focusing solely on speech and language interactions, Irvine's work describes the acceptance of students' communication patterns, along with a constellation of cultural mores such as mutuality, reciprocity, spirituality, deference, and responsibility (King & Mitchell, 1990).

Irvine's work on African American students and school failure considers both micro- and macro-analyses, including teacher and student interpersonal societal contexts, teacher and student expectations, institutional contexts, and the societal contexts. This work is important because of its break with the cultural-deficit or cultural-disadvantage explanations that led to compensatory educational interventions. By carefully analyzing each element in the school and social context, Irvine helped to reveal the complexity of the various factors that contribute to school success or failure.

Lee developed a notion of cultural modeling to describe the way that teachers can use African American students' linguistic strengths to build scaffolding that supports literacy learning. More specifically, Lee describes the use of signifying as a linguistic tool for developing literacy. According to Lee (Lee, 1994, p. 302), "Signifying is a form of oral discourse within the African American community that is characterized by innuendo, double meanings, and rhetorical play on meaning and sounds of words." Lee's work underscores the need for teachers to "place value on the learner's culture" (Lee, 1994, p. 299).

Ladson-Billings (1994) developed a theoretical notion of teaching, termed "culturally relevant pedagogy," that describes an approach to teaching that promotes academic and cultural success in settings where student alienation and hostility characterize the school experience. The propositions on which this theory is based are academic achievement, cultural competence, and sociopolitical consciousness.

Rather than focus on the particular "learning styles" of students, this theory argues that teachers have to adopt a particular set of principles about teaching that can be applied in various school and classroom contexts. The focus on academic achievement argues that teachers must place student learning at the center of all classroom activity. Although there have been many explanations offered for why African American students fail to succeed in school, little research has been done to examine academic success among African American students. The "effective schools" literature (Brookover, 1985; Brookover, Beady, Flood, Schweitzer, & Wisenbaker, 1979; Edmonds, 1979) argued that a group of school-wide correlates were reliable predictors of student success. The basis for judging a school "effective" in this literature was how far above predicted levels students performed on standardized achievement tests. Whether or not scholars can agree on the significance of standardized achievement tests, their meaning in the broader public serves to rank and characterize both schools and individuals. No matter how good a fit develops between a student's home and school cultures, students must achieve. No approach to teaching can escape this reality.

The focus on cultural competence suggests that teachers must help students develop a positive identification with their home culture—an identification that supports student learning. Among the scholarship that has examined academically successful African American students, a disturbing finding has emerged—the students' academic success has come at the expense of their culture and psychosocial well-being (Fine, 1986; Fordham, 1988). Fordham and Ogbu (1986, p. 176) identified a phenomenon entitled "acting white," where African American students who were academically successful were ostracized by their peers. Bacon (1981) found that, among African American high school students identified as gifted in their elementary grades, only about half were continuing to do well at the high school level. A closer examination of the successful students' progress indicated that they were social isolates, with neither African American nor white friends. The students believed that it was necessary for them to separate themselves from other African American students so that teachers would not attribute to them the negative characteristics they may have attributed to low-performing African American students.

Pedagogy must provide a way for students to maintain their cultural integrity while succeeding academically. Many of the self-described African-centered public schools have focused on this notion of cultural competence. To date, little data have been reported on the academic success of students in these school programs.

Finally, teachers must focus on sociopolitical consciousness. This third aspect refers to the kind of civic and social awareness students must develop to work toward equity and justice beyond their own personal advancement, and it has been reflected in successful programs such as Freedom Schools, Citizenship Schools, and Nationalist Schools. This notion of sociopolitical consciousness presumes that teachers themselves recognize social inequities and their causes.

Research by Delpit (1995), Foster (1994, 1995), Irvine (1990), King (1991), Ladson-Billings (1994, 1995), Moll (1988), and Garcia (1988) all suggests that there are some aspects of teaching important to student learning that may be differentially valued and represented in the repertoires of successful teachers in urban, minority contexts.

Foster's (1994, 1995) work identifies cultural solidarity, linking classroom content to students' experiences, a focus on the whole child, a use of familiar cultural patterns, and the incorporation of culturally compatible communication patterns as key elements of success in teaching African American urban students. Irvine's (1990) work has investigated the nested conditions of urban school teaching that require what she terms "cultural synchronization" to produce success.

Ladson-Billings' (1994, 1995) research on successful teachers of African American children found that there is a consensus around how such teachers conceptualize themselves and others (i.e., students, parents, community members), how they conceptualize social relations (both within and outside of the school and classroom), and how they conceptualize knowledge.

Garcia's (1988) work suggests that Latino students benefit from teachers who specify task outcomes and what students must do to accomplish tasks competently, communicate both high expectations and a sense of efficacy about their own ability to teach, exhibit use of "active teaching," communicate clearly, obtain and maintain students' engagement, monitor students' progress, and provide immediate feedback.

Foster (1994, 1995) and Ladson-Billings (1994, 1995) look at specific teacher beliefs and actions. Following are aspects of their work that may be important in understanding the role of teaching in classrooms serving the poor and communities of color.

Cultural Solidarity

Foster (1995, p. 575) argues that although "similar background does not guarantee productive, fluid, or uncomplicated relationships between teacher and student" (Mahiri, 1998), there is evidence that suggests that some of the more successful teaching occurs when teachers do share background and experiences with students (Cazden, 1976, 1988). Siddle-Walker (1993) has demonstrated that a sense of cultural solidarity or connectedness has existed historically, particularly during the era when African Americans were consigned to segregated schools.

The focus on "relationship" in urban schools is particularly important given that urban schools have regularly been described as places where children experience little trust and sense of safety with the adults in the school (Haberman, 1995). But how is a sense of caring and cultural solidarity exhibited in an assessment of teaching? What words, gestures, pieces of evidence can be collected that demonstrate the connection between a teacher and her students? In the case of both Foster and Ladson-Billings, long-term, on-site observations and interviews were used to document this quality. However, nothing in the proposed teacher assessments directly deal with the relationships between teachers and their students. Those relationships are assumed but rarely documented.

Linking Classroom Content with Student Experience

This attribute often relies on how well the previous one (cultural solidarity) is established. The teacher who feels comfortable and has something in common with the students, their community, their language, and their backgrounds has at her disposal a deeper reservoir of skills and abilities on which to draw. For instance, the teacher who attends a church in the community or has had a church experience similar to that of the children in the classroom can more readily make analogues between appropriate behavior at particular times in the school day and appropriate behavior in particular portions of a worship service. These are not necessarily special skills, for indeed we would expect all teachers to be able to provide students with real world examples, but the skills and examples that urban teachers may have can be so familiar to students that their use minimizes conflict and confusion. Ladson-Billings and Henry (1991), in a look at both African American and Afro-Caribbean-Canadian youngsters and their teachers, demonstrated how the teachers' understanding of the specific situations of students allowed them to better manage and teach in classrooms considered difficult by their peers.

Focus on the Whole Child

Foster (1995) points out that successful teachers of African American children typically concern themselves with much more than the children's cognitive growth. Issues of moral ethical, and personal development are a part of their pedagogy. However, the proposed standards-driven assessments for teachers focus primarily on student achievement in specific content areas. The relationship between personal, moral, and ethical growth and cognitive growth has not been clearly established, but successful teachers in urban areas seem to believe this more holistic approach to teaching is key to their success.

Use of Familiar Cultural Patterns

Successful urban teachers know (or quickly learn) the cultural norms and patterns of their students. In Ladson-Billings' (1994) study, teachers describe the ways they used cultural knowledge and/or learned from students in order to facilitate the relationship that would subsequently facilitate learning. Rather than attempt to re-socialize students into a dominant paradigm, successful urban teachers soon learn that qualities such as reciprocity, respect, collectivity, and expressive individualism are vital to being able to work with their students. Foster (1995) asserts that routines and rituals are prevalent in the classrooms of African American teachers who are successful with African American students. These cultural patterns mirror aspects of African American life experiences in music, art, dance, religion, speech, and other forms of communication.

Incorporation of Culturally Compatible Communication Patterns

The area of culturally compatible communication patterns has received the most attention in the research literature. Sociolinguists, such as Cazden and Leggett (1981), Erickson and Mohatt (1982), Mohatt and Erickson (1981), Philips (1983), Au (1980), Au and Jordan (1981), and Jordan (1985), all have devoted considerable research time to examining the interactions between teachers and students who are from different linguistic, racial, ethnic, and cultural groups.

Ladson-Billings' (1994, 1995) work uses a related but different rubric by which to assess effective teaching. In a 3-year study of effective teachers of African American students, she was able to discern a set of general principles that characterize such teachers, which she calls cultural relevant teaching.

Conceptions of Self/Other

Culturally relevant teaching constructs a vision of the teacher and student as capable, efficacious human beings. Rather than succumb to the prevailing beliefs about "at-riskness," culturally relevant teachers make demands for academic success from all students. These teachers, like Kleinfeld's (1974) "warm demanders," did not allow students to avoid work because they were poor or came from single-parent households, or had some other personal/social problems. Sometimes these demands for success can appear harsh. Certainly, a snapshot of the teachers in the classroom (such as those that appear in some assessment exercises) may be a distortion of what the teachers actually are trying to accomplish.

Conceptions of Social Relations

In many urban classrooms there is a strict line of demarcation between students and teachers. In fact, some have likened urban schools to prisons with the students as inmates. However, culturally relevant teachers work to deliberately blur the borders between themselves and their students. The erasing of the borders is not acquiescence to a notion that children and adults are peers. Instead, it is an attempt to erase the distance that exists between and among teachers, students, parents, and the community. To an outside viewer this changed set of social relations might appear as if teachers are overstepping their legal authority. A teacher might speak specifically about a student and his parents. On the surface, this interaction may be interpreted as the teacher behaving inappropriately. However, what may lie beneath the surface is a carefully constructed set of social relations that the teacher has worked out with the student's parents and that allows for a degree of informality.

Additionally, culturally relevant teachers work to stretch the boundaries of the classroom so that they extend out into the community. Such teachers may attend students' church services and sporting events and secure personal goods and services from local merchants and business people to make sure that the latter are a presence in the community.

Conceptions of Knowledge

Culturally relevant teachers take as a given the notion that the curriculum is not working in the best interest of urban, poor children of color. Consequently, these teachers help students to develop counterknowledge that challenges the status quo. This subversive strategy is not likely to show up in an assessment because most such teachers are unlikely to share this strategy publicly. In the classrooms of culturally relevant teachers, knowledge is often very tentatively held because students are charged with the responsibility of deconstructing, reconstructing, and constructing knowledge (Shujaa, 1994). From what we have seen of the new teacher assessments, knowledge construction has been more narrowly defined than what the research on effective teachers in urban settings demonstrates.

What We Still Need to Know

Finally, I believe that there needs to be much more research done on pedagogy. Currently, we have naive and ill-formed notions of pedagogy. Unlike other areas of practice—medicine, law, business, theology—pedagogy lacks a sufficient knowledge foundation on which to base sound practice. The old adage, "those who can't, teach" is not so much a dig at teachers as it is emblematic of the low regard we as a society have for teaching. We believe that almost anyone can do it, and we allow almost anyone to do it. However, with growing numbers of poor students and students of color failing to benefit from schooling, we must begin to examine how and why pedagogy works. Ultimately, we must make a decision about whether there is any power in our pedagogy.

References

Au, K., & Jordan, C. (1981). Teaching reading to Hawaiian children: Finding a culturally appropriate solution. In H. Trueba, G. Guthrie, & K. Au (Eds.), *Culture and the bilingual classroom: Studies in classroom ethnography* (pp. 139–152). Rowley, MA: Newbury House.

Bacon, M. H. (1981, May). *High potential children from Ravenswood Elementary School District* (Follow-up study). Redwood City, CA: Sequoia Union High School District.

Brookover, W. (1985). Can we make schools effective for minority students? *The Journal of Negro Education, 54*, 257–268.

Brookover, W., Beady, C., Flood, P., Schweitzer, J., & Wisenbaker, J. (1979). *School social systems and student achievement: Schools can make a difference.* New York: Praeger.

Cazden, C. (1976). How knowledge about language helps the classroom teacher—or does it? A personal account. *Urban Review, 9*, 74–90.

Cazden, C. (1988). *Classroom discourse: The language of teaching and learning.* Portsmouth, NH: Heinemann.

Cazden, C., & Leggett, C. (1981). Culturally responsive education: Recommendations for achieving Lau remedies II. In H. Trueba, G. Guthrie, & K. Au (Eds.), *Culture and the bilingual classroom: Studies in classroom ethnography* (pp. 69–86). Rowley, MA: Newbury House.

Delpit, L. (1995). *Other people's children: Cultural conflict in the classroom.* New York: The New Press.

Edmonds, R. (1979). Effective schools for the urban poor. *Educational Leadership, 37*, 15–24.

Erickson, F., & Mohatt, G. (1982). Cultural organization and participation structures in two classrooms of Indian students. In G. Spindler (Ed.), *Doing the ethnography of schooling* (pp. 131–174). Prospect Heights, IL: Waveland Press.

Fine, M. (1986). Why urban adolescents drop into and out of high school. *Teachers College Record, 87*, 393–409.

Fordham, S. (1988). Racelessness as a factor in Black students' school success: Pragmatic strategy or pyrrhic victory? *Harvard Educational Review, 58*, 54–84.

Fordham, S., & Ogbu, J. (1986). Black students' school success: Coping with the burden of "acting white." *The Urban Review, 18*, 176–206.

Foster, M. (1995). African American teachers and culturally relevant pedagogy. In J. A. Banks & C. M. Banks (Eds.), *Handbook of research on multicultural education* (pp. 570–581). New York: Macmillan.

Garcia, E. (1988). Attributes of effective schools for language minority students. *Education and Urban Society, 20*, 387–398.

Grant, C. A. (1989). Urban teachers: Their new colleagues and curriculum. *Phi Delta Kappan, 70*, 764–770.

Haberman, M. (1995). *Star teachers of children in poverty.* West Lafayette, IN: Kappa Delta Pi.

Irvine, J. J. (1990). *Black students and school failure.* Westport, CT: Greenwood Press.

Jordan, C. (1985). Translating culture: From ethnographic information to educational program. *Anthropology and Education Quarterly, 16*, 105–123.

King, J. E. (1991). Unfinished business: Black student alienation and Black teachers' emancipatory pedagogy. In M. Foster (Ed.), *Readings on Equal Education Vol. 11* (pp. 245–271). New York: AMS.

King, J. E., & Mitchell, C. (1990). *Black mothers to sons: Juxtaposing African American literature with social practice.* New York: Peter Lang.

Kleinfeld, J. (1974). Effective teachers of Indian and Eskimo high school students. In J. Orvik & R. Barnhardt (Eds.), *Cultural influences in Alaska Native education.* Fairbanks: Center for Northern Educational Research, University of Alaska.

Ladson-Billings, G. (1994). *The dreamkeepers: Successful teaching for African American students.* San Francisco: Jossey Bass.

Ladson-Billings, G. (1995). Toward a theory of culturally relevant pedagogy. *American Educational Research Journal, 32*, 465–491.

Ladson-Billings, G., & Henry, A. (1991). Blurring the borders: Voices of African liberatory pedagogy. *Journal of Education, 172*, 72–88.

Lee, C. D. (1994). African centered pedagogy: Complexities and possibilities. In M. Shujaa (Ed.), *Too much schooling, too little education: A paradox of black life in white societies* (pp. 295–318). Trenton, NJ: Africa World Press.

Macias, J. (1987). The hidden curriculum of Papago teachers: American Indian strategies for mitigating cultural discontinuity in early schooling. In G. Spindler & L. Spindler (Eds.), *Interpretive ethnography at home and abroad* (pp. 363–380). Hillsdale, NJ: Lawrence Erlbaum Associates.

Mahiri, J. (1998). *Shooting for excellence: African American and youth culture in new century schools.* New York: Teachers College Press and NCTE.

Mohatt, G., & Erickson, F. (1981). Cultural differences in teaching styles in an Odawa school: A sociolinguistic approach. In H. Trueba, G. Guthrie, & K. Au (Eds.), *Culture and the bilingual classroom: Studies in classroom ethnography* (pp. 105–119). Rowley, MA: Newbury House.

Moll, L. (1988). Some key aspects in teaching Latino students. *Language Arts, 65*, 465–472.

Siddle-Walker, V. (1993). Caswell County Training School, 1933–1969: Relationships between community and school. *Harvard Educational Review, 63*, 161–182.

Singer, E. (1988). What is cultural congruence, and why are they saying such terrible things about it? (Occasional Paper). East Lansing, MI: Institute for Research on Teaching.

Spindler, G. (1988). *Doing the ethnography of schooling.* Prospect Heights, IL: Waveland Press.

Villegas, A. (1988). School failure and cultural mismatch: Another view. *The Urban Review, 20*, 253–265.

Vogt, L., Jordan, C., & Tharp, R. (1987). Explaining school failure, producing school success: Two cases. *Anthropology and Education Quarterly, 18*, 276–286.

Wilcox, K. (1988). Ethnography as a methodology and its applications to the study of schooling. In G. Spindler (Ed.), *Doing the ethnography of schooling* (pp. 457–488). Prospect Heights, IL: Waveland Press.

Learning Styles of American Indian/Alaska Native Students: A Review of Literature and Implications for Practice

Cornel Pewewardy

Research on learning styles indicates that if a teacher more closely connects teaching, curriculum, and activities with the learning styles of students, students will be more able to participate in learning. However, schools rarely address the learning styles of American Indian or Alaska Native students. As Pewewardy writes in his summary of the "Learning Styles of American Indian/Alaska Native Students," *Journal of American Indian Education* (vol. 41, no. 3, 2002), "Inappropriate and mismatched learning styles are common threads that weave in and out of the literature describing a large number of learners' inability to achieve in the traditional classroom." This selection describes the learning styles of American Indian students, and gives suggestions for approaches to teaching as well as classroom activities that better match those learning styles.

Cornel Pewewardy is Director and Associate Professor of Native American Studies at Portland State University. He is nationally recognized for his research on American Indian education, as well as on helping to develop self-determination policies within sovereign tribal nations. He was named the 2005 Scholars of Color Distinguished Scholar by the American Educational Research Association, and he was named 1992 National Indian Educator of the Year. Pewewardy is also a recording artist, having recorded CDs of Southern Plains Music, being named the 1997 Musician of the Year by the Wordcraft Circle of Native Writers and Storytellers.

Key Concept: learning styles of American Indian students

The purpose of this research was to review the literature on American Indian/Alaska Native learning modalities and cognitive styles in order to draw conclusions that serve as indicators as to how educators may provide instruction/learning opportunities that are compatible with American Indian/Alaska Natives students' learning styles.

Current Approaches and Findings Toward Understanding the Learning Styles of American Indian/Alaska Natives Students

Prior to the 1980s very little information about the learning styles of American Indian/Alaska Natives was documented. Nor was much attention paid as to how to address the needs of these students (Swisher, 1990). Currently, there are numerous ways in which one might approach the topic of learning styles. For the purpose of this article, the learning styles of American Indian/Alaska Native students are approached using the following classifications:

1. Field-Dependence/Field-Independence
2. Perceptual Strengths (Visual, Auditory, and Kinesthetic)
3. Reflectivity Versus Impulsivity
4. Classroom Management and Behavior
5. Role of the Family, Tribe, and Elders
6. Teacher/Pupil Relationships
7. Cooperation Versus Competition

Field-Dependence/Field-Independence

A review of the literature supports the argument that field-dependence or global processing is a learning style tendency among American Indian/Alaskan Native students.

Field-independence and field-dependence refer to how students learn, rather than what they learn. According to Witkin, Moore, Goodenough, and Cox (1977), the field (or one's surroundings) affects the learner's perceptions along a continuum between field-dependence and field-independence. For example, if a learner is field-dependent, he or she is unable to perceive elements or (him or herself) as separate from his or her environment. These learners are holistic or global learners. They begin with the whole picture and establish meaning only in relation to the whole. It is very difficult for the field-dependent student to discern important details from a confusing background. Generally, the field-dependent, global, right brain dominant is highly visual/spatial, integrative, relational, intuitive, and contextual (parts-and-whole-together). The learner's thinking is not linear or hierarchical. This learner is concerned with life and all its relationships. It is not unusual for these learners to listen to the views of others before making quick judgments. Authority figures are often looked to for guidance. In fact, field-dependence is likely to develop in cultures that are highly collective and family-oriented (Nuby, Ehle, & Thrower, 2001).

On the other hand, field-independent learners tend to be analytical, logical, and temporal (sequencing). They prefer to compete to gain individual recognition and are generally task-oriented. These learners often prefer classroom activity that involves abstract, impersonal work (Kinsella, 1995; Worthley, 1987). These learners can easily divide the whole into subcategories based on differences. They can see easily that material can be divided and subdivided into minute pieces and that those pieces add up to the whole. Field-independence often occurs in cultures in which personal autonomy and formal organization in the family are emphasized, as in the White culture (DuBray, 1985; Light & Martin, 1986; Stauss, 1993). And it is often true that in White classrooms information is frequently presented in an analytical, sequential manner. This places the field-dependent learner at a great disadvantage.

Perceptual Strengths: Visual, Auditory, and Kinesthetic

Findings support the view that American Indian/Alaska Native students are visual learners. Visual learners learn best when they are able to see the material they are expected to master. They tend to learn best when the teacher provides a myriad of visual learning opportunities such as graphs, films, demonstrations, and pictures. American Indian/Alaska Native students are taught by observing parents or elders (Red Horse, 1980). When skills are taught, parents or elders generally teach through demonstration. Children watch, and then imitate the skills. For example, the father, mother, or elder might teach the child a skill by modeling. Children are expected to watch, listen and then do. Therefore, many American Indian/Alaska Native students appear to perform best in classrooms with an emphasis on visualization, especially in mathematics.

Mathematics has always been used in situations where American Indian/Alaska Native students count, measure, design, locate, explain, trade, dance, and play. The art of beadwork encompasses all of these behaviors including dancing. Beadwork provides a hands-on demonstration of math in action and can be used as an effective vehicle for teaching mathematics.

Students who speak American Indian/Alaska Native languages should have a chance to learn mathematics terminology in their Native language and then to relate this knowledge to the English language mathematics vocabulary (Davison, 1992). Comparing and contrasting American Indian/Alaska Native mathematics teaches students lessons about the diversity among American Indian/Alaska Native cultures. Mathematics to many American Indian/Alaska Native students is related physically to one's being and religiously to one's soul. Mathematics connects one to his or her universe in many different ways by incorporating language, culture, and daily living practices (Lipka, 1994).

Reflectivity Versus Impulsivity

Research indicates that Native American/Alaska Native students tend to be reflective. Reflection is defined as the tendency to stop to consider options before responding, often resulting in greater accuracy in conceptualizing problems (Hollins, 1999). Conversely, being impulsive is the tendency to respond immediately, more fluently, yet inaccurate problem-solving often occurs. In other words, there is a difference in the time period in which the student contemplates before arriving at conclusions. For example, some students' conversations may have a longer "wait time" between responses. Learning may be enhanced by teachers "tuning in" to the students' rhythms of conversation and movement (MacIvor, 1999). A reflective student does not need immediate closure. Instead, she or he is more open-oriented, delaying decision-making until all evidence is collected before coming to a conclusion or acting in response to a situation. When posed with a question or problem, American Indian/Alaska Native students tend to be reflective learners, examining all sides of an issue, as well as possible implications and solutions related to the problems. Therefore, they are careful to make sure that the answer to a problem is known before responding. It is not uncommon, therefore, for American Indian/Alaska Native students to spend much more time watching and listening and less time talking than do White students (Gilliland, 1999). As Hilliard (2001) pointed out, reluctance to try to solve a problem may be associated with the fear of being shamed if one does not succeed, which may account for the seemingly passive behavior of the American Indian/Alaska Native student. Unfortunately, teachers may mistake this behavior as disinterest or lack of motivation.

Differences in home learning style and school learning style often become manifest when the American

Indian/Alaska Native child goes to school. In the typical White classroom, American Indian/Alaska Native children avoid unfamiliar ground, where trial and error or the inquiry method is employed (Lacy, 2002). Instead, children often begin school believing that a respectful attitude toward a task involves doing a task well (Porter, 1997). Performing an activity according to a recommended or correct form is as important as the purpose or the goal of the activity. If a task cannot be done well, there is no need to engage in the activity at all (Longstreet, 1978).

Classroom Management/Behavior

Studies indicate that people from different cultures attribute disciplinary problems to different causes and use different techniques to motivate students to behave in acceptable ways (McDade, 1993). Some cultural groups rely on the use of rewards and consequences; others do not (Radin, Williams, & Coggins, 1993). Research indicates that American Indian/Alaska Native worldviews and social behaviors are at odds with White values and behaviors.

Research also indicates that more culturally specific management routines are compatible with many American Indian/Alaska Native cultures, especially the Navajo, where ignoring misbehavior or lowering one's eyes, indirectly referring to the misdeed and praising honorable behavior works better than punishment (Bert & Bert, 1992). Navajo youth are unlikely to exhibit the same level and configuration of traditionalism due to the varying impact of mainstream society (Willeto, 1999). Clearly, the question of diversity in traditionalism warrants investigation in some tribal cultures.

Often American Indian/Alaska Native children respond more effectively if the teacher gives the student warnings of bad behavior couched in community terms like, "What would people say—they will laugh at you." Historically in schools, shame or embarrassment were common disciplinary tools with American Indian/Alaska Native children (Cleary & Peacock, 1998).

On the other hand, humor can be a useful teaching strategy when working with American Indian/Alaska Native learners of all ages. Humor is important in bringing Indian students together and reaffirming bonds of kinship (Herring, 1999). Laughter relieves stress and serves to reaffirm and enhance the sense of connectedness that comes from being part of the group (Garrett & Garrett, 1994). Nevertheless, teachers are cautioned to use humor very discreetly and to ensure tribal specificity (Taylor, 2001).

Tribal Role of the Family/Elders

Research indicates that the family, the elders, and the tribe play an important role in the teaching/learning process as related to the American Indian/Alaska Native student. Although the Indian family structure varies from tribe to tribe, some generalizations may be made. In particular, many American Indian/Alaska Native students see the family as an extension of themselves. Relatives like aunts, uncles, and grandparents who may live in separate households often make major contributions in raising children. This extended family concept may also include cousins and sometimes formal adoptees from outside the family unit. It is not unusual for children to stay in a variety of different households. This type of family structure provides a sense of belonging and security, which forms an interdependent system (Pewewardy, 1994). Status and rewards are often derived from adherence to tribal structure. The White teacher who sees the generic "American" family unit as primary often misunderstands the extended family concept of American Indian/Alaska Native students.

American Indian/Alaska Native students are taught to treat family members with respect, especially elders (Cornelius, 1999; Ross, 1996). Social acceptance and approval are sought from older members of the family. They are a source of wisdom and serve as teachers of traditions, customs, legends, and myths. Grandparents, especially, have symbolic leadership positions in family communities.

The tribe is of fundamental importance as related to cultural identity (Haynes Writer, 2001; Mihesuah, 1998; Weaver, 2001; Wildcat, 2001; Yellow Bird, 1995). Problems involving the formulation of an "Indian" identity may be great for many American Indian/Alaska Native students, with youngsters sometimes seeing themselves as primarily "Indian," and sometimes moving in the direction of White values (Garrett & Pichette, 2000). Peer pressure to conform to mainstream school norms causes many American Indian/Alaska Native students to adopt assimilationist values in schools, especially for those students who attend public schools (Pewewardy & Willower, 1993).

Although it is impossible to describe a common set of cultural values that encompass all tribal groups, most share common values of noninterference, time-orientation, sharing, cooperation, coexistence with nature, and extended family structure (Garrett & Wilbur, 1999; Yellow Bird, 2001). For students living on reservations, relationships and tribal affiliation are culturally strong and in many ways quite different from their non-Indian peers or even American Indian/Alaska Native students living in urban areas (Lobo & Peters, 2001). Social stratification and honors are obtained by maintaining conformity to tribal norms. Traditionally the tribe, through the extended-family structure, is responsible for the education of all children (Pewewardy, 1994).

The tendency to place the family, tribe, and elders in such high esteem is very much in contrast with European American culture (Deloria, 2001). Instead of focusing on collectivism, the White culture is highly individualistic, with an emphasis on capitalism, youth, and self (Weenie, 2000). This may very well present a problem in the school setting. American Indian/Alaska Native students have special needs that warrant a teacher's cultural understanding. Differences in language, approaches to learning, cherished cultural values, and familial traditions present special challenges that teachers need to consider in designing instruction and assessment (Lipson & Wixson, 1997).

Teacher/Pupil Relationships

Findings indicate that the teacher of the American Indian/Alaska Native student plays a tremendous role in the teaching and learning process. His or her teaching style or method can have a significant effect on whether students learn or fail. It is apparent that many teachers do not have an understanding of the degree to which culture affects learning styles (Swisher & Dehyle, 1989). Many are not able to identify the learning style differences and to employ culturally responsive techniques to address the needs of culturally different populations. Often teachers view differences in approach to learning as problems inherent in the students themselves, rather than as a lack of understanding by the teacher (Nuby, Ehle, & Thrower, 2001). Unfortunately, many teachers ignore culture and its impact on learning both in "content" and "style," rather than devising methods and techniques through which culturally diverse individuals approach problem-solving.

American Indian/Alaska Native students often encounter difficulties in school because their culturally accepted ways of displaying competencies differ from those expected by the teacher in typical White schools (Ward, 1993). In essence two contrasting learning styles are involved. Traditional American Indian/Alaska Native learning focuses on process over product, legends, and stories as traditional teaching paradigms, knowledge obtained from self, and cognitive development through problem-solving techniques (Tafoya, 1989). This concept is very different than what is expected in the typical White classroom.

Matching teaching styles with learning styles is important for maximizing the learning of Native American/ Alaska Native students. Inappropriate and mismatched learning styles are common threads that weave in out of the literature describing a large number of learners' inability to achieve in the traditional classroom (Shortman, 1990). In fact, two contrasting learning styles are often involved in the education of Native American/Alaska Native students—that of the school and that of the community (Archibald, 1988).

Cooperation Versus Competition

Research indicates that American Indian/Alaska Native students tend to favor cooperation over competition. The typical American Indian/Alaska Native student lives in a world of people. To them, people are all important. Possessions are of value mainly because they can be shared. In contrast to White culture, most students do not equate the accumulation of property as a measure of a person's worth or social status. One's worth is based on the ability and willingness to share. One who has too many personal possessions is suspect. The thought is that getting rich may not be possible or even desirable, especially if one looks after the needs of others.

American Indian/Alaska Native students prefer harmony, unity, and a basic oneness. There is security in being a member of the group rather than being singled out. Students do not want to be shown to be either above or below the status of others. Competition does not produce motivation. American Indian/Alaska Native students often feel "put on the spot" or ashamed if the teacher points out their superior work to the class. They may find it necessary to quit doing good work to regain their place in the group.

On the other hand, many American Indian/Alaska Native students prefer cooperative learning strategies (Cajete, 1999). They find activities enjoyable that bring them together with friends or acquaintances in shared group activities (Ward, 1993). This holds particularly true for athletic events (Ager, 1976; Mills, 1999; Nuby, 1995; Oxendine, 1988; Swisher & Deyhle, 1989). Competition is unfair and situations are avoided if one student is made to look better than another does. As Swisher and Deyhle (1989) pointed out, Indian children hesitate to engage in an individual performance before the public gaze, especially where they sense competitive assessment against their peers and equally do not wish to demonstrate by their individual superiority the inferiority of their peers. In addition, to brag about one's self and personal abilities are, for most tribes, considered to be most ill mannered (Tafoya, 1989). However, as Adams (1995), Mills (1999), and Oxendine (1988) pointed out, in team sports, where performance is socially defined as benefiting the group, American Indian/Alaska Native students can become excellent competitors.

Conclusion

In order to provide a viable educational environment for American Indian/Alaska Native students, teachers should try to identify the learning styles of their students, match their teaching styles to students' learning styles for difficult tasks (Lippitt, 1993), and broaden "deficit thinking" learning styles through easier tasks and drills. All students, regardless of ethnicity, stand to benefit from an understanding of different cultural values. The implementation of programs targeted toward the learning styles of students of varying cultures is consistent with American values, such as tolerance of difference and equality for all. An understanding of cultural values of others such as respect for elders that characterizes the American Indian/Alaska Native cultures is likely to become increasingly desirable as the percentage of elderly Americans increases in the coming years. Similarly, learning the American Indian/Alaska Native value of associating and living in harmony with nature may become essential as we run out of natural resources. As we become an increasingly diverse society, we must learn to understand and know how to work with other cultures that differ from our own.

Last, but certainly not least, when differences in learning styles are addressed, the American Indian/Alaska Native student will become motivated and encouraged to succeed. Personalization of educational programs make learning more meaningful to all involved. Ultimately, American Indian/Alaska Native students must believe that there is respect for their cultural backgrounds. Without this knowledge, the results can be disastrous. "Many educational traditions and practices have been lost or only remain in the memories of survivors of the indigenous peoples' holocaust" (Spring, 2000, p. xi). If Americans are to embrace diversity, the conscious and unconscious expressions of racism within our society must be identified and done away with (Pine & Hilliard, 1990). There is no choice. Schools can no longer afford to cast themselves as the guardians of the status quo, of some idealistic view of mainstream America that ignores the diversity of a multicultural, multiracial, and multitribal society.

References

Adams, D. W. (1995). *Education for extinction: American Indians and the boarding school experience, 1875–1928*. Lawrence, KS: University Press of Kansas.

Ager, L. P. (1976). The reflection of cultural values in Eskimo children's games. In D. Lancy & A. Tindall (Eds.), *The anthropological study of play: Problems and prospects* (pp. 79–86). Cornwall, NY: Leisure Press.

Archibald, J. (1988). *Ourselves, our knowledge, establishing pathways to excellence in Indian education implementation: Challenges and solutions*. Vancouver, BC: University of British Columbia, Faculty of Education, Mokakit Indian Education Research Association. (ERIC Document Reproduction Service No. ED 336 217)

Bert, C. R., & Bert, M. (1992). *The Native American: An exceptionality in education and counseling*. Miami, FL: Independent Native American Development Corp. (ERIC Document Reproduction Service No. ED 351 168)

Cajete, G. A. (1999). The Native American learner and bicultural science education. In K. G. Swisher & J. W. Tippeconnic III (Eds.), *Next steps: Research and practice to advance Indian education* (pp. 133–160). Charleston, WV: ERIC Clearinghouse and Rural Education and Small Schools.

Cleary, L. M., & Peacock, T. D. (1998). *Collected wisdom: American Indian education*. Boston: Allyn and Bacon.

Cornelius, C. (1999). *Iroquois corn in a culture-based curriculum: A framework for respectfully teaching about cultures*. Albany, NY: State University of New York Press.

Davison, D.M. (1992). Mathematics. In J. Reyhner (Ed.), *Teaching American Indian students* (pp. 241–250). Norman, OK: University of Oklahoma Press.

Deloria, V., Jr. (2001). The perpetual education report. In V. Deloria, Jr. & D. R. Wildcat (Eds.), *Power and place: Indian education in America* (pp. 151–161). Golden, CO: Fulcrum Resources.

DuBray, W. H. (1985). American Indian values: Critical factor in casework. *Journal of Contemporary Social Work, 66*(1), 30–37.

Garrett, J. T., & Garrett, M. W. (1994). The path of good medicine: Understanding and counseling Native American Indians. *Journal of Multicultural Counseling and Development, 22*(3), 134–144.

Garrett, M. T., & Pichette, E. F. (2000). Red as an apple: Native American acculturation and counseling with or without reservation. *Journal of Counseling & Development, 78*(1), 3–13.

Garrett, M. T., & Wilbur, M. P. (1999). Does the worm live in the ground? Reflections on Native American spirituality. *Journal of Multicultural Counseling and Development, 27*(4), 193–206.

Gilliland, H. (1999). *Teaching the Native American*. Dubuque, IA: Kendall Hunt.

Haynes Writer, J. (2001). Identifying the identified: The need for critical exploration of Native American identity within educational contexts. *Action in Teacher Education, 22*(4), 40–47.

Herring, R. D. (1999). *Counseling with Native American Indians and Alaska Natives: Strategies for helping professionals*. Thousands Oaks, CA: Sage Publications.

Hilliard, A. G. (2001). Race, identity, hegemony, and education: What do we need to know now? In W. H. Watkins, J. H. Lewis, & V. Chou (Eds.), *Race and education: The roles of history and society in educating African American students* (pp. 7–33). Boston: Allyn and Bacon.

Hollins, E. R. (1999). Becoming a reflective practitioner. In E. R. Hollins & E. I. Oliver (Eds.), *Pathways to success in school: Culturally responsive teaching* (pp. 11–28). Mahwah, NJ: Lawrence Erlbaum Associates.

Kinsella, K. (1995). Understanding and empowering diverse learners in the ESL classroom. In J. Reid (Ed.), *Learning styles in the ESL/EFL classroom* (pp. 170–194). Boston, MA: Hienle & Heinle.

Lacy, L. E. (2002). *Creative planning resource for interconnected teaching and learning*. New York: Peter Lang.

Light, H. K., & Martin, R. E. (1986). American Indian families. *Journal of American Indian Education, 26*(1), 1–5.

Lippitt, L. (1993). *Integrating teaching styles with students' learning styles*. Washington, DC: Department of Education. (ERIC Document Reproduction Service No. ED 406 068)

Lipson, M. Y., & Wixson, K. K. (1997). *Assessment and instruction of reading and writing disability: An interactive approach* (2nd ed.). New York: Longman.

Lobo, S., & Peters, K. (2001). *American Indians and the urban experience*. Walnut Creek, CA: Altamira Press.

Longstreet, W. S. (1978). *Aspects of ethnicity: Understanding differences in pluralistic classrooms*. New York: Teachers College Press.

MacIvor, M. (1999). Redefining science education for aboriginal students. In M. Battiste & J. Barman (Eds.), *First Nations' education in Canada: The circle unfolds* (pp. 73–98). Vancouver, BC: University of British Columbia Press.

McDade, K. (1993). Multi-cultural perspectives on parenting. *Family Perspective, 27*(4), 323–346.

Mihesuah, D. A. (1998). American Indian identities: Issues of individual choices and development. *American Indian Culture and Research Journal, 22*(2), 193–226.

Mills, B. (1999). *Wokini: A Lakota journey to happiness and self-understanding*. Carlsbad, CA: Hay House.

Nuby, J. F. (1995). *Learning styles: A comparative analysis of the learning styles of Native American and African American secondary students*. Unpublished doctoral dissertation, *Tuscaloosa, AL, University of Alabama.*

Nuby, J. F., Ehle, M. A., & Thrower, E. (2001). Culturally responsive teaching as related to the learning styles of Native American students. In J. Nyowe & S. Abadullah (Eds.), *Multicultural education: Diverse perspectives* (pp. 231–271). Victoria, BC: Trafford Publishing Company.

Oxendine, J. B. (1988). *American Indian sports heritage.* Champaigne, IL: Human Kinetics Books.

Pewewardy, C. D. (1994). Culturally responsible pedagogy in action: An American Indian magnet school. In E. R. Hollins, J. E. King, & W. C. Hayman (Eds.), *Teaching diverse populations: Formulating a knowledge base* (pp. 77–92). Albany, NY: State University of New York Press.

Pewewardy, C. D. (1999). Culturally responsive teaching for American Indian students. In E. R. Hollins & E. I. Oliver (Eds.), *Pathways to success in school: Culturally responsive teaching* (pp. 85–100). Mahwah, NJ: Lawrence Erlbaum Associates.

Pewewardy, C. D., & Willower, D. J. (1993). Perceptions of American Indian high school students in public schools. *Equity and Excellence in Education, 26*(1), 52–55.

Pine, G. J., & Hilliard, A. G., III. (1990). Rx for racism: Imperatives for America's schools. *Phi Delta Kappan, 71*(8), 593–600.

Radin, N., Williams, E., & Coggins, K. (1993). Paternal involvement in childrearing and the school performance of Native American children: An exploratory study. *Family Perspective, 27*(4), 375–391.

Red Horse, J. (1980). Family structure and value orientation in American Indians. *Social Casework, 68*(10), 462–467.

Ross, R. (1996). *Returning to the teachings: Exploring aboriginal justice.* New York: Penguin Books.

Shortman, P. V. (1990). Whole brain learning, learning styles and implications on teacher education. In M. M. Dupuis & E. R. Fagan (Eds.), *Teacher education: Reflection and change* (pp. 66–82). (ERIC Document Reproduction Service No. ED 330 647)

Spring, J. (2000). From the series editor. In Maenette Kape'ahiokalani Padeken Ah Nee-Benham & Joanne Elizabeth Cooper (Eds.), *Indigenous educational models for contemporary practice* (pp. xi–xiii). Mahway, NJ: Lawrence Erlbaum Associates.

Stauss, J. H. (1993). Reframing and refocusing American Indian family strengths. *Family Perspective, 27*(4), 311–321.

Swisher, K. G. (1990). Cooperative learning and the education of American Indian/Alaska Native students: A review of the literature and suggestions for implementation. *Journal of American Indian Education, 29*(2), 36–43.

Swisher, K. G., & Dehyle, D. (1989, Special Issue). The styles of learning are different, but the teaching is just the same: Suggestions for teachers of American Indian youth. *Journal of American Indian Education,* 1–14.

Tafoya, T. (1989, Special Issue). Coyote's eyes: Native cognition styles. *Journal of American Indian Education,* 29–42.

Taylor, D. H. (2001). Laughing till your face is red. *Red Ink, 9.2*(10.1), 80–84.

Ward, C. J. (1993). Explaining gender differences in Native American high school dropout rates: A case study of Northern Cheyenne schooling patterns. *Family Perspective, 27*(4), 415–444.

Weaver, H. N. (2001). Indigenous identity: What is it, and who really has it? *American Indian Quarterly, 25*(2), 240–255.

Weenie, A. (2000). Post-colonial recovering and healing. In J. Reyhner, J. Martin, L. Lockard, & W. S. Gilbert (Eds.), *Learn in beauty: Indigenous education for a new century* (pp. 65–70). Flagstaff, AZ: Northern Arizona University, Center for Excellence in Education.

Wildcat, D. R. (2001). Prelude to a dialogue. In V. Deloria, Jr., & D. Wildcat (Eds.), *Power and place: Indian education in America* (p. vii). Golden, CO: Fulcrum Resources.

Willeto, A. A. A. (1999). Navajo culture and family influences on academic success: Traditionalism is not a significant predictor of achievement among young Navajos. *Journal of American Indian Education, 38*(2), 1–24.

Witkin, H. A., Moore, C. A., Goodenough, D. R., & Cox, P. W. (1977). Field dependent and field independent cognitive styles and their educational implications. *Review of Educational Research, 47*(1), 1–64.

Worthley, K. M. E. (1987). *Learning style factors of field dependence/field independence and problem solving strategies of Hmong refugee students.* Unpublished master's thesis, University of Wisconsin, Stout, Wisconsin.

Yellow Bird, M. (1995). Spirituality in First Nations storytelling: A Sahnish-Hidatsa approach to narrative. Reflections: Narratives of professional helping. *A Journal for the Helping Professions, 1*(4), 65–72.

Yellow Bird, M. (2001). Critical values and First Nations peoples. In R. Fong & S. Furuto (Eds.), *Cultural competent social work: Interventions* (pp. 61–74). Boston: Allyn and Bacon.

Educational Issues and Effective Practices for Hispanic Students

Hersh C. Waxman, Yolanda N. Padrón, and Andres García

Hersh C. Waxman is Director of the State of Texas Education Research Center and Professor of Teaching, Learning, and Culture at Texas A&M University. Yolanda N. Padrón is Professor of Educational Psychology at Texas A&M University, after previously serving as Co-Director of the Center for Research on Education, Diversity and Excellence at the University of Houston. Waxman and Padrón have collaborated on a number of publications on Latino and Hispanic Education, Bilingual Education, and Poverty. Andres García was at the University of Houston when the following selection was written.

Waxman, Padrón, and García begin the following selection on "Educational Issues and Effective Practices for Hispanic Students," in Susan J. Paik and Herbert J. Walberg, *Narrowing the Achievement Gap: Strategies for Educating Latino, Black, and Asian Students* (Springer, 2007), with a description of the educational status of Hispanic students in the United States. They lay out statistics that identify underachievement and low educational attainment, while pointing out the concentrated poverty experienced by many Hispanic students who underachieve. The authors list and explain the factors that impede academic achievement of Hispanic students, and then describe a number of factors associated with the educational success of Hispanic students. Waxman, Padrón, and García describe a set of effective teaching practices and overall effective school factors, including both school and parent and community involvement, that contribute to Hispanic student success.

Key Concept: effective educational practices for Hispanic students

The Educational Status of Hispanic Students in the United States

Over the past 20 years, the enrollment of Hispanics in public elementary schools has dramatically increased (over 150%), compared to 20% for African American students and 10% for White students (U.S. Department of Education, 2000). Recent projections are that the Hispanic population and the numbers of preschool, school-age, and college-age populations will continue to dramatically increase (Chapa & De La Rosa, 2004).

The U.S. Hispanic population is quite diverse, representing various countries of origin, levels of primary language proficiency, prior educational experience, and socioeconomic status (García, 2001b). According to the 2000 U.S. Census, 59% of Hispanics were of Mexican origin, 10% were of Puerto Rican origin, and 4% were of Cuban origin. The remaining 28% were designated as "other" Hispanics. Nearly two-thirds (65%) of

all Hispanics live in central cities of metropolitan areas, compared to non-Hispanic Whites (21%) (USDE, 2000). Hispanics constitute about 75% of all students enrolled in programs for limited English proficient students (LEPs), including bilingual education and English as second language (ESL) programs.

In terms of educational achievement, the National Assessment of Educational Progress (NAEP) scores for 17-year-old Hispanic students are well below that of their White peers in mathematics, reading, and science. The dropout rates for Hispanic students are also much higher than other ethnic groups. In 2000, 28% of all Hispanic 16- through 24-year-olds were dropouts (1.4 million)—more than double the dropout rate for African Americans (13%) and more than three times the rate for Whites (7%). Some researchers feel the attrition scores for Hispanics still are undercounted and fail to reveal an accurate picture of the problem (Montecel, Cortez, & Cortez, 2004). Montecel et al. (2004) used the U.S. Census Bureau data to determine that 43% of the Hispanic population did not receive a diploma and 26% dropped out before the ninth grade. Additionally, within the Hispanic student population, immigrants have a 44% dropout rate compared to first generation students (USDE, 2000). Only 64% of Hispanic kindergartners graduate from high school. Twenty-two percent enroll in college; of that 22%, only 10% complete 4 years of college (USDE, 2000).

In addition to the problems of underachievement and low educational attainment, many Hispanic students live in households and communities that experience high and sustained poverty. Thirty-four percent of Hispanic children live in single parent or no parent homes (USDE, 2000). Hispanic children are more than three times as likely to experience poverty than white students (Liagas & Snyder, 2003). Hispanic students also attend schools with more than twice as many poor classmates as those attended by White students (46% vs. 19%). Furthermore, Hispanic students primarily reside in urban cities and are immersed in neighborhoods of concentrated poverty where the most serious educational problems exist. Schools with high concentrations of poor students, for example, tend to be poorly maintained, structurally unsound, fiscally under funded, and staffed with large numbers of uncertified teachers (Garcia, 2001b). Additionally, many Hispanic students are concentrated in campuses where they make up the majority of the student body. In fact, 38% of Hispanic students attend campuses where minority students make up 90% of the student body.

Educational Factors Impacting the Underachievement of Hispanic Students

Need for Qualified Teachers

Estimates have indicated that nearly half of the teachers assigned to teach Hispanic ELLs have not received any preparation specific to the education of ELLs. Presently, about 42% of all public school teachers in the US have at least one ELL student in their class, but less than 3% of these teachers are certified ESL or bilingual teachers (NCES, 2003). In other words, the number of teachers prepared to teach Hispanic ELLs falls far short of the tremendous need for such teachers.

There also have been a number of recent studies that have documented shortcomings in professional development opportunities targeted for teachers of Hispanic ELLs. In a profile showing the quality of our nation's teachers, for example, the National Center for Education Statistics found that most teachers of ELLs or other culturally diverse students did not feel that they were well prepared to meet the needs of their students (Lewis et al., 1999). In another national survey of classroom teachers, 57% of all teachers responded that they either "very much needed" or "somewhat needed" more information on helping students with limited English proficiency achieve to high standards (Alexander, Heaviside, & Farris, 1999). In a large-scale study of over 5,000 teachers in California, Gándara, Maxwell-Jolly, and Driscoll (2005) found that teachers had few professional development opportunities targeted to help them work effectively with ELLs. They also found that many teachers faced barriers communicating with their students and students' parents and there was a lack of appropriate materials and resources to meet their students' needs.

Inappropriate Teaching Practices

Another critical problem related to the underachievement of Hispanic students has to do with current teaching practices. The most common instructional approach found in schools that serve Hispanic students is the direct instructional model, where teachers typically teach to the whole class at the same time and control all of the classroom discussion and decision-making (Waxman & Padrón, 2002). This teacher-directed instructional model emphasizes lecture, drill and practice, remediation, and student seatwork, consisting mainly of worksheets. These instructional practices constitute a "pedagogy of poverty" because they focus on low-level skills and passive instruction (Haberman, 1991; Waxman, Padrón, & Arnold, 2001).

Several studies have examined classroom instruction for Hispanic students and found that this "pedagogy of poverty" orientation exists in many classrooms with Hispanics, ELLs, and other minority students (Padrón & Waxman, 1993; Waxman, Huang, & Padrón, 1995). In a large-scale study examining the classroom instruction of 90 teachers from 16 inner-city middle schools serving predominantly Hispanic students, Waxman et al. (1995) found that students were typically involved in whole-class instruction (not interacting with either their teacher or other students). About two-thirds of the time, for example, students were not involved in verbal interaction with either their teacher or other students. There were very few small group activities and very few interactions with other students. Students rarely selected their own instructional activities, and were generally very passive in the classroom, often just watching or listening to the teacher, even though they were found to be on task about 94% of the time.

In another study examining mathematics and science instruction in inner-city middle-school classrooms serving Hispanic students, Padrón and Waxman (1993) found that questions about complex issues were not raised by any of the mathematics or science teachers. Furthermore, teachers seldom (4% of the time) posed open-ended questions for students in science classes; they never posed these questions in the mathematics classes.

The results of these and other studies have illustrated that classroom instruction in schools serving predominantly Hispanic students often tends to be whole-class instruction with students working in teacher-assigned and generated activities, generally in a passive manner (i.e., watching or listening). In these classrooms, teachers also spend more time explaining things to students rather than questioning, cueing, or prompting students to respond. Teachers were not frequently observed encouraging extended student responses or encouraging students to help themselves or help each other.

At-Risk School Environments

The term "at-risk school environment" describes these phenomena and suggests that the school rather than the individual student should be considered at risk. Waxman (1992) identified several characteristics of an "at-risk environment" that includes: (a) alienation experienced by students and teachers, (b) low standards and low quality of education, (c) low expectations for students, (d) high noncompletion rates for students, (e) classroom practices that are unresponsive to students, (f) high truancy and disciplinary problems, and (g) inadequate preparation of students for the future. Valenzuela (1999), for example, found that many Hispanic students go through a subtractive schooling process that takes away their cultural identity and self-worth. For Hispanic students, these conditions as well as attending poorly maintained schools and having under-qualified teachers places them in an at-risk school environment.

Factors Associated with the Educational Success of Hispanic Students

Effective Teaching Practices for Hispanic Students

Culturally responsive teaching. Culturally responsive teaching emphasizes the everyday concerns of students, such as critical family and community issues, and tries to incorporate these concerns into the curriculum. Culturally responsive instruction helps students prepare themselves for meaningful social roles in their community and larger society by emphasizing both social and academic responsibility. Furthermore, it addresses the promotion of racial, ethnic, and linguistic equality as well as the appreciation of diversity (Boyer, 1993). Culturally responsive instruction: (a) improves the acquisition and retention of new knowledge by working from students' existing knowledge base, (b) improves self-confidence and self-esteem by emphasizing existing knowledge, (c) increases the transfer of school-taught knowledge to

real-life situations, and (d) exposes students to knowledge about other individuals or cultural groups (Rivera & Zehler, 1991). When teachers develop learning activities based on familiar concepts, they help facilitate literacy and content learning and help Hispanic students feel more comfortable and confident with their work (Peregoy & Boyle, 2000).

Cooperative learning. McLaughlin and McLeod (1996) described cooperative learning as an effective instructional approach that stimulates learning and helps students come to complex understandings by discussing and defending their ideas with others. One commonly accepted definition of cooperative learning is "the instructional use of small groups so that students work together to maximize their own and each other's learning" (Johnson & Johnson, 1991, p. 292). Instead of lecturing and transmitting material, teachers facilitate the learning process by encouraging cooperation among students (Bejarano, 1987). This teaching practice is student-centered and creates interdependence among students and the teacher (Rivera & Zehler, 1991).

As an instructional practice, cooperative grouping impacts Hispanic students in several different ways. Cooperative grouping: (a) provides opportunities for students to communicate with each other, (b) enhances instructional conversations, (c) decreases anxiety, (d) develops social, academic, and communication skills, (e) enhances self-confidence and self-esteem through individual contributions and achievement of group goals, (f) improves individual and group relations by learning to clarify, assist, and challenge each other's ideas, and (g) develops proficiency in English by providing students with rich language experiences that integrate speaking, listening, reading, and writing (Calderón, 1991; Christian, 1995; Rivera & Zehler, 1991). Furthermore, cooperative learning activities provide Hispanic students with "the skills that are necessary to function in real-life situations, such as the utilization of context for meaning, the seeking of support from others, and the comparing of nonverbal and verbal cues" (Alcala, 2000, p. 4).

Instructional conversation. Instructional conversation is a teaching practice that provides students with opportunities for extended dialogue in areas that have educational value as well as relevance for students (August & Hakuta, 1998). The instructional conversation is an extended discourse between the teacher and students. It should be initiated by students in order to develop their language and complex thinking skills, and to guide them in their learning process (Tharp, 1995).

August and Hakuta's (1998) comprehensive review of research found that effective teachers of Hispanic students provide students with opportunities for extended dialogue. Rather than avoiding discussion during instruction because students may not have the appropriate language proficiency skills, instructional conversations emphasize dialogue with teachers and classmates

(Durán, Dugan, & Weffer, 1997). Thus, one of the major benefits of the use of instructional conversation for students who are learning English is to provide them with the opportunity for extended discourse, an important activity of second language learning (Christian, 1995).

Cognitively guided instruction. Cognitively guided instruction emphasizes the development of learning strategies that foster students' metacognitive development by the direct teaching and modeling of cognitive learning strategies. In addition, it teaches techniques and approaches that foster students' metacognition and cognitive monitoring of their own learning (Padrón & Knight, 1989; Waxman, Padrón, & Knight, 1991). From an instructional perspective, this approach emphasizes the need for teachers to focus on students' psychological processing as well as what is taught and how it is presented. This instructional approach can be very beneficial for Hispanic students who are not doing well in school because the effective use of cognitive strategies may help to eliminate individual barriers to academic success.

One example of cognitively guided instruction is reciprocal teaching, a procedure where students are instructed in four specific comprehension-monitoring strategies: (a) summarizing, (b) self-questioning, (c) clarifying, and (d) predicting. Studies on reciprocal teaching have found that these cognitive strategies can successfully be taught to Hispanic students and that the use of these strategies increases reading achievement (Padrón, 1992, 1993). Another example of cognitively guided instruction is Chamot and O'Malley's (1987) instructional program for LEP students that focuses specifically on strategy instruction. They found that when cognitive learning strategies are modeled for the student and opportunities to practice the strategy presented, learning outcomes improved.

Technology-enriched instruction. Several studies and reviews of research have found that technology-based instruction is effective for Hispanic students (Cummins & Sayers 1990; Padrón & Waxman, 1996). Web-based picture libraries, for example, can promote Hispanic students' comprehension in content-area classrooms (e.g., science and mathematics) (Smolkin, 2000). Digitized books are now available and allow Hispanic students to request pronunciations of unknown words, request translations of sections, and ask questions (Jiménez & Barrera, 2000). Furthermore, some types of technology (e.g., multimedia) are effective for Hispanic students because they help students connect learning in the classroom to real-life situations, thereby creating a meaningful context for teaching and learning (Means & Olson, 1994). In addition, multimedia technology can be especially helpful for Hispanic students because it can facilitate auditory skill development by integrating visual presentations with sound and animation (Bermúdez & Palumbo, 1994).

In summary, all of these teaching practices incorporate more active student learning and change the teachers' role. Instead of delivering knowledge, the teacher's role is to facilitate learning (Padrón & Waxman, 1999). Glickman

(1998) refers to this approach as "democratic pedagogy," describing it as instruction that "respects the students' own desire to know, to discuss, to problem solve, and to explore individually and with others, rather than learning that is dictated, determined, and answered by the teacher" (p. 52). These student-centered instructional practices represent a model of classroom instruction that has not been very common for Hispanic students and/or Hispanic ELLs.

Effective School Factors for Hispanic Students

Valuing Student's Needs and Culture. Many of the studies on effective schools serving predominantly Hispanic students recognize that their students have unique needs that require more personal attention from teachers. Consequently, schools developed clusters of teachers that work with a particular group of students who are at risk of academic failure (Ancess, 2003; Minicucci et al., 1995). Making home visits, providing parent education, and distributing free school supplies are some of the ways that schools pay personal attention to students. Effective schools serving predominantly Hispanic students also value the students' culture, include it in the academic curriculum, and allow students to develop their own ethnic identity.

Effective Instructional Practices. Another important characteristic found in effective schools serving predominantly Hispanic students is that they provide a number of different instructional practices. A number of effective schools studies have found that the most productive instructional strategy is providing language support in the students' first language (L1) (Gonzalez, Huerta-Macias, & Tinajero, 2001; Miramontes, Nadeau, & Commins, 1997; Mora, 2000; Thomas & Collier, 1997, 2001). According to Thomas and Collier (2001), the academic achievement gap can almost be completely eliminated with instruction in both L1 and L2. English as a Second Language (ESL) instructional programs were also found to be somewhat effective in improving the academic performance of Hispanic ELLs (Miramontes et al., 1997; Thomas & Collier, 2001). Other instructional practices prevalent in effective schools were the use of collaboration, student-centered instruction, incorporating individual learning styles, providing more teacher support and classroom order, and having more instructional interactions with students.

Teachers' professional development. One very important component of effective schools is a collaborative relationship between teachers (Ancess, 2003; Lopez, Scribner, & Mahitivanichcha, 2001; Short, 1994). The teachers in effective schools have been found to work together on curriculum, teaching practices, and other aspects of the school's functioning (Ancess, 2003; Lucas, Henze, & Donato, 1990; Mora, 2000). An important feature of this professional development is that it is ongoing, as well as focused on students' learning (Ancess, 2003; Mora, 2000). Not only does the professional development focus on students' learning needs, but it also emphasizes the teaching skills and practices that serve the students (August & Hakuta, 1998; Lucas, et al., 1990; Mora, 2000; Thomas & Collier, 1997; Waxman & Huang, 1994). Many teachers report that they need long-term professional development in order to: (a) use new methods of classroom instruction (e.g., cooperative grouping), (b) integrate educational technology in the subject they teach, and (c) address the needs of ELLs and other students from diverse cultural backgrounds (Lewis et al., 1999). Classroom teachers desire more: (a) information related to the teaching of Hispanic students, (b) time for training and planning, and (c) opportunities to collaborate and learn from other teachers (Téllez & Waxman, 2006).

Parent and community involvement. Parent and community involvement has been found to be an important component in numerous studies of effective schools for Hispanic students. The effective schools in these studies found ways to actively involve parents in their children's schooling. Furthermore, parent participation was found to be facilitated by empowering parents and other community members to get involved and to be actively engaged in student learning.

Student assessment. The student assessment component of research on effective schools for Hispanic students has two areas of use: (a) program and (b) student. At the program level, effective schools routinely use academic assessments of their students to measure improvements in students' learning as a means for program evaluation. This program level evaluation is then directly linked to teaching practice and professional development (August & Hakuta, 1998). At the student level, assessment is used to monitor individual student progress; however, all three of these studies have different points to make about individual student assessment. Miramontes et al. (1997), for example, found that assessments provide valuable information on students' language proficiency as well as development in L1 and/or L2 in conjunction with academic progress. Reyes, Scribner, & Scribner (1999) found that effective schools serving predominantly Hispanic students used assessment as a way to motivate students to succeed as well as a way to map out individualized learning procedures for students.

School Leadership. Effective school leadership for schools serving predominantly Hispanic students typically includes a self or shared governance structure (Ancess, 2003; Minicucci et al., 1995; Reyes et al., 1999). These studies found that the school community, parents, teachers, and other stakeholders have decision-making responsibility and this shared-decision-making process is linked to the common goal of student success.

The role of the principal in the governance of these effective schools is really that of a supporter (August & Hakuta, 1998; Gonzalez et al., 2001; Maden, 2001; Reyes et al., 1999). Ancess (2003) explains that the principal acts as a guide to the school through changes and is a stabilizing force for the school community so that there is a certain amount of safety in taking risks for school improvement. Gonzalez et al., (2001) describes that the principal plays a pivotal role in student success by focusing on continuous improvement. According to August and Hakuta (1998), not only do these principals support the common vision and shared governance structures, but more specifically they support Hispanic students. Also, Maden (2001) found that a fundamental aspect of school leadership is the hiring, developing, supporting and maintaining of teachers.

School culture and expectations. This final characteristic of effective schools for Hispanic students, school culture and expectations, encompasses three aspects: (a) a caring school climate, (b) a focus on learning, and (c) high expectations. Many studies found that effective schools have caring relationships that are a pervasive part of the school culture (Ancess, 2003; Carter & Chatfield, 1986; Maden, 2001; Waxman & Huang, 1997). The next factor for success in the school culture is the focus on learning. Carter and Chatfield (1986), for example, found that effective schools honored the right to learn through a safe and orderly learning environment. Other studies found that the school faculty and staff held beliefs that education is empowering and thus they were dedicated to empowering Hispanic students through academic achievement (Lucas et al., 1990). The final aspect of school culture and expectations is high expectations. Several studies have found that teachers, administrators, and parents need to set high expectations for academic learning and personal student development (McKissack, 1999; Minicucci et al., 1995).

References

Alcala, A. (2000). A framework for developing an effective instructional program for limited English proficient students with limited formal schools. *Practical Assessment, Research & Evaluation*, 7(9), 1–6.

Alexander, D., Heaviside, S., & Farris, E. (1999). *Status of Education Reform in Public Elementary and Secondary Schools: Teachers' Perspectives*. Washington, DC: U.S. Department of Education, National Center for Education Statistics.

Ancess, J. (2003). *Beating the Odds: High Schools as Communities of Commitment*. New York: Teachers College.

August, D. & Hakuta, K. (eds.) (1998). *Educating Language-minority Children*. Washington, DC: National Academy Press.

Bejarano, Y. (1987). A cooperative small-group methodology in the language classroom. *TESOL Quarterly*, 21, 483–504.

Bermúdez, A.B. & Palumbo, D. (1994). Bridging the gap between literacy and technology: Hypermedia as a learning tool for limited English proficient students. *The Journal of Educational Issues of Language Minority Students*, 14, 165–184.

Boyer, J.B. (1993). Culturally sensitive instruction: An essential component of education for diversity. *Catalyst for Change*, 22(3), 5–8.

Calderón, M. (1991). Benefits of cooperative learning for Hispanic students. *Texas Research Journal*, 2, 39–57.

Carter, T.P. & Chatfield, M.L. (1986). Effective bilingual schools: Implications for policy and practice. *American Journal of Education, 95*, 200–232.

Chamot, A.U. & O'Malley, J.M. (1987). The cognitive academic language learning approach: A bridge to the mainstream. *TESOL Quarterly, 1*, 227–249.

Chapa, J. & De La Rosa, B. (2004). Latino population growth, socioeconomic and demographic characteristics, and implications for educational attainment. *Education and Urban Society, 36*, 130–149.

Christian, D. (1995). Two-way bilingual education. In Montone, C.L. (ed.), *Teaching Linguistically and Culturally Diverse Learners: Effective Programs and Practices.* Santa Cruz, CA: National Center for Research on Cultural Diversity and Second Language Learning, pp. 8–11.

Cummins, J. & Sayers, D. (1990). Education 2001: Learning networks and educational reform. *Computers in the Schools, 7*(1 & 2), 1–29.

Durán, B.J., Dugan, T., & Weffer, R.E. (1997). Increasing teacher effectiveness with language minority students. *The High School Journal, 84*, 238–246.

Gándara, P., Maxwell-Jolly, J., & Driscoll, A. (2005). *Listening to Teachers of English Language Learners: A Survey of California Teachers' Challenges, Experiences, and Professional Development Needs.* Santa Cruz, CA: The Center for the Future of Teaching and Learning.

García, G.N. (2001b). The factors that place Latino children and youth at risk of educational failure. In Slavin, R.E. & Calderón, M. (eds.), *Effective Programs for Latino Students.* Mahwah, NJ: Lawrence Erlbaum, pp. 307–329.

García, S.B. & Guerra, P.L. (2004). Deconstructing deficit thinking: Working with educators to create more equitable learning environments. *Education and Urban Society, 36*, 150–168.

Glickman, C.D. (1998). Educational leadership for democratic purpose! What do we mean? *International Journal of Leadership in Education, 1*(1), 47–53.

Gonzalez, M.L., Huerta-Macias, A., &. Tinajero, J.V. (eds). (2001). *Educating Latino Students: A Guide to Successful Practice.* Lanham, MD: Scarecrow.

Haberman, M. (1991). Pedagogy of poverty versus good teaching. *Phi Delta Kappan, 73*, 290–294.

Hedges, L.V. & Olkin, I. (1980). Vote-counting methods in research synthesis. *Psychological Bulletin, 88*, 359–369.

Jiménez, R.T. & Barrera, R. (2000). How will bilingual/ESL programs in literacy change in the next millennium? *Reading Research Quarterly, 35*, 522–523.

Johnson, D.W. & Johnson, R.T. (1991). Classroom instruction and cooperative grouping. In Waxman, H.C. & Walberg, H.J. (eds.), *Effective Teaching: Current Research.* Berkeley, CA: McCutchan, pp. 277–293.

Lewis, L., Parsad, B., Carey, N., Bartfai, N., Farris, E., & Smerdon, B. (1999). *Teacher quality: A report on the preparation and qualifications of public school teachers* (Report No. 1999-080). Washington, DC: U.S. Department of Education, Office of Educational Research and Improvement, National Center for Education Statistics.

Liagas, C. & Snyder, T.D. (2003). *Status and trends in the education of Hispanics.* Washington, DC: U.S. Department of Education, National Center for Education Statistics.

Lopez, G.R., Scribner, J.D., & Mahitivanichcha, K. (2001). Redefining parental involvement: Lessons from high-performing migrant impacted schools. *American Educational Research Journal, 38*, 253–288.

Lucas, T., Henze, R., & Donato, R. (1990). Promoting the success of Latino language-minority students: An exploratory study of six high schools. *Harvard Educational Review, 60*, 315–340.

Maden, M. (ed.). (2001). *Success Against the Odds—Five Years on: Revisiting Effective Schools in Damaged Areas.* London: Routledge/Falmer.

McKissack, E.A. (1999). *Chicano Educational Achievement: Comparing Escuela Tlatelolco, A Chicanocentric School and a Public High School.* New York: Garland.

McLaughlin, B. & McLeod, B. (1996). *Educating all our students: Improving education for children from culturally and linguistically diverse backgrounds (Vol. 1).* Santa Cruz, CA: National Center for Research on Cultural Diversity and Second Language Learning.

Means, B. & Olson, K. (1994). The link between technology and authentic learning. *Educational Leadership, 51*(7), 15–18.

Minicucci, C., Berman, P., McLaughlin, B., McLeod, B., Nelson, & Woodworth, K. (1995). School reform and student diversity. *Phi Delta Kappan, 77*(1), 77–80.

Miramontes, O.B., Nadeau, A., & Commins, N.L. (1997). *Restructuring Schools for Linguistic Diversity: Linking Decision Making to Effective Programs.* New York: Teachers College.

Montecel, M.R., Cortez, J.D., & Cortez, A. (2004). Dropout-prevention programs: Right intent, wrong focus, and some suggestions on where to go from here. *Education and Urban Society, 36*, 169–188.

Mora, J.K. (2000). Policy shifts in language-minority education: A mismatch between politics and pedagogy. *The Educational Forum, 64*, 204–214.

National Center for Education Statistics (2003). *Overview of Public Elementary and Secondary Schools and Districts: School Year 2001–2002.* Washington, DC: U.S. Department of Education.

Padrón, Y.N. (1992). Strategy training in reading for bilingual students. *Southwest Journal of Educational Research into Practice, 4*, 59–62.

Padrón, Y.N. (1993). The effect of strategy instruction on bilingual students' cognitive strategy use in reading. *Bilingual Research Journal, 16*(3 & 4), 35–51.

Padrón, Y.N. & Knight, S.L. (1989). Linguistic and cultural influences on classroom instruction. In Baptiste, H.P., Anderson, J., Walker de Felix, J., & Waxman, H.C. (eds.), *Leadership, Equity, and School Effectiveness.* Newbury Park, CA: Sage, pp. 173–185.

Padrón, Y.N. & Waxman, H.C. (1993). Teaching and learning risks associated with limited cognitive mastery in science and mathematics for limited English proficient students. In Office of Bilingual Education and Minority Language Affairs (eds.), *Proceedings of the Third National Research Symposium on Limited English Proficient Students: Focus on Middle and High School Issues* (Vol. 2, pp. 511–547). Washington, DC: National Clearinghouse for Bilingual Education.

Padrón, Y.N. & Waxman, H.C. (1996). Improving the teaching and learning of English language learners through instructional technology. *International Journal of Instructional Media, 23*, 341–354.

Padrón, Y.N. & Waxman, H.C. (1999). Effective instructional practices for English language learners. In Waxman, H.C. & Walberg, H.J. (eds), *New Directions for Teaching Practice and Research.* Berkeley, CA: McCutchan, pp. 171–203.

Peregoy, S.F. & Boyle, O.F. (2000). English learners reading English: What we know, what we need to know. *Theory Into Practice*, 39, 237–247.

Reyes, P., Scribner, J., & Scribner, A.P. (1999). *Lessons from High-Performing Hispanic Schools: Creating Learning Communities.* New York: Teachers College.

Rivera, C. & Zehler, A.M. (1991). Assuring the academic success of language minority students: Collaboration in teaching and learning. *Journal of Education*, 173(2), 52–77.

Rolstad, K., Mahoney, K.S., & Glass, G.V. (2005). Weighing the evidence: A meta-analysis of bilingual education in Arizona. *Bilingual Research Journal*, 29(1), 43–67.

Short, D.J. (1994). Expanding middle school horizons: Integrating language, culture, and social studies. *TESOL Quarterly*, 28, 581–608.

Smolkin, L. (2000). How will diversity affect literacy in the next millennium? *Reading Research Quarterly*, 35, 549–550.

Téllez, K. & Waxman, H.C. (eds). (2006). *Improving Educator Quality for English Language Learners: Research, Policies and Practices.* Mahwah, NJ: Lawrence Erlbaum.

Tharp, R.G. (1995). Instructional conversations in Zuni classrooms. In Montone, C.L. (ed.), *Teaching Linguistically and Culturally Diverse Learners: Effective Programs and Practices.* Santa Cruz, CA: National Center for Research on Cultural Diversity and Second Language Learning, pp. 12–13.

Tharp, R.G., Estrada, P., Dalton, S., & Yamauchi, L. (2000). *Teaching Transformed: Achieving Excellence, Fairness, Inclusion, and Harmony.* Boulder, CO: Westview.

Thomas, W.P. & Collier, V. (1997). *School Effectiveness for Language-Minority Students.* Washington, DC: National Clearinghouse for Bilingual Education.

Thomas, W.P. & Collier, V. (2001). *A National Study of School Effectiveness for Language Minority Students' Long Term Academic Achievement.* Santa Cruz, CA: National Center for Research on Education, Diversity & Excellence.

U.S. Department of Education (2000). *Key Indicators of Hispanic Student Achievement: National Goals and Benchmarks for the Next Decade* [on-line]. Available: http://www.ed.gov .pubs/hispanicindicators/

Valencia, R., Valenzuela, A., Sloan; K., & Foley, D.E. (2001). Let's treat the cause, not the symptoms: Equity and accountability in Texas revisited. *Phi Delta Kappan* 83, 321–326.

Valenzuela, A. (1999). *Subtractive Schooling: U.S. Mexican Youth and the Politics of Caring.* Albany, NY: University of New York Press.

Waxman, H.C. (1992). Reversing the cycle of educational failure for students in at-risk school environments. In Waxman, H.C., Walker de Felix, J., Anderson, J., & Baptiste, H.P. (eds). *Students at Risk in At-Risk Schools: Improving Environments for Learning.* Newbury Park, CA: Sage, pp. 1–9.

Waxman, H.C. & Huang, S.L. (1994). *Classroom Instruction Differences Between Effective and Ineffective Inner-City Schools for Language Minority Students.* Paper presented at the annual meeting of the American Educational Research Association Montreal, Quebec.

Waxman, H.C. & Huang, S.L. (1997, April). *Classroom Learning Environment and Instructional Differences Between Effective, Average, and Ineffective Urban Elementary Schools for Latino Students.* Paper presented at the annual meeting of the American Educational Research Association, Chicago, IL.

Waxman, H.C., Huang, S.L., & Padrón, Y.N. (1995). Investigating the pedagogy of poverty in inner-city middle level schools. *Research in Middle Level Education*, 18(2), 1–22.

Waxman, H. C. & Padrón Y.N. (2002). Research-based teaching practices that improve the education of English language learners. In Minaya-Rowe, L. (ed.), *Teacher Training and Effective Pedagogy in the Context of Student Diversity.* Greenwich, CT: Information Age, pp. 3–38.

Waxman, H.C., Padrón, Y.N., & Arnold, K.A. (2001). Effective instructional practices for students placed at risk of failure. In Borman, G.D., Stringfield, S.G., & Slavin R.E. (eds), *Title I: Compensatory Education at the Crossroads.* Mahwah, NJ: Lawrence Erlbaum, pp. 137–170.

Waxman H.C., Padrón, Y.N., & Knight, S.L. (1991). Risks associated with students' limited cognitive mastery. In Wang, M.C., Reynolds M.C., & Walberg, H.J. (eds), *Handbook of Special Education: Emerging Programs* (Vol. 4, pp. 235–254). Oxford, England: Pergamon.

Fighting the Marginalization of Asian American Students with Caring Schools: Focus on Curricular Change

Valerie Ooka Pang

In the following selection titled "Fighting the Marginalization of Asian American Students with Caring Schools: Focus on Curricular Change" (*Race, Ethnicity & Education*, 2006), Valerie Ooka Pang urges educators to create caring-centered education as a way to provide a more inclusive education for all students, including Asian Americans. Pang presents evidence of the marginalization of Asian American students and then follows with suggested teaching strategies and materials for use in elementary schools to create both a caring-centered education and to fight against marginalization of students. She provides suggestions for teaching Social Studies, and Language Arts, and advocates expanding the overall curriculum to include Asian American role models. In such a comprehensive approach, she writes, "The experiences of students in schools is much more than the mastery of basic information, but rather it is the complex development of their intellectual, ethical, emotional, and social well-being."

Pang is a Professor at San Diego State University in California and a Research Fellow at the National Center for Urban School Transformation. She is a former senior fellow of the Annenberg Institute for School Reform, Brown University, in Providence, Rhode Island. She has also served as advisor for various groups that make media productions dealing with children's issues, especially television shows such as *Sesame Street* and *Mister Rogers' Neighborhood.* Her interests are in culturally meaningful teaching, and she has published articles in journals such as *Phi Delta Kappan, Harvard Educational Review,* and *Multicultural Education.* Her book, *Struggling to Be Heard: The Unmet Needs of Asian Pacific American Children,* was selected as Honorable Mention from the 1999 Gustavus Myers Outstanding Book Awards.

Key Concept: caring-centered education and Asian American students

Caring-Centered Education

Caring is a powerful foundation for schooling because the ethic of care as developed by Nel Noddings view's each individual as a precious human being within a country that values social justice, democracy, and moral courage (Hursh & Ross, 2000; Noddings, 1984, 1992; Pang, 2005; Stanley, 2005). These values affirm the belief in human dignity and our commitment to care for each other (Lipman, 1998; Liston & Garrison, 2004). This philosophical orientation affirms the importance of creating a school environment where all students are respected and provided an equitable education so they reach their potential. These values are extremely critical to establish as the foundation for education, because many Asian American students are marginalized in schools. Even though our national values identify equal education as one of its cornerstones, the experiences of many AA students question the reality of this value. Care theory intimately ties caring to our national commitments to freedom and equality within schools. Caring denotes action, therefore when people care, they also act. Our laws, policies, politics, and methods for achieving social justice flow directly from what we care about and our commitment to a socially just society. We are reminded that 'the civil rights movement was such a wonderful movement for social justice because the heart of it was love—loving everyone' (Hooks, 2000, p. 36).

Caring is more fundamental than justice, fairness, and equity (Pang, 2005). When people care about another person, they find ways to treat that person justly, fairly, and equitably. Our nation is strongest when people struggle for justice, freedom, and equality because they care for others and hold human life sacred.

However, schools do not seriously address the inequities of race, class, and gender bias. Why? Sociologist Stanley Aronowitz believes that the US ideology of equal opportunity is so pervasive in the majority culture. Most people think that each individual has an equal chance to make it in society. In addition, if people believe that the USA is an 'Open Society' devoid of a hierarchy based on distinct social class lines, then each person, if she/he works hard enough and long enough, has unlimited opportunities in this country (Aronowitz, 1996).

The paradox of equity influences the daily lives of Asian American students in schools. Many situations concern teacher prejudice and may result in biased institutional policies and practices. In a caring-centered school, teachers and students must tackle issues of racism, ethnocentrism, gender bias, and homophobia because they understand how these biases serve to undermine the integrity of the school and community.

The Paradox of Equity: Marginalization in Schools

Unfortunately, even though our national ideals emphasize equality, there are numerous examples of how prejudicial beliefs, conscious and unconscious, shape the education of Asian Americans. One of the pervasive issues that AA students face is marginalization. This is the practice of placing the needs of a population at the margins of society, therefore their needs are deemed not important. Few schools have curricula where AA issues, history, culture, art, communities, role models, and literature are integrated throughout. Asian Americans are marginalized for four major reasons. First, AA are a numerical minority, composing approximately 4% of the national population. However, many individuals do not understand that this aggregate does not provide an accurate understanding. The number of AAs differs depending on region. For example, in Boston public schools, they made up 9% of the student population in 2005 (Boston Public Schools, 2005); however in a district like Seattle Schools, AAs are a major racial/ethnic group. The category Asian American, which included Pacific Islanders, in the Fall 2003 comprised 23.1% of the total student population, and was about equal to the number of African American youth who made up 22.5% of the district (Seattle Public Schools, 2003). Second, they hold cultural values and behaviors that may differ and sometimes conflict with those of mainstream society. Even in the 21st century, some AA families still teach their children to ascribe to the value of harmonious relationships.

This means that many young people are taught to be collaborative and sometimes deferential toward teachers. In today's school, students who often receive more services and attention are those who are more aggressive and speak up, rather than those who are uncomplaining and conforming.

Third, the AA community is not a politically powerful group whose voice is often heard. Although there are individual organizations such as the Organization for Chinese Americans and the National Congress of Vietnamese Americans, AAs have yet to develop a strong pan-ethnic voice. This may be due to their inherent ethnic and historical differences among groups or because there are few AA organizations with the financial resources to bring such diverse communities together to create common political goals. Finally, because AAs are physically different from mainstream citizens, they are often seen as foreigners and not full members of this nation. Even though some Chinese American and Filipino/a American students may be fifth or sixth generation Americans, they are still viewed as aliens. Because of these four factors, few citizens understand that AAs face serious issues such as immigration, language, employment, housing, transportation, assimilation, identity, racism, and mental health.

Marginalization can also result from the beliefs host members hold about a subgroup. One of the most pervasive themes found in the general community is that Asian Americans are a homogeneous community where few differences exist between groups such as Korean Americans, Cambodian Americans, and Japanese Americans. Teachers may even believe that 'they all look alike'. However, just a cursory look at a world map demonstrates the wide diversity found in Asian ancestral countries. Their geographical distances and topographies can be used to explain cultural differences. However, few classrooms take on a thorough study of the geography of the world, and fewer teachers include discussions of the history and cultures of various nations in Asia.

Language issues are extremely complex in today's schools. Many AA students may come to school speaking a home language, such as Vietnamese, Mandarin, Lao, Korean, or Tagalog. Some students may be provided some bilingual instruction; however many will be placed in transitional classrooms where their home language is replaced with English. The message that students receive is that English is more valued than their home language.

Unconscious and conscious prejudice can also lead to other underlying obstacles to equity. Teachers often do not understand that their views have been shaped by a society in which AAs have been and continue to be marginalized in the USA. Much of the discussion regarding race uses a Black and White paradigm. Therefore, discussions of equity often exclude the participation of AAPI in historical and contemporary periods, leading to their invisibility. In addition, few educators understand that AA students may make up a considerable portion of their student population. For example, in districts such as San Diego City Schools, the category Asian American, which includes Pacific Islanders, makes up the third largest student group, behind Latino/as and Whites, accounting for more than 19% of the total student population. It is critical that AAs are represented in class discussions and guest presentations regarding equity. However, successful AAs are often used as anti-affirmative action poster children. Some groups exploit the success of AA youth to rebuff the claims of Blacks and Latino/as that racism is a present threat to equality. Asian Americans are rarely celebrated for their contributions and hard work within the context of persistent social prejudice and adversity. Rather their success is often seen as supported by mainstream society, though this is not necessarily the case.

Development of the Whole Student: Preparing to Participate in a Democracy

Social Studies

The historical information presented in textbooks about Asian Americans often portray them as marginal participants. For example, in social studies textbooks discussions of AA primarily focus on the following three topics: (1) Chinese immigrants and their role in the gold rush; (2) Chinese immigrants and their role in the building of the transcontinental railroad; and (3) the internment of Japanese Americans. It is important for students to understand the participation of AAs in the building of the USA. However, in most textbooks the discussion of the gold rush and the transcontinental railroad provides only a superficial amount of information. Chinese immigrants become a faceless group, and have been marginalized by the lack of information presented. For example, in discussions of the building of the railroad, not one name of a Chinese immigrant leader is discussed. However, students learn about Leland Stanford, Collis P. Huntington, Charles Crocker, and Mark Hopkins, who headed the Central Pacific Railroad Corporation in 1862 (Chang, 2003). Although there were fifty thousand Chinese workers on the railroad in 1865 and without them the railroad would not have been finished, they remain nameless in textbooks. In 1867, the Chinese conducted a labor strike because they worked more hours yet were paid less than White workers. However, it is disturbing that not one Chinese leader of this strike is named in textbooks. Students are not given the opportunity to learn about an Asian American labor leader who organized and led a critical strike for worker rights during the building of the railroad. Because little information about AAs is found in US social studies and history books, the exclusion of information denies their existence and conveys the idea that their experiences were not important to society in general. Also the manner in which Asian Americans are presented in these texts reinforces stereotypes of Asians as weak and inconsequential, therefore not leaders.

Another example of how AAs are marginalized in the history of their own country is the discussion of immigration and Ellis Island. Most history textbooks include discussion of Ellis Island where many European immigrants were processed before entering the USA. Ellis Island is an important icon to our national ideals of immigration, freedom, and equality. A photo of the Island is often used to represent how the USA willingly accepted oppressed, hard-working immigrants. However, few social studies texts mention Angel Island in the San Francisco Bay, an immigration station in the West. Many Chinese immigrants were segregated from their families and kept over a year in barracks where they had no privacy and little room (Lai *et al.*, 1980). On the island, a large detention center was built to keep Chinese immigrants from being able to talk with members of their families. It was far from the city so no one could swim to the island. The majority of immigrants who were processed through Angel Island were Chinese; people from Japan, Russia, and Korea were also required to go to the detention center.

In desperation, many Chinese immigrants described their incarceration by etching poems on the wooden walls. Today those walls are part of a historical preservation site. An informative website about these writings is presented by the Angel Island Detention Center Foundation. The poems demonstrate the deep desperation and disappointment that Chinese immigrants had when they were imprisoned in the detention center. They held deep frustrations about this new country and their loss of family and freedom.

Language Arts

Curricula in areas such as Literature, Creative Writing, English, Language Arts, Art, and Art History can be naturally integrated with AA experiences and culture, For example, novels by AA writers can provide students with an understanding of the multicultural experiences of immigration and colonization to conflicts in adjustment and acculturation. Artists are able to express in various mediums not only the symbols of AA life, but also present deep understandings of culture, history, and philosophy. For example, Laurence Yep wrote the Newbury Honor winning novel *Dragonwings* (1975) for middle school and above readers. Based on the real life experiences of Joe Fung Guey, an early US aviator, this exceptional story describes the life of a young immigrant. It weaves a wonderful story around the dreams of Windrider and how his Chinese American community dealt with legalized, institutional racism in San Francisco. The book was also turned into a successful play that highlighted the courage and strong cultural values of early Chinese Americans. Yep has written many other novels for young readers and, through his ability to tell stories, he intertwines the richness of family and ethnic cultures.

A well-known picture book writer is Allen Say. His books have received accolades, including the 1994 Caldecott Award for the best picture book *Grandfather's Journey* (1993). This book shares the story of his grandparents from Japan and how they lived a truly bicultural experience. He has also written *Emma's Rug* (1996), *Tree of Cranes* (1991), and *Home of the Brave* (2002). One of the most important aspects of his work is that Say paints accurate visual portrayals of Asian Americans. Their portraits are not 'slant-eyed' stereotypical, comic-like drawings; many of his illustrations are like painted photographs.

Two well-known AA novelists are Amy Tan and Maxine Hong Kingston. Both have extensively included traditional Chinese culture in their novels. Kingston's award-winning *The Woman Warrior: Memoirs of a Girlhood Among Ghosts* (1976) is a powerful piece about the strength of women. Amy Tan's *The Joy Luck Club* (1989) focuses on four Chinese immigrant mothers and how they often conflicted with their US-born daughters. The novel and its film adaptation convey the misunderstandings of mothers and daughters that arose from generational and assimilation levels, reflecting the struggles of many ethnic communities.

For older readers, *No-No Boy* by John Okada (1976) describes the frustration and disappointment of Ichiro who was imprisoned after he answered 'no' to two questions on the loyalty oath during the Second World War. Question 27 was 'Are you willing to serve in the armed forces of the United States on combat duty, wherever ordered?'; question 28 was 'Will you swear unqualified allegiance to the United States and faithfully defend the United States from any or all attack by foreign or domestic forces, and forswear any form of allegiance or obedience to the Japanese emperor, or any other foreign government, power, or organization?' By answering 'no' to both questions, Ichiro served two years in prison. During the early 1940s, there was much pressure from the Japanese American community and leaders to answer 'yes' in order to prove their loyalty to the USA. In spite of their demonstration of loyalty, over 120,000 Japanese Americans were held in internment camps for years.

After the 9/11 attacks in the USA and the subsequent passing of 'The Patriot Act', the issue of civil liberties has become more important today. The book *No-No Boy* (Okada, 1976) is an excellent novel that describes the difficult and complex positions confronted by Japanese Americans during the Second World War and Arab Americans since 2001. An award winning film that demonstrates the racism that both ethnic communities face is *Lest We Forget* (DaSilva, 2003). This film describes the disturbing parallels between what happened in the 1940s and present-day racism.

Internal turmoil and severe disappointment can arise when one's own country discriminates against and imprisons a person. Although some readers assume that the author John Okada was a 'No-No Boy' himself, in actuality Okada served in the US army. For more information about resisters during the internment, there is a documentary called *Conscience and the Constitution: Japanese American Resistance in World War II* (Abe, 2000). This film provides in-depth information about several hundred Japanese Americans who served two years in prison and who stood up for their civil rights when racism was legally enforced. Resistance against racism has been a consistent response by Asian Americans throughout the history of the USA.

This article is too limited to provide an extensive list of names of artists, novelists, and poets. However, teachers should investigate and add to the school curriculum the work of the following: Peter Bacho, Rick Barot, Frank Chin, Marilyn Chin, Jessica Hagedorn, Garret Hongo, Lawson Inada, Gish Jen, Alan Lau, Janice Mirikitani, David Mura, and Cathy Song. The work of these artists should be integrated into the high school English and Literature curriculum since they represent the US experience. In addition, elementary school teachers can add to their language arts lessons and classroom libraries the work by AAPI authors and illustrators, such as Jose Aruego, Dia Cha, Cynthia Kadohata, Lensey Namioka, Yoshiko Uchida, and Janice Wong. A list of recommended multicultural children's literature and annotations of each can be found in *Multicultural Education: A Caring-centered, Reflective Approach* (Pang, 2005).

Civil Rights Role Models

Most schools in the USA highlight the civil rights actions of folks who serve as important role models for young people. There are units presented in schools on individuals such as Martin Luther King, Jr., Harriet Tubman, Malcolm X, and Rosa Parks. Role models serve as important reminders of the courage and strength that people have shown in fighting for equality while simultaneously challenging institutional and social racism.

Students and teachers learn from role models. While it is not advisable to include only 'heroes' of an ethnic group in the curriculum, if little else is presented about the ethnic community, the inclusion of role models does provide all students with some understanding of the contributions that members of a community have made to the larger society. Educators have a responsibility to provide students with information regarding Asian American role models. It is important for *all* students to know that there are numerous Asian Americans who have resisted racism and continually fought against oppression. In spite of being continually marginalized, many AAs fight for the civil rights of all. The story describing the struggle for civil rights in the USA must include role models from diverse groups to demonstrate that the struggle has been a collective one.

A unit on AA civil rights leaders should be comprehensive. For example, the unit could begin with questions, such as 'What does it mean to be equal in society?' This way, students begin to examine the concept of equality and understand the complexities involved. Oliver and Shaver (1966) have carefully outlined three components of equality when looking at controversial issues from a jurisprudence model. First, equality denotes that there are rules that are applied to each person objectively. Second, the rules must not favor one group over another. Third, equality in our country is based on the belief of human dignity in each person. As Oliver and Shaver have explained, 'equality is the basis of liberty; the values of personal freedom and personal choice are guaranteed to all men because all share a common quality: humanity' (Oliver & Shaver, 1966, p. 48). Next, students should read through information on AA civil rights leaders, such as Drith Pran, Philip Vera Cruz, Patsy Mink, Fred Korematsu, and Bill Lann Lee.

Students can begin to discuss elements of a person's life using the following questions: (a) What were the major values of the person?; (b) What problems did the person address?; (c) What actions did they take to address the problems?; (d) What influence did the person have on others?; and (e) What did you learn about equality and democracy from studying the life of this person? The answers to these problems can be put into a data retrieval chart. I suggest that original pieces be read by the students to incorporate the voices of the civil rights leaders. Through this unit, students can be guided to identify and analyze the most important experiences in the life of the leaders and how these experiences influenced their actions. After the person's life has been studied, a storyboard can be drawn by the student in preparation of a documentary of the person's life (Lehman & Khan, 2002). This way, students identify the important beliefs, visions, challenges, and actions of the person. After a thorough study has been undertaken, they can rank in order the characteristics that a civil rights advocate should have. Students should be given the opportunity to present extensive biographies of civil rights leaders orally to the entire class. This is an excellent unit for teachers who may teach in a block setting with Social Studies, Language Arts, and Art.

Conclusion

A caring-centered philosophy of education is critical in schools because it is aimed at providing equal education opportunities to all students including Asian American students. The principles of the framework direct educators towards curricular interventions that emphasize a high quality, effective, and inclusive education. Unfortunately, the needs of AA students are often overlooked or marginalized. In addition, the contributions and experiences of AA communities are often excluded from the total curriculum.

Caring teachers hold students at the heart of what they do.

Caring teachers consider why and how Asian Americans are marginalized in the curriculum, educational

practices, and school policies. They examine how the needs of AA students are often ignored or not addressed. They come to the realization that sometimes their beliefs and actions replicate or reinforce inequitable school practices (Banks, 1995; Gay, 2000; Gordon, 1999; Irvine, 2002; Lee, 1996; Liston & Garrison, 2004; McLaren, 1997; Pang, 1995; Sleeter, 1996; Vinson, 1998). Unfortunately, teachers are often unaware of how their behaviors and responses to students can conflict with their values of equity, justice, and compassion. Many research findings indicate that teachers believe themselves to be caring, but in reality their behaviors and automatic responses reflect deep levels of prejudice (Pang & Park, 2003; Pang & Sablan, 1998).

Curriculum content and strategies can be used in schools to fight the issue of marginalization (Pang *et al.*, 2004), As this article suggests, one approach that K-12 teachers can take is to reflect upon the role they may have played in the marginalization of Asian American students. Have they presented AA role models—those who have risked their lives, livelihood, and security to bring equity to all of us? In addition, a comprehensive curriculum that includes the experiences of Asian Americans must be taught to all students. AAs are *Americans* and their story is an American story. All students and teachers must understand that the USA is a diverse nation and the concept of 'American' is multifaceted.

References

Abe, F. (2000) *Conscience and the Constitution: Japanese American resistance in World War II* (New York, Independent Television Services).

Aronowitz, S. (1996) *The death and rebirth of American radicalism* (New York, Routledge).

Asian Week (2001) The promise of America, February 23–March 1. Retrieved 21 April 2005, http://www.asianweek.com/2001_02_23/feature.html.

Banks, J. A. (1995) Multicultural education: historical development, dimensions, and practice, in: J. A. Banks & C. M. Banks (Eds.), *Handbook of research on multicultural education* (New York, Macmillan), 3–24.

Boston Public Schools (2005) *Facts and figures: enrollment.* Retrieved 18 April 2005, http://boston.kl2.ma.us/bps/enrollment.asp.

Chang, I. (2003) *The Chinese in America* (New York, Penguin).

Cole, M. (1996) *Cultural psychology: a once and future discipline* (Cambridge, MA, Belknap Press of Harvard University).

Cummins, J. (1996) *Negotiating identities: education for empowerment in a diverse society* (Sacramento, California Association for Bilingual Education).

DaSilva, J. (2003) *Lest we forget* (New York, Inface Films).

Dewey, J. (1916) *Democracy and education* (New York, Macmillan).

Gay, G. (2000) *Culturally responsive teaching: theory, research, and practice* (New York, Teachers College Press).

Gordon, E. W. (1999) *Education and justice: a view from the back of the bus* (New York, Teachers College Press).

Hooks, B. (2000) How do we build a community of love? *Shambhala Sun*, 8(3), 32–40.

Hursh, D. W. & Ross, E. W. (2000) *Democratic social education: social studies for social change* (New York, Falmer).

Irvine, J. J. (2002) *In search of wholeness: African American teachers and their culturally specific classroom practices* (New York, Palgrave).

Kingston, M. H. (1976) *The woman warrior: memoirs of a girlhood among ghosts* (New York, Vintage).

Lai, H. M., Lim, G. & Yung, J. (1980) *Island: poetry and history of Chinese immigrants on Angel Island, 1910–1940* (San Francisco, CA, History of Chinese Detained on Island).

Lee, S. (1996) *Unraveling the 'model minority' stereotype: listening to Asian American youth* (New York, Teachers College Press).

Lehman, D. & Khan, J. (2002) Let there be peace: exploring the accomplishments of Nobel Peace Prize recipients, *New York Times,* 11 December. Retrieved 15 April 2005, www.nytimes.com/learning/teachers/lessons/20021211wednesday.html?searchpv=learning_lessons.

Lipman, P. (1998) *Race, class, and power in school restructuring* (Albany, State University of New York Press).

Liston, D. & Garrison, J. (2004) *Teaching, learning, and loving* (New York, Routledge Falmer).

McLaren, P, (Ed.) (1997) *Revolutionary multiculturalism* (Boulder, CO, Westview).

Noddings, N. (1984) *Caring: a feminine approach to ethics and moral education* (Berkeley, CA, University of California Press).

Noddings, N. (1992) *The challenge to care in schools* (New York, Teachers College Press).

Oliver, D. & Shaver, J. (1966) *Teaching public issues in the high school* (Boston, MA, Hougton Mifflin).

Okada, J. (1976) *No-no boy* (Seattle, University of Washington Press).

Pang, V. O. (2005) *Multicultural education: a caring-centered, reflective approach* (2nd edn.) (Boston, MA, McGraw-Hill).

Pang, V. O. & Park, C. (2003) Examination of the self-regulation mechanism: prejudice reduction in pre-service teachers, *Action in Teacher Education,* 25(3), 1–12.

Pang, V. O. & Sablan, V. (1998) Teacher efficacy: how do teachers feel about their ability to teach African American students, in: M. Dilworth (Ed.) *Considerations of culture in teacher education: an anthology on practice* (Washington, D.C., American Association of Colleges for Teacher Education), 39–58.

Pang, V. O., Kiang, P. N. & Pak, Y. (2004) Asian Pacific American students: a diverse and complex population, in: J. A. Banks & C. M. Banks (Eds.) *Handbook of research on multicultural education* (New York, Macmillan), 412–424.

Say, A. (1991) *Tree of cranes* (Boston, Houghton Mifflin).

Say, A. (1993) *Grandfather's journey* (Boston, Houghton Mifflin).

Say, A. (1996) *Emma's rug* (Boston, Houghton Mifflin).

Say, A. (2002) *Home of the brave* (Boston, Houghton Mifflin).

Seattle Public Schools (2003) *Seattle public schools data profile: district summary, December 2003.* Retrieved on 18 April 2005, http://www.seattleschools.org/area/siso/disprof/2003/DP03demog.pdf.

Sleeter, C. (1996) *Multicultural education as social activism* (Albany, NY, State University of New York Press).

Stanley, W. B. (2005) Social studies and the social order: transmission or transformation?, *Social Education,* 69, 282–286.

Tan, A. (1989) *Joy luck club* (New York, Putnam).

Vinson, K. (1998) The traditions revisited: instructional approach and high school social studies teacher, *Theory and Research in Social Education,* 26, 50–82.

Yep, L. (1975) *Dragonwings* (New York, Harper and Row).

SELECTION 26

The Significance of Relationships: Academic Engagement and Achievement Among Newcomer Immigrant Youth

Carola Suárez-Orozco, Allyson Pimentel, and Margary Martin

Carola Suárez-Orozco is Professor of Applied Psychology at New York University's Steinhardt School of Culture, Education, and Human Development and Co-Director of NYU's Immigration Studies. She publishes widely in the areas of cultural psychology and immigrant families and youth. Her 2008 co-authored book *Learning a New Land: Immigrant Students in American Society* received the Harvard University Press Virginia and Warren Stone Award for Best Book on Education. Allyson Pimental is a licensed clinical psychologist who received her doctorate in Human Development and Psychology from Harvard University. Margary Martin is a Senior Research Associate at the Metropolitan Center for Urban Education at New York University whose research focuses on the education of immigrant youth.

In the following selection, titled "The Significance of Relationships: Academic Engagement and Achievement Among Newcomer Immigrant Youth" (*Teachers College Record*, 2009), Suárez-Orozco, Pimentel, and Martin discuss the current educational status of newcomer immigrant youth. The key point of their article is that the development of relationships with both peers and adults has an effect on academic engagement and achievement among these newly immigrated students. As the authors summarize, "The literature suggests that relationships in school play a particularly crucial role in promoting socially competent behavior in the classroom and in fostering academic engagement and achievement." Presenting students' stories to support their recommendations, the authors discuss the positive and negative roles of peers; teachers, school personnel, and adults in the community; and parental and familial relationships.

Key Concept: the effect of relationships on academic achievement

*I*mmigrant children are entering schools in the United States in unprecedented numbers, making them the fastest growing segment of the youth population (Landale & Oropesa, 1995). These children come from highly diverse backgrounds, with over 80% arriving from Latin America, Asia, and the Afro-Caribbean basin (U.S. Bureau of the Census, 2003). Although they bring remarkable strengths, including strong family ties, deep-seated beliefs in education, and optimism about the future, they also face a range of challenges associated with the migration to a new country, including high levels of poverty (Capps, Fix, Ost, Reardon-Anderson, & Passel, 2005), unwelcoming contexts of reception (Portes & Rumbaut, 2001), experiences of racism and discrimination (Szalacha et al., 2004; Suárez-Orozco & Suárez-Orozco, 2001), and exposure to school and community violence (M. Collier, 1998; García-Coll & Magnuson, 1997; Suárez-Orozco & Suárez-Orozco, 2001). These stressors complicate immigrant students' adjustment to new schools and community settings and tax the coping capacities of even the most robust immigrant adolescents, leaving them vulnerable to academic failure.

Consequently, a large segment of immigrant youth struggle to succeed in the American educational system. A number of studies have demonstrated that although immigrant youth have more positive attitudes toward their schools (Suárez-Orozco & Suárez-Orozco, 1995), hold higher aspirations (Fuligini, 1997;

Portes & Rumbaut, 2001), and are more optimistic about the future (Kao & Tienda, 1995; Suárez-Orozco & Suárez-Orozco, 2001) than their native-born peers, many perform poorly on a variety of academic indicators, including achievement tests, grades, dropout rates, and college enrollment (Gándara, 1994; Orfield, 2002; President's Advisory Commission on Educational Excellence for Hispanic American Education, 1996; Ruiz-de-Velasco, Fix, & Clewell, 2001). For nearly all immigrant groups today, length of residence in the United States is paradoxically associated with declining academic achievement and aspirations (Fuligini, 1997; Hernández & Charney, 1998; Portes & Rumbaut, 2001; Steinberg, Brown, & Dornbusch, 1996; Suárez-Orozco & Suárez-Orozco, 1995).

First-generation newcomer immigrant youth share a number of the same challenges as 1.5- and second-generation immigrant youth, but newcomers also face challenges particular to the social and cultural dislocations inherent in the process of migration (Sluzki 1979; Suárez-Orozco & Suárez-Orozco, 2001) and the challenges of language acquisition. Additionally, immigrant parents who have limited English skills often find it difficult to monitor their children's academic progress, keep track of their children's after-school activities, and understand their children's experiences (Cooper, Denner, & Lopez, 1999; Phelan, Davidson, & Yu, 1998; Suárez-Orozco & Suárez-Orozco, 2001). Given the dramatic rise in this school-age population, it is important that we develop models that will shed light on their processes of academic adaptation.

Challenges and Protective Factors

Many immigrant children, especially those who live in urban neighborhoods with concentrated poverty, face a daunting mix of odds in their schools and communities (Waters, 1999). Neighborhoods that combine such features as unemployment (Wilson, 1997), violence, structural barriers (Massey & Denton, 1993), and intense segregation by race and poverty (Orfield, 1998) tend to have schools that are overcrowded and understaffed, face high teacher and staff turnover, and are plagued by violence and hostile peer cultures (García-Coll & Magnuson, 1997; Mehan, Villanueva, Hubbard, & Lintz, 1996; Willis, 1977). Concerns about vulnerability to attacks have a detrimental effect on the school climate and can affect students' readiness and ability to learn (Elliott, Hamburg, & Williams 1998). Exposure to and fear of violence also undermine students' relationships with peers and teachers, weakening their capacities to experience trust (Garbarino, Dubrow, Kostelny, & Pardo, 1992; O'Donnell, Schwab-Stone, & Muyeed, 2002). Because students of color and those attending urban schools are most likely to encounter violence, such concerns affect a disproportionate number of immigrant students.

Mediating Influences on Academic Performance: Relational and Academic Engagement

Successful adaptations among immigrant students appear to be linked to the quality of relationships they forge in their school settings (Portes & Rumbaut, 2001; Zhou & Bankston, 1998). Indeed, social support in the school has been implicated in the academic adaptation of students, and immigrant students appear to be no exception (Cauce, Felmer, & Primavera, 1982; Dubow, 1991; Levitt, Guacci-Franco, & Levitt, 1994; Wetzel, 1999). Social relations provide a variety of protective functions—a sense of belonging, emotional support, tangible assistance and information, cognitive guidance, and positive feedback (Cobb, 1976; Sarason, Sarason, & Pierce, 1990; Wills, 1985). The literature suggests that relationships in school play a particularly crucial role in promoting socially competent behavior in the classroom and in fostering academic engagement and achievement (Fredricks, Blumenfeld, & Paris, 2004; Furrer & Skinner, 2003; Hill & Madhere, 1996; National Research Council, 2004; Suárez-Orozco, Suárez-Orozco, & Todorova, 2007).

Unpacking the Role of Relations in Academic Engagement and Performance

Peers

Children in the study often spoke about the importance of conational peers in their lives as they acclimated to a new country, a new neighborhood, and a new school. Peers were often described as providing an emotional sense of belonging and acceptance, as well as tangible help with homework assignments, language translations, and orientation to school (Gibson et al., 2004; Stanton-Salazar, 2004). To newly arrived immigrant students, the companionship of conational friends seemed to be especially important because these peers served as important sources of information on school culture. "I hung out with friends from my country because they spoke Spanish, because they told me the things I didn't understand," noted a 14-year-old Mexican girl. Similarly, a 16-year-old Dominican girl explained, "When you come here, you don't know English. Your friends help you with English, with classes, and with showing you the school." Hence, peers can act as "vital conduits" (Stanton-Salazar, 2004) of information to disoriented newcomer students.

A 14-year-old Dominican boy echoed and elaborated on these sentiments, introducing the concept that peers can serve as buffers against the violence and drugs that are of special threat to boys in the low-income communities in which so many immigrants live:

> Other students from my country gave me courage to come to school because at the beginning I didn't like to go to school. I found it strange and different. When I missed school, they called to give me the new homework assignment. They would tell me who not to hang around with and they would tell me not to get into bad things like gangs and marijuana.

In addition to the tangible forms of support, guidance, and protection that peers offered one another, students in the study also described the ways in which their peers supported them emotionally, serving as buffers to loneliness and embarrassment and bolstering self-confidence and self-efficacy. Peers were often described as providing important emotional sustenance that supported the development of significant psychosocial competencies. A 16-year-old from Central America noted, "I have a lot of friends and I don't feel alone." A 14-year-old from the Dominican Republic explained,

> When I don't understand, I feel stupid when I ask my teacher. Sometimes even when it's explained several times, I just don't understand how to do it. It makes me feel bad. When I ask my friends, I don't feel as bad because they are my friends and they show me I can do it.

Though many peers were described as modeling positive academic behavior and establishing constructive academic norms, others served to distract their classmates from performing optimally in school (Gándara, 2004). A 17-year-old Mexican girl summed up three of the most commonly cited aspects of negative peer influence on academic performance—"They invite us to cut class, use drugs, and tease us for wanting to study"—thus articulating how peers may encourage maladaptive academic behavior, promote drug use, and discourage competent academic behavior. Furthermore, peers may contribute to unsafe school and community environments, which can undermine students' ability to concentrate, their sense of security, and their ability to experience trusting relationships in school. As a 16-year-old girl from Central America remarked, "Sometimes there are fights in school. This causes problems for me because I think about these fights instead of my work." A 14-year-old from Haiti likewise stated, "I don't like it when kids are bad at school—like to the teachers, when kids don't listen and try to beat up the teachers."

Parents also voiced concerns about the violent environments of the schools that their children attended. The mother of a 15-year-old Central American boy remarked, "The role of the school is to educate the students the best that they can so that they can have a better future. But unfortunately, there are many terrible things going on in schools, many delinquent students killing others. It is very sad because the students feel unsafe."

Teachers, School Personnel, and Adults in the Community

Nonparental adults (Rhodes, 2002) in the school and community served an important role in easing newly arrived immigrant students' cultural transitions. Students also perceived that teachers and other school- and community-based adults offered protection and provided critical encouragement, support, and advice. As a young man from the Dominican Republic put it, "Teachers treat us well and watch out for our safety. When I came here, I didn't speak English and I didn't know how things were here. But one teacher helped me out and would explain things to me in Spanish."

After-school and tutoring programs are of critical importance to immigrant students in providing them with both homework help and information about the college admissions process. A 14-year-old from Haiti noted, "They help you with your homework a lot. When you come home your parents don't have to check it because it's already corrected." These programs also provide information to newcomer students about the American higher education system that immigrant parents, unfamiliar with education in this country, cannot. A 17-year-old Mexican girl commented of Upward Bound, "They told me all I needed to get into the university."

Adults in the community are another source of tangible and emotional support to immigrant youth. Often these adults are conationals who make up an extended network of support for the children, helping them obtain necessary school supplies and offering essential words of encouragement. A 16-year-old Central American girl said of the adults in her neighborhood,

> They ask me if I need anything for school. If we go to a store and I see a notebook, they ask me if I want it. They give me advice, tell me that I should be careful of the friends I choose. They also tell me to stay in school to get prepared. They tell me I am smart. They give me encouragement.

On the other hand, study participants also spoke of the indifference, cultural insensitivity, and the discrimination they experienced while interacting with some adults. Lamentably, all too often, those adults were teachers. Some informants spoke longingly about a desire for a greater sense of closeness and understanding with their teachers, as did a 14-year-old from China, who reported, "Most of my teachers are quite cold. I wish they would care more about my feelings." The mother of a 17-year-old from Central America complained,

> From the moment my daughter arrived at school, her teacher only spoke to her in English. But she didn't know any English. But the teachers—especially the Latino ones—should know you don't learn English in a day, you learn little by little. For this reason, my daughter doesn't want to go to school.

Many parents complained of an unwelcoming context of reception in school (Olsen, 1997) that contributed to their children's academic disengagement. Parents found it particularly distressing when even conational teachers and school personnel did not seem responsive to the needs and struggles of these newly arrived students.

The preceding quotes serve to illustrate the ways in which school-based supportive relationships can either bolster or detract from newcomer students' academic engagement and school performance. From the qualitative data, two distinct yet overlapping types of relational support emerged from the data—tangible school-based support and emotional school-based support. Tangible school-based support reflects the concrete and material supports offered to students, such as help with homework, sharing of resources, and offering of advice. Emotional school-based support is characterized by the emotional connections, or feelings of support and closeness, that students develop with the people around them. Emotional school-based support provides a sense of safety and protection; it helps students build specific skills, confidence, and a sense of self-efficacy. It serves to keep students engaged as they encounter inevitable obstacles in their academic paths.

Parental and Familial Relationships

Although school-based relationships are essential in supporting academic engagement and performance, we found that family relationships also played a critical role in supporting school performance. Many of the students spoke of the complex combination of love, affection, appreciation, gratitude, responsibility, and sense of duty (Fuligini & Pederson, 2002) that characterized their relationships with their families and influenced their academic and behavioral choices. A 15-year-old Dominican girl poignantly articulated,

> One of the most important successes in life is to study, because without a good education there is no life. That is why some of our parents have had to work in factories. They work hard to give us a good education so that we can have a good future, not a future like theirs. Their dream is to see us become lawyers so we can represent our family, our last name, our country.

A 17-year-old Central American girl offered a similar sentiment, highlighting the invaluable impact of parental support:

> My goal is to go to the university and get a career. I'm doing it for myself, for my family, to help them when I have my career. My parents think these are good goals so I can get ahead and earn money for happiness. But I have to do the work. My parents' support is the best inheritance they could give me.

Students in the study repeatedly voiced their keen understanding and appreciation of their parents' sacrifices and struggles on their behalf. A 14-year-old Haitian girl said, "She is a good mother. She fights for us, struggles for us. And she's a single mother so she does it all alone." But although many students described their desire to "give back" to their parents by doing well in school and going on to college, at times their parents had different views about the best ways for their children to meet their familial obligations. An 18-year-old Haitian girl in her senior year of high school explained,

> We have different views on things, like what jobs I should do. They want me to get a job right after high school. They don't want me to go to college. My goal is to go to college, but my mom doesn't want me to. She wants me to get a job instead to make money so I can help them out.

The kinds of relational supports that parents were able to provide varied widely among the participants. Many parents and students described the tangible and emotional support they gave and received in the form of homework help, advice, encouragement, and care. The Central American mother of a 17-year-old remarked, "To help my children succeed in this country, I keep up with their school life, help them study, and feed them good food." Of her parents, a Central American 16-year-old said, "My dad explains things to me if I don't understand. They always want the best for us. They leave us in peace after school so we can keep studying."

Although it was clear from our interview data that the majority of immigrant parents were deeply concerned about their children's education and supported them as best they could, many were challenged in their abilities to help their children with their schoolwork (García-Coll et al., 2002). Because of their limited proficiency with English or limited experience with the educational system in their country of origin and in their new homeland, many immigrant parents were unable to offer academic assistance to their children. Furthermore, because many immigrant parents work long hours in inflexible low-wage jobs, they often are not available to help their children during after-school hours or to attend school meetings during the day. A 14-year-old Chinese boy remarked that he could not ask his mother for help with his assignments because she was "never home." "I seldom see her," he continued, "but as far as I know, she isn't good at my schoolwork. It is impossible for me to ask her to help me with my English. She, herself, is going to night school right now. Her English is not that good." A 14-year-old Dominican boy echoed this sentiment: "I don't ask my parents for help because they are always working and when they get home they are tired and I don't like to bother them much."

The mother of a 14-year-old Chinese girl described a common dilemma faced by immigrant parents when the economic survival of the family is at odds with the educational well-being of their children:

Nowadays, parents are busy making a living, which is very important for them. They work long hours so they are alienated from their kids' schools. Basically, they don't know how their kids are doing in school, they don't know how the school operates. Education is very important for kids. But sometimes I feel that for Chinese families, they work very hard to get here so they don't give much attention to their kids' education. For them the most important thing is to make a living, to survive. How can you talk about education when you don't even have enough to eat? How can you talk about something else when you cannot maintain the basic living level? This is true from a certain perspective. However, if you think deeper, why did you come over here? What did you come here for?

These poignant statements by parents of newly arrived immigrant youth provide insight into why nonparental adults are so critical to easing the journey of recently arrived immigrant youth. They provide not only emotional support in a difficult period of transition but also information and skills that can lead to academic success.

Conclusion

Taken together, these findings suggest that efforts to understand and bolster immigrant students' relational, cognitive, and behavioral engagement are likely to yield important academic payoffs. Any attempts to improve prospects for immigrant youth should consider the importance of caring relationships in supporting academic outcomes. Practices that enrich school-based supportive relationships with both peers and school-based adults, including fostering nurturing safe environments, creating advisory groups, grouping students in smaller multiyear cohorts, and the like, would serve to enhance both the relational and the academic engagement of immigrant youth.

References

Capps, R., Fix, M. E, Ost, J., Reardon-Anderson, J., & Passel, J. S. (2005). *The health and well-being of young children of immigrants*. Washington, DC: The Urban Institute.

Cauce, A. M., Felmer R.D., & Primavera, J. (1982). Social support in high-risk adolescents: structural components and adaptive impact. *American Journal of Community Psychology, 10*, 417–428.

Cobb, S. (1976). Social support as a moderator of life stress. *Psychomatic Medicine, 38*, 300–314.

Collier, M. (1998). *Cultures of violence in Miami-Dade public schools*. Miami: Florida International University.

Dubow, E. F. (1991). A two-year longitudinal study of stressful life events, social support, and social problem-solving skill: Contributions to children's behavioral and academic adjustment. *Child Development, 65*, 583–599.

Elliott, D. S., Hamburg, B. A., & Williams, K. R. (1998). Violence in American schools: An overview. In D. S. Elliott, B. A. Hamburg, & K. R. Williams (Eds.), *Violence in American schools* (pp. 3–28). New York: Cambridge University Press.

Fredricks, J. A., Blumenfeld, P. C., & Paris, A. H. (2004). School engagement: Potential of the concept, state of the evidence. *Review of Educational Research, 74*, 54–109.

Fuligini, A. (1997). The academic achievement of adolescents from immigrant families: The roles of family background, attitudes, and behavior. *Child Development, 69*, 351–363.

Fuligini, A., & Pederson, S. (2002). Family obligation and the transition to young adulthood. *Developmental Psychology, 38*, 856–868.

Furrer, C., & Skinner, E. (2003). Sense of relatedness as a factor in children's academic engagement & performance. *Journal of Educational Psychology, 95*, 148–162.

Gándara, P. (1994). The impact of the educational reform movement on limited English proficient students. In B. McLeod (Ed.), *Language and learning: Educating linguistically diverse students* (pp. 45–70). Albany: State University of New York Press.

Garbarino, J., Dubrow, N., Kostelny, K., & Pardo, C. (1992). *Children in danger: Coping with the consequences of community violence*. San Francisco: Jossey-Bass.

García-Coll, C., Akiba, D., Palacios, N., Silver, R., DiMartino, L., Chin, C., et al. (2002). Parental involvement in children's education: Lessons from three immigrant groups. *Science and Practices 2*, 303–324.

García-Coll, C., & Magnuson, K. (1997). The psychological experience of immigration: A developmental perspective. In A. Booth, A. C. Crouter, & N. Landale (Eds.), *Immigration and the family* (pp. 91–132). Mahwah, NJ: Erlbaum.

Gibson, M. A., & Gándara, P. & Koyma, J. P. (2004). *School connections: U.S. Mexican youth, peers, and school achievement*. New York: Teachers College Press.

Hernández, D., & Charney, E. (Eds.). (1998). *From generation to generation: The health and well-being of children of immigrant families*. Washington, DC: National Academy Press.

Hill, H. M., & Madhere, S. (1996). Exposure to community violence and African American children: A multidimensional model of risks resources. *Journal of Community Psychology, 24*, 26–43.

Kao, G., & Tienda, M. (1995). Optimism and achievement: The educational performance of immigrant youth. *Social Science Quarterly, 76*, 1–19.

Landale, N. S., & Oropesa, R. S. (1995). *Immigrant children and the children of immigrants: Inter- and intra-ethnic group differences in the United States* (Population Research Group PRG Research Paper No. 95-2). East Lansing: Michigan State University.

Levitt, M. J., Guacci-Franco, N., & Levitt, J. L. (1994). Social support and achievement in childhood and early adolescence: A multicultural study. *Journal of Applied Developmental Psychology, 15*, 207–222.

Massey, D., & Denton, N. (1993). *American apartheid*. Cambridge, MA: Harvard University Press.

Mehan, H., Villanueva, I., Hubbard, L., & Lintz, A. (1996). *Constructing school success: The consequences of untracking low achieving students*. New York: Cambridge University Press.

National Research Council. (2004). *Engaging schools: Fostering high school students' motivation to learn*. Washington, DC: National Academies Press.

O'Donnell, D. A., Schwab-Stone, M. E., & Muyeed, A. Z. (2002). Multidimensional resilience in urban children exposed to community violence. *Child Development, 73*, 1265–1282.

Olsen, L. (1997). *Made in America: Immigrant students in our public schools.* New York: New Press.

Orfield, G. (1998). The education of Mexican immigrant children: A commentary. In M. M. Suárez-Orozco (Ed.), *Crossings: Mexican immigration in interdisciplinary perspective* (pp. 276–280). Cambridge, MA: David Rockefeller Center for Latin American Studies/Harvard University Press.

Orfield, G. (2002). Commentary. In M. Suárez-Orozco & M. Paez (Eds.), *Latinos: Remaking America* (pp. 389–397). Berkeley: University of California Press.

Phelan, P., & Davidson, A. L., & Yu, H. C. (1998). *Adolescents' worlds: Negotiating families, peers, and schools.* New York: Teachers College Press.

Portes, A., & Rumbaut, R. G. (2001). *Legacies: The story of the second generation.* Berkeley: University of California Press.

President's Advisory Commission on Educational Excellence for Hispanic American Education. (1996). *Our nation on the fault line: Hispanic American education.* Washington, DC: President's Advisory Commission on Educational Excellence for Hispanic American Education.

Rhodes, J. E. (2002). *Stand by one: The risks and rewards of youth mentoring relationships.* Cambridge, MA: Harvard University Press.

Ruiz-de-Velasco, J., Fix, M., & Clewell, B. C. (2001). *Overlooked and underserved: Immigrant students in U.S. secondary schools.* Washington, DC: Urban Institute.

Sarason, I. G., Sarason, B. R., & Pierce, G. R. (1990). Social support: The search for theory. *Journal of Social and Clinical Psychology, 9,* 133–147.

Sluzki, C. (1979). Migration and family conflict. *Family Process, 18,* 379–390.

Stanton-Salazar, R. (2004). Social capital among working-class minority students. In M. A. Gibson, P. Gándara, & J. P. Koyma (Eds.), *School connections: U.S. Mexican youth, peers, and school achievement* (pp. 18–38). New York: Teachers College Press.

Steinberg, S., Brown, B. B., & Dornbusch, S. M. (1996). *Beyond the classroom.* New York: Simon and Schuster.

Suárez-Orozco, C., & Suárez-Orozco, M. (1995). *Transformations: Immigration, family life, and achievement motivation among Latino adolescents.* Stanford, CA: Stanford University Press.

Suárez-Orozco, C., & Suárez-Orozco, M. (2001). *Children of immigration.* Cambridge, MA: Harvard University Press.

Suárez-Orozco, C., Suárez-Orozco, M., & Todorova, I. (2007). *Learning a new land: Immigrant students in American society.* Cambridge, MA: Harvard University Press.

Szalacha, L. A., Erkut, S., García-Coll, C., Fields, J. P., Alarcón, O., & Ceder, I. (2004). Perceived discrimination and resilience. In S. S. Luthar (Ed.), *Resilience and vulnerability: Adaptation in the context of childhood adversities* (pp. 414–435).

U.S. Bureau of the Census. (2003). *Profile of the foreign-born population in the United States.* Washington, DC: U.S. Government Printing Office.

Waters, M. (1999). *Black identities: West Indian dreams and American realities.* Cambridge, MA: Harvard University Press.

Wetzel, K. R. (1999). Social influences and school adjustment, Commentary. *Educational Psychologist, 34,* 59–69.

Willis, P. (1977). *Learning to labour: How working class kids get working class jobs.* Farnborough, England: Saxon House.

Wills, T. A. (1985). Supportive functions of interpersonal relationships. In S. Cohen & S. L. Syme (Eds.), *Social support and health* (pp. 61–82). Orlando, FL: Academic Press.

Wilson, W. (1997). *When work disappears: The world of the new urban poor.* New York: Vintage Books.

Zhou, M., & Bankston, C. I. (1998). *Growing up American: How Vietnamese children adapt to life in the United States.* New York: Russell Sage Foundation.

Language

Selection 27

JIM CUMMINS, from "Language, Power, and Pedagogy: Bilingual Children in the Crossfire" (Multilingual Matters)

Selection 28

EUGENE E. GARCÍA, from "Education Comes in Diverse Shapes and Forms for U.S. Bilinguals," *Teaching and Learning in Two Languages: Bilingualism & Schooling in the United States*

Language, Power, and Pedagogy: Bilingual Children in the Crossfire

Jim Cummins

Jim Cummins is a professor at the Ontario Institute for Studies in Education, the University of Toronto. His research interests include patterns of language acquisition and academic development among minority students and the effects of teaching practices on the development of language and literacy. Cummins has published a number of articles and over 100 books and book chapters and is considered a leading authority in multicultural education and language development. The following selection is from his book *Language, Power and Pedagogy: Bilingual Children in the Crossfire* (Multilingual Matters, 2000).

Cummins begins by describing the differences between academic and conversational language proficiency, explaining that while recent immigrant children learn conversational English quickly in the school environment, academic language takes much longer to learn. He then speaks of "the positive effects of additive bilingualism." The major portion of this selection is Cummins' presentation of "A Framework for Reversing School Failure," in which he discusses coercive and collaborative relations of power between educators and students. He proposes that "culturally diverse students are empowered or disabled as a direct results of their interactions with educators in the schools."

Key Concept: English language development and interactions with students

Language Interactions in the Classroom: From Coercive to Collaborative Relations of Power

The selection argues that students' identities are affirmed and academic achievement promoted when teachers express respect for the language and cultural knowledge that students bring to the classroom and when the instruction is focused on helping students generate new knowledge, create literature and art, and act on social realities that affect their lives. Only a brief overview of these issues is provided in this chapter. The goal is to sketch a framework for understanding the causes of bilingual students' academic difficulties and the kinds of intervention that are implied by this causal analysis. . . .

Psycholinguistic Principles

Conversational and Academic Proficiency

Research studies since the early 1980s have shown that immigrant students can quickly acquire considerable fluency in the dominant language of the society when they are exposed to it in the environment and at school. However, despite this rapid growth in conversational fluency, it generally takes a minimum of about five years (and frequently much longer) for them to catch up to native-speakers in academic aspects of the language (Collier, 1987; Cummins, 1981b; Hakuta *et al.*, 2000; Klesmer, 1994). Collier's (1987) research among middle-class immigrant students taught exclusively through English in the Fairfax County district suggested that a period of five to ten years was required for students to catch up. The Ramirez Report data illustrate the pattern (Ramirez, 1992): after four years of instruction, Grade 3 Spanish-speaking students in both structured immersion (English-only) and early-exit bilingual programs were still far from grade norms in English academic achievement. Grade 6 students in late-exit programs who had consistently received about 40% of their instruction through their primary language were beginning to approach grade norms. Further analysis of a subset of these data (from a late-exit program in New York City) showed that the rapidity with which bilingual students approached grade norms in English reading by Grade 6 was strongly related to their level of Spanish reading at Grade 3. The better developed their Spanish reading was at Grade 3, the more rapid progress they made in English reading between Grades 3 and 6 (Beykont, 1994).

Gándara (1999), in summarizing data from California, has noted the 'large discrepancy' between the developmental patterns for oral L2 skills (measured by tests) as compared to L2 reading and writing during the elementary school years:

> For example, while listening skills are at 80% of native proficiency by Level 3 (approximately 3rd grade), reading and writing skills remain below 50% of those expected for native speakers. It is not until after Level 5 (or approximately 5th grade) that the different sets of skills begin to merge. This suggests that while a student may be able to speak and understand English at fairly high levels of proficiency within the first three years of school, academic skills in English reading and writing take longer for students to develop. (1999: 5)

Hakuta *et al.*'s analysis of data from two California school districts in the San Francisco Bay area showed that 'even in two California districts that are considered the most successful in teaching English to LEP [limited English proficient] students, oral proficiency [measured by formal tests] takes three to five years to develop, and academic English proficiency can take four to seven years' (2000: iii). They label the one-year time period of 'sheltered English immersion' that Proposition 227 gives ELL students to acquire English 'wildly unrealistic' (2000: 13).

There are two reasons why such major differences are found in the length of time required to attain peer-appropriate levels of conversational and academic skills. First, considerably less knowledge of language itself is usually required to function appropriately in interpersonal communicative situations than is required in academic situations. The social expectations of the learner and sensitivity to contextual and interpersonal cues (e.g. eye contact, facial expression, intonation, etc.) greatly facilitate communication of meaning. These social cues are largely absent in most academic situations that depend on knowledge of the language itself for successful task completion. In comparison to interpersonal conversation, the language of text usually involves much more low frequency vocabulary, complex grammatical structures, and greater demands on memory, analysis, and other cognitive processes.

The second reason is that English L1 speakers are not standing still waiting for English language learners to catch up. A major goal of schooling for all children is to expand their ability to manipulate language in increasingly abstract academic situations. Every year English L1 students gain more sophisticated vocabulary and grammatical knowledge and increase their literacy skills. Thus, English language learners must catch up with a moving target. It is not surprising that this formidable task is seldom complete in one or two years.

By contrast, in the area of conversational skills, most native speakers have reached a plateau relatively early in schooling in the sense that a typical six-year-old can express herself as adequately as an older child on most topics she is likely to want to speak about and she can understand most of what is likely to be addressed to her. While some increase in conversational sophistication can be expected with increasing age, the differences are not particularly salient in comparison to differences in literacy-related skills; compare, for example, the differences in literacy between a twelve-and a six-year-old student in comparison to differences in their conversational skills.

Several obvious implications of these data can be noted. First, educating bilingual/ELL students is the responsibility of the entire school staff and not just the responsibility of ESL or bilingual teachers.

A related implication is that school language policies should be developed in every school to address the needs of *all* students in the school, and in particular, those students who require support in English academic language learning (Corson, 1998a). This also implies that administrators in schools should be competent to provide leadership in addressing issues of underachievement in culturally and linguistically diverse contexts.

A third set of implications concerns assessment issues. District-, state-, or nation-wide assessment programs that assess ELL students who are still in the process of catching up academically in English are likely to give a very misleading impression both of students' academic potential and of the effectiveness of instruction. Students who have been learning English for about three years in a school context perform about one standard deviation (the equivalent of 15 IQ points) below grade norms in academic English skills (Cummins, 1981b). If the interpretation of test results fails to take account of these data, highly effective schools with large numbers of ELL students will appear ineffective to parents and policy-makers. This perception is likely to reduce student and teacher morale. Similarly, assessment of bilingual students who are referred for special education assessment is likely to give distorted results if the assessment is conducted only in students' L2.

In short, the differences between conversational and academic proficiency and the length of time required to catch up academically have major consequences for a variety of curricular and assessment issues. In particular, these data suggest that we should be looking for interventions that will sustain bilingual students' long-term academic progress rather than expecting any short-term 'quick-fix' solution to students' academic underachievement in English.

The Positive Effects of Additive Bilingualism

There are close to 150 empirical studies carried out during the past 30 or so years that have reported a positive association between additive bilingualism and students' linguistic, cognitive, or academic growth. The most consistent findings among these research studies are that bilinguals show more developed awareness of language (metalinguistic abilities) and that they have advantages in learning additional languages. The term 'additive bilingualism' refers to the form of bilingualism that results when students add a second language to their intellectual tool-kit while continuing to develop conceptually and academically in their first language.

The linguistic and academic benefits of additive bilingualism for individual students provide an additional reason to support students in maintaining their LI while they are acquiring English. Not only does maintenance of LI help students to communicate with parents and grandparents in their families, and increase the collective linguistic competence of the entire society, it enhances the intellectual and academic resources of individual bilingual students. At an instructional level, we should be asking how we can build on this potential advantage in the classroom by focusing students' attention on language and helping them become more adept at manipulating language in abstract academic situations.

Interdependence of First and Second Languages

The interdependence principle has been stated as follows (Cummins, 1981a):

> To the extent that instruction in Lx is effective in promoting proficiency in Lx, transfer of this proficiency to Ly will occur provided there is adequate exposure to Ly (either in school or environment) and adequate motivation to learn Ly. (p. 29)

The term *common underlying proficiency (CUP)* has also been used to refer to the cognitive/academic proficiency that underlies academic performance in both languages.

Consider the following research data that support this principle:

- In virtually every bilingual program that has ever been evaluated, whether intended for linguistic majority or minority students, spending instructional time teaching through the minority language entails no academic costs for students' academic development in the majority language (Baker, 1996; Cummins & Corson, 1997).
- An impressive number of research studies have documented a moderately strong correlation between bilingual students' LI and L2 literacy skills in situations where students have the opportunity to develop literacy in both languages. It is worth noting that these findings also apply to the relationships among very dissimilar languages in addition to languages that are more closely related, although the strength of relationship is often reduced (e.g. Arabic–French, Dutch–Turkish, Japanese–English, Chinese–English, Basque–Spanish) (Cummins, 1991c; Cummins *et al.*,

1984; Genesee, 1979; Sierra & Olaziregi, 1991; Verhoeven & Aarts, 1998; Wagner, 1998).

A comprehensive review of US research on cognitive reading processes among ELL students concluded that this research consistently supported the common underlying proficiency model:

> ...considerable evidence emerged to support the CUP model. United States ESL readers used knowledge of their native language as they read in English. This supports a prominent current view that native-language development can enhance ESL reading. (Fitzgerald, 1995:181)

In short, the research data show clearly that within a bilingual program, instructional time can be focused on developing students' literacy skills in their primary language without adverse effects on the development of their literacy skills in English. Furthermore, the relationship between first and second language literacy skills suggests that effective development of primary language literacy skills can provide a conceptual foundation for long-term growth in English literacy skills.

A Framework for Reversing School Failure

The starting point for understanding why students choose to engage academically or, alternatively, withdraw from academic effort is to acknowledge that *human relationships are at the heart of schooling.*

What determines the kinds of relationships that educators establish with culturally diverse students? To answer this question we need to look at the relationships that exist between dominant and subordinated communities in the wider society and how these relationships (henceforth *macro-interactions*) influence both the structures that are set up in schools and the way educators define their roles within the school context.

When patterns of school success and failure among culturally diverse students are examined within an international perspective, it becomes evident that power and status relations between dominant and subordinated groups exert a major influence. Subordinated groups that fail academically have generally been discriminated against over many generations. They react to this discrimination along a continuum ranging from internalization of a sense of ambivalence or insecurity about their identities to rejection of, and active resistance to, dominant group values.

Relations of power in the wider society (macro-interactions), ranging from coercive to collaborative in varying degrees, influence both the ways in which educators define their roles and the types of structures that are established in the educational system. Role definitions refer to the mindset of expectations, assumptions and goals that educators bring to the task of educating culturally diverse students.

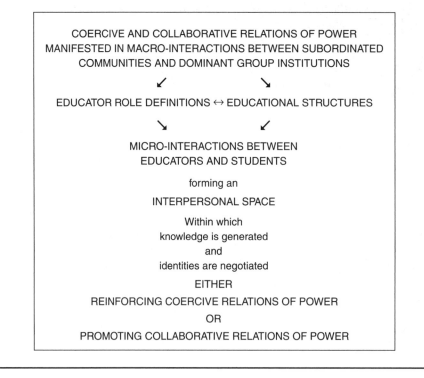

FIGURE 1 Coercive and collaborative relations of power manifested in macro- and micro-interactions

Coercive relations of power refer to the exercise of power by a dominant individual, group, or country to the detriment of a subordinated individual, group or country. For example, in the past, dominant group institutions (e.g. schools) have required that subordinated groups deny their cultural identity and give up their languages as a necessary condition for success in the 'mainstream' society. For educators to become partners in the transmission of knowledge, culturally diverse students were required to acquiesce in the subordination of their identities and to celebrate as 'truth' the perspectives of the dominant group (e.g. the 'truth' that Columbus 'discovered' America and brought 'civilization' to its indigenous peoples).

Collaborative relations of power, by contrast, reflect the sense of the term 'power' that refers to 'being enabled', or 'empowered' to achieve more. Within collaborative relations of power, 'power' is not a fixed quantity but is generated through interaction with others. The more empowered one individual or group becomes, the more is generated for others to share, as is the case when two people love each other or when we really connect with children we are teaching. Within this context, the term *empowerment* can be defined as *the collaborative creation of power*. Students whose schooling experiences reflect collaborative relations of power participate confidently in instruction as a result of the fact that their sense of identity is being affirmed and extended in their interactions with educators. They also know that their voices will be heard and respected within the classroom. Schooling amplifies rather than silences their power of *self*-expression.

Educational structures refer to the organization of schooling in a broad sense that includes policies, programs, curriculum, and assessment. While these structures will generally reflect the values and priorities of dominant groups in society, they are not by any means fixed or static. As with most other aspects of the way societies are organized and resources distributed, educational structures are contested by individuals and groups.

Educational structures, together with educator role definitions, determine the micro-interactions between educators, students, and communities. These micro-interactions form an interpersonal space within which the acquisition of knowledge and formation of identity is negotiated. Power is created and shared within this interpersonal space where minds and identities meet. As such these micro-interactions constitute the most immediate determinant of student academic success or failure.

Micro-interactions between educators, students and communities are never neutral; in varying degrees, they either reinforce coercive relations of power or promote collaborative relations of power. In the former case, they contribute to the disempowerment of culturally diverse students and communities; in the latter case, the micro-interactions constitute a process of empowerment that enables educators, students and communities to challenge the operation of coercive power structures.

The relationships sketched in Figure 1 are elaborated in Figure 2. The term *Exclusionary/Assimilationist* refers to the general orientation to education characteristic of most countries prior to the 1960s and still characteristic of most countries prior to the 1960s and still characteristic of many today. The goal of education was either to exclude certain groups from the mainstream of society or

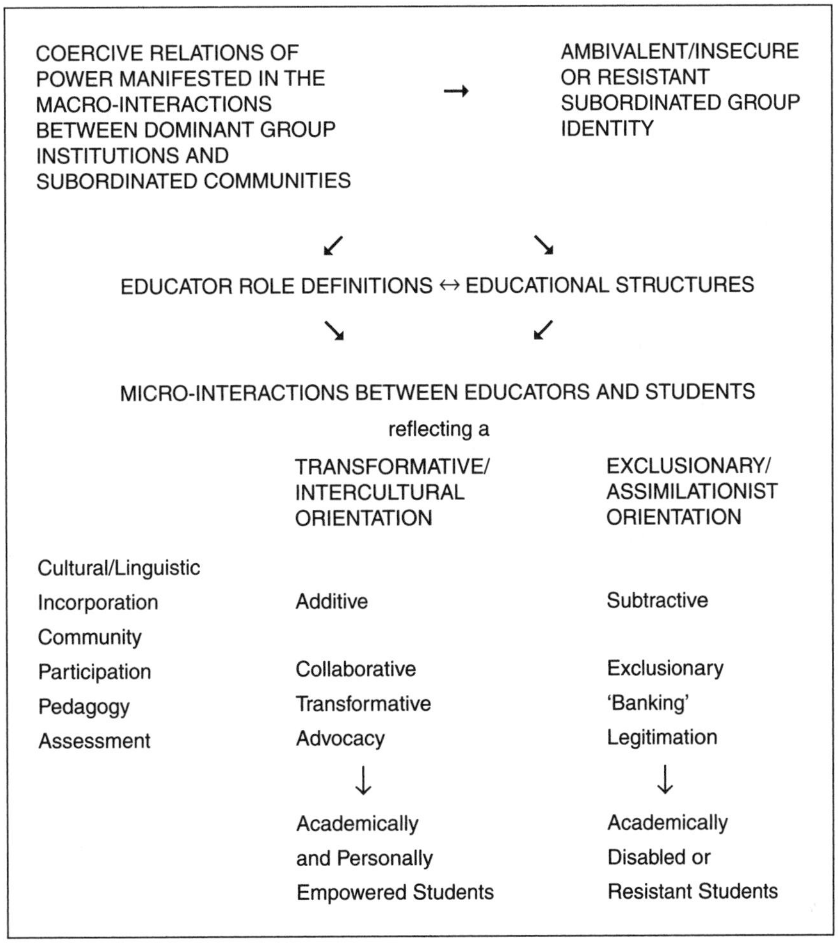

```
┌─────────────────────────────────────────────────────────────────┐
│                                                                   │
│  COERCIVE RELATIONS OF                    AMBIVALENT/INSECURE      │
│  POWER MANIFESTED IN THE                  OR RESISTANT            │
│  MACRO-INTERACTIONS           →           SUBORDINATED GROUP       │
│  BETWEEN DOMINANT GROUP                   IDENTITY                 │
│  INSTITUTIONS AND                                                 │
│  SUBORDINATED COMMUNITIES                                         │
│                                                                   │
│                  ↙              ↘                                │
│     EDUCATOR ROLE DEFINITIONS ↔ EDUCATIONAL STRUCTURES            │
│                  ↘              ↙                                │
│                                                                   │
│     MICRO-INTERACTIONS BETWEEN EDUCATORS AND STUDENTS             │
│                      reflecting a                                 │
│                 TRANSFORMATIVE/        EXCLUSIONARY/              │
│                 INTERCULTURAL          ASSIMILATIONIST            │
│                 ORIENTATION            ORIENTATION               │
│                                                                   │
│  Cultural/Linguistic                                             │
│  Incorporation    Additive             Subtractive               │
│  Community                                                       │
│  Participation    Collaborative        Exclusionary              │
│  Pedagogy         Transformative       'Banking'                 │
│  Assessment       Advocacy             Legitimation              │
│                       ↓                    ↓                     │
│                   Academically         Academically             │
│                   and Personally       Disabled or              │
│                   Empowered Students   Resistant Students        │
│                                                                   │
└─────────────────────────────────────────────────────────────────┘
```

FIGURE 2 Intervention for collaborative empowerment

assimilate them completely. The term *Transformative/Intercultural* refers to the orientation required to challenge the operation of coercive relations of power in the school and wider society. This form of pedagogy entails interactions between educators and students that foster the collaborative creation of power; in other words, *empowerment*. Although *exclusionary* and *assimilationist* may appear to be opposites insofar as 'exclusionary' focuses on segregation of subordinated groups from the mainstream of schools and society while 'assimilationist' focuses on total integration into the society, in reality they are frequently two sides of the same coin: both orientations aspire to make subordinated groups invisible and inaudible.

By contrast, *Transformative/Intercultural* orientations are based on principles of racial and cultural equality and a commitment to educate students for full participation within a democratic society. This implies providing opportunities for students to develop a form of critical literacy where they become capable not only of decoding the words, but also reading between the lines in order to understand how power is exercised through various forms of discourse (advertisements, political rhetoric, textbooks, etc.). The focus is on understanding not only what is said but also whose perspectives are represented and whose have been excluded.

The macro-interactions between dominant and subordinated groups in the wider society give rise to particular forms of educational structures that are designed to reflect the priorities of the society. Since dominant groups, almost by definition, determine the priorities of the society, education has historically tended to reproduce the relations of power in the broader society.

Examples of educational structures that reflect coercive relations of power are:

- submersion programs for bilingual students that actively suppress their L1 and cultural identity;
- exclusion of culturally diverse parents from participation in their children's schooling;
- tracking or streaming practices that place subordinated group students disproportionately in lower-level tracks;
- use of biased standardized tests for both achievement monitoring and special education placement;
- teacher education programs that prepare teachers for a mythical monolingual monocultural white middle-class student population;

- curriculum content that reflects the perspectives and experiences of dominant groups and excludes those of subordinated groups.

These educational structures constitute a frame that sets limits on the kinds of interactions that are likely to occur between educators and students. They *constrict* rather than expand the interactional space.

Societal macro-interactions also influence the ways in which educators define their roles in relation to culturally diverse students and communities; in other words, they influence the mindset of assumptions, expectations and goals that educators bring to the task of educating students. The framework presented [here] argues that culturally diverse students are empowered or disabled as a direct result of their interactions with educators in the schools. These interactions are mediated by the implicit or explicit role definitions that educators assume in relation to four organizational aspects of schooling:

- The extent to which students' language and cultural background are affirmed and promoted within the school; this includes the extent to which literacy instruction in school affirms, builds on, and extends the vernacular literacy practices that many culturally diverse students engage in outside the context of school (see, for example, Hardman, 1998; Heath, 1983; Lotherington *et al.*, 1998; Martin-Jones & Bhatt, 1998; Vasquez, Pease-Alvarez & Shannon, 1994).
- The extent to which culturally diverse communities are encouraged to participate as partners in their children's education and to contribute the 'funds of knowledge' that exist in their communities to this educational partnership (Moll, Amanti, Neff & Gonzalez, 1992; Schecter & Bayley, 1998).
- The extent to which instruction promotes intrinsic motivation on the part of students to use language actively in order to generate their own knowledge, create literature and art, and act on social realities that affect their lives. The alternative is what Freire (1983) termed a *banking education* where the teacher defines her role as depositing information and skills in students' memory banks.
- The extent to which professionals involved in assessment become advocates for students by focusing primarily on the ways in which students' academic difficulty is a function of interactions within the school context rather than legitimizing the location of the 'problem' within students.

These four dimensions, namely, language/culture incorporation, community participation, pedagogy, and assessment represent sets of educational structures that will affect, but can also be influenced by, educators' role definitions.

It is important to note that students (and communities) do not passively accept dominant group attributions of their inferiority. Frequently, they actively resist the operation of the societal power structure as it is manifested in educational settings. An example is the three-day school boycott called by the Latino/Latina community in Santa Barbara when the school board voted to end the city's 25-year-old bilingual program in January 1998. Four hundred families set up their own alternative bilingual academy in a community centre (Hornblower, 1998).

For some students, resistance can contribute to academic development (Zanger, 1994); students work hard to succeed in order to repudiate their teachers' low expectations. However, more typically, resistance takes the form of mentally withdrawing from a coercive educational relationship. Unfortunately, this withdrawal usually entails severe costs with respect to academic success and upward mobility (Fordham, 1990; Willis, 1977).

In summary, a central principle of the present framework is that the negotiation of identity in the interactions between educators and students is central to students' academic success or failure. Our interactions with students are constantly sketching a triangular set of images:

- an image of our own identities as educators;
- an image of the identity options we highlight for our students; consider, for example, the contrasting messages conveyed to students in classrooms focused on collaborative critical inquiry *transformative education)* compared to classrooms focused on passive internalization of information (Freire's *banking education)*;
- an image of the society we hope our students will help form.

In other words, an image of the society that students will graduate into and the kind of contributions they can make to that society is embedded implicitly in the interactions between educators and students. These interactions reflect the way educators have defined their role with respect to the purposes of education in general and culturally diverse students and communities in particular. Are we preparing students to accept the societal status quo (and, in many cases, their own inferior status therein) or are we preparing them to participate actively and critically in the democratic process in pursuit of the ideals of social justice and equity which are enshrined in the constitutions of most democratic countries?

This perspective clearly implies that in situations where coercive relations of power between dominant and subordinated groups predominate, the creation of interpersonal spaces where students' identities are validated will entail a direct challenge by educators (and students) to the societal power structure. For example, to acknowledge that culturally diverse students' religion, culture and language are valid forms of *self*-expression, and to encourage their development, is to challenge the prevailing attitudes in the wider society and the coercive structures that reflect these attitudes.

In summary, empowerment derives from the process of negotiating identities in the classroom. Interactions between educators and culturally diverse students are never neutral with respect to societal power relations. In varying degrees, they either reinforce or challenge coercive relations of power in the wider society. Historically, subordinated group students have been disempowered educationally in the same way their communities have been disempowered in the wider society. In the same way as the attribution of inherent inferiority legitimated the brutalities of slavery, the slaughter of indigenous peoples, and the exploitation of colonized populations in countries around the world, definitions of subordinated group students as 'genetically inferior' (e.g. Dunn, 1987; Jensen, 1969), 'culturally deprived', or simply suffering cognitive confusion as a result of bilingualism have been used to explain their poor academic performance and justify their continued educational exclusion. It follows from this analysis that subordinated group students will succeed academically to the extent that the patterns of interaction in the school challenge and reverse those that have prevailed in the society at large.

References

Baker, C. (1996) *Foundations of Bilingual Education and Bilingualism.* Clevedon: Multilingual Matters.

Beykont, Z.F. (1994) Academic progress of a nondominant group: A longitudinal study of Puerto Ricans in New York City's late-exit bilingual programs. Doctoral dissertation presented to the Graduate School of Education, Harvard University.

Collier, V.P. (1987) Age and rate of acquisition of second language for academic purposes. *TESOL Quarterly* 21, 617–641.

Corson, D. (1998a) *Language Policy in Schools.* Mawah, NJ: Lawrence Erlbaum Associates.

Cummins, J. (1981b) Age on arrival and immigrant second language learning in Canada: A reassessment. *Applied Linguistics* 1, 132–149.

Cummins, J. (1991c) Interdependence of first- and second-language proficiency in bilingual children. In E. Bialystok (ed.) *Language Processing in Bilingual Children* (pp. 70–89). Cambridge: Cambridge University Press.

Cummins, J. and Corson, D. (eds) (1997) *Bilingual Education. Vol. 5. Encyclopedia of Language and Education.* Dordrecht, The Netherlands: Kluwer Academic Publishers.

Cummins, J., Swain, M., Nakajima, K., Handscombe, J., Green, D. and Tran, C. (1984) Linguistic interdependence among Japanese and Vietnamese immigrant students. In C. Rivera (ed.) *Communicate Competence Approaches to Language Proficiency Assessment: Research and Application* (pp. 60–81). Clevedon: Multilingual Matters.

Dunn, L. (1987) *Bilingual Hispanic Children on the US Mainland: A Review of Research on Their Cognitive, Linguistic, and Scholastic Development.* Circle Pines, MN: American Guidance Service.

Fitzgerald, J. (1995) English-as-a-second-language learners' cognitive reading processes: A review of research in the United States. *Review of Educational Research* 65, 145–190.

Fordham, S. (1990) Racelessness as a factor in Black students' school success: Pragmatic strategy or pyrrhic victory? In N.M. Hidalgo, C.L. McDowell and E.V. Siddle (eds) *Facing Racism in Education* (pp. 232–262). Cambridge, MA: Harvard Educational Review.

Freire, P. (1983) Banking education. In H. Giroux and D. Purpel (eds) *The Hidden Curriculum and Moral Education: Deception or Discovery?* Berkeley, CA: McCutcheon Publishing Corporation.

Gándara, P. (1999) *Review of Research on Instruction of Limited English Proficient Students: A Report to the California Legislature.* Santa Barbara, CA: University of California, Linguistic Minority Research Institute.

Genesee, F. (1979) Acquisition of reading skills in immersion programs. *Foreign Language Annals* 12, 71–77.

Hakuta, K., Butler, Y.G. and Witt, D. (2000) *How Long Does It Take English Learners to Attain Proficiency?* Santa Barbara, CA: University of California Linguistic Minority Research Institute.

Hardman, J. (1998) Literacy and bilingualism in a Cambodian community in the USA. In A.Y. Durguno lu and L. Verhoeven (eds) *Literacy Development in a Multilingual Context: Cross-Cultural Perspectives* (pp. 51–81). Mahwah, NJ: Lawrence Erlbaum Associates.

Heath, S.B. (1983) *Ways with Words.* Cambridge: Cambridge University Press.

Hornblower, M. (1998) No habla Español. *TIME* (January 26), 44.

Jensen, A.R. (1969) How much can we boost IQ and scholastic achievement? *Harvard Educational Review* 39, 1–123.

Klesmer, H. (1994) Assessment and teacher perceptions of ESL student achievement. *English Quarterly* 26 (3), 8–11.

Lotherington, H., Ebert, S., Watanabe, T., Norng, S. and Ho-Dac, T. (1998) Biliteracy practices in suburban Melbourne. *Australian Language Matters* 6 (3), 3–4.

Martin-Jones, M. and Bhatt, A. (1998) Literacies in the lives of young Gujerati speakers in Leicester. In A.Y. Durgunoğlu and L. Verhoeven (eds) *Literacy Development in a Multilingual Context: Cross-Cultural Perspectives* (pp. 37–50). Mahwah, NJ: Lawrence Erlbaum Associates.

Moll, L.C., Amanti, C., Neff, D. and González, N. (1992) Funds of knowledge for teaching: Using a qualitative approach to connect homes and classrooms. *Theory Into Practice* 31 (2), 132–141.

Schecter, S.R. and Bayley, R. (1998) Concurrence and complementarity: Mexican-background parents' decisions about language and schooling. *Journal for a Just and Caring Education* 4 (1), 47–64.

Sierra, J. and Olaziregi, I. (1991) *EIFE 3. Influence of Factors on the Learning of Basque. Study of the Models A, B and D in Second Year Basic General Education.* Gasteiz: Central Publications Service of the Basque Country.

Vásquez, O.A., Pease-Alvarez, L. and Shannon, S.M. (1994) *Pushing Boundaries: Language and Culture in a Mexicano Community.* New York: Cambridge University Press.

Verhoeven, L. and Aarts, R. (1998) Attaining functional literacy in the Netherlands. In A.Y. Durgunoğlu and L. Verhoeven (eds) *Literacy Development in a Multilingual Context: Cross-Cultural Perspectives* (pp. 111–134). Mahwah, NJ: Lawrence Erlbaum Associates.

Wagner, D. A. (1998) Putting second language first: Language and literacy learning in Morocco. In L. Verhoeven and A.Y. Durgunoglu (eds) *Literacy Development in a Multilingual Context* (pp. 169–183). Mahway, NJ: Lawrence Erlbaum Associates.

Willis, P. (1977) *Learning to Labor: How Working Class Kids Get Working Class Jobs.* Lexington: D.C. Heath.

Zanger, V.V. (1994) 'Not joined in': Intergroup relations and access to English literacy for Hispanic youth. In B.M. Ferdman, R.-M. Weber and A. Ramírez (eds) *Literacy Across Languages and Cultures* (pp. 171–198). Albany: SUNY Press.

Education Comes in Diverse Shapes and Forms for U.S. Bilinguals

Eugene E. García

There are many different educational approaches to teaching bilingual students in the United States today. The main distinction among such programs is at what level they use the students' native languages during instruction, and to what extent is English used during instruction. In reviewing these programs, Eugene García describes the common characteristics that provide "optimal learning conditions for linguistically and culturally diverse populations that lead to high academic performance." As García documents, many programs have been initiated in the schools, and in order to best educate children, we should consider the features that make some successful, rather than adopting only a single approach.

Eugene García is Vice President for University-School Partnerships at Arizona State University, after serving as Dean of the ASU College of Education. He has served as a Senior Officer and Director of the Office of Bilingual Education and Minority Language Affairs in the U.S. Department of Education. He was also a member of President Obama's Transition Team. García has received grants from the Foundation for Child Development, the National Science Foundation, and from the Irvine Foundation to fund his ongoing research in the areas of bilingual education and effective schooling for Hispanic students. He has also published over 150 books, book chapters, and journal articles. His most recent books include *Hispanic Education in the United States: Raíces y Alas* (Rowman and Littlefield, 2001) and the book from which the current selection is drawn, *Teaching and Learning in Two Languages* (2005).

Key Concept: features of successful bilingual education programs

For a school district staff with bilingual students, there are many program options: Transitional bilingual education, maintenance bilingual education, English as a second language, immersion, sheltered English, and submersion were developed as program types by the U.S. Government Accounting Office in 1987. Ultimately, staff should reject program and model labels and instead answer the following questions:

1. What are the native-language and English-language characteristics of the students, families, and communities we serve?
2. What model of instruction is desired?
    (a) How do we choose to use the native language and English as *mediums of instruction?*
    (b) How do we choose to handle the instruction in the native language and English?
3. What is the nature of staff and resources necessary to implement the desired instruction? (García, 2001a).

These program initiatives can be differentiated by the way they use the native language and English during instruction (Ovando & Collier, 1998; Ovando et al., 2002). In the most recent yet highly outdated (no new national survey has been conducted since 1993) national survey, Development Associates (1993) surveyed 333 school districts in the 19 states that serve over 80% of language-minority students in the United States. For grades K–5, they report the following salient features about the use of language(s) during the instruction of language minority students:

1. Ninety-three percent of the schools reported that the use of English predominated in their programs; 7% indicated that the use of the native language predominated.
2. Sixty percent of the sampled schools reported that both the native language and English were used during instruction.

3. Thirty percent of the sampled schools reported minimal or no use of the native language during instruction.

Programs serving these students have been characterized primarily as bilingual transitional education (Ovando & Collier, 1998). These programs transition students from early-grade, native-language-emphasis instruction to later-grade, English-emphasis instruction and, eventually, to English-only instruction. Other programs that use the primary language emphasize maintaining proficiency in the native language while adding English proficiency—these will be referred to as dual-language programs.

For the one-third of the students receiving little or no instruction in their native language, two alternative types of instructional approaches likely predominate: English-language development/English as a second language (ELD/ESL) and sheltered English immersion (SEI). Each type depends on the primary use of English during instruction but does not ignore the fact that the students are limited in English proficiency. However, these programs do not require instructional personnel who speak the native language of the student. Moreover, they are suited to classrooms in which non-English-speaking students come not from one native-language background but from many.

School district staffs have been creative in developing a wide range of programs for language-minority students. They have answered the above questions differently for (1) different language groups, (2) different grade levels, (3) different subgroups within a classroom, and (4) different levels of language proficiency. The result has been a broad and at times perplexing variety of instructional arrangements (August & Hakuta, 1997; García, 2001a; Ovando & Collier, 1998). This chapter addresses the theoretical and related goals of these diverse instructional arrangements.

What Works: Optimal Instruction and Learning Features

August and Hakuta (1997) provide a comprehensive review of optimal learning conditions for linguistically and culturally diverse populations that lead to high academic performance. Their reviews of 33 case studies identify the following attributes:

> A supportive school-wide climate, school leadership, a customized learning environment, articulation and coordination within and between schools, use of native language and culture in instruction, a balanced curriculum that includes both basic and higher-order skills, explicit skill instruction, opportunities for student-directed instruction, use of instructional strategies that enhance understanding, opportunities for practice, systematic student assessment, staff development, and home and parent involvement. (p. 171)

These features resonate with other recent studies of effectiveness for programs specifically designed for linguistically and culturally diverse populations. California Tomorrow (1995), in a study of early childhood care in California, concluded that a set of principles guided quality child care across a variety of care settings that serve a growing community of linguistically and culturally diverse families:

1. Support the development of ethnic identity and antiracist attitudes among children.
2. Build upon the cultures of families and promote cross-cultural understanding among children.
3. Foster the preservation of children's home language and encourage bilingualism among all children.
4. Engage in on-going reflection and dialogue. (p. 8)

In a state-mandated study of exemplary schools serving the state's linguistically and culturally diverse students, several key attributes were common (Berman, 1992). These features included: (1) *flexibility*—adapting to the diversity of languages, mobility, and special nonschool needs of these students and their families; (2) *coordination*—utilizing sometimes scarce and diverse resources, such as federal and state moneys and local community organizations, in highly coordinated ways to achieve academic goals; (3) *cultural validation*—schools validated their students' cultures by incorporating materials and discussions that built on the linguistic and cultural aspects of the community; and (4) *a shared vision*—a coherent sense of who the students were and what they hoped to accomplish led by a school's principal, staff, instructional aides, parents, and community (Berman, 1992).

Three more recent "effective-exemplary" analyses of schools that serve high percentages of linguistically and culturally diverse students nationally are worthy of mention (Thomas & Collier, 1995). Three key factors are reported as significant in producing academic success for students in studies of five urban and suburban school districts in various regions of the United States. The studies focus on the length of time needed to be academically successful in English and consider factors influencing academic success, such as the student, program, and instructional variables. These studies include about 42,000 student records per school year and from 8 to 12 years of data from each school district.

1. Cognitively complex academic instruction through students' home language for as long as possible and through second language for part of the school day.
2. Use of current approaches to teaching academic curriculum using both students' home language and English through active, discovery, and cognitively complex learning.
3. Changes in the sociocultural context of schooling, such as integrating English speakers, implementation of additive bilingual instructional goals, and

transformation of minority/majority relations to a positive plane (Thomas & Collier, 1995).

A series of case studies of exemplary schools throughout the United States serving highly diverse and poor student populations also illustrates what can be done to promote academic excellence (McLeod, 1996). In these studies, selected schools with demonstrated records of academic success were subjected to intensive site-by-site study with the goal of identifying specific attributes at each site related to the functioning of the school as well as a more ambitious effort to identify common attributes across the sites. Schools in four states (Texas, Illinois, California, and Massachusetts) were particularly successful in achieving high academic outcomes with a diverse set of students and used these common goals for ensuring high-quality teaching.

Foster English acquisition and the development of mature literacy. Schools used native-language abilities to develop literacy that promoted English-literacy development. Programs in these schools were more interested in this mature development than transitioning students quickly into English-language instruction. This approach paid off in English-language development at levels that allowed students to be successful in English instruction.

Deliver grade-level content. Challenging work in the academic disciplines was pursued simultaneously with the goals of English-language learning. Teachers organized lessons to deliver grade-level instruction through a variety of native-language, sheltered English, and ESL activities.

Organize instruction in innovative ways. Examples of innovations included: (1) "schools-within-schools" to more responsively deal with diverse language needs of the students; (2) "families" of students who stayed together for major parts of the schoolday; (3) "continuum classes" in which teachers remained with their students for 2 to 3 years, helping teachers become more familiar with and responsive to student diversity; and (4) grouping of students more flexibly on a continuous basis so as to respond to the developmental differences between their native and second language.

Protect and extend instructional time. Schools used after-school programs, supportive computer-based instruction, and voluntary Saturday schools and summer academies, activities that multiplied the opportunities for students to engage in academic learning. Regular teachers or trained tutors were used to extend this learning time. Not surprisingly, a majority of students took advantage of these voluntary extensions. Care was taken not to erode the daily instructional time that was available—erosion often related to auxiliary responsibilities for teachers that take valuable time away from instruction.

Expand the roles and responsibilities of teachers. Teachers were given much greater roles in curricular and instructional decision making. This decision making was much more collective in nature to ensure cross-grade articulation and coordination. Teachers in these schools became full co-partners, devising more "authentic" assessments that could inform instruction and developing assessment tools and scoring rubrics in reading and mathematics.

Address students' social and emotional needs. Because schools were located in low-income neighborhoods, a proactive stance with regard to issues in these communities was adopted. An after-school activity that was aimed at families—particularly dealing with issues of alcohol and drug abuse, family violence, health care, and related social service needs—brought the school staff together with social service agencies at one school site. Similar examples of actual family counseling and direct medical care were arranged at other sites.

Involve parents in their children's education. Some of the schools were magnet schools to which parents had chosen to send their children and where parental involvement was part of the school contract. Areas of parental involvement included participation in school committees, school festivals and celebrations, and student field trips. In nonmagnet schools, parent outreach services were an integral part of the school operation. In all cases, communication was accomplished on a regular basis in various home languages. Parental participation in governance of the school was a common attribute, although participation levels were highly variable (adapted from McLeod, 1996, pp. 13–33).

Dual-Language Programs

Dual-language (DL) programs are relatively new in the United States. These programs aim to create bilingual, bicultural students without sacrificing these students' success in school or beyond. The goals of DL are to provide high-quality instruction for language-minority students and to provide instruction in a second language for English-speaking students. Schools teach children language through content, with teachers adapting their instruction to ensure children's comprehension and using content lessons to convey vocabulary and language structure. Striving for half language-minority students and half English-speaking students in each classroom, DL programs also aim to teach cross-cultural awareness. Programs vary in terms of the amount of time they devote to each language, which grade levels they serve, how much structure they impose for the division of language and curriculum, and what populations they serve.

There are two main models of language division. In the 50:50 model, instruction is given half the day in English and half the day in Spanish throughout the grades. In the 90:10 model, children spend 90% of their kindergarten schooldays in the minority language, with the percentage gradually dropping to 50% by fourth or fifth grade. Currently, there are more than 225 DL programs in the United States, and the number is growing rapidly (Christian, 1999). While the vast majority offer instruction in Spanish and English, there are also programs that target Korean, Cantonese, Arabic, French, Japanese, Navajo, Portuguese, and Russian (Christian, 1997).

Two-way immersion programs have three major goals: to help language-minority children learn English and succeed in U.S. schools; to help language-majority children learn a foreign language without sacrificing their own success in school; and to promote linguistic and ethnic equity among the children, encouraging children to bridge the gaps between cultures and languages which divide our society. These goals are naturally interdependent. English-speaking children who understand that another language and culture are as important as their own will be more interested in learning about that culture and acquiring that language. Minority-language children who acquire higher school status due to their knowledge of their home language will have more confidence in their ability to learn English. Children who learn the language of their peers are more likely to want to become friends with them, regardless of racial or ethnic background.

English-Language Development in a Bilingual Program

The widely accepted view in the ESL research and pedagogical community is that the ideal for all English-language learners is to maintain or enrich their native languages while acquiring English as a second language (Eisenstein, Bodman, & Carpenter, 1995; Gass & Neu, 1995; Kasper & Blum-Kulka, 1993). Thus, by definition, a bilingual program in which English is to be learned will include a second-language-acquisition component—often referred to as English as a second language. Like bilingual education, second-language acquisition/English as a second language (SLA/ESL) are umbrella terms that can refer to a large number of possible educational models, including not only the more traditional pull-out efforts in which SLA/ESL teachers work outside of the regular classroom but also push-in programs in which SLA/ESL teachers collaborate with regular classroom teachers in their regular classes to promote language development, understanding of content, and sociocultural insights among all students. SLA/ESL alternatives also include self-contained classrooms that offer content through an ESL approach called sheltered English (Stern, 1992).

When it is not possible to provide bilingual education (including some form of English-language development, ELD), then SLA/ESL alone is the next-best alternative to submersion—the option of offering no special assistance to bilingual students. Multilingual populations, small numbers of learners, and/or limited availability of bilingual staff can all contribute to the logistics of such

educational decisions. SLA/ESL specialists are trained to promote additive bilingualism and to provide comprehensible input to learners in a supportive environment. It is a mainstay of the SLA/ESL professional to respect linguistic and cultural diversity and to communicate to all learners that their heritage languages and cultures are treasures to be preserved.

Developing "Academic" English in U.S. Bilinguals

English "academic" proficiency requires a mastery of a more extensive range of features than "everyday" English. An increasing number of children in the United States comes from a non-English background. One of the most important yet difficult aspects of English-language development for students from non-English backgrounds, here referred to as bilinguals, is the development of English in academic contexts (García, 2002).

The advanced language/literacy skills in reading, writing, speaking, and listening needed to succeed in school are often referred to as "academic" English (García, 2001a; Scarcella, 2001; Wong Fillmore & Snow, 1999). A variety of models have been proposed to explain the role of academic language proficiency in educational attainment. Some, like Cummins (1981, 1997), have focused on the cognitive load and degree of context students manipulate as they respond to academic tasks. Some (e.g., Crandall, Dale, Rhodes, & Spanos, 1989) have focused on a close analysis of the language used in specific disciplines, considering academic English as a compilation of many subregisters, such as the language of mathematics. Canale and Swain (1980), in a widely discussed model, propose four key areas to consider: grammatical competence (encompassing lexical, syntactic, and phonological knowledge in an integrated whole), sociolinguistic knowledge (knowing which lexicogrammatical form to choose given the topic, the social setting, and the interlocutor), discourse competence (knowing how to put sentence-level propositions in sequence to form coherent text), and strategic competence (knowing how to negotiate clarification when lack of competence impedes communication). This model implies that unique aspects of language proficiency are tapped by each knowledge type and gives a broader perspective from which to view academic English.

Scarcella (2001, 2003) has undertaken both conceptual and empirical studies in English academic language. Her framework provides an analysis of the various social, cognitive, and linguistic components that students must master to communicate competently in a range of informal and academic situations. She argues that the features that enable students to use English in both everyday situations and academic situations are acquired at different rates over time; that some are easily acquired and some are not; and that most features of academic English depend largely on the development of basic

English proficiency but there are many others (including formulaic expressions and simple word forms and transitional devices) that may depend less on the development of general language proficiency.

In addition, some features may be more important than others. For instance, specific linguistic *functions* (such as persuading, arguing, and hypothesizing) are more characteristic of academic English than of ordinary English. Also, academic English makes more extensive use of reading and writing, while ordinary English makes more extensive use of listening and reading. In addition, Cummins (1981, 1984) points out that academic English, in comparison to ordinary English, is cognitively demanding and relatively decontextualized. All students, including those acquiring English as their second language in a bilingual schooling context, rely on their prior knowledge of words, phraseology, grammar, and pragmatic conventions to understand and interpret it. However—perhaps most importantly—academic English requires a much greater mastery of a wider range of linguistic features than ordinary English. It is important to note that despite these differences, both academic English and ordinary English require proficiency in the same linguistic components: phonological, grammatical, lexical, sociolinguistic, and discourse.

Although there is no consensus regarding the development of academic English in bilingual schooling, considerable agreement is beginning to emerge concerning the factors that affect its development (see, e.g., Fitzgerald, 1995; García, 1999; Snow et al., 1998). The development of academic English is affected by political, social, psychological, and linguistic variables. Instruction also has an enormous effect on the acquisition of academic English. Academic English seems to develop successfully in classrooms in the following circumstances:

1. *Teachers provide students with ample exposure to academic English.* Teachers make regular use of classroom activities and assignments that call on students to use academic English; they provide students with extensive practice in the use of academic English in speech and in writing, including in meaningful academic discussions about the texts that the students use and in writing expository essays.
2. *Teachers get students to attend closely to the features of academic English.* Teachers regularly use classroom activities and assignments that call on students to attend closely to the features of academic English.
3. *Teachers provide direct, explicit language instruction.* Such instruction includes particular features of academic English, including, for instance, word formation skills and specific uses of grammar.
4. *Teachers provide multiple assessments of bilinguals' academic English.* Teachers provide learners with honest feedback concerning their English development. They provide valid, reliable, and frequent

assessments (including entry-level assessment; diagnostic, formative assessments; and summative assessments) using multiple measures. These measures (1) allow teachers to measure their students' developing academic English and to tailor their instruction appropriately, (2) provide parents with information that help them support their children's learning, and (3) give instructional information to all students that helps them learn English.

Specially Designed Academic Instruction

Of particular significance for teachers of non-English-speaking students is the use of Specially Designed Academic Instruction in English (SDAIE) techniques (Becijos, 1997; García, 1999; Krashen, 1999). These strategies attempt to minimize the use of English as the primary mode of delivering instruction while tapping the existing knowledge base of the students during content-based instruction. Students are not asked to learn English before being challenged in subject-matter learning. In particular, SDAIE attempts to match content instruction to students' language/communicative abilities where the instruction is not delivered in the student's primary language. These techniques allow the students to do the following:

- Show their abilities in ways that do not depend only on English proficiency, such as using pictures to depict a science concept
- Connect their real-world experiences to the content material under study (begin with fiction the students have read in their primary language then allow analysis of biological phenomenon present in their lives)
- Utilize talents not normally interjected into academic content learning, such as using music or dramatic presentations
- Seek and receive support from their peers, such as using group projects and community-based data gathering
- Utilize diverse ways to focus on and attack the assigned material, such as journal writing, quick-writes, and graphic organizers
- Connect content-area material through thematic units, such as inter-disciplinary organization of content material around a theme

Although there is little research that specifically addresses the effectiveness of these instructional practices, they are making their way into teacher training programs and classroom instruction in U.S. schools.

Conclusion

This chapter has highlighted theories and related educational practices that provide a broad understanding of important issues in the schooling of bilingual students.

The knowledge base continues to expand but is in no way complete. In addition, it would be incorrect to conclude that the data and theory that have emerged have been primary factors in determining the educational treatment of bilingual students. However, it does seem appropriate to identify possible program, policy, and research implications derived from research and practice as highlighted by this and previous reviews (August & Hakuta, 1997; Ovando & Collier, 1998):

1. One major goal in the education of bilingual students should be the development of the full repertoire of linguistic skills in English, in preparation for participation in mainstream classes. Future research should delineate alternative routes that will allow for effective achievement of this "academic English" goal.

2. Time spent learning the native language is not time lost in developing English. Children can become fluent in a second language without losing the first language, and can maintain the first language without retarding the development of the second language. Presently, it is not clear what processes or mechanisms best facilitate positive transfer. Identifying such processes is a challenge for future researchers.

3. There is no cognitive cost in the development of more than one language in children during the schooling process. Further research that explores specific cognitive/academic functioning of bilingualism is needed.

4. Programs for bilingual students should be flexible enough to adjust to individual and cultural differences among children. Furthermore, educators should recognize that it is not abnormal for some students to need instruction in two languages for relatively long periods of time. We do not yet know how much time in the first language positively or negatively influences academic outcomes in the second language. This type of research will greatly enhance educational outcomes for language-minority students.

5. Educators should expect that young children will take several years to learn a second language at a level comparable to that of a native speaker. At the same time, they should not have lower expectations of older learners, who can typically learn languages quite quickly and often end up speaking them just as well as younger learners. The clear distinction between "young" and "older" learners requires further research.

6. Particularly for children who are at risk of reading failure, reading should be taught in the native language. Reading skills acquired in the native language will transfer readily and quickly to English and result in higher reading achievement in English. Future research should connect overall literacy in the native and second languages.

7. A major problem for minority students in the United States is that many English-speaking children share the negative stereotypes of their parents and the society at large. Any action that upgrades the status of the minority child's language contributes to the child's opportunities for friendship with native English-speaking children. Future research with these children should link issues of ethnic identity, general self-concept, and specific academic status.

References

August, D., & Hakuta, K. (1997). *Improving schooling for language-minority children: A research, policy and practice.* Chicago: Thomas.

Becijos, J. (1997). *SDAIE: Strategies for teachers of English learners.* Boston: Allyn & Bacon.

Berman, P. (1992). *Meeting the challenge of language diversity: An evaluation of California programs for pupils with limited proficiency in English.* San Francisco, CA: American Educational Research Association.

California Tomorrow. (1995). *The unfinished journey: Restructuring schools in a diverse society.* San Francisco: Author.

Canale, M., & Swain, M. (1980). Theoretical bases of communicative approaches to second language teaching and testing. *Applied Linguistics, 1(1),* 1–47.

Christian, D. (1997). *Directory of two-way bilingual education programs.* Washington, DC: Center for Applied Linguistics.

Christian, D. (1999). *Two-way bilingual education: Progress on many fronts.* Washington, DC: Center for Applied Linguistics.

Crandall, J., Dale, T., Rhodes, S., & Spanos, G. (1989). *English skills for algebra.* England Cliffs, NJ: CAL/Prentice-Hall Regents.

Cummins, J. (1981). The role of primary language development in promoting educational success for language minority students. In California Department of Education (Ed.), *Schooling and language minority students: A theoretical framework* (pp. 3–50). Los Angeles: Evaluation, Dissemination, and Assessment Center.

Cummins, J. (1984). *Bilingualism and special education.* San Diego: College Hill Press.

Cummins, J. (1997). Minority status and schooling in Canada. *Anthropology and Education Quarterly, 28(3),* 411–436.

Eisenstein, E. M., Bodman, J., & Carpenter, M. (1995). Cross-cultural realizations of greetings in American English. In S. Gass & J. Neu (Eds.), *Speech Acts Across Cultures.* Hillsdale, NJ: Erlbaum.

Fitzgerald, J. (1995). English-as-a-second-language reading instruction in the United States: A research review. *Journal of Reading Behavior, 27,* 115–152.

García, E. E. (1999), *Understanding and meeting the challenge of student cultural diversity* (2nd ed.). New York: Houghton Mifflin.

García, E. (2001a). *Hispanic education in the United States: Raices y alas.* Lanham, MD: Rowman & Littfield.

García, E. (2002). Bilingualism and schooling in the United States. *International Journal of the Sociology of Language, 155(156),* 1–92.

Gass, S., & Neu, J. (1995). *Speech acts across cultures.* Berlin: Mouton de Gruyter.

Kasper, G., & Blum-Kulka, S. (1993). *Intercultural pragmatics.* New York: Oxford University Press.

Krashen, S. D. (1999). *Condemned without a trial: Bogus arguments against bilingual education.* Portsmouth, NH: Heinemann.

McLeod, B. (1996). *School reform and student diversity: Exemplary schools for language minority students.* Washington, DC: Institute for the Study of Language and Education, George Washington University.

Ovando, C., & Collier, V. (1998). *Bilingual and ESL classrooms* (2nd ed.). New York: McGraw Hill.

Scarcella, R. (2001). *Key issues in accelerating English language development.* Berkeley: University of California Press.

Scarcella, R. (2003). *Academic English: A conceptual framework.* Santa Barbara: University of California Language Minority Research Institute.

Snow, C. E., Burns, S., & Griffin, P. (1998). *Preventing reading difficulties in young children.* Washington, DC: National Academy Press.

Stern, H. H. (1992). *Issues and options in language teaching.* Oxford, UK: Oxford University Press

Thomas, W. P., & Collier, V. P. (1995). *A longitudinal analysis of programs serving language minority students.* Washington, DC: National Clearinghouse on Bilingual Education.

Wong Fillmore, L., & Snow, C. E. (1999). *What educators—especially teachers—need to know about language: The bare minimum.* Santa Barbara: Language Minority Research Institute.

Religion

Selection 29

IRA C. LUPU, DAVID MASCI, AND ROBERT W. TUTTLE, from *Religion in the Public Schools*

Selection 30

KHYATI Y. JOSHI, from "Religious Oppression of Indian Americans in the Contemporary United States," in Maurianne Adams, Warren J. Blumenfeld, Carmelita Cateñeda, Heather W. Hackman, Madeline L. Peters, and Ximena Zúñiga, *Readings for Diversity and Social Justice*

Religion in the Public Schools

Ira Lupu, David Masci, and Robert W. Tuttle

Ira Lupu is F. Elwood and Eleanor Davis Professor of Law at George Washington University Law School. David Masci is a Senior Research Fellow at the Pew Forum on Religion and Public Life. Robert Tuttle is the David R. and Sherry Kirschner Berz Professor of Law at George Washington University Law School. The Pew Research Center's Forum on Religion and Public Life, launched in 2001, seeks to promote a deeper understanding of issues at the intersection of religion and public affairs. The Pew Forum conducts surveys, demographic analyses, and other social science research on important aspects of religion and public life in the United States and around the world.

Religion in the Public Schools is a 2007 report by The Pew Forum on Religion and Public Life laying out some of the key court cases and laws in the twentieth and twenty-first centuries related to religion and public schools. The authors describe the context leading to each court case, explain the case itself, and give a follow-up to how some of the cases have affected education in the years following the cases. The cases they describe include those related to school prayer; the Pledge of Allegiance in schools; creationism and evolution in the curriculum; study of the Bible in schools; school holiday programs; multiculturalism; and the religious rights of students, parents, teachers, and administrators.

Key Concept: laws regarding religion in public schools

*N*early a half-century after the Supreme Court issued its landmark ruling striking down school-sponsored prayer, Americans continue to fight over the place of religion in public schools. Indeed, the classroom has become one of the most important battlegrounds in the broader conflict over religion's role in public life.

Some Americans are troubled by what they see as an effort on the part of federal courts and civil liberties advocates to exclude God and religious sentiment from public schools. Such an effort, these Americans believe, infringes upon the First Amendment right to the free exercise of religion.

Civil libertarians and others, meanwhile, voice concern that conservative Christians are trying to impose their values on students of all religious stripes. Federal courts, the civil libertarians point out, have consistently interpreted the First Amendment's prohibition on the establishment of religion to forbid state sponsorship of prayer and most other religious activities in public schools.

Prayer and the Pledge

School Prayer

The most enduring and controversial issue related to school-sponsored religious activities is classroom prayer. In *Engel v. Vitale* (1962), the Supreme Court held that the Establishment Clause prohibited the recitation of a school-sponsored prayer in public schools. *Engel* involved a simple and seemingly nonsectarian prayer composed especially for use in New York's public schools. In banning the prayer exercise entirely, the court did not rest its opinion on the grounds that unwilling students were coerced to pray; that would come much later. Rather, the court emphasized what it saw as the wrongs of having the government create and sponsor a religious activity.

The following year, the high court extended the principle outlined in *Engel* to a program of daily Bible reading. In *Abington School District v. Schempp*, the court ruled broadly that school sponsorship of religious exercises violates the Constitution. *Schempp* became the source of the enduring constitutional doctrine that all government action must have a predominantly secular purpose— a requirement that, according to the court, the Bible-reading exercise clearly could not satisfy. By insisting that religious expression be excluded from the formal curriculum, the Supreme Court was assuring parents that public schools would be officially secular and would not compete with parents in their children's religious upbringing.

With *Engel* and *Schempp*, the court outlined the constitutional standard for prohibiting school-sponsored religious expression, a doctrine the court has firmly maintained. In *Stone v. Graham* (1980), for instance, it found unconstitutional a Kentucky law requiring all public schools to post a copy of the Ten Commandments. And in *Wallace v. Jaffree* (1985), it overturned an Alabama law requiring public schools to set aside a moment each day for silent prayer or meditation.

School sponsorship of student-led prayer has fared no better. In 2000, the Supreme Court ruled in *Santa Fe Independent School District v. Doe* that schools may not sponsor student-recited prayer at high school football games.

More sweeping in its consequences is *Lee v. Weisman* (1992), which invalidated a school-sponsored prayer led by an invited clergyman at a public school commencement in Providence, R.I. The court's 5–4 decision rested explicitly on the argument that graduating students were being forced to participate in a religious ceremony. The case effectively outlawed a practice that was customary in many communities across the country, thus fueling the conservative critique that the Supreme Court was inhospitable to public expressions of faith.

The Pledge of Allegiance

In 1954, Congress revised the Pledge of Allegiance to refer to the nation as "under God," a phrase that has since been recited by generations of schoolchildren. In 2000, Michael Newdow filed suit challenging the phrase on behalf of his daughter, a public school student in California. Newdow argued that the words "under God" violated the Establishment Clause because they transformed the pledge into a religious exercise.

The case, *Elk Grove Unified School District v. Newdow*, reached the Supreme Court in 2004, but the justices did not ultimately decide whether the phrase was acceptable. Instead, the court ruled that Newdow lacked standing to bring the suit because he did not have legal custody of his daughter. In concurring opinions, however, four justices expressed the view that the Constitution permitted recitation of the pledge—with the phrase "under God"—in public schools.

Since then, the issue has not again reached the Supreme Court but is still being litigated in the lower courts. In *Myers v. Loudoun County Public Schools* (2005), the 4th U.S. Circuit Court of Appeals upheld the reciting of the pledge in Virginia, but a U.S. district court in California ruled the other way in a new suit involving Michael Newdow and other parents. The court ruling in California, *Newdow v. Congress of the United States* (2005), is on appeal in the 9th U.S. Circuit Court of Appeals.

Religion in the Curriculum

Creationism and Evolution

Courts have long grappled with attempts by school boards and other official bodies to change the curriculum in ways that directly promote or denigrate a particular religious tradition. Best known among these curriculum disputes are those involving the conflict between proponents and opponents of Darwin's theory of evolution, which explains the origin of species through evolution by means of natural selection. Opponents favor teaching some form of creationism, the idea that life came about as described in the biblical book of Genesis or evolved under the guidance of a Supreme Being. A recent alternative to Darwinism, intelligent design, asserts that life is too complex to have arisen without divine intervention.

The Supreme Court entered the evolution debate in 1968, when it ruled, in *Epperson v. Arkansas*, that Arkansas could not eliminate from the high school biology curriculum the teaching of "the theory that mankind descended from a lower order of animals." Arkansas' exclusion of that aspect of evolutionary theory, the court reasoned, was based on a preference for the account of creation in the book of Genesis and thus violated the state's constitutional obligation of religious neutrality. Almost 20 years later, in *Edwards v. Aguillard* (1987), the Supreme Court struck down a Louisiana law that required "balanced treatment" of evolution science and "Creation science," so that any biology teacher who taught one also had to teach the other. The court said the law's purpose was to single out a particular religious belief—in this case, biblical creationism—and promote it as an alternative to accepted scientific theory. The court also pointed to evidence that the legislation's sponsor hoped that the balanced treatment requirement would lead science teachers to abandon the teaching of evolution.

Lower courts have consistently followed the lead of *Epperson* and *Edwards*. As a result, school boards have lost virtually every fight over curriculum changes designed to challenge evolution, including disclaimers in biology textbooks. One of the most recent and notable of these cases, *Kitzmiller v. Dover Area School District* (2005), involved a challenge to a Pennsylvania school district's policy of informing high school science students about intelligent design as an alternative to evolution. After lengthy testimony from both proponents and opponents of intelligent design, a federal district court in Pennsylvania concluded that the policy violates the Establishment Clause because intelligent design is a religious, rather than scientific, theory.

The *Kitzmiller* ruling has received an unusually large amount of attention, in part because it is the first decision to address the constitutionality of teaching intelligent design. But *Kitzmiller* also has been noted for its forceful analysis, and the ruling is likely to be highly influential if and when courts hear other cases involving alternatives to Darwinian evolution.

Study of the Bible

Courts have also expended significant time and energy considering public school programs involving Bible study. Although the Supreme Court has occasionally referred to the permissibility of teaching the Bible as literature, some school districts have instituted Bible study programs that courts have found unconstitutional. Frequently, judges have concluded that these courses are thinly disguised efforts to teach a particular understanding of the New Testament.

In a number of these cases, school districts have brought in outside groups to run the Bible study program. The groups, in turn, hired their own teachers, in some cases Bible college students or members of the clergy who did not meet state accreditation standards.

Such Bible study programs have generally been held unconstitutional because, the courts conclude, they teach the Bible as religious truth or are designed to inculcate particular religious sentiments. For a public school class to study the Bible without violating constitutional limits, the class would have to include critical rather than devotional readings and allow open inquiry into the history and content of biblical passages.

Holiday Programs

Christmas-themed music programs also have raised constitutional concerns. For a holiday music program to be constitutionally sound, the courts maintain, school officials must ensure the predominance of secular considerations, such as the program's educational value or the musical qualities of the pieces. The schools also must be sensitive to the possibility that some students will feel coerced to participate in the program (*Bauchman v. West High School*, 10th U.S. Circuit Court of Appeals, 1997; *Doe v. Duncanville Independent School District*, 5th Circuit, 1995). Moreover, the courts have said, no student should be forced to sing or play music that offends his religious sensibilities. Therefore, schools must allow students to choose not to participate.

Multiculturalism

Not all the cases involving religion in the curriculum concern the promotion of the beliefs of the majority. In a number of recent cases, challenges have come from Christian

groups arguing that school policies discriminate against Christianity by promoting cultural pluralism.

In a recent example, the 2nd U.S. Circuit Court of Appeals considered a New York City Department of Education policy regulating the types of symbols displayed during the holiday seasons of various religions. The department allows the display of a menorah as a symbol of Hanukkah and a star and crescent as a symbol of Ramadan but permits the display of only secular symbols of Christmas, such as a Christmas tree; it explicitly forbids the display of a Christmas nativity scene in public schools.

Upholding the city's policy, the Court of Appeals reasoned in *Skoros v. Klein* (2006) that city officials intended to promote cultural pluralism in the highly diverse setting of the New York City public schools. The court concluded that a "reasonable observer" would understand that the menorah and star/crescent combination had secular as well as religious meanings. The judicial panel ruled that the policy, therefore, did not promote Judaism or Islam and did not denigrate Christianity.

In another high-profile case, *Citizens for a Responsible Curriculum v. Montgomery County Public Schools* (2005), a Maryland citizens' group successfully challenged a health education curriculum that included discussion of sexual orientation. Ordinarily, opponents of homosexuality could not confidently cite the Establishment Clause as the basis for a complaint, because the curriculum typically would not advance a particular religious perspective. However, the Montgomery County curriculum included materials in teacher guides that disparaged some religious teachings on homosexuality as theologically flawed, and contrasted those teachings with what the guide portrayed as the more acceptable and tolerant views of some other faiths. The district court concluded that the curriculum had both the purpose and effect of advancing certain faiths while denigrating the beliefs of others. The county has now rewritten these materials to exclude any reference to the views of particular faiths. These new materials will be more difficult to challenge successfully in court because the lessons do not condemn or praise any faith tradition.

Rights in and out of the Classroom

Rights of Students

The leading Supreme Court decision on freedom of student speech is *Tinker v. Des Moines School District* (1969), which upheld the right of students to wear armbands protesting the Vietnam War. The court ruled that school authorities may not supress expression by students unless the expression significantly disrupts school discipline or invades the rights of others.

This endorsement of students' freedom of speech did not entirely clarify things for school officials trying to determine students' rights. *Tinker* supported student expression, but it did not attempt to reconcile that right of expression with the Supreme Court's earlier decisions forbidding student participation in school-sponsored prayer and Bible reading. Some school officials responded to the mix of student liberties and restraints by forbidding certain forms of student-initiated religious expression such as the saying of grace before lunch in the school cafeteria, student-sponsored gatherings for prayer at designated spots on school property or student proselytizing aimed at other students.

After years of uncertainty about these matters, several interest groups devoted to religious freedom and civil liberties drafted a set of guidelines, "Religious Expression in Public Schools," which the U.S. Department of Education sent to every public school superintendent in 1995. The department revised the guidelines in 2003, placing somewhat greater emphasis on the rights of students to speak or associate for religious purposes. The guidelines highlight these four general principles:

- Students, acting on their own, have the same right to engage in religious activity and discussion as they do to engage in comparable secular activities.
- Students may offer a prayer or blessing before meals in school or assemble on school grounds for religious purposes to the same extent as other students who wish to express their personal views or assemble with others.
- Students may not engage in religious harassment of others or compel other students to participate in religious expression, and schools may control aggressive and unwanted proselytizing.
- Schools may neither favor nor disfavor students or groups on the basis of their religious identities.

A case recently decided by the 9th U.S. Circuit Court of Appeals underscores the difficulties that school officials still can face when students exercise their right to religious expression on school property. In this case, gay and lesbian students in a California high school organized a Day of Silence, in which students promoting tolerance of differences in sexual orientation refrained from speaking in school. The following day, Tyler Harper, a student at the school, wore a T-shirt that on the front read, "Be Ashamed, Our School Has Embraced What God Has Condemned," and on the back, "Homosexuality Is Shameful, Romans 1: 27." School officials asked him to remove the shirt and took him out of class while they attempted to persuade him to do so.

The Court of Appeals, in *Harper v. Poway Unified School District* (2006), rejected Harper's claim that the school officials violated his First Amendment rights. Judge Stephen Reinhardt, writing for a 2–1 majority and citing *Tinker*, argued that students' constitutional rights may be limited to prevent harming the rights of other students. He concluded that the T-shirt could be seen as violating school policies against harassment based on sexual orientation.

Writing in dissent, Judge Alex Kozinski asserted that the school's sexual harassment policy was far too vague and sweeping to support a restriction on all anti-gay speech. He also argued that the school district had unlawfully discriminated against Harper's freedom of speech. By permitting the Gay and Lesbian Alliance to conduct the Day of Silence, Kozinski said, the district was choosing sides on a controversial social issue and stifling religiously motivated speech on one side of the issue.

Harper petitioned the Supreme Court to review the appeals court decision. But Harper graduated from high school, and the case took a different turn. The Supreme Court, in early 2007, ordered the lower court to vacate its ruling and dismiss the case on the grounds that it had become moot.

Although the case appears to be over, it highlights a conflict—one likely to recur—between the rights of students to engage in religious expression and the rights of other students to be educated in a nonhostile environment. Indeed, Tyler Harper's sister, Kelsie Harper, filed suit in a federal district court arguing that the school district's "anti-hate behavior" policies violate the First Amendment as well as California law. The district court rejected Kelsie Harper's argument, and her case is now being appealed to the U.S. 9th Circuit Court of Appeals. The Supreme Court eventually may clarify school officials' power to suppress speech as a means of protecting the rights of other students. For now, cases like *Harper* illustrate the difficulties for school officials in regulating student expression.

Rights of Parents

Parents sometimes complain that secular practices at school inhibit their right to direct the religious upbringing of their children. These complaints typically rest on both the Free Exercise Clause of the First Amendment and the 14th Amendment's Due Process Clause, which forbids the state to deprive any person of "life, liberty or property without due process of law." The Supreme Court has interpreted them as protecting the right of parents to shape and control the education of their children. When they object to certain school practices, the parents often seek permission for their children to skip the offending lesson or class—to opt out—rather than try to end the practice schoolwide.

The first decision by the Supreme Court on parents' rights to control their children's education came in *Pierce v. Society of Sisters* (1925), which guarantees to parents the right to enroll their children in private rather than public schools, whether the private schools are religious or secular. In *West Virginia State Board of Education v. Barnette* (1943), the court upheld the right of public school students who were Jehovah's Witnesses to refuse to salute the American flag. The students said the flag represented a graven image and that their religion forbade them from recognizing it. The court's decision rested on the right of *all* students, not just those who are religiously motivated, to resist compulsory recitation of official orthodoxy, political or otherwise.

Of all the Supreme Court rulings supporting religious opt-outs, perhaps the most significant came in *Wisconsin v. Yoder* (1972), which upheld the right of members of the Old Order Amish to withdraw their children from formal education at the age of 14. The court determined that a state law requiring children to attend school until the age of 16 burdened the free exercise of their families' religion. The Amish community had a well-established record as hardworking and law-abiding, the court noted, and Amish teens would receive home-based training. The worldly influences present in the school experience of teenagers, the court said, would undercut the continuity of agrarian life in the Amish community.

In later decisions, lower courts recognized religious opt-outs in other relatively narrow circumstances. Parents successfully cited religious grounds to win the right to remove their children from otherwise compulsory military training (*Spence v. Bailey*, 1972) and from a coeducational physical education class in which students had to dress in "immodest apparel" (*Moody v. Cronin*, 1979). In *Menora v. Illinois High School Association* (1982), the 7th U.S. Circuit Court of Appeals ruled that the Illinois High School Association was constitutionally obliged to accommodate Orthodox Jewish basketball players who wanted to wear a head covering, despite an association rule forbidding headgear. The *Menora* case involves a narrow exception from the dress code, rather than a broader right to opt-out of a curriculum requirement.

A great many school districts, meanwhile, have recognized the force of parents' religious or moral concerns on issues of sexuality and reproduction and have voluntarily provided opt-outs from classes devoted to those topics. Under these opt-out programs, parents do not have to explain their objection, religious or otherwise, to participation by their children. On other occasions, however, parental claims that the Constitution entitles them to remove their children from part or all of a public school curriculum have fared rather poorly.

The issue of home schooling is a good example. Before state legislatures passed laws allowing home schooling, parents seeking to educate their children at home were often unsuccessful in the courts. Many judges distinguished these home schooling cases from *Yoder* on the grounds that *Yoder* involved teenagers rather than young children. The judges also noted that *Yoder* was concerned with the survival of an entire religious community—the Old Order Amish—rather than the impact of education on a single family. Indeed, in virtually all of the cases decided over the past 25 years, courts have found that the challenged curriculum requirement did not unconstitutionally burden parents' religious choices.

The most famous of the cases is *Mozert v. Hawkins County Board of Education* (1987), in which a group of Tennessee parents complained that references to mental telepathy, evolution, secular humanism, feminism, pacifism and magic in a series of books in the reading curriculum offended the families' Christian beliefs. The school board originally allowed children to choose alternative reading materials but then eliminated that option.

The 6th U.S. Circuit Court of Appeals ruled in the county's favor on the grounds that students were not being asked to do anything in conflict with their religious obligations. Furthermore, the court said, the school board had a strong interest in exposing children to a variety of ideas and images and in using a uniform series of books for all children. Because the books did not explicitly adopt or denigrate particular religious beliefs, the court concluded, the parents could insist neither on the removal of the books from the schools nor on their children opting out.

The 1st U.S. Circuit Court of Appeals reached a similar conclusion in a case involving a public high school in Massachusetts that held a mandatory assembly devoted to AIDS and sex education. In that case, *Brown v. Hot, Sexy, and Safer Productions* (1995), the court rejected a complaint brought by parents who alleged that exposure to sexually explicit material infringed on their rights to religious freedom and control of the upbringing of their children. The court concluded that this onetime exposure to the material would not substantially burden the parents' freedom to rear their children and that the school authorities had strong reasons to inform high school students about "safe sex."

Rights of Teachers and Administrators

Without question, public school employees retain their rights of free exercise. When off duty, school employees are free to engage in worship, proselytizing or any other lawful faith-based activity. When they are acting as representatives of a public school system, however, courts have said their rights are constrained by the Establishment Clause.

This limitation on religious expression raises difficult questions. The first is what limits school systems may impose on the ordinary and incidental expression of religious identity by teachers in the classroom. Most school systems permit teachers to wear religious clothing or jewelry. Similarly, teachers may disclose their religious identity; for instance, they need not refuse to answer when a student asks, "Do you celebrate Christmas or Hanukkah?" or "Did I see you at the Islamic center yesterday morning?"

At times, however, teachers act in an uninvited and overtly religious manner toward students and are asked by school administrators to refrain. When those requests have led to litigation, the administrators invariably have prevailed, on the grounds that they are obliged (for constitutional and pedagogical reasons) to be sensitive to a teacher's coercive potential.

In *Roberts v. Madigan* (1990), a federal district court similarly upheld the authority of a public school principal in Colorado to order a fifth-grade teacher to take down a religious poster from the classroom wall and to remove books titled *The Bible in Pictures* and *The Life of Jesus* from the classroom library. The court also backed the principal's order that the teacher remove the Bible from his desktop and refrain from silently reading the Bible during instructional time. The court emphasized that school principals need such authority to prevent potential violations of the Establishment Clause and to protect students against a religiously coercive atmosphere.

That much is clear. What is less clear is how public school systems should draw the line between teachers' official duties and their own time. That was the key question in *Wigg v. Sioux Falls School District* (8th U.S. Circuit Court of Appeals, 2004), in which a teacher sued the South Dakota school district for refusing to allow her to serve as an instructor in the Good News Club (an evangelical Christian group) that met after school hours at various public elementary schools in the district.

A federal district court ruled that the teacher, Barbara Wigg, should be free to participate in the club but said the school district could insist that the teacher not participate at the school where she was employed. The appellate court affirmed the decision but went further in protecting the teacher's rights, concluding that the school district could not exclude her from the program at her own school. The court reasoned that once the school day ended, Wigg became a private citizen, leaving her free to be a Good News Club instructor at any school, including the one where she worked. The court ruled that no reasonable observer would perceive Wigg's after-school role as being carried out on behalf of the school district, even though the club met on school property.

In general, then, the courts have ruled that public schools have substantial discretion to regulate the religious expression of teachers during instructional hours, especially when students are required to be present. The courts have also ruled, however, that attempts by schools to extend that control into noninstructional hours constitute an overly broad intrusion on the teachers' religious freedom.

Religious Oppression of Indian Americans in the Contemporary United States

Khyati Y. Joshi

Khyati Joshi is Associate Professor at Farleigh Dickinson University. She is an internationally recognized scholar on cultural and religious pluralism in America, and in particular on issues involving race, religion, and immigrant communities. In 2009, the Organization for Security and Cooperation in Europe invited her to address legislators from its 56 member nations on the development of hate crimes legislation to address the European region's growing religious and racial pluralism.

Joshi uses the term "*religious oppression* to refer to the historic and systemic pattern of domination and subordination of religious minorities at cultural, institutional, and interpersonal levels" in the following selection "Religious Oppression of Indian Americans in the Contemporary United States" (from Maurianne Adams, Warren J. Blumenfeld, Carmelita Cateñeda, Heather W. Hackman, Madeline L. Peters, and Ximena Zúñiga, *Readings for Diversity and Social Justice*, 2nd ed., Routledge, 2010). Yoshi describes levels of privilege afforded Christianity in America and describes the experiences of Muslims, Hindus, and Sikhs within the Christian-dominated society of contemporary United States. Her key points are that because Christians have the power to define normalcy in the United States, the beliefs of non-Christians are misrepresented or discounted and harassment, discrimination, and violence against those non-Christians are legitimized through that Christian privilege.

Key Concept: religious oppression of non-Christians

eligious discrimination is not a post 9/11 phenomenon. Indeed, it is not even a 21st century phenomenon, nor has it been limited to non-Christian faiths. The United States has a history of religious intolerance from its beginnings. Native Americans, Catholics, Quakers, Mennonites, and Eastern Orthodox Christians faced religious persecution in 17th, 18th and 19th century America. Here, I use the term *religious oppression* to refer to the historic and systemic pattern of domination and subordination of religious minorities at cultural, institutional, and interpersonal levels—and focus my attention here on the experiences of Hindus, Muslims, and Sikhs within the dominant U.S. Christian milieu. This subordination is a product of the unequal power relationships among religious groups within American society and is supported by the actions of individuals, and by institutional structures *religious discrimination*), as well as by cultural norms *religious prejudice*) and societal practices. Through religious oppression, Christianity is used to marginalize, exclude, and deny the members and institutions of non-Christian religious groups in society the privileges and

access that accompany a Christian affiliation. Using the term *religious oppression* to refer to a social system operating at these three levels—individual, institutional, and cultural/societal—recognizes that the disadvantages of non-Christianity exist not merely at the one-on-one level but also at a societal and institutional level where individuals are socialized, punished, rewarded and guided in ways that maintain and perpetuate oppressive structures.

In the context of America's racial schema, religious oppression sets up a dichotomy between the privilege and normativity associated with Whiteness and Christianity, and the othering of dark skin and non-Christian-ness. For Indian American Hindus, Muslims, and Sikhs who are not white and not Christian, religious discrimination may be exacerbated by racial discrimination. This privileging and othering takes place at the overarching level of society and culture, where norms are perpetuated implicitly and explicitly. By comparison with these hegemonic (or assumed and every-day) norms, these non-Christian "other" religions come to be seen as evil, wrongful, deviant and/or sick. In the act of defining Hinduism, Islam and

Sikhism as exotic and illegitimate, and thereby excluding them from society American white Christians are able to represent themselves as good, normal, and righteous. Moreover, because systemic racialization of religion reinforces this pattern of religious exclusion and inferiority, that same discourse serves to reinforce the inclusion and superiority of white Christianity.

Societal norms are reproduced through written laws and policies as well as inscribed in the daily behaviors of the populace. Christian holidays—"holy days"—are endorsed institutionally through a calendar that serves the convenience and priorities of Christians, as in a Monday-Friday workweek and Sunday worship, or official days off for Christmas. Government sanction reinforces the dominant status of Christianity and the implied illegitimacy of other faiths. The mindset of rightness and privilege is manifested in the treatment of religious minorities by members of the majority—whether that treatment is meant to harm and threaten members of the target religion (as does the assumption that Muslims or Sikhs are terrorists), or "save" them (by Christian proselytizing). These attitudes and behaviors, whether conscious or not, maintain systemic religious oppression.

Let me be clear. I am not saying Christianity, as a faith or a belief system, is to be held accountable for religious oppression, or that all Christians consciously or purposely harbor prejudice toward non-Christians or approve of institutional religious discrimination. But I am saying that Christianity and Christian identity in the U.S. functions as a tool of oppression in the largely unconscious privileging of Christians through a hegemonic culture and social system. The issue at hand here is not one of intention, but one of consequences, of noticing the effects on religious minorities of the many instances of marginalization and disadvantage, despite our pluralistic society.

In the case of Hindus, Muslims, and Sikhs, the phenomenon of religious oppression in the U.S. exists and is perpetuated by and through a specific combination of facts and acts each building upon its precedent. These include: (1) in the sociocultural and historical context of the United States, Christians have the power to define normalcy; (2) because Christianity has been normalized, the belief systems of Hinduism, Islam, and Sikhism are misrepresented and/or discounted; (3) the normalization of Christianity within social institutions leads to harassment, discrimination, and other forms of unequal treatment towards non-Christians; (4) religious oppression justifies violence or the threat of violence.

1. Christian Groups Have The Power To Define Normalcy

To be nominally Christian requires no conscious thought or effort on the part of Christian Americans. "Business as usual" follows their schedule and reflects their theological understandings. Social norms and rituals, language, and institutional rules and rewards all presume the existence of a Christian sociopolitical history and sociocultural norms of dress, behavior, and worship. America's vocabulary of faith, practice, prayer, belief, sites of worship and religious history largely ignore the existence of other religions, some of which are older than Christianity (for example, Buddhism, Hinduism, Judaism, and Native American spiritual practices).

We can observe Christianity's normative nature at three levels of society: institutional, societal/cultural, and individual. At the institutional and societal levels, there are examples in federal and state law and policy. Clearly, the First Amendment requires that the state allow and accommodate individual religious practices, and forbids the government to show hostility toward any particular religion. While acknowledging that this is nominally true, we must look at which religion is accommodated and which religions are not. The United States Senate and House of Representatives each employ chaplains whose salaries are paid for by all U.S. taxpayers; both are Christian. An image of Moses with the Ten Commandments, along with other "law-givers," is etched in stone on the wall of the Supreme Court of the United States of America. The vacation schedules of most public schools are structured around Christian holidays, particularly Christmas and Easter. "Spring Break," for example, often coincides with the week between Palm Sunday and Easter. Policies like these permit Christian children to accompany their parents to worship and participate in the festivities leading up to each holiday without missing school or having to make up work.

Christian hegemony at the cultural and societal level is maintained in American society via the exercise of Christian privilege. In the United States, Christian privilege, like white privilege, exists through the cultural power norms that are largely invisible and thus unquestioned. Some examples of the norms underlying Christian privilege are:

- WORSHIP. The idea that it is something that occurs in a church, led by a member of the clergy. Here, the church represents both a place outside the home to go and pray, and the idea that prayer, properly performed, is done in groups and led by a person imbued by an institution with special theological authority.
- IMAGES of God, derived from western (i.e., Christian) art and literature. This god is anthropomorphized in a particular manner: singular, male, white, often elderly, and usually bearded, with two arms and two legs.
- ARCHITECTURE. The norms for houses of worship in which, for example, a steeple is "normal" but a minaret is something foreign.
- PRAYER. The Western image involves an act of worship performed in a seated or kneeling position, in silence, and with crossed hands.

- SACRED STORIES. In American society, Biblical stories, however fantastical, are treated as credible . . . Stories based in the Christian tradition, such as the Virgin birth are believed to be credible and true, whereas stories based in the Muslim tradition, such as Mohammed's midnight flight to heaven, or the Hindu tradition, such as Vishnu's periodic visitation upon earth in different incarnations, are not believed and considered to be incredible and fantastical.
- HOLIDAYS. State and federal holidays, including the position of the "weekend" on Saturday and Sunday, are structured around the Christian calendar.
- SAFETY. Most Christians are able to pray publicly and visibly in safety, without fear of violence or mockery. Also, Christian congregations can build their houses of worship without opposition from neighbors and local authorities.

Christian privilege benefits not only people who identify with Christianity or consider themselves "religious," but also those born Christian who are no longer observant. Christian privilege involves a legacy of public acceptance from which Christians benefit whether they want to or not, and whether they know it or not. It is an unearned perquisite of their identity as Christians. They can live their lives unaware of the daily exclusions, insults, and assaults endured by Hindus, Muslims, and Sikhs.

Contrariwise, non-Christians find themselves forced to explain their religions not in their own terms but by reference to a Christian vocabulary: "What is your church like. What is your Bible? When is your Christmas?" The conveniences of life as a Christian are lost to the Hindu who must leave work to observe a Hindu New Year, the Sikh who must cut his hair in order to join the military, or the Muslim student who must participate in gym class while fasting for Ramadan.

2. The Belief Systems Of Hinduism, Islam, And Sikhism, Along With Their Respective Histories And Cultures Are Delegitimized, Misrepresented And/Or Discounted

By exacerbating the "otherness" of Indian American Hindus, Muslims, and Sikhs, the racialization of religion contributes to the delegitimization of these three faiths in a number of ways. First, in everyday interactions the Christian norm is applied, and Hinduism, Islam and Sikhism are compared to this norm. Second, differences, real or imagined, from the Christian norm are highlighted, such as the Christian posture of "prayer" (kneeling, with the fingers of both hands interlaced) compared to Muslim bowing eastward or to Hindu *aarti* (fire offering). In terms of belief, the power of the norm is found at the line

between what the western mind views as "credible" and what it considers "incredible." Consider these three stories: A Jewish virgin gives birth to the child of God, after an angel visits her at night and tells her what to name the child. A prophet rides a flying horse to Heaven, accompanied by an angel. God comes to earth in the form of a dwarf and saves the world from a demon king. The first of these stories is the Biblical story of the Annunciation and the birth of Jesus to the Virgin Mary. What makes it more credible or "believable" an idea than Mohammed's midnight flight from Jerusalem, or Vishnu's periodic visitation of the Earth in different incarnations? Yet in the United States, it is. Biblical stories, however fantastical, are treated as fact, or at least as "faith." The beliefs of other religions are viewed as silly (at best) or heretical (at worst); they are branded with the more dismissive terminology of "myth" or "superstition."

Christian norms are reinforced by the Christian majority who assume these norms, and also assume without question the illegitimacy of other different faith traditions by comparison. The perception of illegitimacy grows out of ignorance, contempt, and mischaracterization of Hinduism, Islam, and Sikhism by the mass media as well as social and political institutions and individuals. Its negative effect is felt most dramatically by children and adolescents from marginalized faith traditions, whose home belief systems are invalidated and even actively contested by educators, other adults, and peers, and whose invisibility is manifested in the absence of news coverage or the congratulatory public service announcements aired around Christmas, Easter, and other "recognized" holidays. Disrespect is shown by the co-option of holy images and prayers to sell candles, perfume, and other commercial goods.

3. Harassment, Discrimination, And Other Forms Of Differential Treatment Are Institutional And Unchallenged

Another dimension of Christian privilege appears in the non-acceptance, disrespect, and invisibility of minority religious traditions, despite the Constitutional guarantee of the free exercise of religion. Christian privilege in this case involves both legal "freedom" (which is shared, at least in theory, by members of other religions) and social sanction, which is not available to marginalized faith traditions. As Christians are made to be confident, comfortable, and oblivious to their privilege because of the omnipresence of Christianity in the American culture and social system, other religious groups are made unsure, uncomfortable and alienated. Being Christian protects one from many kinds of hostility, distress and violence, which—even when subtle—are part of daily experience for people of Hindu, Sikh, Muslim, and other non-western religious backgrounds. While society's endorsement may be tacit, and even invisible to the Christian eye, it's absence is conspicuous and visible to these religious minorities.

4. Violence And The Threat of Violence

Many South Asian and Arab Americans and other "double minorities"—non-White and non-Christian—experience verbal attacks and physical threats and attacks from people who are both White and Christian. Students in the K-12 school setting are threatened because of their religious identity (often signified by turban or hijab) and racialized phenotype. While hate crimes and threats of violence against these populations did in fact increase during the weeks and months after September 11, 2001, they were not confined to this "9/11 backlash" and in fact have occurred both before and since that time.

Indian American Hindus, Muslims and Sikhs are part of immigrant communities, and for these communities, although experiencing racism, the experience of religion is paramount. The communities are built on the edifice of religion, and while they also encounter racism, the experience of religious oppression is critical and must not be ignored. The impact of racial oppression takes on *religious* dimensions, arising from the belief in religion as something especially profound and "never changing." Religious oppression results in Indian American Sikhs, Muslims and Hindus identifying more closely with their home religion, magnifying religion's role in one's life and increasing the likelihood the individual will identify as "religious" and engage in worship, ritual, and religious study in adulthood.

Social Class

Social Class and School Knowledge

Jean Anyon

Jean Anyon is Professor at the Graduate Center, the City University of New York. She received the American Educational Research Association Lifetime Achievement Award in 2010. Anyon has published extensively on how social class affects schooling, especially in inner-city settings. Her book *Radical Possibilities: Public Policy, Urban Education, and a New Social Movement* (Routledge, 2005) offers practical and theoretical insights into securing economic and educational justice for America's poor families and students.

Anyon presents a study of four types of schools in the following selection from "Social Class and School Knowledge," *Curriculum Inquiry* (vol. 11, no. 1, 1981). She found that social stratification of knowledge is clear, with sharp differences between the different schools. As Anyon defines the four types of schools studied, she explains that the differences lie not only along economic levels but also along the types of work the parents do. The types of schools were "working-class," "middle-class," "affluent professional," and "executive elite" schools. Anyon was especially interested in the reproductive aspects of knowledge, or those that contribute directly to the legitimation and perpetuation of existing ideologies and practices, and the nonreproductive aspects, or those that facilitate transformation of ideologies and practices. Her findings show that the schools differ with regard to whose history is taught, what the main goal of life is taught to be, the acceptability of the expression of creative ideas, and access to how to control ideas that dominate society. Anyon also found that within all schools there are possibilities for students to become transformative.

Key Concept: social stratification of knowledge

When Max Weber and Karl Marx suggested that there were identifiable and socially meaningful differences in the educational knowledge made available to literati and peasant, aristocrat and laborer, they were of course discussing earlier societies. Recent scholarship in political economy and sociology of knowledge has also argued, however, that in advanced industrial societies such as Canada and the U.S., where the class structure is relatively fluid, students of different social class backgrounds are still likely to be exposed to qualitatively different types of educational knowledge. Students from higher social class backgrounds may be exposed to legal, medical, or managerial knowledge, for example, while those of the working classes may be offered a more "practical" curriculum (e.g., clerical knowledge, vocational training) (Rosenbaum 1976; Karabel 1972; Bowles and Gintis 1976). It is said that such social class differences in secondary and postsecondary education are a conserving force in modern societies, an important aspect of the reproduction of unequal class structures (Karabel and Halsey 1977; Apple 1979; Young and Whitty 1977).

The present article examines data on school knowledge collected in a case study of five elementary schools in contrasting social class settings in two school districts in New Jersey. The data suggest, and the article will argue, that while there were similarities in curriculum topics and materials, there were also subtle as well as dramatic differences in the curriculum and the curriculum-in-use among the schools. The study reveals that even in an elementary school context, where there is a fairly "standardized" curriculum, social stratification of knowledge is possible. The differences that were identified among the schools suggest as well that rather than being simply conserving or "reproductive," school knowledge embodies contradictions that have profound implications for social change. The reproductive and nonreproductive possibilities of school knowledge involve theoretical implications of the data and will be delineated after the data have been presented....

The terminology defining social classes and differentiating the schools in this study is to be understood in a technical sense, as reflected in the process by which the sample of schools was selected. Thus, the schools in this study were differentiated not only by income level as an indicator of parent access to capital, but also by the kind of *work* that characterized the majority of parents in each school.

The first three schools were in a medium-size city district in northern New Jersey, and the final two were in a nearby New Jersey suburban district. In each of the three city schools, approximately 85% of the students were white. In the fourth school, 90% were white, and in the last school, all were white.

The first two schools are designated *working-class schools*, because the majority of the students' fathers (and approximately one-third of their mothers) were in unskilled or semiskilled occupations, with somewhat less than one-third of the fathers being skilled workers. Most family money incomes were at or below $12,000 during the period of the study, as were 38.6% of all U.S. families (U.S. Bureau of the Census 1979, p. 2, Table A). The third school is designated the *middle-class school*, although because of residence patterns the parents were a mixture of highly skilled, well-paid blue collar and white collar workers, as well as those with traditional middle-class occupations such as public school teachers, social workers, accountants, and middle-managers. There were also several local doctors and town merchants among the parents. Most family money incomes were between $13,000 and $25,000 during the period of the study, as were 38.9% of all U.S. families (U.S. Bureau of the Census 1979, p. 2, Table A).

The fourth school is designated the *affluent professional school*, because the bulk of the students' fathers were highly-paid doctors such as cardiologists; television or advertising executives; interior designers; or other affluent professionals. While there were a few families less affluent than the majority (e.g., the families of the superintendent of schools and of several professors at nearby universities, as well as several working-class families), there were also a few families who were more affluent. The majority of family money incomes were between $40,000 and $80,000 during the period of the study, as were approximately 7% of all U.S. families.[1]

The final school is called the *executive elite school*. The majority of pupils' fathers in this school were vice presidents or more advanced corporate executives in U.S.-based multinational corporations or financial firms on Wall Street. Most family money incomes were over $100,000 during the period of the study, as were less than 1% of U.S. families (see Smith and Franklin 1974). . . .

Conclusion and Implications

I would conclude that despite similarities in some curriculum topics and materials, there are profound differences in the curriculum and the curriculum-in-use in the sample of schools in this study. What counts as knowledge in the schools differs along dimensions of structure and content. The differences . . . will be assessed for social and theoretical implications. The assessment will focus on reproductive and nonreproductive aspects of knowledge in each social-class setting. "Reproductive" will refer to aspects of school knowledge that contribute directly to the legitimation and perpetuation of ideologies, practices, and privileges constitutive of present economic and political structures. "Nonreproductive" knowledge is that which facilitates fundamental transformation of ideologies and practices on the basis of which objects, services, and ideas (and other cultural products) are produced, owned, distributed, and publicly evaluated. The present definition of social change as fundamental transformation transcends the goals of, but does not deny the importance of, humanitarian efforts and practices in institutions such as the school. As we shall see, however, the genesis of truly transformative activity is in the contradictions within and between social settings.

In the working class schools there are two aspects of school knowledge that are reproductive. First, and quite simply, students in these schools were not taught their own history—the history of the American working class and its situation of conflict with powerful business and political groups, e.g., its long history of dissent and struggle for economic dignity. Nor were these students taught to value the interests which they share with others who will be workers. What little social information they were exposed to appears to provide little or no conceptual or critical understanding of the world or their situation in the world. Indeed, not knowing the history of their own group—its dissent and conflict—may produce a social amnesia or "forgetting" (Jacoby, 1975). Such "forgetting" by the working class has quietistic implications in the social arena and potentially reproductive consequences.

A second reproductive aspect of school knowledge in these working-class schools was the emphasis in curriculum and in classrooms on mechanical behaviors, as opposed to sustained conception. This is important to a reproduction of the division of labor at work and in society between those who plan and manage (e.g., technical professionals, executives) and the increasing percentage of the work force whose jobs entail primarily carrying out the policies, plans, and regulations of others. These working-class children were not offered what for them would be *cultural capital*—knowledge and skill at manipulating ideas and symbols in their own interest, e.g., historical knowledge and analysis that legitimates their dissent and furthers their own class in society and in social transformation.

These aspects of school knowledge in the working-class schools contribute to the reproduction of a group in society who may be without marketable knowledge; a reserve group of workers whose very existence, whose availability for hire, for example, when employed workers strike, serves to keep wages down and the work force disciplined. A reserve group is, of course, essential to capitalism because lower wages permit profit accumulation, which is necessary to the viability of firms, banks, state budgets and other bank-financed budgets of, one could argue, the entire system.

On the other hand, however, there is a major contradiction in school knowledge in these working-class schools, and from this may emerge a situation that is potentially socially transformative. Teacher control of students is a high priority in these schools, as in other schools. What the teachers attempted, in these two working-class schools, however, was *physical* control. There was little attempt to win the hearts and minds of these students. Now, our own era in history is one in which social control is achieved primarily through the dominant ideology and the perceived lack of ideological alternatives. But the working-class children in the schools studied here were taught very little of the ideology that is central to stable reproduction of the U.S. system, e.g., traditional bodies of knowledge that include the ideologies of an alleged lack of social alternatives to capitalist organization, patriotism and nationalism, faith in one's own chance of "making it big," and belief that the economy and polity are indeed designed in the interests of the average man and woman. In some cases, children in this study gave evidence that they had already rejected the ideologies of patriotism and of equal chances for themselves.

The absence of traditional bodies of knowledge and ideology may make these children vulnerable to alternative ideas; the children may be more open to ideas that support fundamental social change. Indeed, some of the children were already engaged in a struggle against what was to them an exploitative group—the school teachers and administrators. They were struggling against the imposition of a foreign curriculum. They had "seen through" that system. The children's struggle, however, was destructive to themselves. Really *useful* knowledge for these students, e.g., honest "citizenship" education, would authenticate students' own meanings and give them skills to identify and analyze their own social class and to transform a situation that some already perceive is not in their own interest.

A social and theoretical implication of the education of the working-class students in this study, then, is that while a reserve pool of marginally employed workers is perhaps assured by modern schooling, ideological hegemony is not. Ideological hegemony is, rather, extremely tenuous, and the working class may be less ideologically secured than some other social groups. What is important is to make available to working-class students the cultural and ideological tools to begin to transform perspicacity into power.[2]

In the middle-class school, the children I observed were not taught the history of workers or of dissent, nor were they instructed to unify around common interests they will have as wage earners in a system in which many middle-class jobs are becoming increasingly like industrial and clerical jobs—mechanical and rote (for example, computer, technical, and social work; other service jobs;

perhaps teaching; nursing and other formerly professional jobs). There were, however, distinguishing characteristics of knowledge in this middle-class school that are important primarily because of the social-class location of the families. For example, the notion of knowledge as originating in external and externally approved sources, as generated and validated by experts, may yield a passive stance before ideas and ideology and before the creation or legitimation of new ideas. This, of course, has implications of intellectual passivity, and ideological quietude. Moreover, school knowledge in the middle-class school was highly commodified. The reification of ideas and knowledge into given facts and "generalizations" that exist separately from one's biography or discovery contributes to the commodification of knowledge. It is true that knowledge in the working-class schools was reified as well. However, in order to be a commodity, a product must have some value in the marketplace and must be perceived as having some value, or no one would "buy" it. That is, it must have an exchange value. Traditional conceptual or academic knowledge in the working-class schools is not perceived by many teachers or students as having exchange value in the marketplace, or workplace, of working-class jobs. Therefore, it does not have commodity status. In the social class position of the present middle-class school, however, the teachers and students perceive the knowledge to have market value: there is a perceived chance that if one can accumulate facts, information, and "generalizations," one can exchange them for college entrance or for a white-collar (perhaps even professional) job. But as is true of all commodities, when one exchanges an object, one gives up its use for oneself. Furthermore, a commodity is useful only in an exchangeable, objectified form. Forms in which knowledge is useful for reflection, critical thought, or making sense do not generate as much value in the competition for college entrance and the majority of U.S. jobs.

Commodification of knowledge in the middle-class school is reproductive in part because it helps to legitimate and reproduce the ideology of production for consumption, for example, production of knowledge and other cultural products for the market rather than for personal use or for social transformation. (An actively consuming public is, of course, a material necessity in a capitalist system, and thus legitimation of the ideology of consumption—of production *for* consumption—has direct economic reproductive consequences as well.)

There is a second aspect of knowledge in the middle-class school that is reproductive. This is also a part of the apparent acceptance or belief in the possibility of success for oneself. It is a social fact of major importance that the U.S. middle class is a group whose recent history has shown rapidly decreasing economic stability for individual families. There is, thus, material reason for the reification of knowledge into accumulatable form and for the anxiety which the children manifest concerning tests, college, and jobs. For example, the amount of attention one must pay to "getting ahead" not only leaves little interest or time for critical attention, but it also actively fosters and strengthens belief in the ideologies of upward mobility and success. For example, "If I do not believe that there is a chance for me, and that I can succeed, why should I try so hard? Why go along?" I must *believe* in order to work hard; and to work hard increases the personal (psychological) necessity of my belief. So, the perception of social possibilities for the middle class hinted at in this study and the ideologized and reified school knowledge found in their schooling contribute not only to some of them "getting ahead," but to the production of a class with perhaps the highest degree of mystification and ideological internalization. This, of course, is reproductive.

There is, however, a potentially nonreproductive contradiction to be foreseen regarding school knowledge and the lives of these children. Many of those whose schooling and families have promised them a high reward for working hard and doing well will actually *not* succeed in the job market. This situation, after years of schooling in ideology and promises, may serve to generate cynicism or, more constructively, a critical view of the system. Also, the fact that many of these students will go to college may expose them to alternative ideas. They may be exposed to authors and professors who present alternative views and critical assessments of the social order. From this new knowledge and social perspective, they may, perhaps, be moved to utilize their own curiosity, to begin to use knowledge to question what is. Such questioning is a beginning of any socially transformative activity.

In the affluent professional school there are several aspects of school knowledge that are reproductive. First, the children are taught what is, for most of them, their own history—the history of the wealthy classes. They are taught that the power of their own group is legitimate. They are, as well, taught ways of expressing and using such ideas—that ideology—in their own interests. They are being provided with cultural capital. Indeed, the fact that the knowledge of their own group is socially prestigious knowledge enhances the exchange value of their knowledge as capital. Moreover, because many affluent professional jobs (doctor, lawyer, professor, scientist) still require conception and creativity and independent thought, many of the children in this school will be in the privileged position of having the *use* value of their knowledge (for personal creativity, for example) be at the same time its *exchange* value (for example, they will get paid for doing creative, conceptual work).

A second aspect of school knowledge that is reproductive here is its nascent empiricism (by empiricism I refer to the emphasis in adult science on basing knowledge on experience and on appearances, on observable data this experience produces). As the basis for knowledge or explanations, empiricism is socially reproductive when it provides a framework for allegedly independent thought. Empiricism uses characteristics of observable data and characteristics of the observed relationships between data

for its explanations; empiricism eschews explanations and analyses which are based on transcendent and nonempirical knowledge (see Bernstein 1978). This mode of inquiry thus uses categories and explanations that are confined to what already exists, to what can be observed. This mitigates against challenges to the necessity or naturalness of these categories and of what exists. School science programs and math manipulables make a small contribution, then, to the legitimation of empiricism as a way of seeking and testing knowledge, and to the acceptance of what is, as opposed to what could be. The programs are, in this case, a potential invisible boundary of the social thought of these children.

Accompanying the nascent empiricism in this affluent professional school is the emphasis on individual development as a primary goal of education (as opposed, for example, to the development of the priority of collective goals). A priority on personal expression, personal "meaning making" and the "construction of reality" mitigates against collectivistic values and meanings and solutions; it is thereby reproductive of values important to an individualistic, privately owned, and competitive economy.

Finally, the emphasis in the curriculum and classrooms on active use of concepts and ideas by students, as opposed to a stress on mechanics or rote behaviors, facilitates the perpetuation of an unequal division of labor in U.S. society, where some (these children?) will plan and others (working-class and middle-class children?) will have jobs that entail carrying out the plans.

There are, however, basic contradictions apparent in the school knowledge of these affluent professional children. In these conflicts one can see powerful implications for social transformation. For example, the contradiction between attempting as a student, and making sense as an adult, presumably later in one's professional creative labors, in a society where many things do *not* make sense and are irrational is a conflict which may generate political radicalism. Such a conflict may lead to intellectuals who are highly critical of the system and who attempt to persuade others by disseminating their own views. Or, it may lead to political activism, to overt attempts to take physical action against perceived political and economic irrationalities, as, for example, the students in Students for a Democratic Society (SDS)—a radical, anti-Vietnam War group—a majority of whom were from affluent professional families. Indeed, as Alvin Gouldner points out (1979), almost all leaders of social revolutions in the modern era have come from families of comparatively high standing in their society who were exposed to large amounts of cultural capital (e.g., Marx, Engels, the majority of the early Bolsheviks, Mao Tse-tung, Chou En-Lai, Ho Chi Minh, and Fidel Castro).

It is probably true that the conflict inherent in attempting to make sense in a world that is in many ways irrational is present for all children in all schools and social classes. What makes the conflict a potentially powerful force in the affluent professional school, however, is first the social-class position of these children, their cultural capital, and future access to information, power, and further cultural capital afforded to them by their social position. A second factor important here is the nature of their schooling. These children were told, and encouraged, more than the children in any other school to be creative, to think for themselves, and to make sense. It is indeed because of such encouragement to the young that the increasingly ideological notions of freedom and democracy can be turned back upon the economically and politically powerful and made into truly transformative demands.

Another contradiction to the school knowledge of these children that is nonreproductive is the contradiction between the value placed on creativity and personal decision making, and the systematic, increasingly rationalized nature of school and professional work in U.S. society. This conflict, already apparent in the use of science and reading programs in this school, is a contradiction that suggests possible later conflicts between the use and exchange values of knowledge in adult work, for example, between one's own creativity and the increasing rationalization and control of professional work by technology, bureaucratic trends, and centralization. It also suggests class conflict between affluent professionals, with their own interests and skills and relative power in the bureaucracy on one hand, and the capitalists, who are their "bosses" and who hold the purse strings, on the other. Conflict between the educated classes and the ruling class has long been a source of movement for social transformation. Indeed, as Gouldner (1979) reminds us, it has been this class—the educated, the intellectuals—who have, to date, taken control in periods of revolutionary upheaval, e.g., in the early Soviet Union and China. It is, then, important to provide the children of the affluent professional class with school knowledge that is not just conceptual, analytical, and expressive, but that is also critical and collective. Such knowledge would foster responsiveness not only to the needs of individual "meaning making" and development, but to the development of a wider social collectivity that, not coincidentally, would affirm the needs of the working and middle classes as well.

The executive elite school offers cultural capital to its children, whose families as a class have the major portion of available physical capital in society. These children are taught the history of "ruling" groups, and that rule by the wealthy and aristocratic is rational and natural, going back, for example, to the Ancient Greeks. Such knowledge is, for them, symbolic capital. They are provided with other kinds of symbolic capital as well—practice in manipulating socially prestigious language and concepts in systematic ways. They are told the importance of controlling ideas and given some insight into controlling ideas in their own (Western) culture. The fact that the culture of their social class is the dominant and most prestigious one enhances the exchange value or "worth" of their knowledge in the marketplace.

Some of these children had a fair amount of class consciousness, if this is defined as knowledge of themselves as part of a group in society and in history, and an appreciation of their own group's interests as opposing the interests of other groups in society (e.g., plebs, strikers). While class consciousness among the working classes is likely to be nonreproductive, such a consciousness among the capitalist class is, of course, likely to increase their efforts to win conflicts, to conserve culture, and to maintain their social position, e.g., to prevent what [English historian Arnold] Toynbee said was the "decay of civilization from within."

School knowledge in the executive elite school was the most "honest" about society, U.S. social problems, and social irrationalities. It was sometimes expressive of liberal concerns, as well. Indeed, it came the closest to being socially critical. The children were given analytical and unsentimental insight into the system. Whereas, for example, middle-class children might see a pluralism of equal or competing ethnic cultures, the children of the executive elite might perceive social class and economic conflict. Thus, these children may be less ideologically mystified than, for example, the middle-class students. The executive elite students—in different and more socially profitable ways than the working class students—may see more clearly through the rhetoric of nationalism and equal opportunity to the raw facts of class and class conflict.

There is a potential contradiction here in the "clarity" of understanding the system that may, in the particular context of the social-class position of these children, have transformative possibilities. This is the contradiction for them between the use and exchange values in their knowledge: the contradiction between using knowledge for pleasure and enjoying one's class privilege, for example, and the exchange value of knowledge when it must be used to maintain that privilege. Two particular characteristics that empower this contradiction for these children (because the contradiction does appear in weaker forms in other schools) are, first, that extreme pressure is necessary, and excruciating struggle is demanded in a capitalist political democracy to actually maintain one's position of economic power and privilege. To grow up in the modern capitalist class is not only to enjoy travel, luxury, good schools, and financial wealth; it is also to have to maintain power in the face of others competing with you, within an irrational economic system that is increasingly difficult to predict, manage, and control—not only in the U.S. but in a rebellious Third World, as well. To be the "best," one must continually "beat the best." This is severe pressure. Second, to be a powerful capitalist, one must cause suffering and actually exploit others. Indeed, one's wealth and power are possible only because there are others (e.g., a reserve "pool" of workers) who do not have power and resources. These two "facts of life" of "being a capitalist" mean that if one is not ideologically secured, one may reject these demands. In contrapuntal fashion, the pressures, the irrationalities, and the exploitative characteristics of one's role in the system may one day cause the system to be perceived as the enemy—to be destroyed, rather than exploited. One thinks, as examples, of ruling class "children" who have rejected their privileges for radical politics and who have attempted to destroy members of their own class (the Baader-Meinhoff Group in Germany, the Red Brigades in Italy, or, indeed, the Weathermen in the U.S.). While such efforts at social transformation are violent and irrational and are not condoned, they must be acknowledged as nonreproductive in intent.

By situating school knowledge in its particular social location, we can see how it may contribute to contradictory social processes of conservation and transformation. We see the schools reproducing the tensions and conflicts of the larger society. It becomes apparent as well that an examination of only one social site may blur the distinctions and subtleties that a comparative study illuminates. That is, a social phenomenon may differ by social class; and indeed similar (or the same) phenomena may have different meanings in different social contexts.

This study has suggested, as well, that there are class conflicts in educational knowledge and its distribution. We can see class conflict in the struggle to impose the knowledge of powerful groups on the working class and in student resistance to this class-based curriculum. We can see class conflict in the contradictions within and between school knowledge and its economic and personal values, and in attempts to impose liberal public attitudes on children of the rich.

Class conflict in education is thus not dormant, nor a relic of an earlier era; nor is the outcome yet determined. No class is certain of victory, and ideological hegemony is not secure. Those who would struggle against ideological hegemony must not confuse working-class powerlessness with apathy, middle-class ideology with its inevitability, or ruling-class power and cultural capital with superior strength or intelligence. Just as blacks were not the happy-go-lucky fellows of former stereotypes, so the working class is not dull or acquiescent, and the rich are not complacent or secure. Indeed, perhaps the most important implication of the present study is that for those of us who are working to transform society, there is much to do, at all levels, in education.

Notes

1. This figure is an estimate. According to the Bureau of the Census, only 2.6% of families in the United States had money incomes of $50,000 or over in 1977 (U.S. Bureau of the Census 1979, Table A, p. 2). For figures on income at these higher levels, see Smith and Franklin (1974).

2. It is interesting to note (as information that supports my interpretation of a "perspicacious" working class) that several academic surveys in the 1960s (reported the Vietnam War) and throughout the war, Americans with only a grade-school education were much stronger for withdrawal from the war than Americans with a college education. Zinn argues that "the regular polls, based on samplings, underestimated the opposition to the war among lower-class people" (p. 482). Just as the earliest anti-Vietnam protests came out of the Civil Rights movement as blacks began being drafted, so opposition was stronger earlier in working-class communities as young men from these communities were drafted.

References

Apple, Michael. *Ideology and curriculum.* Boston: Routledge and Kegan Paul, 1979.

Bernstein, Richard. *The restructuring of social and political theory.* Philadelphia: University of Pennsylvania Press, 1978.

Bowles, Samuel, and Gintis, Herbert. *Schooling in capitalist America: Educational reform and the contradictions of economic life.* New York: Basic Books, 1976.

Gouldner, Alvin. *The future of intellectuals and the rise of the new class.* New York: Seabury Press, 1979.

Jacoby, Russell. *Social amnesia.* Boston: Beacon Press, 1975.

Karabel, Jerome. "Community colleges and social stratification." *Harvard Educational Review* 42, no. 4 (November 1972): 521–562.

_____, and Halsey, A.H. *Power and ideology in education.* New York: Oxford University Press, 1977.

Rosenbaum, James. *Making inequality: The hidden curriculum of high school tracking.* New York: Wiley, 1976.

Smith, James, and Franklin, Stephan. "The concentration of personal wealth, 1922–1969." *American Economic Review* 64, no. 4 (May 1974): 162–167.

United States Bureau of the Census. "Money income in 1977 of families and persons in the United States." In *Current population reports,* Series P–60, no. 118. Washington, D.C.: United States Government Printing Office, 1979.

Young, Michael, and Whitty, Geoff. *Society, state and schooling.* Sussex, England: Falmer Press, 1977.

Zinn, Howard. *A people's history of the United States.* New York: Harper and Row, 1980.

The Importance of Class in Multiculturalism

Joe L. Kincheloe and Shirley R. Steinberg

In the following selection, "The Importance of Class in Multiculturalism" (*Changing Multiculturalism*, Open University Press, 1997), Joe L. Kincheloe and Shirley R. Steinberg argue that class differences are increasing and that any efforts to disregard discussions of class in society are attempts to perpetuate the status quo. They propose what they call "a critical multicultural pedagogy of empowerment for the poor." Such an education would need to include several features. There must be a recognition of class bias within education, with an understanding of the nature and effects of the polarization of wealth. There must be a political vision and an ability to organize the poor into resistance. And there must be the development of the knowledge and skills required to escape poverty.

After previously serving on the faculty at the Graduate Center, City University of New York, both authors are now at McGill University. Kincheloe is Canada Research Chair in Education and Steinberg is Associate Professor in Education. While each has published a number of articles and books individually, Kincheloe and Steinberg have written or edited a number of books together. Together, they have edited the books *Cutting Class: Social Class and Education* (Rowman & Littlefield, 2007), *Kinderculture: The Corporate Construction of Childhood* (Westview, 1997), and the book from which the following selection is drawn, *Changing Multiculturalism* (Open University Press, 1997). Kincheloe focuses his research on pedagogy, popular culture, and issues of race, class, and gender. Steinberg focuses on the construction of childhood consciousness and the corporate curriculum.

Key Concept: education for empowering the poor

The study of class as an important social force in Western society has never been more important than it is at the end of the twentieth century, with the massive redistribution of wealth from the poor to the wealthy. In 1980, for example, the average corporate chief executive officer (CEO) in the USA earned 38 times the salary of the average factory worker. By 1990 the average CEO earned 72 times as much as a teacher and 93 times as much as a factory worker (Coontz 1992; West 1993; Sleeter and Grant 1994).

The Intensification of Class Inequality

When such unequal realities exist and continue to grow, the importance of the study of class and the need for class analysis in a critical multiculturalism expands. When the specific dynamics of the polarization of wealth in the USA are analysed in further detail, new insights into mobility are uncovered. Americans have always placed great value on hard work. People who work hard should be rewarded for their effort—indeed, Americans believe that the backbone of society rests upon hard work. Most Americans would be surprised to find out, therefore, that the redistribution of wealth of the past fifteen years has been accomplished inversely in relation to hard work. Much of the new wealth created in the 1980s and 1990s did not come from inventing a better mousetrap or long hours of study or working overtime. Most new wealth befell those with enormous assets who were able to reap 'instant wealth' from rapidly fluctuating return rates on their speculative investments. Dividends, tax shelters, interest and capital gains were at the centre of the action—not hard work (Coontz 1992). The connection between class position and one's willingness to work hard may be less direct than many Americans have assumed. The attempt to dismiss class as an American issue must be exposed for what it is—an instrumental fiction designed to facilitate the perpetuation of the status quo by pointing to the poor's laziness and incompetence as the causes of their poverty. . . .

A Critical Multicultural Pedagogy of Empowerment for the Poor

. . . [C]ritical multiculturalists advocate a politically informed, socially contextualized, ethically grounded, power-sensitive pedagogy for students from poor backgrounds. Such a cultural and institutional education would possess several features.

(1) The recognition of class bias within education. Teachers, students, cultural critics and political leaders must understand the subtle and hidden ways in which class bias filters into educational policy, schooling and the cultural curriculum. Schools, media, religious groups and politicians often maintain that Western capitalist societies are lands of wealth and opportunity open to all who are willing to work. Lessons are taught daily that former communist nations in Eastern Europe and Third World societies in Africa, Asia and Latin America are stricken by poverty and its concurrent social problems, but that Western societies are above such pathology. Indeed, countries like the USA, Britain, Canada, Australia and New Zealand constantly use their expertise to repair the problems of other, less developed nations. Implicitly embedded in such a curriculum is the notion that Western societies are at their essence white and middle class nations. They are populated by upwardly mobile white men who are the smartest, most industrious people in the world. Their main concern is to make a prosperous life for themselves and their families—an objective that operates in the best interests of everyone on the planet.

In the school curriculum the poor are rarely studied. In elementary and secondary social studies curricula the contributions of workers are erased, as textbooks and curriculum guides depict a world where factory and business owners and politicians do all the work. At an implicit, subtextual level such teaching inscribes irrelevancy on the lives of the working classes. The study of the past is an examination of 'the lives of the rich and famous'. One can almost hear Robin Leach's grating voice uncritically enshrining and ennobling the behaviours of the privileged, especially when they are engaged in morally reprehensible practices such as slavery, conquest of indigenous peoples, political and economic colonization and urbanization. Such activities are often presented unambiguously as heroic acts of 'progress' that brought honour and wealth to the motherland. The brutal, often genocidal, features of these practices are too often ignored. Students and citizens involved in a pedagogy of empowerment gain the ability to expose features of the class-biased curriculum that operate daily in their lives (Swartz 1993; Sleeter and Grant 1994).

(2) The appreciation of the nature and effects of the polarization of wealth. Again, everyone benefits, the poor in particular, from an understanding of the way power works and poverty develops. Such knowledge empowers the poor not only to escape such forces themselves but to initiate public, institutional and private conversations about the relationship between poverty and wealth. Such knowledge empowers the poor to 'call' media commentators and political leaders on the superficial and misleading pronouncements that pass for an analysis of the causes of poverty (Jones 1992). Western peoples—Americans in particular—have yet to discuss the social, political and economic aspects of privilege *vis-à-vis* deprivation. In this context students and citizens will learn that the polarization of wealth and the economic perspectives that allowed it to happen have created a situation where our society's economic machine no longer needs young inexperienced people. Adolescence as a preparatory stage for adulthood is obsolete. In the 1990s it has become a corral for unneeded young people drifting in a socio-economic purgatory (for more information on these changing conditions of youth in the late twentieth century see Steinberg and Kincheloe 1997). Demographers report that elderly men have the highest suicide rate. Perceived by society and themselves as socially superfluous, old men are removed from the workforce, stripped of a future and left to wait for death. Over the past quarter century the group that witnessed the fastest growing suicide rate was males aged fifteen to nineteen (Gaines 1990). Stripped of their hopes for socio-economic mobility and burdened with the masculine expectation for self-sufficiency, these young men reflect the Western social dilemma in the 1990s. Critical multiculturalism must provide a voice of hope, an avenue of participation for students and citizens victimized by contemporary economic strategies and youth policies.

(3) The articulation of a political vision. Any pedagogy of empowerment that fails to produce a political vision that grounds the political organization of the economically marginalized will fail. The poor must gain the political savvy to uncover hegemonic ideological attempts to disempower them. In this context they will turn such political knowledge into the political clout to resist those who attempt to undermine their solidarity by appealing to their racial, gender, ethnic or religious prejudices (Jennings 1992). A critical multicultural political vision understands that the traditional route to socio-economic mobility has, contrary to the prevailing wisdom, involved first achieving income stability and then investing in education (Coontz 1992). In the light of this understanding the basis of an economic empowerment policy should revolve around job creation/full employment policies that provide child care for workers and reward and punish businesses on the basis of their contributions to the creation of good jobs and democratic workplaces in poor areas. The critical multicultural political vision calls for an increase in wages and a commitment to end welfare by providing jobs to welfare recipients. In two-parent families where one or two of the parents is a full-time worker or in single-parent families where the parent works either full-time or part-time, work should be rewarded. Health care for such workers should be guaranteed and tax burdens should be reduced (Ellwood 1988; West 1992; Nightingale 1993). Obviously, such a political vision is not popular in Western societies at the end of the century. Thus, it will take a monumental effort on the part of the poor and their allies to generate support for the policies demanded by the vision.

(4) The development of the knowledge and skills required to escape poverty.   The core of the critical multicultural pedagogy of empowerment revolves around an understanding of the impediments to social and economic mobility and the specifics of how one gets around such social, cultural and educational roadblocks. As a rigorous multidimensional course of study, the empowerment curriculum views men and women in more than simply egoistic, self-centred and rationalist terms. Individuals, especially poor ones, need help making meaning in their lives, developing sense of purpose, constructing a positive identity and cultivating self-worth. Unlike previous forms of conservative and liberal education, the pedagogy of empowerment would address these issues, using the categories covered in this [selection] as the programme's theoretical basis. Understanding socio-economic class in the larger context of historical power relations, students would understand that poverty is not simply a reflection of bad character or incompetence. In this context students would appreciate the organizational dynamics necessary to the effort to 'pull oneself up by one's bootstraps'—an undertaking often referenced but infrequently explained. The empowerment curriculum would help poor individuals to develop strategies to take control of schools, social agencies, health organizations and economic organizations. Understanding how these organizations work to undermine the interests of the poor, with their narrow and often scientifically produced definitions of normality, intelligence, family stability etc., the curriculum helps students to devise strategies to resist the imposition of policies grounded on such definitions (Ellwood 1988; Jennings 1992; West 1992).

The curriculum begins with the personal experiences of working class students but moves to understandings far beyond them; teachers constantly relate what is being learned back to student experience. Concepts and information about the world are integrated into what students already know. Such data are then analysed in the light of questions of economic justice, environmental/ecological connections to class bias, an understanding of Western modernist ways of seeing the world and the needs of democracy. Such understandings help to create a critical consciousness grounded on an appreciation of both the way ideology works to convince the marginalized of their own inferiority and how empowered people are capable of generating democratic change. Students with a critical consciousness are able to point out the ways the power bloc enforces its dominance and how in the electronic world of postmodernity the process takes on new degrees of impact and complexity. Empowered students who possess a critical multicultural consciousness draw upon the reality of everyday conflict in their lives, their recognition of the gap between the promise of democracy and the despair they have experienced as members of the low socio-economic class to illustrate to all the reality of injustice. In this emotional connection of lived experience to larger conceptual understanding, students and teachers begin to get in touch with their passion, the lived impact of their encounter with critical multiculturalism (Sleeter and Grant 1994; Britzman and Pitt 1996; Giroux 1997a).

In the light of the engagement with this passionate new consciousness, all forms of knowledge are opened to question. Here, an important skill for poor students involves the ability to reveal the power interests hidden within allegedly neutral knowledge forms. Thus, a central feature of any critical multicultural curriculum involves an analysis of existing literary works, important philosophical, political and religious texts and particular accounts of history that shape a curriculum—the Eurocentric canon, for example. In this analysis students explore where such knowledge comes from, why particular knowledge forms have not been included and the strengths and limitations of the ways of knowing that accompany the canonical discourse. What we are describing here is rigorous scholarly activity that refuses to dispense information to students dispassionately, but insists on engaging students in the discovery of personal meanings within knowledge and in the production of knowledge. As subjugated groups begin to make sense of their histories and their personal worlds, critical multiculturalists display their respect for the intellect of members of such groups by not simply accepting any meaning they make or knowledge they produce as authentic. Critical multicultural teachers and cultural workers engage the knowledge production of particular individuals, inducing them to become more and more aware of the socio-political, cultural and moral dynamics embedded within their constructions. It is not uncommon to find racist and sexist undercurrents that undermine the dignity of nonwhites and women. In this context critical multiculturalists have no problem challenging the assumptions behind such knowledge. Such engagements with canon, meaning making and critiques provide not only empowerment and cognitive development, but also a form of cultural capital that emerges from an understanding of the discourse of education. Education can be thought of as a discourse community with its own rules of knowledge, decorum and success. In the process of engaging students with the issues discussed here, critical multicultural teachers from elementary school to college are consciously involved in introducing students to this educational discourse community. Students from subjugated groups typically feel that they are not a part of the school community, that they don't possess the secret knowledge that will let them into the club. The type of critical education discussed here provides students from lower socio-economic class backgrounds with a sense of belonging that holds implications not only for their lives in school but for vocational, spiritual and interpersonal domains as well (Darder 1991; Harred 1991; Hauser 1991).

(5) Awareness of the liabilities and possibilities of resistance. When marginalized students come to the conclusion—and most of them eventually do—that education is set up to reward the values of the already successful, those whose culture most accurately reflects the mainstream, they have to negotiate how they react to this realization. Most lower socio-economic class students are, understandably, confused and dislocated because of this reality. Critical multiculturalism is devoted to helping marginalized students make sense of this reality and facilitating the formulation of the resistance to it. A central lesson for angry marginalized students involves developing an awareness of the costs of various forms of resistance. Rejection of middle class propriety often expresses itself as an abrasive classroom behaviour antithetical to mutual respect and focused analysis. Critical multiculturalists believe that the outcome of marginalized student resistance does not have to be disempowerment. To formulate an emancipatory form of resistance we draw upon the world of cultural analyst John Fiske (1993). Fiske argues that marginalized peoples comprise localized power groups who typically produce popular forms of knowledge. Such knowledge forms are powerful and can be drawn upon for psychic protection from the ideological teachings of the power bloc. Marginalized knowledge forms or, as we described them earlier, subjugated knowledge allow the oppressed to make sense of their social and educational experiences from a unique vantage point and in the process to reconstruct their identities. Critical multiculturalists both study these knowledge forms and encourage their students to explore their origins and effects. Without such understanding and encouragement, we fear that lower socio-economic class anger over the unfairness and oppression they encounter will turn violent.

Obviously, it already has in many places, but what we have observed so far may simply represent the tip of the iceberg. Marginalized peoples become violent when they are not heard. Obviously racial and class violence has a plethora of causes, but one of the most important involves the fact that the power bloc often does not listen to non-white or poor people. In this context studies indicate that while violence can be observed at all socio-economic levels, it is concentrated among males from poor backgrounds. As the disparity of wealth increases, the impulse for violence also grows. We can see such an impulse quite clearly in a variety of popular cultural forms consumed by working class men and women,

young males in particular, including heavy metal music, violent movies and professional wrestling (Gaines 1990; Fiske 1993). To avoid the escalation of violence among the oppressed, issues of social and economic justice will have to be taken seriously by individuals from various social sectors. Without dramatic action, Western societies face a violent opening of the new millennium. Constructive, non-violent strategies of resistance must be carefully studied in the coming years.

(6) Emphasis on the ability to organize the poor. Many observers consistently underestimate the localizing power of the poor to assert themselves. The localizing power of the poor is a social resource typically misunderstood by the power bloc that helps to define the parameters of what the power bloc can or cannot do. When thoughtfully organized, the poor can extend the influence of such power and move it in an emancipatory direction. Such organization increases the odds that the poor will be able to draw upon the subversive power of their localized or subjugated knowledge. An empowering aspect of such knowledge involves the insight it can provide into the connections between the actions of various power blocs—consistencies in the ways such power wielders attempt to maintain the status quo. One of the roles of critical multiculturalists . . . involves pointing out and conceptually extending such subjugated understandings. For example, an organized group of poor people would understand the class elitism at work both in a school curriculum that focused on the 'great contributions' of business, industrial and political leaders and in newspapers and TV reports that provide business news and not labour news. Though they occur in different social venues, these realities work to undermine the power and importance of the poor and working class. Such an understanding leads to the possibility of an informed resistance.

Any organizational efforts for the empowerment of the marginalized must understand that power does not flow in some unidirectional hierarchy from the powerful to the oppressed. Though their power is weak in relation to the power bloc, the oppressed possess a variety of means of eluding the control of oppressors—in many historical cases this bottom-up power has led to the overthrow of the power bloc. Organizational efforts to mobilize the disempowered must always be mindful of this potential and appreciate the marginalized individual's capacity to use his or her creativity and localized knowledge to question dominant ideologies and the hegemonic purposes of its institutions. The very lower socio-economic class students who are saddled with the disempowering burden of a low IQ, for example, are the students who because of their social location are empowered to recognize the foibles and naiveté of privileged individuals with high IQs. On many occasions we have heard the oppressed laugh at the incompetence of high-status individuals whom they had encountered at some point during their lives. Such a subjugated knowledge can serve as a conceptual basis for rejecting the cognitive essentialism of intelligence tests and the psychic scars and socio-economic disempowerment that accompany them. Such understandings can be used as a foundation for the development of a counter-hegemonic and empowered consciousness. They can experientially ground the development of counter-organizations that produce counter-histories and counter-knowledges of the relationships between the marginalized and the privileged. New forms of political organizations and pedagogical interventions must be formulated that draw upon both subjugated understandings of the privileged and critical multicultural understandings of how power works (Wartenberg 1992; Fiske 1993; West 1993; Britzman and Pitt 1996; Carspecken 1996).

References

Britzman, D. and Pitt, A. (1996) On refusing one's place: The ditchdigger's dream, in J. Kincheloe, S. Steinberg and A. Gresson (eds.) *Measured Lies: The Bell Curve Examined.* New York: St. Martin's Press.

Carspecken, P. (1996) The set-up: Crocodile tears for the poor, in J. Kincheloe, S. Steinberg and A. Gresson (eds.), *Measured Lies: The Bell Curve Examined.* New York: St. Martin's Press.

Coontz, S. (1992) *The Way We Never Were: American Families and the Nostalgia Trap.* New York: Basic Books.

Darder, A. (1991) *Culture and Power in the Classroom: A Critical Foundation for Bicultural Education.* Westport, CT: Bergin and Garvey.

Ellwood, D. (1988) *Poor Support: Poverty in the American Family.* New York: Basic Books.

Fiske, J. (1993) *Power Plays, Power Works.* New York: Verso.

Gaines, D. (1990) *Teenage Wasteland: Suburbia's Dead End Kids.* New York: Harper Perennial.

Giroux, H. (1997a) *Pedagogy and the Politics of Hope: Theory, Culture, and Schooling.* Boulder, CO: Westview Press.

Harred, J. (1991) Collaborative learning in the literature classroom: old problems revisited, paper presented at the Conference on College Composition and Communication, Boston.

Hauser, J. (1991) Critical inquiries, uncertainties and not faking it with students, paper presented at the Annual Conference of the Center for Critical Thinking and Moral Critique, Rohnert Park, CA.

Jennings, J. (1992) Blacks, politics, and the human service crisis, in J. Jennings (ed.) *Race, Politics, and Economic Development: Community Perspectives.* New York: Verso.

Jones, M. (1992) The black underclass as systematic phenomenon, in J. Jennings (ed.) *Race, Politics, and Economic Development: Community Perspectives.* New York: Verso.

Nightingale, C. (1993) *On the Edge: A History of Poor Black Children and Their American Dreams.* New York: Basic Books.

Sleeter, C. and Grant, C. (1994) *Making Choices from Multicultural Education: Five Approaches to Race, Class, and Gender.* New York: Merrill.

Steinberg, S. and Kincheloe, J. (1997) *Kinderculture: Corporate Constructions of Childhood.* Boulder, CO: Westview Press.

Swartz, E. (1993) Multicultural education: Disrupting patterns of supremacy in school curricula, practices, and pedagogy, *Journal of Negro Education*, 62(4): 493–506.

Wartenberg, T. (1992b) Situated social power, in T. Wartenberg (ed.) *Rethinking Power.* Albany, NY: SUNY Press.

West, C. (1992) Nihilism in black America, in G. Dent (ed.) *Black Popular Culture.* Seattle: Bay Press.

West, C. (1993) *Race Matters.* Boston: Beacon Press.

Multicultural Classrooms and Schools

Empowering Children to Create a Caring Culture in a World of Differences

Louise Derman-Sparks

Louise Derman-Sparks is Professor Emeritus at Pacific Oaks College in Pasadena, California. She has focused on antibias and antiracist education, especially for early childhood. She has written articles and books on the topics, including a teacher's guide for implementing an antibias curriculum into an early childhood classroom called *Anti-Bias Curriculum: Tools for Empowering Young Children*. Her works give recommendations to teachers for implementing new ideas. The following selection is from an article titled "Empowering Children to Create a Caring Culture in a World of Differences," *Childhood Education* (Winter 1993/1994).

In the following selection, Derman-Sparks focuses on working with young children to create a climate of antibias. She begins by describing how early—between two and four years old—children pick up on gender and racial bias. Using the words of young children, she describes how schools and teachers can unintentionally create and reinforce racial, gender, and cultural biases. She then lays out how teachers can create a curriculum and an environment that is purposefully antibiased and antiracist. To be effective, says Derman-Sparks, there must be "a caring culture in which children can be empowered." And she emphasizes that teachers need to actively engage themselves in this effort in their own lives as well. Teachers' attempting to become antiracist is where the efforts need to begin, according to Derman-Sparks. In this effort, teachers need to engage in reflective thinking, planning, and locating resources, and then they must create the same experiences for children by using the students' own experiences and interests.

Key Concept: creating an antiracist climate for young children

Racism, sexism, classism, heterosexism and ableism are still deeply entrenched and pervasive in society, making it very difficult for millions of children to be "Freedom's Child." What must we do as educators to ensure that all children can develop to their fullest potential—can truly become "Freedom's Child"?

Children's Development of Identity and Attitudes

Take a moment to listen to the voices of children. Members of the Anti-Bias Curriculum Task Force developed the anti-bias approach after a year spent collecting and analyzing children's thinking and trying out activities. They collected the following anecdotes:

- Steven is busy being a whale on the climbing structure in the 2-year-old yard. Susie tries to join him. "Girls can't do that!" he shouts.

- Robby, 3 years old, refuses to hold the hand of a dark-skinned classmate. At home, he insists, after bathing, that his black hair is now "white because it is clean."

- "You aren't really an Indian," 4-year-old Rebecca tells one of her child care teachers. "Where are your feathers?"

- "Malcolm can't play with us. He's a baby," Linda tells their teacher. Malcolm, another 4-year-old, uses a wheelchair.

Those voices reflect the impact of societal bias on children. Now, listen to voices of children in programs that practice anti-bias curriculum:

- Maria, 4 years old, sees a stereotypical "Indian warrior" figure in the toy store. "That toy hurts Indian people's feelings," she tells her grandmother.

- Rebecca's kindergarten teacher asks the children to draw a picture of what they would like to be when they grow up. Rebecca draws herself as a surgeon—in a pink ball gown and tiara.

- After hearing the story of Rosa Parks and the Montgomery bus boycott, 5-year-old Tiffany, whose skin is light brown, ponders whether she would have had to sit in the back of the bus. Finally, she firmly asserts, "I'm Black and, anyway, all this is stupid. I would just get off and tell them to keep their old bus."
- In the school playground, 5-year-old Casey and another white friend, Tommy, are playing. Casey calls two other boys to join them. "You can't play with them. They're Chinese eyes," Tommy says to him. Casey replies, "That's not right. All kinds of kids play together. I know. My teacher tells me civil rights stories."

Children do not come to preschool, child care centers or elementary school as "blank slates" on the topic of diversity. Facing and understanding what underlies their thoughts and feelings are key to empowering children to resist bias. . . .

What Empowering Children to Create a Caring Culture Requires of Us

Clarity About Goals

The following goals are for *all* children. The specific issues and tasks necessary for working toward these goals will vary for children, depending on their backgrounds, ages and life experiences.

Nurture each child's construction of a knowledgeable, confident self-concept and group identity.   To achieve this goal, we must create education conditions in which all children are able to like who they are without needing to feel superior to anyone else. Children must also be able to develop biculturally where that is appropriate.

Promote each child's comfortable, empathic interaction with people from diverse backgrounds.   This goal requires educators to guide children's development of the cognitive awareness, emotional disposition and behavioral skills needed to respectfully and effectively learn about differences, comfortably negotiate and adapt to differences, and cognitively understand and emotionally accept the common humanity that all people share.

Foster each child's critical thinking about bias.   Children need to develop the cognitive skills to identify "unfair" and "untrue" images (stereotypes), comments (teasing, name-calling) and behaviors (discrimination) directed at one's own or others' identities. They also need the emotional empathy to know that bias hurts.

Cultivate each child's ability to stand up for her/himself and for others in the face of bias.   This "activism" goal requires educators to help every child learn and practice

a variety of ways to act: a) when another child acts in a biased manner toward her/him, b) when a child acts in a biased manner toward another child, c) when an adult acts in a biased manner. Goal 4 builds on goal 3 as critical thinking and empathy are necessary components of acting for oneself or others in the face of bias.

These four goals interact with and build on each other. We cannot accomplish any one goal without the other three. *Their combined intent is to empower children to resist the negative impact of racism and other "isms" on their development and to grow into adults who will want and be able to work with others to eliminate all forms of oppression.* In other words, the underlying intent is not to end racism (and other "isms") in one generation by changing children's attitudes and behaviors, but rather to promote critical thinkers and activists who can work for social change and participate in creating a caring culture in a world of differences.

Preparing Ourselves

Effective anti-bias education requires every teacher to look inward and commit to a lifelong journey of understanding her/his own cultural beliefs, while changing the prejudices and behaviors that interfere with the nurturing of all children. Teachers need to know:

- how to see their own culture in relationship to society's history and current power realities
- how to effectively adapt their teaching style and curriculum content to their children's needs
- how to engage in cultural conflict resolution with people from cultural backgrounds other than their own
- how to be critical thinkers about bias in their practice
- how to be activists—engaging people in dialogue about bias, intervening, working with others to create change.

Achieving these goals takes commitment and time, and is a developmental process for adults as well as for children. One must be emotionally as well as cognitively involved and ready to face periods of disequilibrium and then reconstruction and transformation.

Implementation Principles and Strategies

To create a caring culture in which children can be empowered, teachers must be "reflective practitioners" who can think critically about their own teaching practice and adapt curriculum goals and general strategies to the needs of their children.

Critical Thinking

Be aware of "tourist multicultural curriculum" and find ways to eliminate tourism from your program. Tourist multicultural curriculum is the most commonly practiced approach in early childhood education and elementary school today. The majority of commercial curriculum materials currently available on the market and many published curriculum guides reflect a tourist version of multicultural education. Unfortunately, tourist multicultural curriculum is a simplistic, inadequate version of multicultural education.

In a classroom practicing a tourist approach, the daily "regular" curriculum reflects mainstream European American perspectives, rules of behavior, images, learning and teaching styles. Activities about "other" cultures often exhibit the following problems:

Disconnection: Activities are added on to the curriculum as special times, rather than integrated into all aspects of the daily environment and curriculum.

Patronization: "Other" cultures are treated as "quaint" or "exotic." This form of tourism does not teach children to appreciate what all humans share in common.

Trivialization: Cultural activities that are disconnected from the daily life of the people trivialize the culture. A typical example is multicultural curriculum that focuses on holidays—days that are different from "normal" days. Children do not learn about how people live their lives, how they work, who does what in the family—all of which is the essence of a culture. Other forms of trivialization include: turning cultural practices that have deep, ritual meaning into "arts and crafts" or dance activities, or asking parents to cook special foods without any further lessons about the parents' cultures.

Misrepresentation: Too few images of a group oversimplifies the variety within the group. Use of images and activities based on traditional, past practices of an ethnic group rather than images of contemporary life confuse children. Misusing activities and images that reflect the culture-of-origin of a group to teach about *the life of cultures in the U.S.* conveys misconceptions about people with whom children have little or no face-to-face experience.

In sum, tourist multicultural curriculum does not give children the tools they need to comfortably, empathetically and fairly interact with diversity. Instead, it teaches simplistic generalizations about other people that lead to stereotyping, rather than to understanding of differences. Moreover, tourist curriculum, because it focuses on the unusual and special times of a culture and neglects how people live their daily lives, does not foster children's understanding and empathy for our common humanity. Moving beyond tourist multicultural curriculum is key to our profession's more effective nurturing of diversity.

Incorporate Multicultural and Anti-Bias Activities into Daily Curriculum Planning

Diversity and anti-bias topics are integral to the entire curriculum at any education level. One practical brainstorming technique for identifying the numerous topic possibilities is "webbing."

Step one is determining the center of the "web." This can be: 1) an issue raised by the children (e.g., a person who is visually impaired cannot work); 2) any number of traditional preschool "units" (e.g., my body, families, work); 3) High/Scope's (Weikart, 1975) "key experiences" (e.g., classification or seriation); 4) any of the traditional content areas of the primary curriculum (science, math, language arts, physical and health curriculum).

Step two involves brainstorming the many possible anti-bias, multicultural issues that stem from the subject at the web's center. *Step three* involves identifying specific content for a particular classroom based on contextual/developmental analysis. *Step four* involves listing possible activities that are developmentally and culturally appropriate for your particular class.

Cultural Appropriateness: Adult/Child Interactions

Effective teaching about diversity, as in all other areas, *is a continuous interaction between adults and children.* On the one hand, teachers are responsible for brainstorming, planning and initiating diversity topics, based on their analyses of children's needs and life experiences. On the other hand, careful attention to children's thinking and behavior, and to "teachable moments," leads educators to modify initial plans.

Find ways to engage children in critical thinking and the planning and carrying out of "activism" activities appropriate to their developmental levels, cultural backgrounds and interests.

Critical thinking and activism activities should rise out of real life situations that are of interest to children. The purpose of such activities is to provide opportunities for children, 4 years old and up, to build their empathy, skills and confidence and to encourage their sense of responsibility for both themselves and for others. Consequently, activities should reflect *their* ideas and issues, not the teacher's. The following two examples are appropriate activism activities.

In the first situation, the children's school did not have a "handicapped" parking space in their parking lot. After a parent was unable to attend open school night because of this lack, the teacher told the class of 4- and 5-year-olds what had happened and why. They then visited other places in their neighborhood that had "handicapped" parking and decided to make one in their school lot. After they did so, they then noticed that teachers were inappropriately parking in the "handicapped" spot (their classroom overlooked the parking lot), so they decided to make tickets. The children dictated their messages, which their teacher faithfully took down, and drew pictures to accompany their words. They then ticketed those cars that did not have "handicapped parking" plaques in their windows.

In the second example, a class of 1st- through 3rd-graders visited a homeless shelter and talked to the director to find out what people needed. They started a toy and blanket collection drive, which they promoted using posters and flyers. They visited several classrooms to talk about what they were doing. They also wrote to the Mayor and the City Council to say that homeless people needed more houses and jobs.

Parents and Family Involvement

Find ways to involve parents and other adult family members in all aspects of anti-bias education. Education and collaboration with parents is *essential*. Educators have to be creative and ingenious to make this happen. Parents can help plan, implement and evaluate environmental adaptations and curricular activities. They can serve on advisory/planning committees with staff, provide information about their lifestyles and beliefs, participate in classroom activities and serve as community liaisons. Teachers can send home regular short newsletters to share ongoing plans and classroom activities, and elicit parent advice and resources. Parent meetings on child-rearing and education issues should also incorporate relevant diversity topics.

When a family member disagrees with an aspect of the curriculum, it is essential that the teachers listen carefully and sensitively to the issues underlying the disagreement. Objections may include: 1) family's belief that learning about differences will "make the children prejudiced" ("color-blind" view), 2) parent's belief that teaching about stereotyping and such values belongs in the home, not at school, 3) family members' strong prejudices against specific groups.

Staff need to find out all they can about the cultural and other issues that influence the family's concerns, and then work with family members to find ways to meet their needs while also maintaining the goals of anti-bias education. The techniques for working with parents on anti-bias issues are generally the same as those used for other child development and education topics. The difference, however, lies in the teachers' level of comfort about addressing such topics with other adults.

Teacher Education and Professional Development

Teacher training must incorporate liberating pedagogical techniques that:

- engage students on cognitive, emotional and behavioral levels

- use storytelling to enable students to both name and identify the ways that various identity contexts and bias have affected their lives
- use experiential activities that engage learners in discovering the dynamics of cultural differences and the various "isms"
- provide new information and analysis that give deeper meaning to what is learned through storytelling and experiential activities
- create a balance between supporting and challenging students in an environment of safety, not necessarily comfort.

The most useful way to work on our own development is to join with others (staff, or staff and parents) in support groups that meet regularly over a long period of time. By collaborating, sharing resources and providing encouragement, we can work on our self-awareness issues, build and improve our practices, strengthen our courage and determination and maintain the joy and excitement of education.

In sum, children of the 21st century will not be able to function if they are psychologically bound by outdated and narrow assumptions about their neighbors. To thrive, even to survive, in this more complicated world, children need to learn how to function in many different cultural contexts, to recognize and respect different histories and perspectives, and to know how to work together to create a more just world that can take care of all its people, its living creatures, its land.

Let's remember the African American novelist Alice Walker's call to "Keep in mind always the present you are constructing. It should be the future you want" (Walker, 1989, p. 238).

References

Walker, A. (1989). *The temple of my familiar.* New York: Pocket Books.

Weikart, D. (1975). *Young children in action.* Ypsilanti, MI: High Scope Press.

Transforming the Mainstream Curriculum

James A. Banks

James A. Banks is the Kerry and Linda Killinger Endowed Chair in Diversity Studies and Director of the Center for Multicultural Education at the University of Washington, Seattle. He is past president of the American Educational Research Association (AERA) and the National Council for Social Studies. As a world-renowned scholar in the field of multicultural education, he has received a number of honors and awards, including the Distinguished Career Contribution Award from the AERA Committee on the Role and Status of Minorities in Educational Research and Development. He has also received fellowships from the National Academy of Education, the Kellogg Foundation, and the Rockefeller Foundation. While he writes on virtually all areas related to multicultural education, much of Banks' work focuses on teaching strategies and curriculum development for multicultural education and for social studies.

The following selection is from "Transforming the Mainstream Curriculum," *Educational Leadership* (May 1994). In it, Banks describes five popular dimensions of a multicultural classroom, then provides a different dimension that he recommends for helping students to better understand the complexities of a multicultural society. In the five dimensions of multicultural education that already exist, Banks expresses concern that the curriculum remains dominated by mainstream perspectives. Thus, he recommends a different dimension of instruction for the multicultural classroom: the *transformation approach*. The basic assumptions of the curriculum under this approach are changed to include the perspectives of many groups. To demonstrate this approach, Banks presents a lesson in which the Montgomery bus boycott, which followed Rosa Parks' refusal to give up her seat on the bus, is reinterpreted. In this way, he shows how the transformation approach can result in a much greater and deeper understanding of an event in history by including different perspectives on the event, often the perspectives that have been left out of the traditional interpretation of that event.

Key Concept: approaches to making the curriculum more multicultural

Schools today are rich in student diversity. A growing number of American classrooms and schools contain a complex mix of races, cultures, languages, and religious affiliations.

Two other sources of diversity are becoming increasingly prominent as well. The widening gap between rich and poor students is creating more social class diversity, and an increasing number of gay students and teachers are publicly proclaiming their sexual orientations.

Toward an Authentic *Unum*

The increasing recognition of diversity within American society poses a significant challenge: how to create a cohesive and democratic society while at the same time allowing citizens to maintain their ethnic, cultural, socioeconomic, and primordial identities.

Our ideal as a nation has been and continues to be *e pluribus unum*—out of many, one. In the past, Americans have tried to reach this goal by eradicating diversity and forcing all citizens into a white Anglo-Saxon Protestant culture (Higham 1972).

This coerced assimilation does not work very well. An imposed *unum* is not authentic, is not perceived as legitimate by nonmainstream populations, does not have moral authority, and is inconsistent with democratic ideals. To create an authentic, democratic *unum* with moral authority and perceived legitimacy, the *pluribus* (diverse peoples) must negotiate and share power.

Even with its shortcomings, the United States has done better in this regard than most nations. Still, citizen expectations for a just *unum* are far outpacing the nation's progress toward its ideal. Many citizens of color, people with low incomes, or speakers of languages other than English feel alienated, left out, abandoned, and forgotten.

Our society has a lot to gain by restructuring institutions in ways that incorporate all citizens. People who now feel disenfranchised will become more effective and productive citizens, and new perspectives will be added to the nation's mainstream institutions. The institutions themselves will then be transformed and enriched.

In the past two decades, multicultural education has emerged as a vehicle for including diverse groups and transforming the nation's educational institutions (Banks 1994a, Banks and Banks 1992). Multicultural education tries to create equal educational opportunities for all students by ensuring that the total school environment reflects the diversity of groups in classrooms, schools, and the society as a whole.

Considering the Dimensions of Multicultural Education

The following five dimensions of multicultural education can help educators implement and assess programs that respond to student diversity (Banks 1993, 1994b).

1. The first dimension, *content integration*, deals with the extent to which teachers illuminate key points of instruction with content reflecting diversity. Typically, teachers integrate such content into curriculum in several different ways (Banks 1991b). One common approach is the recognition of contributions—that is, teachers work into the curriculum various isolated facts about heroes from diverse groups. Otherwise, lesson plans and units are unchanged. With the additive approach, on the other hand, the curriculum remains unchanged, but teachers add special units on topics like the Women's Rights Movement, African Americans in the West, and Famous Americans with Disabilities. While an improvement over the passing mention of contributions, the additive approach still relegates groups like women, African Americans, and disabled people to the periphery of the curriculum.

2. A second dimension of multicultural education is *knowledge construction*, or the extent to which teachers help students understand how perspectives of people within a discipline influence the conclusions reached within that discipline. This dimension is also concerned with whether students learn to form knowledge for themselves.

3. The *prejudice reduction* dimension has to do with efforts to help students to develop positive attitudes about different groups. Research has revealed a need for this kind of education and the efficacy of it. For example, researchers have shown that while children enter school with many negative attitudes and misconceptions about different racial and ethnic groups (Phinney and Rotheram 1987), education can help students develop more positive intergroup attitudes, provided that certain conditions exist. Two such conditions are instructional materials

with positive images of diverse groups and the use of such materials in consistent and sustained ways (Banks 1991a).

4. The *equitable pedagogy* dimension concerns ways to modify teaching so as to facilitate academic achievement among students from diverse groups. Research indicates, for example, that the academic achievement of African-American and Mexican-American students improves when teachers use cooperative (rather than competitive) teaching activities and strategies (Aronson and Gonzalez 1988).

5. The *empowering school culture and social structure* dimension concerns the extent to which a school's culture and organization ensure educational equality and cultural empowerment for students from diverse groups. Some of the variables considered are grouping practices, social climate, assessment practices, participation in extracurricular activities, and staff expectations and responses to diversity.

Knowledge Construction and Transformation

I would like to suggest an alternative to the contributions and additive approaches that are used in the content integration dimension. This alternative, the *transformation approach*, changes the structure, assumptions, and perspectives of the curriculum so that subject matter is viewed from the perspectives and experiences of a range of groups. The transformation approach changes instructional materials, teaching techniques, and student learning.

This approach can be used to teach about our differences as well as our similarities. Teachers can help students understand that, while Americans have a variety of viewpoints, we share many cultural traditions, values, and political ideals that cement us together as a nation.

The transformation approach has several advantages. It brings content about currently marginalized groups to the center of the curriculum. It helps students understand that how people construct knowledge depends on their experiences, values, and perspectives. It helps students learn to construct knowledge themselves. And it helps students grasp the complex group interactions that have produced the American culture and civilization.

Reinterpreting the Montgomery Bus Boycott

The history of the Montgomery (Alabama) bus boycott, which began on December 5, 1955, can be used to illustrate how the transformation approach works. Viewing this event from different perspectives shows how historians construct interpretations, how central figures can be omitted from historical records, how history can be rewritten, and how students can create their own interpretations.

Textbook accounts of the Montgomery bus boycott generally conclude that: (1) when a bus driver asked Rosa Parks to give up her seat to a white person, she refused because she was tired from working hard all day, and (2) the arrest of Rosa Parks triggered the planning and execution of the boycott.

Two important accounts by women who played key roles in the boycott contradict important aspects of the textbook conclusions. The two memoirs are those of Rosa Parks (with Haskins 1992) and Jo Ann Gibson Robinson (Garrow 1987). Robinson was an Alabama State College English professor and president of the Women's Political Council.

Students can compare mainstream accounts of the events (such as those in textbooks) with transformative accounts (such as those by Robinson and Parks). This activity presents an excellent opportunity both to learn content about diverse groups and to gain insights about the construction of knowledge.

According to Robinson, professional African-American women in Montgomery founded the Women's Political Council in 1946 to provide leadership, support, and improvement in the black community and to work for voting rights for African Americans. Many council members were Alabama State College professors. Others were black public school teachers.

In 1953, the council received more than 30 complaints concerning bus driver offenses against African Americans. For instance, black people (even when seated in the "Negro" section of the bus) were asked to give up their seats to whites. Further, blacks often had to pay their fares in the front of the bus, exit, and reenter through the back door—and sometimes when they stepped off the bus, the driver left them.

Robinson and other council members worked with city leaders to improve the treatment of black bus riders, but to no avail. African Americans continued to experience intimidating, demeaning, and hostile encounters with bus drivers.

As the negative pattern of incidents persisted, the council concluded that only a boycott against the bus system would end the abuse of black bus riders and bus segregation. A boycott was thought to have good potential for success because about 70 percent of Montgomery's bus riders were African American. The council planned the boycott and then waited for the right time to launch it.

The year 1955 presented three choices for the "right time." On March 2, 1955, Claudette Colvin, a 15-year-old high school student seated in the "Negro" section of a bus, was arrested after refusing to give up her seat to a white rider. Next, Robinson said:

> They dragged her, kicking and screaming hysterically, off the bus. Still half-dragging, half-pushing, they forced her into a patrol car that had been summoned, put handcuffs on her wrists so she would do no physical harm to

the arresting police, and drove her to jail. There she was charged with misconduct, resisting arrest, and violating the city segregation laws (Garrow 1987).

Claudette Colvin was later found guilty and released on probation. The conviction enraged the African-American community. Six months after the Colvin incident, Mary Louise Smith, 18, was arrested on a similar charge. Smith was fined.

Then, on December 1, Rosa Parks was arrested for refusing to give up her seat. She gives quite a different reason for her intransigence than has commonly been reported:

> People always say that I didn't give up my seat because I was tired, but that isn't true. I was not tired physically, or no more tired than I usually was at the end of a working day. I was not old, although some people have an image of me being old then. I was 42. No, the only tired I was, was tired of giving in.
>
> The driver of the bus saw me still sitting there, and he asked was I going to stand up. I said, "No." He said, "Well, I'm going to have you arrested." Then I said, "You may do that." These were the only words we said to each other.
>
> . . . People have asked me if it occurred to me that I could be the test case the NAACP had been looking for. I did not think about that at all. In fact if I had let myself think too deeply about what might happen to me, I might have gotten off the bus. But I chose to remain.

Fed up with mistreatment, the African-American women of Montgomery, led by their council, called for a boycott of city buses. Robinson described the preparations for the boycott:

> I sat down and quickly drafted a message and then called a good friend and colleague, John Cannon, chairman of the business department of the college, who had access to the college's mimeograph equipment. When I told him that the WPC was staging a boycott and needed to run off the notices, he told me that he too had suffered embarrassment on the city buses. Like myself, he had been hurt and angry. He said that he would happily assist me.
>
> Along with two of my most trusted students, we quickly agreed to meet almost immediately, in the middle of the night, at the college's duplicating room. We were able to get three messages to a page, greatly reducing the number of pages that had to be mimeographed in order to produce the tens of thousands of leaflets we knew would be needed. By 4 A.M. on Friday, the sheets had been duplicated, cut in thirds, and bundled (Garrow 1987).

Part of Robinson's leaflets read:

> Another Negro woman has been arrested and thrown in jail because she refused to get up out of her seat on the bus for a white person to sit down. . . . This has to be stopped. Negroes have rights, too, for if Negroes did not ride the buses, they could not operate. Three-fourths of the riders are Negroes, yet we are arrested, or have to stand over empty seats. If we do not do something to stop the arrests, they will continue. The next time it may be you, your daughter, or mother. This woman's case will come

up on Monday. We are, therefore, asking every Negro to stay off the buses Monday in protest of the arrest and trial. Don't ride the buses to work, to town, to school, or anywhere else on Monday (Garrow 1987).

Reinterpreting the Past

Robinson's and Parks' accounts of the Montgomery bus boycott reveal that significant players in historical events can be virtually ignored in written history. For instance, most textbook accounts of the Montgomery bus boycott emphasize the work of men (like Martin Luther King Jr. and Ralph D. Abernathy) or organizations headed by men. The work of women like Robinson and her female colleagues in the Women's Political Council simply cannot be found in most textbooks.

Further, Rosa Parks' stated reason for refusing to give up her seat helps students understand that recorded history can be wrong. Students can also see that when people who have been excluded from the construction of historical knowledge begin to play active roles in interpreting history, the resulting accounts can be strikingly different and much more accurate. As Robert Merton (1972) observed, insiders and outsiders often have different perspectives on the same events, and both perspectives are needed to give the total picture of social and historical reality.

Incorporating New Scholarship

Since the 1970s, people of color—who have historically been outsiders and transformative scholars—have produced a prodigious amount of scholarship on multicultural education. Their thoughtful and informative works include Ronald Takaki's *A Different Mirror: A History of Multicultural America* (1993); John Hope Franklin's *The Color Line: Legacy for the Twenty-First Century* (1993); Gloria Anzaldua's *Borderlands: La Frontera* (1987); Patricia Hill Collins's *Black Feminist Thought: Knowledge, Consciousness, and the Politics of Empowerment* (1991); and Paula Gunn Allen's *The Sacred Hoop* (1986).

Because men of color have often been as silent on women's issues as white men have been (hooks [sic] and West 1991), a special effort should be made to include works by women (such as those by Anzaldua, Collins, and Allen). Two important new books edited by women are Carol Dubois and Vicki Ruiz's *Unequal Sisters: A Multicultural Reader in U.S. Women's History* (1990) and Darlene Clark Hine and her colleagues' *Black Women in America: A Historical Encyclopedia* (1993).

Teaching Civic Action

One of multicultural education's important goals is to help students acquire the knowledge and commitment needed to think, decide, and take personal, social, and civic action. Activism helps students apply what they

have learned and develop a sense of personal and civic efficacy (Banks with Clegg 1990).

Action activities and projects should be practical, feasible, and attuned to the developmental levels of students. For instance, students in the primary grades can take action by refusing to laugh at ethnic jokes. Students in the early and middle grades can read about and make friends with people from other racial, ethnic, and cultural groups. Upper-grade students can participate in community projects that help people with special needs. Lewis (1991) has written a helpful guide that describes ways to plan and initiate social action activities and projects for students.

When content, concepts, and events are studied from many points of view, all of our students will be ready to play their roles in the life of the nation. They can help to transform the United States from what it is to what it could and should be—many groups working together to build a strong nation that celebrates its diversity.

References

Aronson E., and A. Gonzalez. (1988). "Desegregation, Jigsaw, and the Mexican-American Experience." In *Eliminating Racism: Profiles in Controversy*, edited by P. A. Katz and D. A. Taylor. New York: Plenum Press.

Banks, J. A. (1991a). "Multicultural Education: Its Effects on Students' Racial and Gender Role Attitudes." In *Handbook of Research on Social Teaching and Learning*, edited by J. P. Shaver. New York: Macmillan.

Banks, J. A. (1991b). *Teaching Strategies for Ethnic Studies*. 5th ed. Boston: Allyn and Bacon.

Banks, J. A. (1993). "Multicultural Education: Historical Development, Dimensions and Practice." In *Review of Research in Education*, vol. 19, edited by L. Darling-Hammond. Washington, D.C.: American Educational Research Association.

Banks, J. A. (1994b). *Multiethnic Education: Theory and Practice*. 3rd ed. Boston: Allyn and Bacon.

Banks, J. A., with A. A. Clegg Jr. (1990). *Teaching Strategies for the Social Studies: Inquiry, Valuing, and Decision-Making*. 4th ed. New York: Longman.

Banks, J. A., and C. A. McGee Banks, eds. (1992). *Multicultural Education: Issues and Perspectives*. 2nd ed. Boston: Allyn and Bacon.

Garrow, D. J., ed. (1987). *The Montgomery Bus Boycott and the Women Who Started It: The Memoir of Jo Ann Gibson Robinson*. Knoxville: The University of Tennessee Press.

Higham, J. (1972). *Strangers in the Land: Patterns of American Nativism 1860–1925*. New York: Atheneum.

hooks, b., and West, C. (1991). *Breaking Bread: Insurgent Black Intellectual Life*. Boston: South End Press.

Lewis, B. A. (1991). *The Kid's Guide to Social Action*. Minneapolis: Free Spirit Publishing.

Merton, R. K. (1972). "Insiders and Outsiders: A Chapter in the Sociology of Knowledge." *The American Journal of Sociology* 78, 1:9–47.

Parks, R., with J. Haskins. (1992). *Rosa Parks: My Story*. New York: Dial Books.

Phinney, J. S., and M. J. Rotheram, eds. (1987). *Children's Ethnic Socialization: Pluralism and Development*. Beverly Hills, Calif.: Sage Publications.

Creating Multicultural Learning Communities

Sonia Nieto

Sonia Nieto puts multicultural education in a sociopolitical context. She encourages educators to make multicultural education a comprehensive education that is schoolwide and that is good education for all students. According to Nieto, a comprehensive, schoolwide, multicultural education would be antiracist education, would understand that all students have strengths, would proceed on the notion that a student's community should be involved in education, that there should be high expectations for all learners, and that school reform must be empowering and just for all students.

Nieto is Professor Emerita in Language, Literacy, and Culture at the University of Massachusetts, Amherst. She taught in public schools in Brooklyn, New York, and the Bronx before moving to the college level. She writes on multicultural and Puerto Rican education and curriculum and is probably best known for her books preparing teachers for multicultural education. Her book *Affirming Diversity: The Sociopolitical Context of Multicultural Education* (Longman) is now in its 5th edition. The following selection is from her book *The Light in Their Eyes: Creating Multicultural Learning Communities* (Teachers College Press, 1999). Nieto has served on many boards of organizations that focus on educational equity and social justice. She has also received numerous awards, including the Human and Civil Rights Award from the Massachusetts Teachers Association in 1989, the Críticas Spanish Language Community Advocate of the Year Award in 2003, and the 2006 Enrique T. Trueba Lifetime Achievement Award for Scholarship, Mentorship, and Service.

Key Concept: characteristics of a schoolwide multicultural education

Conditions That Promote Student Learning: Systemic School Reform with a Multicultural Perspective

Educational reform cannot be envisioned without taking into account both micro- and macro-level issues that may affect student learning. Micro-level issues include the cultures, languages, and experiences of students and their families, and how these are taken into account in determining school policies and practices. Macro-level issues include the racial, social class, and gender stratification that helps maintain inequality, and the resources and access to learning that are provided or denied by schools. In addition, the way that students and their families view their status in schools and society also needs to be considered.

Five kinds of school reform can substantially improve student learning:

1. School reform that is antiracist and antibias

2. School reform that reflects an understanding of all students as having talents and strengths that can enhance their education
3. School reform that is based on the notion that those most intimately connected with students need to be meaningfully involved in their education
4. School reform that is based on high expectations and rigorous standards for all learners
5. School reform that is empowering and just

School Reform That Is Antiracist and Antibias

An antiracist and antibias perspective is at the very heart of multicultural education. Although some educators may believe that having a multicultural education approach will automatically take care of racism, this is far from the case. In fact, multicultural education without a clear antiracist focus may end up maintaining rigid stereotypes if it focuses on only superficial aspects of culture or the addition of ethnic tidbits to the curriculum. In contrast, being antiracist means paying attention to all areas in which some students may be favored over others, including the curriculum, choice of materials, sorting policies, and teachers' interactions and relationships with students and their communities.

Educators committed to multicultural education with an antiracist perspective need to closely examine both school policies and the attitudes and behaviors of the staff to determine how these might be complicitous in causing academic failure. The kinds of expectations held for students, whether using their native language is permitted or punished, how sorting takes place, and how classroom organization, pedagogy, and curriculum might influence student learning all need to be considered. For example, during her graduate studies, [a teacher's] reactions to films, readings, and class discussions concerning White privilege were, as she said, "hard work." But it is only when teachers undergo this kind of hard work, whether in their schools or through personal encounters or professional development, that they can learn to identify how racism and other kinds of institutional discrimination operate in schools and society to the detriment of some students and the advantage of others.

Institutional power is a significant consideration here because discussions of racism tend to focus on individual biases and negative perceptions toward members of other groups. This perception conveniently skirts the issue of how institutions themselves, which are far more powerful than individuals, develop harmful policies and practices that victimize American Indians, African Americans, Latinos, immigrants, poor European Americans, females, gay and lesbian students, and others from powerless groups. The major difference between individual and institutional discrimination is precisely the wielding of power, because it is primarily through the power of the people who control institutions such as schools that oppressive policies and practices are reinforced and legitimated (Tatum, 1992; Weinberg, 1990). That is, when racism and other forms of discrimination are understood as *systemic* problems, not just as individual dislikes for a particular group of people, we can better understand their negative and destructive effects.

School Reform That Reflects an Understanding of All Students as Having Talents and Strengths That Can Enhance Their Education

Even many well-meaning educators approach their role in teaching bicultural students with the assumption that these students bring little of value to their education. Too often, they are considered to be deficient for social, cultural, or genetic reasons. The potential inherent strengths of many students may be overlooked when teachers feel that they need to begin educating students by first doing away with their prior learning. The role of "teacher as missionary" is the unfortunate result.

Beginning with a more positive view of students' strengths is in the long run not only a better policy, but indeed a more hopeful strategy. Teachers who begin by first learning about their students and then building on their students' talents and strengths change dramatically the nature of the teaching/learning dynamic and the climate in which education takes place. Rather than feeling that their students have nothing to give, the perspective that students are active, engaged, and motivated co-constructors of learning is the result.

School Reform That Is Based on the Notion That Those Most Intimately Connected with Students Need to Be Meaningfully Involved in Their Education

Research on involvement by parents, students, and teachers in decisions affecting education has indicated consistently that such involvement can dramatically improve student learning (Henderson & Berla, 1995). Yet the people who are closest to learners and learners themselves frequently are excluded from discussions, policy implications, and implementation of school reform measures. Although schools give lip service to parent, teacher, and student involvement, schools usually are not organized to encourage the involvement of these groups.

For instance, Jim Cummins (1996) reviewed programs that included student empowerment as a goal and concluded that students who are encouraged to develop a positive cultural identity through interactions with their teachers experience a sense of control over their own lives and develop the confidence and motivation to succeed academically. In the case of teachers, a study of secondary schools reported that teachers who had more control over classroom conditions considered themselves more efficacious (Lee, Bryk, & Smith, 1993). Regarding parents, an analysis of a number of programs stressing effective parent involvement found that all of the programs reviewed shared, among others, the following components: a commitment to involve low-income parents, family empowerment as a major goal, and a stated desire to reduce the gap between home and school cultures by designing programs that respond to and build on the values, structures, languages, and cultures of students' homes (Fruchter, Galletta, & White, 1993).

School reform measures that stress the meaningful involvement of students, teachers, and families look quite different from traditional approaches to school improvement. Rather than thinking of ways to circumvent the ideas of students, teachers, and parents, school reformers actively seek their involvement in developing, for instance, disciplinary policies, curriculum development, and decisions concerning ability grouping and the use of tests.

There are many ways in which parents and students can be involved, and governance is only one of them. Helping to make decisions about curriculum content, the hiring of new staff, or grouping policies is an important role, but not all parents or students feel equally comfortable, nor do they have the time, to be involved in this way. Even the simple process of listening to, respecting, and affirming families' ideas can be a big step in involving them. Questions to parents about their children is an example of this. Although seemingly basic, the mere act of bringing parents into their children's education through questions about the children proved to be a powerful mechanism for letting families know that their insights and ideas were valued. Similarly, when students' viewpoints are seriously considered, they may feel more connected to schools, which in turn may help them to define themselves as capable and worthy of learning.

School Reform That Is Based on High Expectations and Rigorous Standards for All Students

Many young people struggle on a daily basis with tremendous odds, concerning not only their school lives, but their very existence. These odds include personal, family, and social problems such as poverty, racism, violence, drug abuse, and lack of health care and appropriate housing. As we reach the start of the twenty-first century, these problems are becoming even more severe and complicated as families experience great distress and our society undergoes monumental structural changes. Add to this the fact that the very identities of some students are thought to be a barrier to their learning—including their social class, race, ethnicity, and native language— and many teachers feel themselves at a loss to teach their students effectively.

In many cases students' identities and the conditions in which they live are used as a justification for having low expectations, or as a reason for "watering down" the curriculum. I maintain that just the opposite should happen. That is, because schools in our society historically have been expected to provide an equal and equitable education for all students, not just for those who are White or middle-class, or who speak English fluently, it is with even greater urgency that the mission of schools needs to be redefined to support students who might not be identified as potentially academically capable. If schools are purposeful about giving all students more options in life, particularly students from communities that do not have the necessary resources with which to access these options, then we need to begin with the assumption that these students are academically able, individually and as a group.

I am not suggesting that it is easy to have equally high standards for all students. I have seen many examples of

young people for whom teachers and schools seem to be doing the very best they can, and yet these young people face such massive personal and family problems that the situation seems hopeless. But as educators, we have no other choice than to believe that school conditions *can* be created in which all students can become successful learners. There have been too many examples of academic success in the face of tremendous adversity to conclude that intelligence and ability are handed out sparingly or based on only genetic endowments, or that they cannot be affected by educational environments. These examples are powerful reminders that great potential exists in all students. What needs changing first are the attitudes, beliefs, and values with which teachers approach their students, and the conditions in schools to support the high-level learning of all students. As stated simply "Being nice is not enough." Although being nice to students may be a good start, if unaccompanied by a deep belief and trust that bicultural students are capable and worthy, it will not necessarily lead to improved learning. Forging a deep and committed connection to their students, is the key to motivating students to become learners.

School Reform That Is Empowering and Just

When educational reform is perceived to be a bureaucratic procedure, or when technical processes take precedence in school restructuring, then crucial questions related to social justice and student empowerment are swept aside. But school reform that has as its primary goal the improvement of learning for all students needs to concern more than just changing schedules, or buying new textbooks, or adding ethnic content to curriculum. While these reforms in fact may improve conditions for learning among a greater number of students, they will not by themselves change the nature of learning that takes place in classrooms. A case in point is the educational reform known as *block scheduling,* the realignment of school schedules in middle and secondary schools from 40-minute slots to 1½-, 2- or 3-hour-long segments. Block scheduling has become a popular reform and it makes sense for a lot of reasons: Students have more time to tackle important issues in greater depth; teachers can build significant relationships with students when they work closely and intensively with them; and teachers have the opportunity to work collaboratively with one another. However, if the content of what students learn in their blocks does not change, or if the way in which they are expected to learn is not affected, then block scheduling may not provide the improvements promised.

School reform measures that have as their underlying focus both the empowerment of students and the creation of socially just learning environments are based on the view that critical reflection and analysis are fundamental to the development and maintenance of a democratic society. Without this perspective, learning can be defined as simply "banking education," or as the depositing of knowledge in otherwise empty receptacles. But if we expect schools to be living laboratories for democracy, where all students know that they are worthy and capable of learning and where they develop a social awareness and responsibility to their various communities, then classrooms and schools need to become just and empowering environments for all students.

Conclusion

In the end, if teachers believe that students cannot achieve at high levels, that their backgrounds are riddled with deficiencies, and that multicultural education is a frill that cannot help them to learn, the result will be school reform strategies that have little hope for success. On the other hand, if teachers begin by challenging societal inequities that inevitably place some students at a disadvantage over others; if they struggle against institutional policies and practices that are unjust; if they begin with the strengths and talents of students and their families; if they undergo a process of personal transformation based on their own identities and experiences; and, finally, if they engage with colleagues in a collaborative and imaginative encounter to transform their own practices and their schools to achieve equal and high-quality education for all students, then the outcome is certain to be a more positive one than is currently the case. A critical and comprehensive approach to multicultural education can provide an important framework for rethinking school reform, and it is a far more promising scenario for the effective learning of students. When teachers understand the light in the eyes of their students as evidence that they are capable and worthy human beings, then schools can become places of hope and affirmation for students of all backgrounds and all situations.

Connecting with Families and Communities

Selection 36

JOYCE EPSTEIN, from "School/Family/Community Partnerships: Caring for the Children We Share," *Phi Delta Kappan*

Selection 37

LUIS C. MOLL, CATHY AMANTI, DEBORAH NEFF, AND NORMA GONZALEZ, from "Funds of Knowledge for Teaching: Using a Qualitative Approach to Connect Homes and Classrooms," *Theory Into Practice*

School/Family/Community Partnerships: Caring for the Children We Share

Joyce Epstein

In the following selection from "School/Family/Community Partnerships: Caring for the Children We Share," *Phi Delta Kappan* (May 1995), Joyce Epstein emphasizes the importance of creating collaborative partnerships between schools, families, and communities. She lays out her well-known framework of six types of school-community involvement, which range from the school teaching parenting schools through to involving parents and community members in school-related decisions. Epstein then goes on to problematize those six types of involvement, raising questions and challenges to current practices in this area. And finally, she lays out a process of creating action teams to plan for, and engage in, partnerships between schools and communities.

Joyce Epstein is renowned as a leading scholar and educator in the area of school, family, university, and community partnerships. She is a Professor and the Director of the Center on School, Family, and Community Partnerships at Johns Hopkins University. As part of her work, Epstein also is Founder and Director of the National Network of Partnership Schools, which works to help schools, universities, and communities work better collaboratively to best educate children. As a result of her studies and her efforts in the area of partnerships, she has won several awards and has over 100 publications in the field, including the book *School, Family, and Community Partnerships: Preparing Educators and Improving Schools* (Westview Press, 2001).

Key Concept: framework of six types of school-community involvement

The way schools care about children is reflected in the way schools care about the children's families. If educators view children simply as *students*, they are likely to see the family as separate from the school. That is, the family is expected to do its job and leave the education of children to the schools. If educators view students as *children*, they are likely to see both the family and the community as partners with the school in children's education and development. Partners recognize their shared interests in and responsibilities for children, and they work together to create better programs and opportunities for students.

There are many reasons for developing school, family, and community partnerships. They can improve school programs and school climate, provide family services and support, increase parents' skills and leadership, connect families with others in the school and in the community, and help teachers with their work. However, the main reason to create such partnerships is to help all youngsters succeed in school and in later life. When parents, teachers, students, and others view one another as partners in education, a caring community forms around students and begins its work.

What do successful partnership programs look like? How can practices be effectively designed and implemented? What are the results of better communications, interactions, and exchanges across these three important contexts? These questions have challenged research and practice, creating an interdisciplinary field of inquiry into school, family, and community partnership with "caring" as a core concept.

Six Types of Involvement; Six Types of Caring

A framework of six major types of involvement has evolved from many studies and from many years of work by educators and families in elementary, middle, and high schools. The framework (summarized in the accompanying tables)

Table 1 Epstein's Framework of Six Types of Involvement and Sample Practices

Type 1, Parenting	Type 2, Communicating	Type 3, Volunteering	Type 4, Learning at Home	Type 5, Decision Making	Type 6, Collaborating with Community
Help all families establish home environments to support children as students.	Design effective forms of school-to-home and home-to-school communications about school programs and children's progress.	Recruit and organize parent help and support.	Provide information and ideas to families about how to help students at home with homework and other curriculum-related activities, decisions, and planning.	Include parents in school decisions, developing parent leaders and representatives.	Identify and integrate resources and services from the community to strengthen school programs, family practices, and student learning and development.
Sample Practices	**Sample Practices**	**Sample Practices**	**Sample Practices**	**Sample Practices**	**Sample Practices**
Suggestions for home conditions that support learning at each grade level.	Conferences with every parent at least once a year, with follow-ups as needed.	School and classroom volunteer program to help teachers, administrators, students, and other parents.	Information for families on skills required for students in all subjects at each grade.	Active PTA/PTO or other parent organizations, advisory councils, or committees (e.g., curriculum, safety, personnel) for parent leadership and participation.	Information for students and families on community health, cultural, recreational, social support, and other programs or services.
Workshops, video tapes, computerized phone messages on parenting and child rearing at each age and grade level.	Language translators to assist families as needed.	Parent room or family center for volunteer work, meetings, resources for families.	Information on homework policies and how to monitor and discuss schoolwork at home.	Independent advocacy groups to lobby and work for school reform and improvements.	Information on community activities that link to learning skills and talents, including summer programs for students.
Parent education and other courses or training for parents (e.g., GED, college credit, family literacy).	Weekly or monthly folders of student work sent home for review and comments.	Annual postcard survey to identify all available talents, times, and locations of volunteers.	Information on how to assist students to improve skills on various class and school assessments.	District-level councils and committees for family and community involvement.	Service integration through partnerships involving school; civic, counseling, cultural, health, recreation, and other agencies and organizations; and businesses.
Family support programs to assist families with health, nutrition, and other services.	Parent/student pickup of report card, with conferences on improving grades.	Class parent, telephone tree, or other structures to provide all families with needed information.	Regular schedule of homework that requires students to discuss and interact with families on what they are learning in class.	Information on school or local elections for school representatives.	Service to the community by students, families, and schools (e.g., recycling, art, music, drama, and other activities for seniors or others).
Home visits at transition points to preschool, elementary, middle, and high school. Neighborhood meetings to help families understand schools and to help schools understand families.	Regular schedule of useful notices, memos, phone calls, newsletters, and other communications.	Parent patrols or other activities to aid safety and operation of school programs.	Calendars with activities for parents and students at home.	Networks to link all families with parent representatives.	Participation of alumni in school programs for students.
	Clear information on choosing schools or courses, programs, and activities within schools.		Family math, science, and reading activities at school.		
	Clear information on all school policies, programs, reforms, and transitions.		Summer learning packets or activities.		
			Family participation in setting student goals each year and in planning for college or work.		

Table 2 Challenges and Redefinitions for the Six Types of Involvement

Type 1, Parenting	Type 2, Communicating	Type 3, Volunteering	Type 4, Learning at Home	Type 5, Decision Making	Type 6, Collaborating with Community
Challenges	**Challenges**	**Challenges**	**Challenges**	**Challenges**	**Challenges**
Provide information to *all* families who want it or who need it, not just to the few who can attend workshops or meetings at the school building.	Review the readability, clarity, form, and frequency of *all* memos, notices, and other print and nonprint communications.	Recruit volunteers widely so that *all* families know that their time and talents are welcome.	Design and organize a regular schedule of interactive homework (e.g., weekly or bimonthly) that gives *students* responsibility for discussing important things they are learning and helps families stay aware of the content of their children's classwork.	Include parent leaders from all racial, ethnic, socioeconomic, and other groups in the school.	Solve turf problems of responsibilities, funds, staff, and locations for collaborative activities.
Enable families to share information with schools about culture, background, children's talents and needs.	Consider parents who do not speak English well, do not read well, or need large type.	Make flexible schedules for volunteers, assemblies, and events to enable parents who work to participate.	Coordinate family-linked homework activities, if students have several teachers.	Offer training to enable leaders to serve as representatives of other families, with input from and return of information to all parents.	Inform families of community programs for students, such as mentoring, tutoring, business partnerships.
Make sure that all information for and from families is clear, usable, and linked to children's success in school.	Review the quality of major communications (newsletters, report cards, conference schedules, and so on).	Organize volunteer work: provide training, match time and talent with school, teacher, and student needs, and recognize efforts so that participants are productive.	Involve families and their children in all important curriculum-related decisions.	Include students (along with parents) in decision-making groups.	Assure equity of opportunities for students and families to participate in community programs or to obtain services.
	Establish clear two-way channels for communications from home to school and from school to home.				Match community contributions with school goals; integrate child and family services with education.
Redefinitions	**Redefinitions**	**Redefinitions**	**Redefinitions**	**Redefinitions**	**Redefinitions**
"Workshop" to mean more than a *meeting* about a topic held at the school building at a particular time. "Workshop" may also mean making information about a topic available in a variety of forms that can be viewed, heard, or read anywhere, any time, in varied forms.	"Communications about school programs and student progress" to mean two-way, three-way, and many-many channels of communication that connect schools, families, students, and the community.	"Volunteer" to mean anyone who supports school goals and children's learning or development in any way, at any place, and at any time—not just during the school day and at the school building.	"Homework" to mean not only work done alone, but also interactive activities shared with others at home or in the community, linking schoolwork to real life. "Help" at home to mean encouraging, listening, reacting, praising, guiding, monitoring, and discussing—not "teaching" school subjects.	"Decision making" to mean a process of partnership, of shared views and actions toward shared goals, not just a power struggle between conflicting ideas. Parent "leader" to mean a real representative, with opportunities and support to hear from and communicate with other families.	"Community" to mean not only the neighborhoods where students' homes and schools are located but also any neighborhoods that influence their learning and development. "Community" rated not only by low or high social or economic qualities, but by strengths and talents to support students, families, and schools. "Community" means all who are interested in and affected by the quality of education, not just those with children in the schools.

Table 3 Expected Results of the Six Types of Involvement for Students, Parents, and Teachers

Type 1, Parenting	Type 2, Communicating	Type 3, Volunteering	Type 4, Learning at Home	Type 5, Decision Making	Type 6, Collaborating with Community
Results for Students	**Results for Students**	**Results for Students**	**Results for Students**	**Results for Students**	**Results for Students**
Awareness of family supervision: respect for parents.	Awareness of own progress and of actions needed to maintain or improve grades.	Skill in communicating with adults.	Gains in skills, abilities, and test scores linked to homework and classwork.	Awareness of representation of families in school decisions.	Increased skills and talents through enriched curricular and extracurricular experiences.
Positive personal qualities, habits, beliefs, and values, as taught by family.	Understanding of school policies on behavior, attendance, and other areas of student conduct.	Increased learning of skills that receive tutoring or targeted attention from volunteers.	Homework completion.	Understanding that student rights are protected.	Awareness of careers and of options for future education and work.
Balance between time spent on chores, on other activities, and on homework.	Informed decisions about courses and programs.	Awareness of many skills, talents, occupations, and contributions of parents and other volunteers.	Positive attitude toward schoolwork.	Specific benefits linked to policies enacted by parent organizations and experienced by students.	Specific benefits linked to programs, services, resources, and opportunities that connect students with community.
Good or improved attendance.	Awareness of own role in partnerships, serving as courier and communicator.		View of parent as more similar to teacher and of home as more similar to school.		
Awareness of importance of school.			Self-concept of ability as learner.		
For Parents	**For Parents**	**For Parents**	**For Parents**	**For Parents**	**For Parents**
Understanding of and confidence about parenting, child and adolescent development, and changes in home conditions for learning as children proceed through school.	Understanding school programs and policies.	Understanding teacher's job, increased comfort in school, and carryover of school activities at home.	Know how to support, encourage, and help student at home each year.	Input into policies that affect child's education.	Knowledge and use of local resources by family and child to increase skills and talents or to obtain needed services.
Awareness of own and others' challenges in parenting.	Monitoring and awareness of child's progress.	Self-confidence about ability to work in school and with children or to take steps to improve own education.	Discussions of school, classwork, and homework.	Feeling of ownership of school.	Interactions with other families in community activities.
Feeling of support from school and other parents.	Responding effectively to students' problems.	Awareness that families are welcome and valued at school.	Understanding of instructional program each year and of what child is learning in each subject.	Awareness of parents' voices in school decisions.	Awareness of school's role in the community and of community's contributions to the school.
	Interactions with teachers and ease of communication with school and teachers.	Gains in specific skills of volunteer work.	Appreciation of teaching skills.	Shared experiences and connections with other families.	
			Awareness of child as a learner.	Awareness of school, district, and state policies.	
For Teachers	**For Teachers**	**For Teachers**	**For Teachers**	**For Teachers**	**For Teachers**
Understanding families' backgrounds, cultures, concerns, goals, needs, and views of their children.	Increased diversity and use of communications with families and awareness of own ability to communicate clearly.	Readiness to involve families in new ways, including those who do not volunteer at school.	Better design of homework assignments.	Awareness of parent perspectives as a factor in policy development and decisions.	Awareness of community resources to enrich curriculum and instruction.
Respect for families' strengths and efforts.	Appreciation for and use of parent network for communications.	Awareness of parents' talents and interests in school and children.	Respect of family time.	View of equal status of family representatives on committees and in leadership roles.	Openness to and skill in using mentors, business partners, community volunteers, and others to assist students and augment teaching practice.
Understanding of student diversity.	Increased ability to elicit and understand family views on children's programs and progress.	Greater individual attention to students, with help from volunteers.	Recognition of equal helpfulness of single-parent, dual-income, and less formally educated families in motivating and reinforcing student learning.		Knowledgeable, helpful referrals of children and families to needed services.
Awareness of own skills to share information on child development.			Satisfaction with family involvement and support.		

can guide the development of a balanced, comprehensive program of partnerships, including opportunities for family involvement at school and at home, with potentially important results for students, parents, and teachers.

Action Teams for School, Family, and Community Partnerships

Who will work to create caring school communities that are based on the concepts of partnership? How will the necessary work on all six types of involvement get done? Although a principal or a teacher may be a leader in working with some families or with groups in the community, one person cannot create a lasting, comprehensive program that involves all families as their children progress through the grades.

From the hard work of many educators and families in many schools, we have learned that, along with clear policies and strong support from state and district leaders and from school principals, an Action Team for School, Family, and Community Partnerships in each school is a useful structure. The action team guides the development of a comprehensive program of partnership, including all six types of involvement, and the integration of all family and community connections within a single, unified plan and program.

Step 1: Create an Action Team

A team approach is an appropriate way to build partnerships. The Action Team for School, Family, and Community Partnerships can be the "action arm" of a school council, if one exists. The action team takes responsibility for assessing present practices, organizing options for new partnerships, implementing selected activities, evaluating next steps, and continuing to improve and coordinate practices for all six types of involvement. Although the members of the action team lead these activities, they are assisted by other teachers, parents, students, administrators, and community members.

The action team should include at least three teachers from different grade levels, three parents with children in different grade levels, and at least one administrator. Teams may also include at least one member from the community at large and, at the middle and high school levels, at least two students from different grade levels. Others who are central to the school's work with families may also be included as members, such as a cafeteria worker, a school social worker, a counselor, or a school psychologist. Such diverse membership ensures that partnership activities will take into account the various needs, interests, and talents of teachers, parents, the school, and students.

Step 2: Obtain Funds and Other Support

A modest budget is needed to guide and support the work and expenses of each school's action team. Funds for state coordinators to assist districts and schools and funds for district coordinators or facilitators to help each school may come from a number of sources. These include federal, state, and local programs that mandate, request, or support family involvement, such as Title I, Title II, Title VII, Goals 2000, and other federal and similar state funding programs. In addition to paying the state and district coordinators, funds from these sources may be applied in creative ways to support staff development in the area of school, family, and community partnerships; to pay for lead teachers at each school; to set up demonstration programs; and for other partnership expenses. In addition, local school/business partnerships, school discretionary funds, and separate fund-raising efforts targeted to the schools' partnership programs have been used to support the work of their action teams. At the very least, a school's action team requires a small stipend (at least $1,000 per year for three to five years, with summer supplements) for time and materials needed by each subcommittee to plan, implement, and revise practices of partnership that include all six types of involvement.

The action team must also be given sufficient time and social support to do its work. This requires explicit support from the principal and district leaders to allow time for team members to meet, plan, and conduct the activities that are selected for each type of involvement. Time during the summer is also valuable—and may be essential—for planning new approaches that will start in the new school year.

Step 3: Identify Starting Points

Assessments of starting points may be made in a variety of ways, depending on available resources, time, and talents. For example, the action team might use formal questionnaires or telephone interviews to survey teachers, administrators, parents, and students (if resources exist to process, analyze, and report survey data). Or the action team might organize a panel of teachers, parents, and students to speak at a meeting of the parent/teacher organization or at some other school meeting as a way of initiating discussion about the goals and desired activities for partnership. Structured discussions may be conducted through a series of principal's breakfasts for representative groups of teachers, parents, students, and others; random sample phone calls may also be used to collect reactions and ideas, or formal focus groups may be convened to gather ideas about school, family, and community partnerships at the school.

- *Present strengths.* Which practices of school/family/ community partnerships are now working well for the school as a whole? For individual grade levels? For which types of involvement?

- *Needed changes.* Ideally, how do we want school, family, and community partnerships to work at this school three years from now? Which present practices should continue, and which should change? To reach school goals, what new practices are needed for each of the major types of involvement?

- *Expectations.* What do teachers expect of families? What do families expect of teachers and other school personnel? What do students expect their families to do to help them negotiate school life? What do students expect their teachers to do to keep their families informed and involved?

- *Sense of community.* Which families are we now reaching, and which are we not yet reaching? Who are the "hard-to-reach" families? What might be done to communicate with and engage these families in their children's education? Are current partnership practices coordinated to include all families as a school community? Or are families whose children receive special services (e.g., Title I, special education, bilingual education) separated from other families?

- *Links to goals.* How are students faring on such measures of academic achievement as report card grades, on measures of attitudes and attendance, and on other indicators of success? How might family and community connections assist the school in helping more students reach higher goals and achieve greater success? Which practices of school, family, and community partnerships would directly connect to particular goals?

Step 4: Develop a Three-Year Plan

From the ideas and goals for partnerships collected from teachers, parents, and students, the action team can develop a three-year outline of the specific steps that will help the school progress from its starting point on each type of involvement to where it wants to be in three years. This plan outlines how each subcommittee will work over three years to make important, incremental advances to reach more families each year on each type of involvement.

In addition to the three-year outline of goals for each type of involvement, a detailed one-year plan should be developed for the first year's work. It should include the specific activities that will be implemented, improved, or maintained for each type of involvement.

In short, based on the input from the parents, teachers, students, and others on the school's starting points and desired partnerships, the action team will address these issues.

- *Details.* What will be done each year, for three years, to implement a program on all six types of involvement? What, specifically, will be accomplished in the first year on each type of involvement?

- *Responsibilities.* Who will be responsible for developing and implementing practices of partnership for each type of involvement? Will staff development be needed? How will teachers, administrators, parents, and students be supported and recognized for their work?

- *Costs.* What costs are associated with the improvement and maintenance of the planned activities? What sources will provide the needed funds? Will small grants or other special budgets be needed?

- *Evaluation.* How will we know how well the practices have been implemented and what their effects are on students, teachers, and families? What indicators will we use that are closely linked to the practices implemented to determine their effects?

Step 5: Continue Planning and Working

Each year, the action team updates the school's three-year outline and develops a detailed one-year plan for the coming year's work. It is important for educators, families, students, and the community at large to be aware of annual progress, of new plans, and of how they can help.

In short, the action team addresses the following questions. How can it ensure that the program of school/family/community partnership will continue to improve its structure, processes, and practices in order to increase the number of families who are partners with the school in their children's education? What opportunities will teachers, parents, and students have to share information on successful practices and to strengthen and maintain their efforts?

Characteristics of Successful Programs

As schools have implemented partnership programs, their experience has helped to identify some important properties of successful partnerships.

- *Incremental progress.* The development of a partnership is a process, not a single event. All teachers, families, students, and community groups do not engage in all activities on all types of involvement all at once. Not all activities implemented will succeed with all families. But with good planning, thoughtful implementation, well-designed activities, and pointed improvements, more and more families and teachers can learn to work with one another on behalf of the children whose interests they share. Similarly, not all students instantly improve their attitudes or achievements when their families become involved in their education. After all, student learning depends mainly on good curricula and instruction and on the work completed by students. However, with a well-implemented program of partnership, more students will receive support from their families, and more will be motivated to work harder.

- *Connection to curricular and instructional reform.* A program of school/family/community partnerships that focuses on children's learning and development is an important component of curricular and instructional reform. Aspects of partnerships that aim to help more students succeed in school can be supported by federal, state, and local funds that are targeted for curricular and instructional reform. Helping families understand, monitor, and interact with students on homework, for example, can be a clear and important extension of classroom instruction, as can volunteer programs that bolster and broaden student skills, talents, and interests. Improving the content and conduct of parent/teacher/student conferences and goal-setting activities can be an important step in curricular reform; family support and family understanding of child and adolescent development and school curricula are necessary elements to assist students as learners.
- *Redefining staff development.* The action team approach to partnerships guides the work of educators by restructuring "staff development" to mean colleagues working together and with parents to develop, implement, evaluate, and continue to improve practices of partnership. This is less a "dose of in-service education" than it is an active form of developing staff talents and capacities. The teachers, administrators, and others on the action team become the "experts" on this topic for their school. Their work in

this area can be supported by various federal, state, and local funding programs as a clear investment in staff development for overall school reform. Indeed, the action team approach as outlined can be applied to any or all important topics on a school improvement agenda. It need not be restricted to the pursuit of successful partnerships.

It is important to note that the development of partnership programs would be easier if educators came to their schools prepared to work productively with families and communities. Courses or classes are needed in preservice teacher education and in advanced degree programs for teachers and administrators to help them define their professional work in terms of partnerships. Colleges and universities that prepare educators and others who work with children and families should identify where in their curricula the theory, research, policy, and practical ideas about partnerships are presented or where in their programs these can be added.

Next Steps: Strengthening Partnerships

Collaborative work and thoughtful give-and-take among researchers, policy leaders, educators, and parents are responsible for the progress that has been made over the past decade in understanding and developing school, family, and community partnerships. Similar collaborations will be important for future progress in this and other areas of school reform.

Funds of Knowledge for Teaching: Using a Qualitative Approach to Connect Homes and Classrooms

Luis C. Moll, Cathy Amanti, Deborah Neff, and Norma Gonzalez

The article "Funds of Knowledge for Teaching: Using a Qualitative Approach to Connect Homes and Classrooms" (*Theory Into Practice,* 1992) is considered to be a classic example of how teachers can learn about the home life and background experiences of their students within their families and communities. The authors discuss the importance of learning about students' backgrounds and household knowledge, and provide a portion of a transcript in which an anthropologist and a teacher-researcher discuss their new understandings of students through their home visits with parents. They then describe how they created lessons based on their new knowledge of one particular Mexican American student and his family, and included family members to help strengthen the connections between school and home.

Luis C. Moll is Professor of Language, Reading and Culture and Associate Dean of Academic Affairs at the College of Education, University of Arizona. He has long directed research in the field of study come to be known as "Funds of Knowledge." In this series of studies, researchers and teachers study the household knowledge and experiential background of Mexican American families and students. Cathy Amanti, having served as a teacher in the Tucson, AZ, Unified School District, was one of the researchers who speaks in this article through the transcript of her experiences entering the households of her students to learn about their cultural and experiential background. Deborah Neff was Professor of Anthropology at the University of Arizona when this study was conducted, and she is currently an Instructor at Skagit Valley College. She has also co-authored *Desert Indian Woman: Stories and Dreams.* Norma Gonzalez is Professor of Teaching, Learning & Sociocultural Studies at University of Arizona and is President of the Council of Anthropology and Education. Gonzalez, Moll, and Amanti have published a book to gather much of the studies on "Funds of Knowledge" since their original 1992 article. The book is titled *Funds of Knowledge: Theorizing Practices in Households, Communities, and Classrooms* (Lawrence Erlbaum Associates, 2005).

Key Concept: learning about students' household and family knowledge

We form part of a collaborative project between education and anthropology that is studying household and classroom practices within working-class, Mexican communities in Tucson, Arizona. The primary purpose of this work is to develop innovations in teaching that draw upon the knowledge and skills found in local households. Our claim is that by capitalizing on household and other community resources, we can organize classroom instruction that far exceeds in quality the rote-like instruction these children commonly encounter in schools (see, e.g., Moll & Greenberg, 1990; see also Moll & Diaz, 1987).

To accomplish this goal, we have developed a research approach that is based on understanding households (and classrooms) qualitatively. We utilize a combination of ethnographic observations, open-ended interviewing strategies, life histories, and case studies that, when combined analytically, can portray accurately the complex functions of households within their socio-historical contexts. Qualitative research offers a range of methodological alternatives that can fathom the array of cultural and intellectual resources available to students and teachers within these households. This approach is particularly important in dealing with students whose households are usually viewed as being "poor," not only economically but in terms of the quality of experiences for the child.

Our research design attempts to coordinate three interrelated activities: the ethnographic analysis of household dynamics, the examination of classroom practices, and the development of after-school study groups with teachers. These study groups, collaborative ventures between teachers and researchers, are settings within which we discuss our developing understanding of households and classrooms. These study groups also function as "mediating structures" for developing novel classroom practices that involve strategic connections between these two entities (see Moll et al., 1990).

Some Basic Findings

As noted, central to our project is the qualitative study of households. This approach involves, for one, understanding the history of the border region between Mexico and the United States and other aspects of the sociopolitical and economic context of the households (see, e.g., Vélez-Ibáñez, in press; see also Heyman, 1990; Martínez, 1988). It also involves analyzing the social history of the households, their origins and development, and most prominently for our purposes, the labor history of the families, which reveals the accumulated bodies of knowledge of the households (see Vélez-Ibáñez & Greenberg, 1989).

With our sample, this knowledge is broad and diverse, as depicted in abbreviated form in Table 1. Notice that household knowledge may include information about farming and animal management, associated with households' rural origins, or knowledge about construction and building, related to urban occupations, as well as knowledge about many other matters, such as trade, business, and finance on both sides of the border (see, e.g., Moll & Greenberg, 1990). We use the term "funds of knowledge" to refer to these historically accumulated and culturally developed bodies of knowledge and skills essential for household or individual functioning and well-being (Greenberg, 1989; Tapia, 1991; Vélez-Ibáñez, 1988).

Our approach also involves studying how household members use their funds of knowledge in dealing with changing, and often difficult, social and economic circumstances. We are particularly interested in how families develop social networks that interconnect them with their social environments (most importantly with other households), and how these social relationships facilitate the development and exchange of resources, including knowledge, skills, and labor, that enhance the households' ability to survive or thrive (see, e.g., Moll & Greenberg, 1990; Vélez-Ibáñez & Greenberg, l989; see also Keefe & Padilla, 1987).

Two aspects of these household arrangements merit emphasis here, especially because they contrast so sharply with typical classroom practices. One is that these networks are flexible, adaptive, and active, and may

Table 1 A Sample of Household Funds of Knowledge

Agriculture and Mining	Material & Scientific Knowledge
Ranching and farming	Construction
Horse riding skills	Carpentry
Animal management	Roofing
Soil and irrigation systems	Masonry
Crop planting	Painting
Hunting, tracking, dressing	Design and architecture
Mining	Repair
Timbering	Airplane
Minerals	Automobile
Blasting	Tractor
Equipment operation and maintenance	House maintenance

Economics	Medicine
Business	Contemporary medicine
Market values	Drugs
Appraising	First aid procedures
Renting and selling	Anatomy
Loans	Midwifery
Labor laws	
Building codes	Folk medicine
Consumer knowledge	Herbal knowledge
Accounting	Folk cures
Sales	Folk veterinary cures

Household Management	Religion
Budgets	Catechism
Childcare	Baptisms
Cooking	Bible studies
Appliance repairs	Moral knowledge and ethics

involve multiple persons from outside the homes; in our terms, they are "thick" and "multi-stranded," meaning that one may have multiple relationships with the same person or with various persons. The person from whom the child learns carpentry, for example, may also be the uncle with whom the child's family regularly celebrates birthdays or organizes barbecues, as well as the person with whom the child's father goes fishing on weekends.

Thus, the "teacher" in these home-based contexts of learning will know the child as a "whole" person, not merely as a "student," taking into account or having knowledge about the multiple spheres of activity within which the child is enmeshed. In comparison, the typical teacher-student relationship seems "thin" and "single-stranded," as the teacher "knows" the students only from their performance within rather limited classroom contexts.

Additionally, in contrast to the households and their social networks, the classrooms seem encapsulated, if not isolated, from the social worlds and resources of the community. When funds of knowledge are not readily available within households, relationships with individuals outside the households are activated to meet either household or individual needs. In classrooms, however, teachers rarely draw on the resources of the "funds of knowledge" of the child's world outside the context of the classroom.

A second, key characteristic of these exchanges is their reciprocity. As Vélez-Ibáñez (1988) has observed, reciprocity represents an "attempt to establish a social relationship on an enduring basis. Whether symmetrical or asymmetrical, the exchange expresses and symbolizes human social interdependence" (p. 142). That is, reciprocal practices establish serious obligations based on the assumption of "confianza" (mutual trust), which is reestablished or confirmed with each exchange, and leads to the development of long-term relationships. Each exchange with relatives, friends, and neighbors entails not only many practical activities (everything from home and automobile repair to animal care and music) but constantly provides contexts in which learning can occur—contexts, for example, where children have ample opportunities to participate in activities with people they trust (Moll & Greenberg, 1990).

A related observation, as well, is that children in the households are not passive bystanders, as they seem in the classrooms, but active participants in a broad range of activities mediated by these social relationships (see La Fontaine, 1986). In some cases, their participation is central to the household's functioning, as when the children contribute to the economic production of the home, or use their knowledge of English to mediate the household's communications with outside institutions, such as the school or government offices. In other cases they are active in household chores, such as repairing appliances or caring for younger siblings.

Our analysis suggests that within these contexts, much of the teaching and learning is motivated by the children's interests and questions; in contrast to classrooms, knowledge is obtained by the children, not imposed by the adults. This totality of experiences, the cultural structuring of the households, whether related to work or play, whether they take place individually, with peers, or under the supervision of adults, helps constitute the funds of knowledge children bring to school (Moll & Greenberg, 1990).

Funds of Knowledge for Teaching

Our analysis of funds of knowledge represents a positive (and, we argue, realistic) view of households as containing ample cultural and cognitive resources with great, *potential* utility for classroom instruction (see Moll & Greenberg, 1990; Moll et al., 1990). This view of households, we should mention, contrasts sharply with prevailing and accepted perceptions of working-class families as somehow disorganized socially and deficient intellectually; perceptions that are well accepted and rarely

challenged in the field of education and elsewhere (however, see McDermott, 1987; Moll & Díaz, 1987; Taylor & Dorsey-Gaines, 1988; see also Vélez-Ibáñez, in press).

In what follows we present a case example from our most recent work that addresses these questions. The goal of the study was to explore teacher-researcher collaborations in conducting household research and in using this information to develop classroom practices.

Rather than provide further technical details about this project, however, we present an edited transcript from a recent presentation by a teacher (Cathy Amanti) and an anthropologist (Deborah Neff) who collaborated in the study. They describe their experiences conducting the research, and provide a revealing glimpse of the process of using qualitative methods to study households and their funds of knowledge.

Studying Household Knowledge

In their presentation, Amanti and Neff first described some of their concerns in conducting the work, including how their assumptions and previous experiences may have influenced their observations.

DN: We are going to share with you some of our experience in working as a team doing household interviews. We have chosen the López family, a pseudonym, as the focus of this brief talk. The Lópezes are the parents of one of Cathy's students, whom we will call Carlos.

In going into the homes, we carry with us cultural and emotional baggage that tends to color our understanding of interviews and observations. We have fears and assumptions, and perhaps misunderstandings. I for one did not know exactly what to expect when I first went into the López home with Cathy. I had heard talk of dysfunctional homes, lack of discipline, lack of support systems and so forth, but remained skeptical of these negative characterizations. Having done fieldwork before, I was accustomed to this kind of uncertainty.

CA: I, however, was nervous because I was going out in the field for the first time with someone who's had experience doing this type of research. Deborah had experience doing ethnography, I did not, and I was concerned about balancing doing interviews and observations with establishing and maintaining rapport. I was glad, though, that she was there, and I wanted her feedback to make sure I was getting what I should from the visit.

In 2 years of teaching, I had visited only a handful of homes. So, I had been into some of these homes before but only for school-related reasons, for example, delivering a report card, but I'd only visited for a brief period of time. These research visits were to be different—I had to observe, ask questions, take notes, and establish rapport—it was a lot to assimilate, with many activities to coordinate at the same time.

CA: Once we began the interview, it seemed that Ms. López was really enjoying talking about her family, her children, and her life. They had told us this in training, that people would open up once they get talking.

For instance, when she got on the subject of the difference between Mexican and U.S. schools, she just kept talking, and we let her go with it, and got more out of it than if we had stayed strictly with the questionnaire. But we had to balance that with our agenda, and for the first interview the main thing was to get the family history so we would have a baseline for discussing literacy, parenting, attitudes towards school, and funds of knowledge.

CA: As we progressed asking questions about family background and labor history, I began to relax, although I was concerned with whether I was getting enough material that would be useful later in developing a learning module. Actually I never totally disengaged from my role as a teacher and when such things as cross-border trade came up, I thought this would be a great topic to use in my classroom and I tried to figure out how I could capture this resource for teaching.

Seeing Beyond Stereotypes

An important aspect of the teachers' participation in the household research became the more sophisticated understanding they developed about the children and their experiences. There is much teachers do not know about their students or families that could be immediately helpful in the classroom, as the following comments illustrate.

DN: One of the things that we learned about the Lópezes that we didn't know before was the depth of the multicultural experiences their son, Carlos, had in cross-border activities. It wasn't just a superficial experience for him.

CA: Half of the children in my classroom are international travelers and yet this experience is not recognized or valued because they are Mexican children going to Mexico. Anglo children may spend a summer in France and we make a big deal about it, by asking them to speak to the class about their summer activities! Carlos spends summers in Magdalena, Mexico, yet he's probably rarely been asked to share his experiences with anyone.

Carlos's father's parents are involved in the import/export of major appliances between Sonora and Arizona and there are regular visits of relatives back and forth. His dad says they really live in both places. I'll read some of the notes from my interview with Carlos that describe his life in Sonora:

"In Magdalena he and his family stay with different relatives. When he is there he plays with his cousins. They are allowed to wander freely around most of the town. They like to play hide-and-seek and sometimes they are taken places by older relatives. They like to visit a pharmacy that one of his aunts owns and one of his older cousins is married to someone who works on three ranches.

"Sometimes he goes to visit the ranches. Once he got to ride a horse. One thing he likes to do when he visits a ranch is play with bow and arrow. He says his cousin's husband will give him and his cousins a thousand pesos if they find the arrows." Carlos also reports playing cards when he visits Magdalena and that he has gone fishing near Santa Ana with older cousins and an uncle.

DN: It is precisely through information of these kinds of social activities that we identify funds of knowledge that can be used in the classroom to help improve his academic development.

CA: Furthermore, because of these experiences, Carlos and many of my other students show a great deal of interest in economic issues, because they have seen the difference in the two countries, in immigration law, but also in laws in general; they would ask me why there are so many laws here that they don't have in Mexico. These children have had the background experiences to explore in-depth issues that tie in with a sixth grade curriculum, such as the study of other countries, different forms of government, economic systems, and so on.

Carlos himself is involved in what we could call international commerce. He's a real entrepreneur. Not only does he sell candy from Mexico but, according to his mother, he'll sell anything he can get anyone to buy, for example, bike parts. His mother says Carlos got the idea to sell candy from other children.

We didn't uncover this only through questioning but from being there when one child came over to buy some candy from Carlos. He was really proud when he gave us each a piece to take home. Here was Carlos right in front of our eyes enacting a family fund of knowledge. This experience later turned out to be the seed for the learning module I developed for the project.

The two presenters then discuss how the specific qualitative methods of study influenced not only the nature of the information collected from the family, yielding data about their experiences and funds of knowledge, but provided them with a more sophisticated understanding of the student, his family, and their social world. This more elaborate understanding helped the teacher transform this information into a useful instructional activity.

DN: It is so important to learn how culture is expressed in students' lives, how students live their worlds. We can't make assumptions about these things. Only a part of that child is present in the classroom. We had little idea of what Carlos's life was really like outside of the classroom, and what he knew about the world.

DN: We learned a lot during these three interviews that fractured stereotypes that we had heard others say about these households. Carlos's parents not only care, but have a very strong philosophy of child-rearing that is supportive of education, including learning English. They have goals of a university education for their children, instill strong values of respect for others, and possess a tremendous amount of pride and a strong sense of identity—in addition to the more practical knowledge in which their children share on a regular basis. These values are not unique to this family. All of the households we visited possess similar values and funds of knowledge that can be tapped for use in the classrooms.

Experimenting with Practice

The presentation concluded with a description by Cathy, the teacher, of the development of a theme study, or learning module, as we called them, based on information gathered from the households. Notice the emphasis on the inquiry process, on the students becoming active learners, and on strategically using their social contacts outside the classroom to access new knowledge for the development of their studies. Here is her summary:

CA: After we had completed our field work and written field notes for all our interviews, it truly was left up to us, the teachers, to decide how we were going to use the knowledge we had gained about our students and their families. We spent 2 days with consultants and everyone else who had been working on the project and brainstormed and bounced ideas off each other. I worked with two other teachers from my school and together we developed a learning module with a rather unusual theme—candy. You've already heard that Deborah and I witnessed Carlos selling Mexican candy to a neighbor. The fifth grade teacher I worked with also uncovered this theme. He interviewed a parent who is an expert at making all kinds of candy. In a truly collaborative effort, we outlined a week's worth of activities we could use in our classes.

To focus students' thinking on the theme, I had students free associate with the topic. I recorded their ideas on a large piece of white paper on the board. Next, I had them come up with a definition for the word candy. This was not as easy as you might think. They'd mentioned gum and sunflower seeds while brainstorming, which I wasn't sure should be included in this category. But I didn't tell them this because I wanted them to use their analytical skills to come up with their own definition. Actually, they got stuck deciding if salty things like *picalimón* and *saladitos* (Mexican snacks that include salt and spices) were candy. Next they categorized all the candies they'd mentioned.

After that we used the KWL method to organize our unit. For those not familiar with this method, we used a three-column chart. In the first column, we recorded everything the students "know" about the topic. In the next column, we recorded what they "want" to know. The third column, the "L" column, is to be used at the end of the unit to record what the students learned during the study. After working with the project consultant, I added another W at the end of the chart—a fourth column, something new for me—to record new questions students had, to help them see that learning is ongoing, that it does not consist of discrete chunks of knowledge. We then surveyed and graphed favorite candies of the class.

CA: Next, we became a research team. Students chose one of the questions they'd generated to answer. They chose, "What ingredients are used in the production of candy?" I framed the pursuit of the answer using the version of the scientific method we use in schools. After writing their question on the board, the students developed a procedure to answer their question; then they hypothesized what ingredients they'd find on the candy labels they brought in the next day.

The next day, after students had made a class list of ingredients in the candy samples they'd brought in, they graphed the frequency of occurrence of the ingredients they'd found. Then I had them divide the ingredients into two lists—one of ingredients they'd found in the Mexican candy samples and one of ingredients they'd found in U.S. candy samples. We all learned something that day. We were all surprised to see that fewer ingredients are used in Mexican candies and that they don't use artificial flavors or coloring—just vegetable dyes and real fruit.

The next day one of the parents of my students, Mrs. Rodríguez, came in to teach us how to make *pipitoria*, a Mexican candy treat. This turned out to be the highlight of our unit. Before she came in that morning, the students divided up to make advertising posters and labels for the candy because we were going to sell what we made at the school talent show. When Mrs. Rodríguez arrived, she became the teacher. While the candy was cooking, she talked to the class for over an hour and taught all of us not only how to make different kinds of candy but also such things as the difference in U.S. and Mexican food consumption and production, nutritional value of candy, and more. My respect and awe of Mrs. Rodríguez grew by leaps and bounds that morning. Finally, the students packaged and priced their candy.

CA: The last day of the unit, students wrote summaries of what they'd learned and we recorded it on our chart. Then they began to formulate new questions. Examples of their new questions are: "What is candy like in Africa?" and "What candy do they eat in China?" As you can see, if we'd had time to continue our unit, our studies would have taken us all over the world. We did, however, cover many areas of the curriculum in one short week—math, science, health, consumer education, cross-cultural practices, advertising, and food production.

From the questions the students came up with alone, we could have continued investigating using innumerable research and critical thinking skills for a considerable part of the year. If we had continued this type of activity all year, by the end we would have been an experienced research team and my role would have been to act as facilitator helping the students answer their own questions.

Conclusion

Our concept of funds of knowledge is innovative, we believe, in its special relevance to teaching, and contrasts with the more general term "culture," or with the concept of a "culture sensitive curriculum," and with the latter's reliance on folkloric displays, such as storytelling, arts, crafts, and dance performance. Although the term "funds of knowledge" is not meant to replace the anthropological concept of culture, it is more precise for our purposes because of its emphasis on strategic knowledge and related activities essential in households' functioning, development, and well-being. It is specific funds of knowledge pertaining to the social, economic, and productive activities of people in a local region, not "culture" in its broader, anthropological sense, that we seek to incorporate strategically into classrooms.

One of the hallmarks of qualitative research is that strategies often evolve within the process of doing. As teachers, administrators, and parents become more aware of the linkages that can be created utilizing this methodology, and become comfortable with the redefinition of roles that it entails, new strategies of implementation will emerge that are driven by the needs of the target community. As the research unfolds, the constitutive nature of the inquiry process becomes apparent, as teacher, researcher, parent, child, and administrator jointly create and negotiate the form and function of the exploration.

References

Greenberg, J.B. (1989, April). *Funds of knowledge: Historical constitution, social distribution, and transmission.* Paper presented at the annual meetings of the Society for Applied Anthropology, Santa Fe, NM.

Heyman, J. (1990). The emergence of the waged life course on the United States-Mexico border. *American Ethologist, 17,* 348–359.

Keefe, S., & Padilla, A. (1987). *Chicano ethnicity.* Albuquerque: University of New Mexico Press.

La Fontaine, J. (1986). An anthropological perspective on children in social worlds. In M. Richards & P. Light (Eds.), *Children of social worlds: Development in a social context* (pp. 10–30). Cambridge, U.K.: Polity Press.

Martínez, O.J. (1988). *Troublesome border.* Tucson: The University of Arizona Press.

McDermott, R.P. (1987). The explanation of minority school failure, again. *Anthropology and Education Quarterly, 18,* 361–364.

Moll, L.C., & Díaz, S. (1987). Change as the goal of educational research. *Anthropology and Education Quarterly, 18,* 300–311.

Moll, L.C., & Greenberg, J. (1990). Creating zones of possibilities: Combining social contexts for instruction. In L.C. Moll (Ed.), *Vygotsky and education* (pp. 319–348). Cambridge, U.K.: Cambridge University Press.

Moll, L.C., Vélez-lbáñez, C., Greenberg, J., Whitmore, K., Saavedra, E., Dworin, J., & Andrade, R. (1990). *Community knowledge and classroom practice: Combining resources for literacy instruction* (OBEMLA Contract No. 300-87-0131). Tucson: University of Arizona, College of Education and Bureau of Applied Research in Anthropology.

Tapia, J. (1991). *Cultural reproduction: Funds of knowledge as survival strategies in the Mexican American community.* Unpublished doctoral dissertation, University of Arizona, Tucson.

Taylor, D., & Dorsey-Gaines, C. (1988). *Growing up literate: Learning from inner city families.* Portsmouth, NH: Heinemann.

Vélez-lbáñez, C.G. (1988). Networks of exchange among Mexicans in the U.S. and Mexico: Local level mediating responses to national and international transformations. *Urban Anthropology, 17(1),* 27–51.

Vélez-lbáñez, C.G. (in press). U.S. Mexicans in the borderlands: Being poor without the underclass. In J. Moore & R. Rivera (Eds.), *Issues of Hispanic poverty and underclass.* Los Angeles: Sage.

Vélez-lbáñez, C.G., & Greenberg, J. (1989). *Formation and transformation of funds of knowledge among U.S. Mexican households in the context of the borderlands.* Paper presented at the annual meeting of the American Anthropological Association, Washington, DC.

Acknowledgments

Chapter 1

SELECTION 1   From Joel Spring, "The Great Civil Rights Movement and the New Culture Wars," *Deculturalization and the Struggle for Equality: A Brief History of the Education of Dominated Cultures in the United States*, 4th ed. (McGraw-Hill, 2004).

SELECTION 2   From Maxine Greene, "The Passions of Pluralism: Multiculturalism and the Expanding Community," *Educational Researcher*, vol. 22, no. 1 (January–February 1993), pp. 13–18.

SELECTION 3   From Kathy Hytten, "The Promise of Cultural Studies of Education," *Educational Theory*, vol. 49, no. 4 (Fall 1999), pp. 527–543.

Chapter 2

SELECTION 4   From Samuel Bowles, "Unequal Education and the Reproduction of the Social Division of Labor," in Martin Carnoy, ed., *Schooling in a Corporate Society: The Political Economy of Education in America*, 2nd ed. (David McKay, 1972).

SELECTION 5   From John U. Ogbu, "Adaptation to Minority Status and Impact on School Success," *Theory Into Practice*, vol. 31, no. 4 (Autumn 1992), pp. 287–295.

Chapter 3

SELECTION 6   From Jonathan Kozol, *Savage Inequalities: Children in America's Schools* (Crown Publishers, 1991).

SELECTION 7   From Penelope Eckert, *Jocks and Burnouts: Social Categories and Identity in the High School* (Teachers College Press, 1989).

SELECTION 8   From Guadalupe Valdés, "The Town, the School, and the Students," *Learning and Not Learning English: Latino Students in American Schools* (Teachers College Press, 2001).

Chapter 4

SELECTION 9   From Edward T. Hall, "What Is Culture?" *The Silent Language* (Doubleday, 1981).

SELECTION 10   Excerpted with permission from Lisa D. Delpit, "The Silenced Dialogue: Power and Pedagogy in Educating Other People's Children," *Harvard Educational Review,* 88:3 (August 1988), pp. 280–298. Copyright © by the President and Fellows of Harvard College. All rights reserved. For more information, please visit www. harvardeducationalreview.org.

Chapter 5

SELECTION 11   From Cornel West, *Race Matters* (Beacon Press, 1993).

SELECTION 12   From Peggy McIntosh, "White Privilege: Unpacking the Invisible Knapsack," *Peace and Freedom* (July/ August 1988). This essay is excerpted from her working paper "White Privilege and Male Privilege: A Personal Account of Coming to See Correspondences Through Work in Women's Studies."

SELECTION 13   From Jana Noel, "Stereotyping, Prejudice, and Racism," *Developing Multicultural Educators* (Waveland Press, 2005).

Chapter 6

SELECTION 14   From Jean S. Phinney, "Ethnic Identity in Adolescents and Adults: Review of Research," *Psychological Bulletin*, vol. 108, no. 3 (1990), pp. 499–514.

SELECTION 15   From Beverly Daniel Tatum, "Teaching White Students About Racism: The Search for White Allies and the Restoration of Hope," *Teachers College Record*, vol. 95, no. 4 (Summer 1994), pp. 462–476.

Chapter 7

SELECTION 16   From Arthur M. Schlesinger, Jr., "The Disuniting of America," *American Educator* (Winter 1991). Adapted and reprinted from *The Disuniting of America: Reflections on a Multicultural Society* (W. W. Norton, 1992).

SELECTION 17   From William J. Bennett, Chester E. Finn, Jr., and John T. E. Cribb, Jr., *The Educated Child: A Parent's Guide from Preschool through Eighth Grade* (The Free Press, 1999).

Chapter 8

SELECTION 18   From Paulo Freire, *Pedagogy of the Oppressed* (Continuum, 1970).

SELECTION 19   From Daniel G. Solorzano, "Images and Words that Wound: Critical Race Theory, Racial Stereotyping, and Teacher Education," *Teacher Education Quarterly*, (Summer, 1997), pp. 5–19.

Chapter 9

SELECTION 20   From Christianne Corbett, Catherine Hill, and Andresse St. Rose, from *Where the Girls Are: The Facts About Gender Equity in Education* (American Association of University Women, 2008).

SELECTION 21   From Stuart Biegel, *The Right to Be Out: Sexual Orientation and Gender Identity in America's Public Schools* (University of Minnesota, 2010).

Chapter 10

SELECTION 22   From Gloria Ladson-Billings, "The Power of Pedagogy: Does Teaching Matter?" in William H. Watkins, James H. Lewis, and Victoria Chow, eds., *Race and Education: The Roles of History and Society in Educating African American Students* (Allyn & Bacon, 2001).

SELECTION 23   From Cornel Pewewardy, "Learning Styles of American Indian/Alaska Native Students: A Review of Literature and Implications for Practice," *Journal of American Indian Education*, vol. 41, no. 3 (2002), pp. 22–56.

SELECTION 24   From Hersh C. Waxman, Yolanda N. Padrón, and Andres García, "Educational Issues and Effective Practices for Hispanic Students," Susan J. Paik and Herbert J. Walberg, *Narrowing the Achievement Gap: Strategies for Educating Latino, Black, and Asian Students* (Springer, 2007).

SELECTION 25   From Valerie Ooka Pang, "Fighting the Marginalization of Asian American Students with Caring Schools: Focus on Curricular Change," *Race, Ethnicity & Education*, vol. 9, no. 1 (2006), pp. 67–83.

SELECTION 26   From Carola Súarez-Orozco, Allyson Pimentel, and Margary Martin, "The Significance of Relationships: Academic Engagement and Achievement Among Newcomer Immigrant Youth," *Teachers College Record*, vol. 111, no. 3 (2009), pp. 712–749.

Chapter 11

SELECTION 27   From Jim Cummins, *Language, Power, and Pedagogy: Bilingual Children in the Crossfire* (Multilingual Matters, 2000).

SELECTION 28   From Eugene E. García, "Education Comes in Diverse Shapes and Forms for U.S. Bilinguals," *Teaching and Learning in Two Languages: Bilingualism & Schooling in the United States* (Teachers College Press, 2005).

Chapter 12

SELECTION 29   From Ira C. Lupu, David Masci, Robert W. Tuttle, *Religion in the Public Schools* (The Pew Forum on Religion and Public Life, 2007)

SELECTION 30   From Khyati Y. Joshi, "Religious Oppression of Indian Americans in the Contemporary United States," in Maurianne Adams, Warren J. Blumenfeld, Carmelita Cateñeda, Heather W. Hackman, Madeline L. Peters, and Ximena Zúñiga, *Readings for Diversity and Social Justice* (2nd ed., Routledge, 2010).

Chapter 13

SELECTION 31   From Jean Anyon, "Social Class and School Knowledge," *Curriculum Inquiry*, vol. 11, no. 1 (1981), pp. 3–42.

SELECTION 32   From Joe L. Kincheloe and Shirley R. Steinberg, "The Importance of Class in Multiculturalism," *Changing Multiculturalism* (Open University Press, 1997).

Chapter 14

SELECTION 33   From Louise Derman-Sparks, "Empowering Children to Create a Caring Culture in a World of Differences," *Childhood Education* (Winter 1993/1994), pp. 66–71.

SELECTION 34   From James A. Banks, "Transforming the Mainstream Curriculum," *Educational Leadership*, vol. 51, no. 8 (May 1994), pp. 4–8.

SELECTION 35   From Sonia Nieto, "Creating Multicultural Learning Communities," *The Light in Their Eyes: Creating Multicultural Learning Communities* (Teachers College Press, 1999).

Chapter 15

SELECTION 36   From Joyce Epstein, "School/Family/Community Partnerships: Caring for the Children We Share," *Phi Delta Kappan*, vol. 76 (May 1995), pp. 701–712.

SELECTION 37   From Luis C. Moll, Cathy Amanti, Deborah Neff, and Norma Gonzalez, "Funds of Knowledge for Teaching: Using a Qualitative Approach to Connect Homes and Classrooms," *Theory Into Practice*, vol. 31, no. 2 (Spring 1992), pp. 132–141.